THE TENDER BAR

0

THE TENDER BAR

A MEMOIR BY J.R. MOEHRINGER

SCEPTRE

First published in Great Britain in 2006 by Sceptre
A division of Hodder Headline

A Sceptre Book

1

A CIP catalogue record for this title is
available from the British Library

ISBN 0 340 82882 X

Printed and bound in Great Britain by
Mackays of Chatham plc, Chatham, Kent

Hodder Headline's policy is to use papers that are natural,
renewable and recyclable products and made from wood grown in
sustainable forests. The logging and manufacturing processes are expected
to conform to the environmental regulations of the country of origin.

Hodder and Stoughton
A division of Hodder Headline
338 Euston Road
London NW1 3BH

For my mother

THE TENDER BAR

PROLOGUE

Where no sea runs, the waters of the heart
Push in their tides

—Dylan Thomas, "Light breaks where no sun shines"

prologue | ONE OF MANY

WE WENT THERE FOR EVERYTHING WE NEEDED. WE WENT there when thirsty, of course, and when hungry, and when dead tired. We went there when happy, to celebrate, and when sad, to sulk. We went there after weddings and funerals, for something to settle our nerves, and always for a shot of courage just before. We went there when we didn't know what we needed, hoping someone might tell us. We went there when looking for love, or sex, or trouble, or for someone who had gone missing, because sooner or later everyone turned up there. Most of all we went there when we needed to be found.

My personal list of needs was long. An only child, abandoned by my father, I needed a family, a home, and men. Especially men. I needed men as mentors, heroes, role models, and as a kind of masculine counterweight to my mother, grandmother, aunt and five female cousins with whom I lived. The bar provided me with all the men I needed, and one or two men who were the last thing I needed.

Long before it legally served me, the bar saved me. It restored my faith when I was a boy, tended me as a teenager, and when I was a young man the bar embraced me. While I fear that we're drawn to what abandons us, and to what seems most likely to abandon us, in the end I believe we're defined by what embraces us. Naturally I embraced the bar right back, until one night the bar turned me away, and in that final abandonment the bar saved my life.

There had always been a bar on that corner, by one name or another, since the beginning of time, or the end of Prohibition, which were the same thing in my hard-drinking hometown—Manhasset, Long Island. In the 1930s the bar was a stop-off for movie stars on their way to the nearby yacht clubs and posh ocean resorts. In the 1940s the bar was a haven for soldiers coming home from the wars. In the 1950s the bar was a lounge for greasers and their poodle-skirted girlfriends. But the bar didn't become a landmark, a patch of hallowed ground, until 1970, when Steve bought the place and re-named it Dickens. Above the door Steve hung a silhouette of Charles Dickens, and below the silhouette he spelled out the name in Old English lettering: 𝕯𝖎𝖈𝖐𝖊𝖓𝖘. Such a blatant display of Anglophilia didn't sit well with every Kevin Flynn and Michael Gallagher in Manhasset. They let it slide only because they so thoroughly approved of Steve's Cardinal Rule of the Bar-room: Every third drink free. Also, it helped that Steve hired seven or eight members of the O'Malley clan to bus his tables, and that he took pains to make Dickens look as though it had been shipped brick by brick from County Donegal.

Steve intended his bar to look like a European public house, but to feel quintessentially American, an honest-to-god house for the public. His public. In the heart of Manhasset, a pastoral suburb of eight thousand people, sev-enteen miles southeast of Manhattan, Steve wanted to create a sanctuary where his neighbors and friends and fellow drinkers, and especially his high-school buddies coming home from Vietnam, could savor a feeling of safety and return. In every venture Steve was confident of success—confidence was his most attractive quality and his tragic flaw—but with Dickens he surpassed his greatest expectations. Manhasset quickly came to see Steve's bar as *the* bar. Just as we said The City to mean New York City, and The Street to mean Wall Street, we always said The Bar, presumptively, and there was never any confusion about which bar we meant. Then, imperceptibly, Dickens became something more than The Bar. It became The Place, the preferred shelter from all life's storms. In 1979, when the nuclear reactor at Three Mile Island melted down and fear of apocalypse swept the Northeast, many Manhas-setites phoned Steve to reserve space in the airtight basement below his bar.

Of course everyone had their own basements. But there was just something about Dickens. People thought of it first whenever doomsday loomed.

Along with sanctuary, Steve provided nightly lessons in democracy, or the special plurality of alcohol. Standing in the middle of his barroom, you could watch men and women from all strata of society educating and abusing one another. You could hear the poorest man in town discussing "market volatility" with the president of the New York Stock Exchange, or the local librarian lecturing a New York Yankees Hall of Famer about the wisdom of choking up on the bat. You could hear a feebleminded porter say something so off-the-wall, and yet so wise, that a college philosophy professor would jot it on a napkin and tuck it in his pocket. You could hear bartenders—in between making bets and mixing Pink Squirrels—talk like philosopher kings.

Steve believed the corner bar to be the most egalitarian of all American gathering places, and he knew that Americans have always venerated their bars, saloons, taverns, and "gin mills," one of his favorite expressions. He knew that Americans invest their bars with meaning and turn to them for everything from glamour to succor, and above all for relief from that scourge of modern life—loneliness. He didn't know that the Puritans, upon landing in the New World, built a bar even before they built a church. He didn't know that American bars descend directly from the medieval inns of Chaucer's *Canterbury Tales,* which descended from the Saxon alehouses, which descended from the *tabernae* along the roads of ancient Rome. Steve's bar could trace its lineage all the way back to the painted caves of Western Europe where Stone Age elders initiated young boys and girls into the ways of the tribe nearly fifteen thousand years ago. Though Steve didn't know these things, he sensed them in his blood and enacted them in everything he did. More than most men, Steve appreciated the importance of place, and on the cornerstone of this principle he was able to build a bar so strange and shrewd and beloved and wondrously in tune with its customers that it came to be known well beyond Manhasset.

My hometown was famous for two things—lacrosse and liquor. Year in, year out, Manhasset produced a disproportionate number of superb lacrosse players and a still-greater number of distended livers. Some people also knew Manhasset as the backdrop for *The Great Gatsby*. While composing portions of his masterpiece, F. Scott Fitzgerald sat on a breezy veranda in Great Neck and gazed across Manhasset Bay at our town, which he turned into the fictional East Egg, a historic distinction that gave our bowling alley and pizzeria a certain archaeological grandeur. We strode each day across Fitzgerald's abandoned stage set. We romanced one another among his ruins. It was a kick—an honor. But like Steve's bar it was merely an offshoot of Manhasset's famous fondness for drink. Anyone familiar with Manhasset understood why liquor surged through Fitzgerald's novel like the Mississippi across a floodplain. Men and women throwing raucous parties and boozing until they blacked out or ran someone down with their car? Sounded to us like a typical Tuesday night in Manhasset.

Manhasset, site of the largest liquor store in New York State, was the only town on Long Island with a cocktail named after it (a Manhasset is a Manhattan, with more alcohol). The town's half-mile-long main drag, Plandome Road, was every drinker's street of dreams—bar after bar after bar. Many in Manhasset likened Plandome Road to a mythical country lane in Ireland, a gently winding procession of men and women brimming with whiskey and good cheer. Bars on Plandome Road were as numerous as stars on Hollywood's Walk of Fame, and we took a stubborn, eccentric pride in their number. When one man torched his bar on Plandome Road to collect the insurance, cops found him in another bar on Plandome Road and told him he was wanted for questioning. The man put a hand over his heart like a priest accused of burning a cross. "How could I," he asked, "how could anyone—*burn down a bar*?"

With its curious division of upper class and working class, its ethnic mix of Irish and Italian, and its coterie of some of the wealthiest families in the United States, Manhasset was forever struggling to define itself. It was a town where dirty-faced urchins gathered at Memorial Field—to play "bicycle polo;" where neighbors hid from one another behind their perfect hedgerows—yet still kept careful track of one another's stories and foibles; where everyone departed at sunrise on the trains to Manhattan—but no one ever really left for good, except in a pine box. Though Manhasset felt like a small farm community, and though real estate brokers tended to call it a bedroom community, we cleaved to the notion that we were a barroom community. Bars gave us identity and points of intersection. The Little League, softball league, bowling league, and Junior League not only held their meetings at Steve's bar, they often met on the same night.

Brass Pony, Gay Dome, Lamplight, Kilmeade's, Joan and Ed's, Popping Cork, 1680 House, Jaunting Car, The Scratch—the names of Manhasset's bars were more familiar to us than the names of its main streets and founding families. The life spans of bars were like dynasties: We measured time by them, and found some primal comfort in the knowledge that whenever one closed, the curtain would rise on another. My grandmother told me that Manhasset was one of those places where an old wives' tale was accepted as fact—namely, that drinking at home was the mark of an alcoholic. So long as you drank publicly, not secretly, you weren't a drunk. Thus, bars. Lots and lots of bars.

Of course many bars in Manhasset, like bars everywhere, were nasty places, full of pickled people marinating in regret. Steve wanted his bar to be different. He wanted his bar to be sublime. He envisioned a bar that would cater to Manhasset's multiple personalities. A cozy pub one minute, a crazy after-hours club the next. A family restaurant early in the evening, and late at night a low-down tavern, where men and women could tell lies and drink until they dropped. Essential to Steve was the idea that Dickens would be the opposite of the outside world. Cool in the dog days, warm from the first frost until spring. His bar would always be clean and well-lighted, like the den of that perfect family we all believe exists but doesn't and never did. At Dickens everyone would feel special, though no one would stand out. Maybe my favorite story about Steve's bar concerned the man who found his way there after escaping a nearby mental hospital. No one looked askance at the man. No one asked who he was, or why he was dressed in pajamas, or why he had such a feral gleam in his eye. The gang in the barroom simply threw their arms around him, told him funny stories, and bought him drinks all day long. The only reason the poor man was eventually asked to leave was that he suddenly and for no apparent reason dropped his pants. Even then the bartenders only chided him gently, using their standard admonition: "Here now—you can't be doing *that*!"

Like love affairs, bars depend on a delicate mix of timing, chemistry, lighting, luck and—maybe above all—generosity. From the start Steve declared that no one at Dickens would feel slighted. His burgers would be three-inch soufflés of filet mignon, his closing time would be negotiable, no matter what the law said, and his bartenders would give an extra—*extra*—long pour. A standard drink at Dickens would be a double anywhere else. A double would leave you cross-eyed. A triple would "cream your spinach," according to my mother's younger brother, my Uncle Charlie, the first bartender Steve ever hired.

A true son of Manhasset, Steve believed in booze. Everything he was, he owed to booze. His father, a Heineken distributor, died and left Steve a small fortune when he was young. Steve's daughter was named Brandy, his speedboat was named *Dipsomania,* and his face, after years of homeric drinking, was that telltale shade of scarlet. He saw himself as a Pied Piper of Alcohol, and the pie-eyed residents of Manhasset saw him that way, too. Through the years he developed a fanatic following, a legion of devotees. A Cult of Steve.

Everyone has a holy place, a refuge, where their heart is purer, their mind clearer, where they feel closer to God or love or truth or whatever it is they happen to worship. For better or worse my holy place was Steve's bar. And because I found it in my youth, the bar was that much more sacred, its image clouded by that special reverence children accord those places where they feel safe. Others might feel this way about a classroom or playground, a theater or church, a laboratory or library or stadium. Even a home. But none of these places claimed me. We exalt what is at hand. Had I grown up beside a river or an ocean, some natural avenue of self-discovery and escape, I might have mythologized it. Instead I grew up 142 steps from a glorious old American tavern, and that has made all the difference.

I didn't spend every waking minute in the bar. I went into the world, worked and failed, fell in love, played the fool, had my heart broken and my threshold tested. But because of Steve's bar each rite of passage felt linked to the last, and the next, as did each person I met. For the first twenty-five years of my life everyone I knew either sent me to the bar, drove me to the bar, accompanied me to the bar, rescued me from the bar, or was in the bar when I arrived, as if waiting for me since the day I was born. Among this last group were Steve and the men.

I used to say I'd found in Steve's bar the fathers I needed, but this wasn't quite right. At some point the bar itself became my father, its dozens of men melding into one enormous male eye looking over my shoulder, providing that needed alternative to my mother, that Y chromosome to her X. My mother didn't know she was competing with the men of the bar, and the men didn't know they were vying with her. They all assumed that they were on the same page, because they all shared one antiquated idea about manhood. My mother and the men believed that being a good man is an art, and being a bad man is a tragedy, for the world as much as for those who depend on the tragic man in question. Though my mother first introduced me to this idea, Steve's bar was where I saw its truth demonstrated daily. Steve's bar attracted all kinds of women, a stunning array, but as a boy I noticed only its improbable assortment of good and bad men. Wandering freely among this unlikely fraternity of alphas, listening to the stories of the soldiers and ballplayers, poets and cops, millionaires and bookies, actors and crooks who leaned nightly against Steve's bar, I heard them say again and again that the differences among them were great, but the reasons they had come to be so different were slight.

A lesson, a gesture, a story, a philosophy, an attitude—I took something from every man in Steve's bar. I was a master at "identity theft" when that crime was more benign. I became sarcastic like Cager, melodramatic like Uncle Charlie, a roughneck like Joey D. I strived to be solid like Bob the Cop, cool like Colt, and to rationalize my rage by telling myself that it was no worse than the righteous wrath of Smelly. Eventually I applied the mimicry I'd learned at Dickens to those I met outside the bar—friends, lovers, parents, bosses, even strangers. The bar fostered in me the habit of turning each person who crossed my path into a mentor, or a character, and I credit the bar, and blame it, for my becoming a reflection, or a refraction, of them all.

Every regular at Steve's bar was fond of metaphors. One old bourbon drinker told me that a man's life is all a matter of mountains and caves—mountains we must climb, caves where we hide when we can't face our mountains. For me the bar was both. My most luxuriant cave, my most perilous mountain. And its men, though cavemen at heart, were my Sherpas. I loved them, deeply, and I think they knew. Though they had experienced everything—war and love, fame and disgrace, wealth and ruin—I don't think they ever had a boy look at them with such shining, worshipful eyes. My devotion was something new to them, and I think it made them love me, in their way, which was why they kidnapped me when I was eleven. But now I can almost hear their voices. *Whoa, kid, you're getting ahead of yourself.*

Steve would have me say it like this: I fell in love with his bar, and it was reciprocal, and it was this romance that shaped all my others. At a tender age, standing in Dickens, I decided that life is a sequence of romances, each new romance a response to a previous romance. But I was only one of many romantics in Steve's bar who had reached this conclusion, who believed in this chain reaction of love. It was this belief, as much as the bar, that united us, and this is why my story is just one strand in the cord that braided all our love stories together.

PART I

Slumbering in every human being lies an infinity of possibilities, which one must not arouse in vain. For it is terrible when the whole man resonates with echoes and echoes, none becoming a real voice.

—Elias Canetti, *Notes from Hampstead*

one | THE MEN

I F A MAN CAN CHART WITH ANY ACCURACY HIS EVOLUTION FROM small boy to barfly, mine began on a hot summer night in 1972. Seven years old, driving through Manhasset with my mother, I looked out the window and saw nine men in orange softball uniforms racing around Memorial Field, the silhouette of Charles Dickens silk-screened in black on their chests. "Who is that?" I asked my mother.

"Some men from Dickens," she said. "See your Uncle Charlie? And his boss, Steve?"

"Can we watch?"

She pulled over and we found seats in the stands.

The sun was setting, and the men cast long shadows, which seemed made of the same black ink as the silhouettes on their chests. Also, the men sported cummerbunds of blubber that stretched their XXL jerseys until those silhouettes looked like splatter stains caused by the men stomping in their own shadows. Everything about the men had this surreal, cartoonish quality. With their scant hair, giant shoes, and overdeveloped upper bodies, they looked like Blutos and Popeyes and steroidal Elmer Fudds, except my lanky Uncle Charlie, who patrolled the infield like a flamingo with sore knees. I remember that Steve wielded a wooden bat the size of a telephone pole, and every home run he clouted hovered in the sky like a second moon.

Standing at the plate, the Babe Ruth of the beer league, Steve dug at the dirt and growled at the pitcher to give him something he could pulverize. The pitcher looked scared and amused at the same time, because even while barking at him, Steve never stopped smiling. His smile was like the strobe from a lighthouse, making everyone feel a little safer. It was also a command. It bade everyone to smile also. It was irresistible, and not just to those around him. Steve himself seemed unable to stop baring his teeth.

Steve and the men of Dickens were fierce competitors, but the game never once got in the way of their main goal in life—laughter. Regardless of the score, they never stopped laughing, they couldn't stop laughing, and the fans in the stands couldn't either. I laughed harder than anyone, though I didn't get the joke. I laughed at the sound of the men's laughter, and at their comic timing, as fluid and quicksilver as their turning of a double play.

"Why do those men act so silly?" I asked my mother.

"They're just—happy."

"About what?"

She looked at the men, thinking.

"Beer, sweetheart. They're happy about beer."

Each time the men ran past, they left a scented cloud. Beer. Aftershave. Leather. Tobacco. Hair tonic. I inhaled deeply, memorizing their aroma, their essence. From then on, whenever I smelled a keg of Schaeffer, a bottle of Aqua Velva, a freshly oiled Spalding baseball glove, a smoldering Lucky Strike, a flask of Vitalis, I would be there again, beside my mother, gazing at those beery giants stumbling around the diamond.

That softball game marked for me the beginning of many things, but particularly time. Memories before the softball game have a disjointed, fragmentary quality; after, memories move forward, smartly, single file. Possibly I needed to find the bar, one of the two organizing principles of my life, before I could make a linear, coherent narrative of my life. I remember turning to the other organizing principle of my life and telling her I wanted to watch the men forever. We can't, babe, she said, the game is over. What? I stood, panicked. The men were walking off the field with their arms around each other.

As they faded into the sumacs around Memorial Field, calling to one another, "See you at Dickens," I started to cry. I wanted to follow.

"Why?" my mother asked.

"To see what's so funny."

"We're not going to the bar," she said. "We're going—home."

She always tripped over that word.

My mother and I lived at my grandfather's house, a Manhasset landmark nearly as famous as Steve's bar. People often drove by Grandpa's and pointed, and I once heard passersby speculating that the house must suffer from some sort of "painful house disease." What it really suffered from was comparisons. Set among Manhasset's elegant Gingerbread Victorians and handsome Dutch Colonials, Grandpa's dilapidated Cape Cod was doubly appalling. Grandpa claimed he couldn't afford repairs, but the truth was, he didn't care. With a touch of defiance and a perverse pride he called his house the Shit House, and paid no attention when the roof began to sag like a circus tent. He scarcely noticed when paint peeled away in flakes the size of playing cards. He yawned in Grandma's face when she pointed out that the driveway had developed a jagged crack, as if lightning had struck it—and in fact lightning had. My cousins saw the lightning bolt sizzle up the driveway and just miss the breezeway. Even God, I thought, is pointing at Grandpa's house.

Under that one sagging roof my mother and I lived with Grandpa, Grandma, my mother's two grown siblings—Uncle Charlie and Aunt Ruth—and Aunt Ruth's five daughters and one son. "Huddled masses yearning to breathe rent-free," Grandpa called us. While Steve was creating his public sanctuary at 550 Plandome Road, Grandpa was running a flophouse at 646.

Grandpa could have nailed a silhouette of Charles Dickens above his door too, since the conditions were comparable to a Dickensian workhouse. With one usable bathroom and twelve people, the waits at Grandpa's were often excruciating, and the cesspool was constantly backed up ("Shit House" was sometimes more than a flippant nickname). The hot water ran out each morning in the middle of Shower Number Two, made a brief cameo during Shower Number Three, then teased and cruelly abandoned the person taking Shower Number Four. The furniture, much of which dated to Franklin Roosevelt's third term, was held together with duct tape and more duct tape. The only new objects in the house were the drinking glasses, "borrowed" from Dickens, and the Sears living room sofa, upholstered in a hypnotically hideous pattern of Liberty Bells, bald eagles, and faces of the Founding Fathers. We called it the bicentennial sofa. We were a few years ahead of ourselves, but Grandpa said the name was right and fitting, since the sofa looked as if George Washington had used it to cross the Delaware.

The worst thing about life at Grandpa's house was the noise, a round-the-clock din of cursing and crying and fighting and Uncle Charlie bellowing that he was trying to sleep and Aunt Ruth screaming at her six kids in the nerve-shredding key of a seagull. Just beneath this cacophony was a steady percussion, faint at first, louder as you became more aware of it, like the heartbeat deep inside the House of Usher. In the House of Grandpa the heartbeat was supplied by the screen door opening and closing all day long as people came and went—*squeak bang, squeak bang*—and also by the peculiar thudding way that everyone in my family walked, on their heels, like storm troopers on stilts. Between the screaming and the screen door, the fighting and the stomping feet, by dusk you'd be barking and twitching more than the dog, who ran off every chance she got. But dusk was the crescendo, the loudest and most tension-filled hour of the day, because dusk was dinnertime.

Seated around the lopsided dining room table, we'd all talk at once, trying to distract ourselves from the food. Grandma couldn't cook, and Grandpa gave her almost no money for groceries, so what came out of that kitchen in chipped serving bowls was both toxic and comical. To make what she called "spaghetti and meatballs," Grandma would boil a box of pasta until it was glue, saturate it with Campbell's cream of tomato soup, then top it with chunks of raw hot dog. Salt and pepper to taste. What actually brought on the indigestion, though, was Grandpa. A loner, a misanthrope, a curmudgeon with a stutter, he found himself each night at the head of a table with twelve uninvited guests, counting the dog. A Shanty Irish reenactment of the Last Supper. As he looked us up and down we could hear him thinking, *Each of you has betrayed me tonight*. To his credit Grandpa never turned anyone away. But he never made anyone feel welcome either, and he often wished aloud that we'd all just "clear the hell out."

My mother and I would have left, gladly, but we had nowhere else to go. She made very little money, and she got none from my father, who wanted no part of his wife and only child. He was a hard case, my father, an unstable mix of charm and rage, and my mother had no choice but to leave him when I was seven months old. He retaliated by disappearing, and withholding all help.

Because I was so young when he disappeared, I didn't know what my father looked like. I only knew what he sounded like, and this I knew too well. A popular rock 'n' roll disc jockey, my father would speak each day into a large microphone somewhere in New York City, and his plummy baritone would fly down the Hudson River, tack across Manhasset Bay, zoom up Plandome Road and burst a millisecond later from the olive green radio on Grandpa's kitchen table. My father's voice was so deep, so ominous, it made my ribs vibrate and the utensils tremble.

Adults in Grandpa's house would try to protect me from my father by pretending he didn't exist. (Grandma wouldn't even refer to him by name—Johnny Michaels—but simply called him The Voice.) They would lunge for the dial whenever they heard my father and sometimes hide the radio altogether, which made me wail in protest. Surrounded by women, and two remote men, I saw The Voice as my only connection to the masculine world. Moreover it was my only means of drowning out all the other hateful voices in Grandpa's house. The Voice, hosting a party every night in the same olive green box as Stevie Wonder and Van Morrison and the Beatles, was the antidote to all the discord around me. When Grandma and Grandpa went to war over the grocery money, when Aunt Ruth threw something against the wall in anger, I'd press my ear close to the radio and The Voice would tell me something funny or play me a song by Peppermint Rainbow. I listened so ardently to The Voice, achieved such mastery at shutting out other voices, that I became a prodigy at selective listening, which I thought was a gift, until it proved to be a curse. Life is all a matter of choosing which voices to tune in and which to tune out, a lesson I learned long before most people, but one that took me longer than most to put to good use.

I remember feeling particularly lonely one day as I tuned in my father's show. For his first song my father played the Four Seasons, "Working My Way Back to You," then said in his smoothest, silkiest tone, in which you could hear the smile on his face, "I *am* working my way back to you, Momma—but be patient, 'cause I've only got a paper route." I closed my eyes and laughed and for a few moments I forgot who and where I was.

two | THE VOICE

MY FATHER WAS A MAN OF MANY TALENTS, BUT HIS ONE TRUE genius was disappearing. Without warning he would change shifts or switch stations. I'd counter by taking a portable radio outside to the stoop, where the reception was better. With the radio on my lap I'd wiggle the antenna and slowly turn the dial, feeling lost until I found The Voice again. One day my mother caught me. "What are you doing?" she asked.

"Looking for my father."

She frowned, then turned and went into the house.

I knew that The Voice didn't have the same tranquilizing effect on my mother. In her mind my father's voice was "full of money," as Fitzgerald wrote of another careless voice in Manhasset. Hearing my father boom from the radio, my mother didn't hear his jokes, his charm, his voice. She heard every child-support payment he'd failed to make. After I'd spent the day listening to The Voice I'd often see my mother looking through the mail for The Voice's check. Dropping the stack of envelopes on the dining room table she'd give me a blank face. Nothing. Again.

For my mother's sake I would try to keep the radio volume low. Now and then I would even try to give up The Voice altogether, but it was hopeless. Everyone in Grandpa's house had at least one vice—drinking, smoking, gambling, lying, cursing, sloth. The Voice was mine. As my dependence grew, so did my tolerance, until it was no longer enough merely to listen. I began talking back. I'd tell The Voice about school, Little League, my mother's health. She was exhausted every night after work, I told The Voice, and I worried about her constantly. If I timed it just right—listening when The Voice was speaking, speaking when The Voice was not—it almost felt like a conversation.

Eventually my mother caught me. "Who are you talking to?" she asked.

"No one."

She put a hand to her mouth and looked stricken. I turned the volume lower.

One afternoon, just after The Voice had signed off the air, the phone rang in Grandpa's living room. "Answer it," my mother said, her tone strange. I picked up the receiver. "Hello?"

"Hello," said The Voice.

I swallowed. "Dad?"

I'd never used that word before. I felt a release of pressure inside me, as if a cork had popped. He asked how I was. What grade are you in? That so? You like your teachers? He didn't ask about my mother, who had secretly arranged the call after overhearing my latest conversation with the radio. He didn't explain where he was or why he never visited. He made small talk as though we were old army buddies. Then I heard him take a long puff on a cigarette and exhale so hard that I thought a jet of smoke would spurt through the phone. I could hear the smoke in his voice, and thought his voice *was* smoke. This was how I pictured my father—as talking smoke.

"So," he said, "how'd you like to go to a baseball game with your old man?"

"Wow! Really?"

"Sure."

"Mets or Yankees?"

"Mets, Yankees, whoever."

"Uncle Charlie says the Mets came into Dickens the other night."

"How is your Uncle Charlie? How's he doing down at the bar?"

"They play the Braves tomorrow night."

"Who?"

"The Mets."

"Oh. Right."

I heard the click-clock of ice cubes in a glass. "Sure," he said. "Tomorrow night. I'll pick you up at your grandfather's—six-thirty."

"I'll be ready."

I was ready at four-thirty. Sitting on the stoop, wearing my Mets cap, slugging my fist into the pocket of my new Dave Cash mitt, I peered at every car that approached the house. I was waiting for my father, but I didn't know what that meant. My mother hadn't saved any photos of him, and I hadn't yet been to New York City to see his face on billboards and buses. I didn't know if my father had a glass eye, a toupee, a gold tooth. I couldn't have picked him out of a police lineup, something my grandmother often suggested I'd need to do one day.

At five Grandma appeared at the door. "I thought he was coming at six-thirty," she said.

"I want to be ready. In case he's early."

"Your father? Early?" She made a tsk-tsk sound. "Your mother called from work. She told me to tell you to bring a jacket."

"It's too hot."

Again she made a sound and walked off. Grandma was no fan of my father, and she wasn't alone. The whole family boycotted my parents' wedding, except my mother's rebellious brother, Uncle Charlie, four years younger, who walked my mother down the aisle. I felt ashamed to be so excited about my father's visit. I knew it was wrong to welcome him, to think about him, to love him. As the man of my family, as my mother's protector, I should have been prepared to demand money from my father the moment he showed his face. But I didn't want to scare him off. I longed to see him even more than I longed to see my beloved Mets in person for the first time.

I bounced a rubber ball on the front stoop and tried to concentrate on the good things I knew about my father. My mother had told me that before he went into radio my father had been a "stand-up," and people "rolled in the aisles" when he performed. "What's a stand-up?" I asked. "Someone who stands up in front of people and makes them laugh," she said. I wondered if my father would stand up in front of me and make me laugh. Would he look like my favorite comedian, Johnny Carson? I hoped so. I promised God I'd never ask for another thing if my father looked like Johnny Carson—those twinkly eyes, that kindly trace of a smile always playing at the corners of his mouth.

A terrifying thought made me stop throwing the ball against the stoop. What if my father, knowing how the whole family felt about him, didn't want to pull into the driveway? What if he slowed down on Plandome Road, checked to see if I was there, then sped away? I sprinted to the sidewalk. Now I could jump through his window as he slowed down and away we'd go. Leaning sideways like a hitchhiker I stared at each man who drove by, trying to decide if that could be my father. Each man looked back, concerned, irritated, wondering why that seven-year-old boy was staring at him so intently.

Just after eight I returned to the stoop and watched the sunset. The horizon turned the same orange as the uniforms of the Dickens softball team and the NY on my Mets cap. Uncle Charlie left for the bar. Striding across the lawn, his head down, he was so intent on polishing his sunglasses with a Kleenex that he didn't see me.

At eight-thirty Grandma appeared at the door. "Come in and eat something," she said.

"No."

"You have to eat."

"No."

"A bite."

"We're going to have hot dogs at the stadium."

"Hm."

"He's just late. He'll be here."

I heard Grandpa tuning in the Mets on channel 9. Normally, because of his poor hearing and all the noise in the house, he blared the TV. That night, for my sake, he kept the volume low.

At nine I tried something new. If I don't look at this next car, I thought, if I don't so much as glance at the driver, it will be my father for sure. I employed this strategy, in which I had full confidence, on thirty cars.

At nine-thirty I made small concessions to the inevitable. I took off my Mets hat. I took off my mitt and used it as a seat cushion. I ate a piece of Grandma's chicken.

At ten I ran inside to pee. Hurrying down the hall I heard the crowd at Shea Stadium roar as someone hit a home run.

At eleven the game ended. I went inside, put on my pajamas and climbed under the covers. Seconds after I turned off the light Grandpa appeared at the foot of my bed. If Lyndon Johnson had appeared at the foot of my bed I couldn't have been more astonished.

"I'm sorry," he said. "About your father."

"Oh," I said, nonchalant, pulling at a loose thread in my security blanket. "I'm glad he didn't come. I didn't like those pants I was wearing anyway."

Grandpa nodded, then left the room.

I lay in the dark and listened to Grandma and Grandpa in the kitchen, talking about my father "standing up JR." They stopped talking as a car pulled into the driveway. I heard gravel crackling under tires, an engine idling. My father! I bounded out of bed and ran out of the bedroom. At the end of the narrow hall that led to the front door was my mother. "Oh no," she said. "What are you doing here? Didn't you go to the game?"

I shook my head. She walked quickly toward me and I wrapped my arms around her, startled by how much I loved her and how intensely I needed her. As I held my mother, clung to her, cried against her legs, it struck me that she was all I had, and if I didn't take good care of her I'd be lost.

three | SECURITY BLANKET

WHEN NOT CROUCHED OVER THE RADIO, LISTENING TO THE Voice, I was tuned to my mother's frequencies, monitoring her moods. I watched her, analyzed her, followed her from room to room. It was more than attachment, more than protectiveness. It was partly a pursuit, because no matter how intently I watched and listened, my mother was often a complete mystery to me.

When happy, when expressing joy or love, my mother could be marvelously loud. But when sad or hurt, when frightened or worried about money, my mother would fall silent and her face would go blank. Some people interpreted this tendency as coldness. They couldn't have been more wrong. Even at seven years old I understood that my mother's silences and blank faces concealed an emotional cauldron. What seemed a lack of feeling was an overflow, a surge. My mother would slip behind her mask of feigned calm for the sake of discretion, as someone might step behind a screen when changing.

There had always been a trace of the unfathomable about my mother, according to Grandma, who told me a story by way of explanation. When my mother was in second grade, the teacher asked the class a question and my mother shot her hand in the air. She knew that answer and couldn't wait to shout it out. But the teacher called on someone else. After a few minutes the teacher noticed my mother's hand still hovering. Dorothy, she said, put down your hand. I can't, my mother said. Put down your hand, the teacher said. My mother's eyes filled with tears. The teacher sent my mother to the principal, who sent my mother to the nurse, who concluded that my mother wasn't faking. Her hand and arm were truly stuck in the upright and locked position.

Grandma was summoned to school, and she described to me with some wonderment that long, strange walk home, my mother a half step behind, her hand rigidly aloft. Grandma sent my mother to bed—the only thing she could think to do—and in the morning, when the sadness or disappointment presumably had worn off, my mother's arm fell to her side.

Though she was mysterious by nature, some of my mother's mystery was by design. The most honest person I've ever known, she was a beautiful liar. To avoid giving pain, to cushion the blow of bad news, she'd fib or baldly fabricate without the slightest hesitation. Her lies were so well crafted, so expertly told, that I never gave them a second thought. As a result, every now and then, sorting through childhood memories, I still come upon one of my mother's lies, like an elaborately painted Easter egg that was hidden too well and forgotten.

The earliest lie I can remember came about when my mother and I had moved into a small apartment five minutes from Grandpa's house. At last, she said, we've escaped. She was loudly, riotously happy, until she got laid off from her job. Soon I found food stamps in her purse. "What are these?" I asked.

"Coupons," she said brightly.

She didn't want me to know we were broke. She didn't want me to worry more than I already did. For this same reason she lied when I asked if we could buy a TV. "You know, I've been meaning to buy us a TV," she said. "If only the TV makers weren't on strike."

I nagged her for weeks about the TV strike, and she concocted detailed stories on the fly about picketers at the factory and breakdowns in the negotiations. When she'd saved enough for a used black-and-white Zenith, she came to me and announced that management had caved. For years I believed there had been a bitter work stoppage among Long Island's TV makers, until I heard myself telling people about it at a dinner party and saw them staring at me.

On those rare occasions when my mother was caught in a lie, she was refreshingly unrepentant. She had a "relationship" with the truth, she explained coolly, and like all relationships it required compromises. Lying, she believed, was no greater sin than turning down the volume on the radio to protect me from The Voice. She merely notched down the volume on the truth.

Her most inspired lie marked a watershed in our relationship, because it concerned my most cherished possession, my security blanket. Made of mint green satin, quilted with thick white thread, the blanket was my other addiction, besides The Voice. I grew edgy when it was out of reach. I wore it as a poncho, a sash, a scarf, and sometimes as a bridal train. I regarded my blanket as a loyal friend in a cruel world, while my mother saw it as an adult emotional disorder in the making. Seven was too old for a security blanket, she said, trying to reason with me, but when did reason stand a chance against obsessive love? She tried seizing the blanket, but I howled as though she were hacking off my arm at the joint. Finally I woke one night to find her on the edge of my bed. "What's wrong?" I asked.

"Nothing. Go back to sleep."

Over the next few weeks I noticed my security blanket getting smaller. I asked my mother. "Maybe it's shrinking in the wash," she said. "I'll use colder water." Many years later I learned that my mother had crept into my room each night and taken a scissor to my security blanket, snipping off an imperceptible slice, until it became a security shawl, a security washcloth, a security swatch. Over time there would be more security blankets, people and ideas and particularly places to which I would form unhealthy attachments. Whenever life snatched one from me, I would recall how gently my mother pared away my first.

The one thing my mother couldn't lie about was how deeply Grandpa's house offended her. She said Grandpa's house made the Amityville Horror look like the Taj Mahal. She said Grandpa's house should be burned down and the soil plowed with salt. She said Grandpa's house was Manhasset's answer to Alcatraz, except with lumpier mattresses and worse table manners. She'd escaped that house at nineteen, literally flew away, joining United Airlines as a stewardess, jetting around the country in her aqua blue uniform and cap. She'd sampled other fun jobs, including a stint as a girl Friday at Capitol Records, meeting Nat King Cole, eavesdropping at the switchboard on phone conversations between her boss and Frank Sinatra. Now, thirty-three years old, a penniless single mother, she'd returned to Grandpa's house, a bitter defeat and a sad step backward. She juggled three jobs—secretary, waitress, baby-sitter—and saved constantly for what she called Our Next Great Escape. But every escape was foiled. Within six or nine months our savings would run out, our rent would go up, and we'd be back in the Shit House. By the time I was seven we'd moved out of Grandpa's house three times, and back three times.

Though I didn't love the Shit House, I didn't despise it the way my mother did. The sagging roof, the duct-taped furniture, the exploding cesspool and bicentennial sofa—all seemed a fair trade for being with my cousins, whom I adored. My mother understood, but Grandpa's house sapped her energy to such an extent that she couldn't take any pleasure in the compensations it held for me. She was so tired, she said. So terribly tired.

More than returning to Grandpa's house, more than moving our stuff yet again, what seemed to devastate my mother was the moment she realized that our next return was inevitable. I remember waking in yet another one-bedroom apartment, going out to the kitchen and finding my mother pecking at her calculator. I could tell she'd been pecking at it since dawn, and she looked as if the calculator had been pecking at her. I'd long suspected she had conversations with her calculator, as I did with the radio, and that morning I caught her red-handed. "Who are you talking to?" I asked. She looked up and gave me her blank face. Mom? Blank. Before my eyes she was reverting to that catatonic schoolgirl with her hand in the air.

Each time we returned to Grandpa's, my mother would insist that we take regular mental-health breaks. Sunday afternoons we'd climb into our rust-spackled 1963 T-Bird, which sounded like a Civil War cannon, and go for a drive. We'd start on Shore Drive, the finest street in Manhasset, where the white-columned houses were bigger than Town Hall, and several had Long Island Sound as their front lawns. "Imagine living in one of these showplaces," my mother would say. She'd park in front of the grandest house, the one with the golden yellow shutters and the wraparound porch. "Imagine lying in bed on a summer morning," she'd say, "with the windows open, and a warm breeze off the water blowing the curtains in and out."

It always seemed as if a misty rain was falling during our drives, so my mother and I couldn't get out of the car for a closer look. We'd sit with the engine and heater running and the windshield wipers slinging back and forth. My mother would study the house and I would study my mother. She had lustrous auburn hair, which she wore to her shoulders, and green-brown eyes that turned a shade greener whenever she smiled. Her most common facial expression, however, was one of enormous self-command, like a young aristocrat posing for her coming-out portrait. It was the look of a woman who could be gentle, and fragile, but who would assuredly be fierce when protecting those she loved. I see in some photos of my mother that she was aware of her ability, in hard times, to set aside her delicate qualities, to fight like hell, and she took a certain pride in it. The camera captured her pride in a way my seven-year-old eye couldn't. The only pride I noticed as a boy was the pleasure she took in her sense of style. Petite and slim, my mother knew what looked good on her. Even when we were broke she managed to look classic, which probably had more to do with her carriage than with her clothes.

After we'd been sitting there for some time, the owners of the house would hear the T-Bird and peer through their windows at us. My mother would then jerk the T-Bird into drive and we'd rumble south on Plandome Road, through the commercial district that started at Dickens and ended at St. Mary's Church. I liked the way Manhasset was bracketed by its two most sacred sites, each a house of furtive adult communion. At St. Mary's we'd hang a left onto Northern Boulevard, then a quick right onto Shelter Rock Road, passing Shelter Rock itself, the 1,800-ton glacier that had skittered downstate many millennia before, like one of the marbles I pitched on the playground at Shelter Rock Elementary School, a mile away. Legends surrounded Shelter Rock. For centuries its sharp outcrop, a natural canopy of stone, had shielded people from animals and elements and enemies. Revered by Native Americans who lived along Manhasset Bay, the rock was then prized by Dutch cow farmers who came to Manhasset seeking their fortune in the 1600s, then adopted by British colonists who came seeking religious freedom in the 1700s, then co-opted by millionaires who built their grand estates along Shelter Rock Road in the 1800s. If things got really bad at Grandpa's, I figured, my mother and I could live alongside Shelter Rock. We could sleep under the canopy and cook our meals over an open fire, and though it would be rough, how much rougher could it be?

Just beyond the rock my mother and I would come to a stretch of rolling hills where the houses were even more astonishing than those on the water. Prettiest houses in the world, my mother said. Every few hundred yards, through a tall padlocked wrought-iron gate, we'd glimpse another lawn wider and greener than the outfield at Shea Stadium, stretching toward another replica of the Irish castles in my storybooks. "This is where the Whitneys live," she said. "And that's where the Paleys live. And that's where the Paysons live. Isn't that lovely?"

Hanging a U-turn at the last mansion, heading back to Grandpa's, my mother would invariably start to sing. She'd warm up with "I Got You Babe," because she liked the line, "They say our love won't pay the rent—before it's earned our money's all been spent." Then she'd belt out her favorite, an old Tin Pan Alley tune.

Oh! we ain't got a barrel of money,
Maybe we're ragged and funny,
But we'll travel along,
Singin' a song,
Side by side

She always sang at the top of her voice, but volume couldn't mask her frustration. Those mansions tormented my mother as much as they fascinated her, and I understood. I felt the same way. Pressing my forehead against the car window as the mansions flew by, I'd think: *So many beautiful places in the world, and we're barred from them all.* Obviously the secret of life was *getting in.* Why couldn't my mother and I figure out how it was done? My mother deserved a home. It didn't even need to be a mansion, just a little cottage with a rose garden and cream-colored curtains and rugs that were soft and clean and kissed your bare feet as you walked across them. That would be plenty. It made me mad that my mother didn't have nice things, madder still that I couldn't provide them for her, and furious that I couldn't say any of this aloud, because my mother was singing, striving to stay upbeat. Taking care of my mother meant saying nothing to disrupt her fragile optimism, so I would press my forehead against the window, harder, until it hurt, and shift my focus from the mansions to my reflection in the glass.

Though I kept my feelings bottled tight, eventually those feelings fermented, then fizzed to the surface in the form of odd behavior. I turned overnight into a compulsive and neurotic child. I set about trying to fix Grandpa's house—straightening rugs, restacking magazines, retaping furniture. My cousins laughed and called me Felix, but I wasn't being neat, I was going crazy. Besides doing what I could to make the house less offensive to my mother, I was trying to put order to chaos, a quest that led me ultimately to seek a more dramatic rearrangement of reality.

I began dividing life into absolutes. Manhasset was this way, I thought—why not the world? In Manhasset you were either Yankees or Mets, rich or poor, sober or drunk, church or bar. You were "Gaelic or garlic," as one schoolmate told me, and I couldn't admit, to him or myself, that I had both Irish and Italian ancestors. Life was governed by polar opposites, I decided, as proved by the stark contrast between the Shit House and the Whitney mansion. Things and people were either perfectly bad, or perfectly good, and when life didn't obey this black-or-white rule, when things or people were complex or contradictory, I pretended otherwise. I turned every defeat into a disaster, every success into an epic triumph, and separated all people into heroes or villains. Unable to bear ambiguity, I built a barricade of delusions against it.

My other delusions were more obvious and therefore more troubling to my mother. I became extravagantly superstitious, collecting phobias as other boys collected baseball cards. I avoided ladders and black cats, threw salt over my shoulder, knocked on wood, held my breath walking past cemeteries. So determined was I not to step on a crack, for fear of breaking my mother's back, that I weaved down the sidewalk like a drunk. I spoke "magic" words three times to ward off dangers, and watched for signs and omens from on high. While listening for my father's voice I also listened for the voice of the universe. I communed with rocks and trees and inanimate objects, especially the T-Bird. Like a horse whisperer I petted its dashboard and begged it to keep running. If the T-Bird broke down, I worried, my mother would break down. Irrational fears hounded me, and the worst was the fear of being the last one to fall asleep in Grandpa's house. If everyone but me was asleep, I felt unbearably alone, and my limbs went cold and rigid. It may have had something to do with the absence of all voices. When I confided this fear to my cousin Sheryl, five years older than I, she put her arm around me and said the perfect thing. "Even if we're all asleep you can be sure Uncle Charlie and everyone down at Dickens will be awake."

My mother hoped I'd outgrow my odd behavior. Instead I grew worse, and when I began throwing tantrums she took me to a child psychiatrist.

"What's the boy's name?" the psychiatrist asked as my mother and I settled into chairs across from his desk. He was jotting notes on a legal pad.

"JR," my mother said.

"His real name."

"JR."

"Those are his initials, no?"

"No."

"Well." The psychiatrist dropped his legal pad on his desk. "There's your answer."

"Pardon?" my mother said.

"The boy is obviously suffering an identity crisis. He has no identity, which causes rage. Give him a name—a *proper* name—and you'll have no more tantrums."

Rising, my mother told me to put my jacket back on, we were leaving. She then gave the psychiatrist a look that could have cracked Shelter Rock in two and in measured tones informed him that seven-year-olds do not suffer identity crises. Driving back to Grandpa's she gripped the steering wheel tightly and ran through her repertoire in three-quarter time. Suddenly she stopped singing. She asked what I thought of the doctor's remarks. Did I dislike my name? Did I suffer from an identity crisis? Was something or someone causing me to feel—rage?

I peeled my eyes from the mansions flying by, turned slowly from the window to my mother, and gave her my own blank face.

four | GRANDPA

IT HIT ME ONE DAY. I REALIZED THAT MY MOTHER WASN'T OF-fended so much by Grandpa's house as by its owner. The needed repairs saddened her because they reminded her of the man who refused to make them. Catching her glance in Grandpa's direction, then seeing her sink into a bottomless gloom, I got it, though I assumed her problem with Grandpa had something to do with how he looked.

Along with his house, Grandpa let himself go to pot. He wore pants with patches, shoes with holes, shirts wet with his saliva and leavings from his breakfast, and he went days without combing his hair or putting in his teeth or bathing. He used and reused his razor so many times that his cheeks looked as if he'd been clawed by a wild cat. He was crusty, rumpled, sour-smelling, and one other thing that my mother could never tolerate—lazy. Grandpa had long since stopped trying. As a young man he'd lost or shed whatever ambition he'd possessed. When his dreams of becoming a professional baseball player crumbled to dust he drifted into the insurance business, enjoying a success that turned his stomach. How cruel of fate, he thought, to make him excel at a job he loathed. He got his revenge on fate. The moment he amassed enough money to generate a dependable income for the rest of his life, he quit. From then on he did little more than watch his house fall apart and make his family cringe.

We cringed that much more when he took his act on the road. Every day at dusk Grandpa would walk uptown to greet the rush-hour trains from the city. As commuters stepped onto the platform and discarded their final-edition newspapers, Grandpa would dive into one of the garbage cans and fish a newspaper out, intent on saving himself a few cents. Seeing him with his legs sticking out of a garbage can, no commuter could have imagined why that poor old hobo wanted that final edition in the first place—to check the closing prices on his sizable portfolio of stocks and bonds.

Grandpa had a photographic memory, an astounding vocabulary, a firm command of Greek and Latin, but his family wasn't able to enjoy his intellectual gifts because he never engaged us in actual conversations. He kept us at bay with a ceaseless patter of TV jingles, advertising slogans and non sequiturs. We'd tell him about our day and he'd shout, "It's a free country!" We'd ask him to pass the beans and he'd say, "Tastes good like a cigarette should." We'd mention that the dog had fleas and he'd say, "Don't tell everybody—they'll all want one!" His private language was a fence he put around himself, a fence that grew a few inches taller the day he overheard one of my cousins urging the constipated dog to "do boo-boo." Thus was born Grandpa's signature phrase. At least a dozen times a day he'd say, "Do boo-boo," which might mean hello or let's eat or the Mets lost—or nothing at all. It's possible that Grandpa talked this way to compensate for his stutter, rehearsed phrases being easier to say. It's also possible, however, that he was moderately insane.

Grandpa had two passions, one a secret, one not. Every Saturday morning he'd come downstairs with his hair brushed, his teeth in, his clothes pressed and spotless. From the pocket of his blue pinstripe suit a lace handkerchief would rise like a fresh orchid. Without a word he'd get into his Ford Pinto and putter away, not returning until late, sometimes not until the next day. No one asked where Grandpa went. His Saturday rendezvous was like the cesspool, so obviously foul it didn't require comment.

His nonsecret passion was words. For hours Grandpa would sit in his bedroom, solving crossword puzzles, reading books, gazing at a dictionary under a magnifying glass. He considered Shakespeare the greatest man who ever lived, "because he *invented* the Eng, Eng, English language—when he couldn't find a word, he made one up." Grandpa credited his etymological passion to his Jesuit schoolteachers, who, when they couldn't make him memorize a word, beat it into him. Though the beatings worked, Grandpa believed they also caused his stutter. Priests made him love words, and made it hard for him to say words. My first example of irony.

One of the few tender moments I ever shared with Grandpa came about because of a word. It happened when he accidentally answered the phone. With his stutter and poor hearing he tended to avoid the phone, but he chanced to be walking past just as it rang, and picked up. A reflex, maybe. Or else he was bored. Unable to hear what the caller was saying, he waved me over. "Translate," he said, shoving the phone at me.

The caller was conducting a survey for a consumer-research company. She rattled off a list of products, cars and foods, none of which Grandpa had ever used, driven or tasted. Grandpa offered his opinion about each one, lying merrily.

"Now then," the caller said. "What's the best thing about the town where you live?"

"What's the best thing about Manhasset?" I translated.

Grandpa thought carefully, as though being interviewed by the *Times*. "Its proximity to Manhattan," he said.

I relayed his answer to the caller.

"Fine," the caller said. "And lastly, what is your annual income?"

"What's your annual income?" I translated.

"Hang up."

"But—"

"Hang up."

I set the phone on the cradle. Grandpa sat in silence, his eyes closed, and I stood before him, rubbing my hands together, my habit whenever I couldn't think of something to say.

"What's 'proximity'?" I asked.

He stood. He put his hands in his pockets and jiggled some coins. "Closeness," he said. "For in, for in, for instance, I have too much prox, prox, proximity to my family." He laughed. A chortle at first, then a raucous haw-haw, which made me laugh. We were both laughing, cackling, until Grandpa's laughter became a coughing fit. He pulled a handkerchief from his pocket and hocked it full of phlegm, then patted me on the head and walked away.

After that brief exchange I felt a new emotional proximity to my grandfather. I started to get ideas about winning him over. Maybe I could ignore his faults, focus on his good points, whatever those might be. I just needed to climb over his linguistic fence. I wrote a poem about him, which I grandly presented to him one morning in the bathroom. He was lathering his jaws for a shave, using a beaver-hair brush that looked like a giant mushroom. He read the poem, handed it back to me and turned back to his reflection in the mirror. "Thanks for the pl, pl, plug," he said.

Later I had a pang. Would befriending Grandpa mean betraying my mother? I realized I should get her permission before I went any farther, and so at bedtime I sounded her out, asked her to tell me again why we hated Grandpa. She tucked my atrophying security blanket under my chin and chose her words carefully. We didn't hate Grandpa, she explained. In fact she hoped I could find a way to get along with him as long as we lived under his roof. I should continue talking to Grandpa, she said, even when he didn't answer me. And I shouldn't pay too much attention to the fact that she didn't talk to him. Ever.

"But why don't you?" I asked. "Why do you get so sad whenever you look at him?"

She stared at the peeling wallpaper. "Because," she said, "Grandpa is a real-life Scrooge, and not just with money."

Grandpa hoarded love, my mother said, as if he were afraid of one day running out. He'd ignored her and Aunt Ruth and Uncle Charlie while they were growing up, gave them no attention or affection whatsoever. She described one family outing at the beach when she was five. Seeing how sweetly the father of her cousin Charlene played with his children, my mother asked Grandpa to put her on his shoulders in the ocean. He did, but then carried her past the waves, and when they were out far, when she could barely see the shore, she became frightened and pleaded with him to let her down. So he threw her. Down she went, plunging to the bottom, gulping seawater. She fought her way to the surface, gasped for air and saw Grandpa—laughing. You wanted to be let down, he told her, oblivious to her tears. Staggering out of the surf, alone, my mother had a precocious epiphany: Her father was not a good man. In that realization, she told me, came a release. She felt independent. I asked her what "independent" meant. "Free," she said. She looked again at the peeling wallpaper and said more softly, "Free."

But there was one other thing, she said, which cut deeper. Grandpa had forbidden my mother and Aunt Ruth to attend college, and he did so at a time when there were no student loans or financial aid available, so they couldn't circumvent him. More than his neglect, this was the blow that altered the trajectory of my mother's life. She'd longed to attend college, prepare for some exciting career, but Grandpa denied her that chance. Girls become wives and mothers, he decreed, and wives and mothers don't need college. "That's why you're going to get the education I didn't," my mother said. "Harvard or Yale, babe. Harvard or Yale."

It was an outrageous statement for a woman who earned twenty dollars a day. And she didn't stop there. After college, she added, I would attend law school. I didn't know what a lawyer was, but it sounded awfully boring, and I mumbled words to this effect. "No, no," she said. "You're going to be a lawyer. That way I can hire you to sue your father for child support. Ha." She smiled, but she didn't look as if she were kidding.

I cast my mind into the future. After I became a lawyer, maybe my mother could pursue her long-deferred dream of attending college. I wanted that for her. If my being a lawyer could make that happen, I'd be a lawyer. Meanwhile I'd forget about befriending Grandpa.

Rolling onto my side, away from my mother, I promised her that with my first paycheck as a lawyer I would send her to college. I heard a gasp, or a gulp, as if she were fighting her way up from the bottom of the ocean, and then I felt her lips on the back of my head.

five | JUNIOR

DAYS BEFORE MY EIGHTH BIRTHDAY THERE WAS A KNOCK AT Grandpa's door and The Voice was coming out of a man in the breeze-way. The sun was behind the man, shining directly into my eyes, which made it impossible to discern his features. I could see only the outline of his torso, a massive block of pale white muscle in a tight white T-shirt, set atop two bowed legs. The Voice was a giant tooth.

"Give your father a hug," The Voice commanded. I reached up, tried to wrap my arms around him, but his shoulders were too wide. It was like hug-ging the garage. "That's no hug," he said. "Give your father a proper hug." I stood on my toes and squeezed. "Harder!" he said. I couldn't squeeze any harder. I hated myself for being so weak. If I couldn't hug my father hard enough, if I couldn't grab hold, he wouldn't come back.

After a sidebar with my mother, who stole nervous looks at me the whole time, my father said he was driving me into the city to meet his family. Along the way he entertained me with a dizzying Babel of accents. Apparently The Voice wasn't his only voice. Besides being a stand-up, he said, he'd once been an "impressionist," a word that was new and beautiful to me. He demon-strated. He was a Nazi commandant, he was a French chef. Now he was a Mafia thug, now a British butler. Jumping abruptly from voice to voice, my father sounded like the radio when I turned the dial quickly back and forth, a trick that made me nervous even as it made me laugh.

"So," he said, lighting a cigarette, "you like living at your grandfather's house?"

"Yes," I said. "I mean, no."

"Little of both?"

"Yes."

"Your grandfather's a good man. Marches to his own drummer, but I like that about him."

I wasn't sure what to say about that.

"What do you *not* like about living at your grandfather's?" my father asked.

"It makes my mother sad."

"And what do you *like* about living there?"

"Its proximity to my mother."

My father whipped his head toward me, took a drag of his cigarette, and stared.

"Your mother says you listen to your old man on the radio a lot."

"Yes."

"What do you think?"

"You're funny."

"Would you like to be a disc jockey when you grow up?"

"I'm going to be a lawyer."

"A lawyer? Jesus, of all things. Why?"

I didn't answer. He blew a cloud of smoke at the windshield and we both watched it curl up the glass and roll back upon itself like a wave.

I have only hazy memories of my father's face that day. I was too nervous to look at him for more than a second at a time, and I was too captivated by his voice. Also, I was too focused on the speech I was about to deliver. I was going to demand that my father give me money. If I could choose the perfect words, if I could say them just right, I would return to my mother with a fistful of cash and we could escape Grandpa's house and she would never again have to sing in anger or peck at her calculator. I rehearsed in my head, while taking deep breaths and steeling myself. It's like diving off the high board at the public swimming pool, I told myself, closing my eyes. One. Two. Three.

I couldn't. I didn't want to say anything that would make The Voice disappear again. Instead I stared out the window, at the slums and liquor stores and snowdrifts of paper along the side of the road. We must be a long way from Manhasset, I thought, wondering vaguely what I would do if my father kept driving and never brought me back, and feeling guilty that this scenario caused a shiver of excitement.

We arrived at someone's brick town house, which smelled of stewed tomatoes and grilled sausages. I was put in a corner of the kitchen, where I stared up at a row of enormous female rumps. Five women, including one called Aunt Fatty, stood at a stove, fixing lunch. After bolting several helpings of Aunt Fatty's eggplant my father took me to a nearby apartment to meet his "gang." Again I was put in a corner and told to amuse myself. Instead I watched my father and three couples sit around a table, playing cards and drinking. Soon they began to take off their clothes.

"You're bluffing," someone said.

"You're right! Glad I wore my clean underwear today."

"Glad I'm wearing *any* underwear today," my father said, to peals of laughter.

My father was down to his boxer shorts and one black sock. Then he lost the sock. He studied his cards, crooked an eyebrow, made everyone gasp with laughter as he pretended to be in a panic about losing his last article of clothing.

"Johnny," someone said to him, "what you got?"

"Momma, I ain't wearing any clothes—you can see what I got!"

"Johnny's got nothing."

"Aw, shit, I don't want to see Johnny's thing."

"Absolutely. I second that. Johnny's out."

"Wait!" my father said. "The boy! I'll bet the boy!" He called to me and I stepped forward. "Look at this fine young specimen. Wouldn't you rather have this nice little boy than a look at my manhood? Wouldn't you rather have this fruit of my loins than my Fruit of the Looms! I'll see your bet and raise you—Junior!"

My father lost the hand. His friends slid off their chairs, whooping with laughter, and there was some breathless discussion of who would pay for my education, and who would explain things to my mother when my father didn't bring me home.

I don't remember anything after my father bet me, which felt worse than if he'd beaten me. I don't remember him sobering up, putting on his clothes, or driving me home, and I don't remember what I said to my mother about the visit. I know only that I didn't tell her the truth.

Some weeks later I was warming up the radio, waiting for my father's show to start. I planned to tell The Voice about a troubling rumor that the Mets were going to trade my idol, Tom Seaver. Handsome, clean-cut, a former marine who was the ace of the Mets pitching staff, Seaver began his windup with his hands under his chin, as if praying, then drove his powerful body forward, kneeling on his right knee, as if he were going to propose to the batter. That the Mets might trade Seaver was too awful to contemplate. I wondered what The Voice would say. But the time came for The Voice and

The Voice wasn't there. My father had switched shifts or changed stations again. I took the radio to the stoop and slowly turned the dial back and forth. Nothing. I went and found my mother and asked if she knew what had happened to The Voice. She didn't answer. I asked again. Blank face. I asked urgently. She exhaled and looked at the clouds.

"You know I've been asking your father for years to help us," she said. "Right?"

I nodded.

She'd hired lawyers, filed court papers, appeared before judges, and still my father hadn't paid. So she'd made one last effort. She'd sworn out a warrant for my father's arrest. The next day two cops handcuffed and dragged my father away from a live microphone while a stunned audience listened on. When they released my father from jail the following day, my mother said, he was insane with anger. He paid a fraction of what he owed us and failed to appear in court a week later. His lawyer told the judge that my father had fled the state.

My mother waited for all this to sink in. She then told me that within the last twenty-four hours she'd gotten a call from my father. He wouldn't say where he was, and he threatened that if she didn't stop dunning him for money, he'd have me kidnapped. Years later I would learn that my father had also threatened to put a contract on my mother's life, and his voice was so menacing she didn't dare call his bluff. For weeks she couldn't start the T-Bird without her hands shaking.

My father didn't want to see me, but he might kidnap me? It didn't make any sense. I squinted at my mother.

"He's probably just trying to scare me," she said. "But if your father shows up at Shelter Rock, or if someone says he'll take you to see your father, you mustn't go with them." She took me by the shoulders and turned me toward her. "Do you hear?"

"Yes."

I pulled away and walked back to the stoop, back to the radio. Maybe she was wrong. Maybe my father was working at a new station, doing one of his funny voices so he couldn't be recognized. I turned the dial, wiggled the antenna, analyzed each voice, but none was funny like my father, none was deep enough to make my ribs vibrate or utensils tremble. My mother came and sat beside me.

"Talk about it?" she said.

"No."

"You never say how you feel."

"You either."

She blanched. I hadn't meant to be so abrupt. Tears started to run down my cheeks. I thought my mother was telling me the whole truth about my father, which was why it hurt so much, but of course she was editing, holding back the worst. Over the next few years she would gradually reveal the facts, gently paring away the illusion I'd conjured from The Voice, one piece at a time. Still, I always remember the whole story there on the stoop, on that bleak afternoon, because that was when she made the first painful cut.

My father was an improbable combination of magnetic and repellent qualities. Charismatic, mercurial, sophisticated, suicidal, hilarious, short-tempered—and dangerous from the start. He got into a fistfight at their wedding. Drunk, my father shoved my mother, and when his best man objected to such treatment of the bride, my father decked him. Several guests jumped my father, trying to restrain him, and when the cops arrived they found my father running up and down the sidewalk, assaulting passersby.

For their honeymoon my father took my mother to Scotland. When they returned she discovered that the trip was supposed to have been the grand prize in a contest for listeners at his radio station. My father was lucky not to be arrested. In the two years they were married he was always verging into lawlessness, befriending mobsters, threatening cabdrivers and waiters, beating up one of his bosses. Toward the end he turned his outlaw ways on my mother. When I was seven months old my father threw my mother on their bed and tried to suffocate her with a pillow. She broke free. Two weeks later he did it again. She broke free again, but this time he chased her and cornered her in the bathroom with his straight razor. He described in gruesome detail how he was going to carve up her face. He lunged for her and only my crying in the next room broke the spell of his rage. That was the day we left him. That was the day we arrived at Grandpa's house, with nowhere else to go.

"Why did you marry him?" I asked her that day on the stoop.

"I was young," she said. "I was dumb."

I didn't want her to say another word. There was just one more thing I needed to know before I dropped the subject of my father for good.

"Why does my father have a different name than us?"

"He uses an alias on the radio."

"What's an alias?"

"A pretend name."

"What's his *real* name?"

"John Joseph Moehringer."

"My father called me Junior," I said. "Why?"

"Oh." She frowned. "Okay. Your legal name is John Joseph Moehringer, Jr. But I didn't like the name John, and I didn't want to call you Joseph. Or Junior. So your father and I agreed to call you JR. As in Junior."

"You mean, my real name is the exact same as my father's?"

"Yes."

"And JR stands for—Junior?"

"Yes."

"Does anyone know?"

"Well, Grandma. And Grandpa. And—"

"Can we not tell anyone else? Ever? Can we please just tell people that my real name is JR? Please?"

She looked at me with the saddest look I'd ever seen on her face.

"Sure," she said.

She hugged me, and we linked pinkies. Our first mutual lie.

six | MR. SANDMAN

I WAS ONLY TRYING TO REPLACE A VOICE, SO I DIDN'T NEED MUCH. Just another masculine entity, another pretend father. Still, I realized that even a pretend father would be better if I could see him. Manhood is mimesis. To be a man, a boy must see a man. Grandpa hadn't panned out. Naturally I turned next to the only other man in my vicinity, Uncle Charlie—and Uncle Charlie was something to see.

When he was in his early twenties, the hair on Uncle Charlie's head began to fall out, first in small tufts, then clumps, then divots, followed by the hair on his chest and legs and arms. Finally his eyelashes and eyebrows and pubic hair blew away one day like dandelion spores. Doctors diagnosed alopecia, a rare disease of the immune system. The disease devastated Uncle Charlie, but its ravages were more internal than external. After denuding his body, alopecia stripped his psyche clean. He became pathologically self-conscious, unable to leave the house without a hat and dark glasses, a disguise that actually made him more conspicuous. He looked like the Invisible Man.

Personally I loved the way Uncle Charlie looked. Long before bald became fashionable, long before Bruce Willis, Uncle Charlie was sleek—cool. But Grandma told me that Uncle Charlie hated the sight of himself, that he recoiled from every mirror as if it were a loaded gun.

To me, the unique thing about Uncle Charlie wasn't the way he looked, but the way he talked, a crazy, jazzy fusion of SAT words and gangster slang that made him sound like a cross between an Oxford don and a Mafia don. Stranger yet, after blithely issuing a torrent of vulgar words he would apologize for using one fancy word, as though his erudition were more shocking than his profanity. "You don't mind if I say 'verisimilitude,' do you?" he'd ask. "You don't mind if I say 'perspicacious'?" Uncle Charlie had inherited Grandpa's love of words, but unlike Grandpa he pronounced each word precisely, with a flourishing roll of the tongue. I thought sometimes that Uncle Charlie might be showing off, rubbing Grandpa's nose in the fact that *he* didn't stutter.

Just after The Voice disappeared I began taking more notice of Uncle Charlie. When he came to the dinner table I would stop chewing and stare, hanging on his every word. He sometimes went a whole meal in silence, but when he did talk, it was always the same topic. Finishing dinner he would push his plate forward, light a Marlboro Red, and give us a story about Dickens to go with dessert. He told us about two men at Dickens who made a "life-or-death" wager on an arm-wrestling match: The loser had to wear a Boston Red Sox cap for nine full innings at Yankee Stadium. "That's the last we'll ever hear of that guy," Uncle Charlie said, chuckling. He told us one night about Steve and the men from the bar "hijacking" an Entenmann's truck. They heisted hundreds of pies and waged a pitched battle in and around the bar, hurling custards and meringues at each other and at innocent bystanders on Plandome Road. An Entenmann's Gettysburg, Uncle Charlie called it—the wounded bled jelly. Another time Uncle Charlie described how Steve and the gang bought a fleet of old jalopies and tricked them out as stock cars. They filled the trunks with cement, welded the doors shut, and parked the cars along Plandome Road. They were going to find a field the next day and stage their own demolition derby, but they got to drinking and Steve couldn't wait. At three in the morning they went careering up and down Plandome Road, ramming into one another at breakneck speeds. The cops were not amused. Cops were seldom amused by goings-on at Dickens, Uncle Charlie boasted. The men at the bar had a running feud with one cop in particular, a tight-ass who manned a police booth near Memorial Field. Late one night they got up a posse and attacked the empty police booth with flaming arrows, burning it to the ground.

Flaming arrows? Demolition derbies? Pie fights? Dickens sounded both silly and sinister, like a children's birthday party on a pirate ship. I wished my mother would go there once in a while, and bring my grandparents, since they all needed a dose of silly. But my mother hardly drank at all, and Grandma only drank daiquiris on her birthday, and Grandpa drank two generic beers with dinner, never more, never less. He was too cheap to be an alcoholic, my mother said, though he also had no tolerance. On holidays, after a glass of Jack Daniel's, he'd start to sing, "Chicky in the car and the car won't go— that's how you spell Chicago!" Then he'd pass out on the bicentennial sofa, his snores louder than the T-Bird.

On the surface Uncle Charlie didn't seem like someone who would go in for the silliness of Dickens. He was too melancholy, too full of long rolling sighs. Like my mother, he was a mystery to me. And the more I studied him the deeper that mystery grew.

Every afternoon a man with a sandpapery voice would phone the house for Uncle Charlie. "Chas there?" the man would say, speaking rapidly, as if he were being chased. Uncle Charlie slept most of the day, and my cousins and I knew the rule. If someone from Dickens calls for Uncle Charlie, take a message. If Mr. Sandman calls, wake Uncle Charlie immediately.

It usually fell to me. I liked answering the phone—thinking it might be The Voice—and when it was Mr. Sandman I would ask him to wait, please, then hurry down the hall to Uncle Charlie's bedroom. Knocking softly I would open the door a crack. "Uncle Charlie?" I'd say. "That man is on the phone."

From the humid darkness I'd hear the creak of his bedsprings. Then a groan, then a loud sigh. "Tell him I'm coming."

By the time Uncle Charlie came to the phone—pulling on his robe, clenching an unlit cigarette in his teeth—I'd be crouched behind the bicentennial sofa. "Hey," Uncle Charlie would say to Mr. Sandman. "Yeah, yeah, here goes. Rio wants Cleveland five times. Tony wants Minnesota ten times. Everybody's doing the Jets fifteen times. Give me the Bears with the points. They're due to cover. Yeah. Eight and a half, right? Right. And what's the under on the Sonics? Two hundred? Uh-huh. Give me the under. Good. See you at Dickens."

My older cousins told me Uncle Charlie was a "gambler," that he was doing something illegal, but I didn't think it could be all that illegal—probably like jaywalking, I figured—until I discovered that the world of gambling, and the special myopia of the gambler, were beyond my comprehension. It happened when I called on my friend Peter. His mother answered the door. "Guess you can't wear *that* anymore," she said, pointing to my chest. I looked down. I was wearing my favorite sweatshirt—WORLD CHAMPION NEW YORK KNICKS—which I loved nearly as much as my security blanket.

"Why not?" I asked, aghast.

"The Knicks lost last night. They're not the champs."

I burst into tears. I ran home and crashed through Grandpa's back door, then stormed into Uncle Charlie's bedroom, an unthinkable breach, barging into the sanctum sanctorum even though Mr. Sandman wasn't on the phone. Uncle Charlie shot up in bed. "Who's there!" he shouted. He was wearing a Lone Ranger mask, except it had no eyeholes. I told him what Peter's mother had said. "The Knicks didn't lose last night!" I cried. "Did they? They couldn't have lost! Could they?"

He flipped up his mask, lay back in bed and reached for the box of Marlboros that was always on his nightstand. "It's worse than that," he said with a sigh. "They didn't cover."

In the summer Uncle Charlie and the men from Dickens would commandeer Grandpa's garage and stage high-stakes poker games that lasted for days. Men would play cards for six hours, walk down to Dickens for food, go home, make love to their wives, sleep, shower, and return to find the game still roaring. I liked to lie in bed late at night, the windows open, listening to the voices raising, calling, and folding. I'd hear cards shuffling, poker chips clicking, bushes rustling as players looked for someplace to pee. The voices were more soothing than a lullaby. For a few days, at least, I would not have to worry about being the last one awake.

While I observed Uncle Charlie's gambling with growing interest, adults in Grandpa's house pretended it didn't exist. Especially Grandma. The phone rang one day and I didn't reach it in time, so she answered. Since it wasn't Mr. Sandman, she refused to wake Uncle Charlie. The caller pleaded. Grandma held firm. "Message?" she said, reaching into the pocket of her housecoat for her grocery list and a pencil stub. "Go ahead. Yes. Uh-huh. Boston ten times? Pittsburgh—five times? Kansas City—how many times?" Of course it's possible she had no idea what the message meant. But I suspect she simply didn't want to know.

In Grandma's eyes Uncle Charlie could do no wrong. He was her only son, and they had a bond that looked familiar to me. Unlike my mother, however, Grandma didn't insist on respect and courtesy from her son. No matter how Uncle Charlie spoke to Grandma—and when hungover he could be vicious—she coddled him, doted on him, called him her "poor boy," because his bad luck evoked in her an inexhaustible pity. Thank God for Steve, she often said. Steve gave Uncle Charlie a job in that nice dark bar when Uncle Charlie was getting dozens of painful and ultimately useless injections in his scalp. Uncle Charlie needed a place to hide, and Steve came to the rescue. Steve saved Uncle Charlie's life, Grandma said, and I gathered that she was doing the same thing by letting Uncle Charlie hide in his boyhood bedroom, with the wallpaper—cartoon baseball players—that had been hung when Uncle Charlie was my age.

Many nights when Uncle Charlie was down at Dickens I'd hang out in his bedroom, looking through his stuff. I'd sift through his betting slips, smell his Dickens T-shirts, tidy up his dresser, which was blanketed with cash. Fifties and hundreds lay everywhere, in a house where Grandma didn't always have enough money for milk. I'd think about taking some money and giving it to my mother, but I knew that my mother would refuse it and be mad at me. I'd stack the bills in neat piles, noticing that Ulysses Grant looked like one of the men I'd seen at the Dickens softball game. Then I'd stretch out in Uncle Charlie's bed, propped up on his goose-feather pillows, and be Uncle Charlie. I'd watch the Mets and pretend I had what Uncle Charlie called "heavy timber" on the game. I'd wonder if Uncle Charlie ever bet heavy timber against the Mets. A thing like that would bother me more than knowing he was breaking the law.

During a rain delay one night I changed the channel, hoping for an old Abbott and Costello movie, and happened upon *Casablanca*. "I'm shocked—*shocked*—to find that gambling is going on in here." I sat up. That man in the tuxedo—he was Uncle Charlie. That hound-dog face, that wistful squint, that furrowed brow. And not only was Humphrey Bogart a dead ringer for Uncle Charlie—except with hair—he also talked like Uncle Charlie, lips never wider than the width of a cigarette. When Bogart said, "Here's looking at you, kid," the hairs on the back of my neck tingled, because it sounded as if Uncle Charlie were in the room with me. Bogart even walked like Uncle Charlie, that flamingo-with-sore-knees gait. Then the topper: Bogart spent every waking hour in a bar. He too had suffered a run of bad luck, apparently, and a bar was where he chose to lie low, along with scores of other refugees playing hide-and-seek with the world. I didn't need much help romanticizing Dickens, but after discovering *Casablanca* I became a hopeless case. At eight years old I began to dream of going to Dickens as other boys dream of visiting Disneyland.

seven | NOKOMIS

WHENEVER SHE FOUND ME IN UNCLE CHARLIE'S ROOM, Grandma would try to lure me out. Walking in with a stack of clean Dickens T-shirts for Uncle Charlie's dresser, she'd see me stretched across his bed and give me a look. Then she'd scan the room—stacks of money, betting slips, hats and dice and cigarette butts—and her ice blue eyes would darken. "I've got Entenmann's coffee cake," she'd say. "Come have a piece with me."

Her words would be clipped, her movements hurried, as if there were something contagious in that room and we were both at risk. I didn't give it much thought, because Grandma was always afraid of something. She set aside time each day for dread. And not nameless dread. She was quite specific about the various tragedies stalking her. She feared pneumonia, muggers, riptides, meteors, drunk drivers, drug addicts, serial killers, tornadoes, doctors, unscrupulous grocery clerks, and the Russians. The depth of Grandma's dread came home to me when she bought a lottery ticket and sat before the TV as the numbers were called. After her first three numbers were a match, she began praying feverishly that she wouldn't have the next three. She dreaded winning, for fear her heart would give out.

I pitied Grandma, and rolled my eyes at her, and yet when we spent time together I found myself dreading right along with her. On my own I was a terrible worrier—I knew this about myself and worried about it—and now and then I worried that if I spent too much time with Grandma, added her dreads to my worries, I'd eventually become paralyzed by fear. Also, Grandma was always teaching me girly things, like how to iron and needlepoint, and while I liked to learn anything new, I worried what these skills would make me.

Still, no matter how much I feared Grandma's influence, I craved her attention, because she was the kindest person in that house. So when she invited me to the kitchen for cake I always abdicated my throne on Uncle Charlie's bed and followed close on her heels.

Before the first bite of cake was in my mouth she'd be well into a story. Uncle Charlie was a superb storyteller, as was my mother, but Grandma was the master. She'd learned her craft as a young girl, haunting movie houses in Hell's Kitchen. After watching over and over whichever western or romance was playing, she'd walk home at dusk and be set upon by poorer kids in the neighborhood who couldn't afford a ticket. Surrounded by this mob—whom I pictured as a mix of Bowery Boys and Little Rascals—Grandma would recreate dialogue and reenact scenes, and the kids would ooh and aah and applaud, making little Margaret Fritz feel momentarily like a movie star.

Grandma knew her audience. She always stressed a moral sure to have special meaning for her listeners. With me, for instance, she talked about her brothers, three beefy Irishmen straight out of *Grimm's Fairy Tales*. "Those boys didn't take any crap," Grandma would say, her version of "Once upon a time . . ." Her classic story about the Brothers Fritz concerned the night they came home and caught their father punching their mother. They were just young boys, my age, but they took their old man by the throat and told him, "Touch Momma again and we'll kill you." Moral: Real men take care of their mothers.

From her brothers Grandma would segue to stories about my other set of cousins, the Byrnes, who lived farther east on Long Island. (I couldn't keep straight in my head how they were related to me—they were the grandchildren of Grandma's sister.) There were ten Byrne kids—one daughter and nine sons, whom Grandma put on the same pedestal as her brothers. The Byrne Boys had that same combination of brawn and grace, she said, holding them up to me as "perfect gentlemen," which I resented. Easy for them to be perfect, I'd think—they have a father. Uncle Pat Byrne was dark and Black Irish handsome and played touch football with his boys every night after work.

At eight years old I was unusually gullible, and yet I was still able to divine the ulterior motive behind many of Grandma's stories. Though she disliked my father, Grandma understood what I got from his voice and what I lost when his voice vanished, and she was doing what she could to summon new male voices for me. I was grateful, and also vaguely conscious that this wasn't the only substitution taking place during our cake-and-story sessions. Grandma was being called upon to fill in for my mother, who was working longer hours, more determined than ever to get us out of Grandpa's house.

As Grandma and I spent more time together, as we grew closer, we both worried that she would run out of material. Eventually our worry came true. Her archive of stories exhausted, she was forced to reach into literature, reciting lyrical passages from Longfellow, her favorite poet, whom she'd memorized as a schoolgirl. I liked Longfellow even better than the Brothers Fritz. I stopped breathing when Grandma recited *The Song of Hiawatha*, stared in awe as she described how the Indian boy's father vanished soon after he was born, and how Hiawatha's mother then died, which left the boy to be raised by his grandmother, Nokomis. Despite the warnings of Nokomis, despite her sense of dread, Hiawatha set off in search of his father. The boy had no choice. He was haunted by his father's voice on the wind.

I enjoyed Grandma's recollections about her epic brothers, and her poetry recitals about heroic men, but I felt embarrassed, even ashamed, because my favorite stories were about a woman—her mother, Maggie O'Keefe. The oldest of thirteen, Maggie was forced to care for her siblings while her mother was sick or pregnant, and she became a folk hero in County Cork for her many sacrifices, including carrying her baby sister piggyback to school when the sister was too lazy to walk. Maggie vowed that her sister would learn to read and write, something Maggie had always longed to do.

What it was that made Maggie leave Ireland, forsake her siblings and parents and flee to New York in the 1800s, we never knew. We yearned to know, because she was the first in a long line of leavers, the matriarch of a clan of men and women who made mysterious and dramatic exits. But her reason for leaving must have been too awful, too painful, because Maggie was said to be a born storyteller, and that story was the one she would never tell.

For her secret torment, for her many fine qualities, Maggie deserved a bit of happiness when she docked at Ellis Island. Instead life got harder. Working as a maid in one of the grand estates on Long Island, she was passing an upstairs window one day when she spotted a gardener beneath a tree, reading a book. He was "despicably handsome," she said years later, and obviously educated. Maggie fell hard. She confided her love to a friend, another maid, and they conceived a plan. The friend, who knew how to write, would take down Maggie's thoughts and turn them into love letters, which Maggie would sign and slip into the gardener's book while he pruned the roses. Naturally the gardener was awed by Maggie's letters, seduced by her soaring prose, and after a whirlwind courtship he and Maggie married. When he learned that Maggie was illiterate, however, the gardener felt cheated, and thus was born a lifelong resentment, which he used to justify drinking and beating her—until their three boys caught him and took him by the throat.

While Grandma was telling me stories late one night, Grandpa appeared in the kitchen. "Give me some cake," he said to her.

"I'm right in the middle of a story," she said.

"Give me a piece of goddamned cake and don't make me ask you twice, you goddamned stupid woman!"

Where Grandpa was merely cold with his children, and off-putting with his grandchildren, he was ugly to Grandma. He belittled her, bullied her, tormented her for sport, and his cruelty was crystallized in his name for her. I never once heard him call her Margaret. He called her Stupid Woman, which sounded like a perversion of certain Indian names—Great Bear and Laughing Water—in *Hiawatha*. I didn't understand why Grandma allowed Grandpa to mistreat her, because I didn't understand the depth of her dependence on him, emotional and financial. Grandpa understood, and exploited it, keeping her in rags to match his own. Out of the forty dollars he gave her each week for food and household expenses, there was nothing left over for a new dress or shoes. Her daily outfit was a tattered housecoat. It was her garb of submission, her sackcloth.

After Grandpa left the kitchen—after Grandma had served him his cake—there was a dreadful silence. I watched Grandma, her gaze riveted on her plate. She removed her thick glasses and touched her left eye, which was now fluttering, twitching, a nervous tic. A photo taken when Grandma was nineteen shows her blue eyes calm and steady, her round face framed by crinkly blond hair. It wasn't a conventionally pretty face, but the features were harmonized by vitality, and when that vitality was gone—dreaded away, bullied away—the features fell out of tune. Along with the twitching eye, the nose sagged, the lips retracted, the cheeks sank. Every day of degradation and shame showed. Even when she was silent, Grandma's face was telling a story.

Though I didn't understand why Grandma couldn't fight back, why she didn't heed her genetic legacy and leave, I understood quite well after that visitation from Grandpa why she told all those stories about men. It wasn't for my benefit alone. She was her own best audience, reminding herself, reassuring herself, that good men do exist, that they might ride to our rescue any moment. As she continued to stare at the crumbs I felt that I should say something, that someone should say something before we were both swallowed by the silence. So I asked, "Why are there so many bad men in our family?"

Without looking up she said, "It's not just our family. There are bad men everywhere. That's why I want you to grow up to be good." Slowly she raised her eyes. "That's why I want you to stop being so angry all the time, JR. No more tantrums. No more security blankets. No more asking for TV sets and toys your mother can't afford. You need to take care of your mother. Do you hear?"

"Yes."

"Your mother works so hard, and she's so tired, and she has no one but you to help her. No one else can do it. She's counting on you. I'm counting on you."

Each time she said the word "you," it sounded like a drum. My mouth went dry, because I was trying my best, but Grandma was saying that my worst fear, the thing I worried about most, was coming true. I was falling short. Failing my mother. I promised Grandma that I would do more, then asked to be excused and went quickly back down the hall to Uncle Charlie's room.

eight | McGRAW

WHAT ARE YOU DOING?" MY COUSIN McGRAW ASKED. He was standing in the middle of the backyard, swinging a bat at an imaginary pitch, making a sound—*koosh*—like the ball connecting. I was sitting on the stoop, the radio in my lap. I was nearly nine and McGraw was seven.

"Nothing," I said.

A few minutes passed.

"No, really," he said. "What are you doing?"

I lowered the volume. "Trying to see if my father is back on the radio."

After shooting another pretend pitch into the gap, McGraw adjusted his plastic Mets batting helmet, which he never took off, and said, "What if there was a machine that let you see or hear your father whenever you wanted? How cool would *that* be?"

McGraw's father, my Uncle Harry, hardly ever came around, but his absence seemed more pointed than my father's because Uncle Harry lived just one town over. And his appearances were scarier, because he sometimes hit Aunt Ruth and the cousins. He once poured a bottle of wine over Aunt Ruth's head in front of McGraw. Another time he pulled Aunt Ruth by her hair along the floor in front of all the cousins. He even slapped me, across my face, which gave me a cold dead feeling deep inside my chest.

McGraw was my best friend and closest ally in Grandpa's house, after my mother. I often introduced him as my brother, and I wasn't lying. I was searching for something truer than the truth. How could McGraw not be my brother, when he led the same life, steered by the same coordinates? Absent father. Weary mother. Shady uncle. Sad grandparents. One-of-a-kind first name that prompted teasing and confusion. Also, as with my name, there was some mystery about the origins of McGraw's. Aunt Ruth told Grandpa that

McGraw's name was inspired by John McGraw, the legendary baseball manager, but I also overheard her telling my mother that she'd picked the most rugged name she could find, to ensure that McGraw, surrounded by sisters, wouldn't be a sissy.

I shared Aunt Ruth's concern. I too feared that McGraw and I were doomed to sissyhood. When McGraw, who was more easygoing than I, didn't worry about such things, I forced him to. I initiated McGraw into my neuroses, drilled into his head the notion that we were growing up without the manly arts, like auto repair and hunting, camping and fishing, and especially boxing. For McGraw's own good I commanded him to help me stuff Uncle Charlie's golf bag with dishrags and newspapers, and with this makeshift punching bag we taught each other to throw left-right combinations. I dragged McGraw against his will to the duck pond by the railroad tracks, where we cast hooks baited with Wonder Bread into the scummy water. We actually caught something, a speckled fish that looked like Barney Fife, which we brought to Grandpa's. We put it in the bathtub and forgot about it. When Grandma found it she scolded us severely, which confirmed my paranoia that we were living under a tyranny of the feminine.

Despite our identical lives McGraw and I were different boys, and our differences seemed to grow out of our relationships with our mothers. McGraw tended to fume at his, whom he called Ruth, while I clung to mine, whom I never once called Dorothy. She was always Mom. My mother let me wear my hair like Keith Partridge, McGraw's mother gave him a military buzz cut every two weeks. I was intense, McGraw was laid back. I was prone to brood, McGraw was a giggler, and his giggle was a distinctive, symphonic trill that conveyed an irrepressible joy. I was finicky about food, McGraw ate everything in sight and washed it down with gallons of milk. "McGraw," Grandma would cry, "I don't have a cow in the backyard!" To which he'd respond with a fit of giggles. I was dark and skinny, McGraw was blond and big, and bigger all the time. He grew like a boy in a fairy tale, breaking chairs, hammocks, beds, the basketball hoop on the garage. Since Uncle Harry was a giant, it seemed logical to me that McGraw was growing like a beanstalk.

McGraw wouldn't talk about his father, and wouldn't talk about why he wouldn't talk about his father. I suspected, however, that whenever a train went across the trestle spanning Manhasset Bay, making a clacking sound audible from one end of Manhasset to the other, McGraw couldn't help but think about his father, a conductor on the Long Island Railroad. Though McGraw wouldn't say so, I believed the sound of the train affected him the way radio static affected me. Somewhere in that white noise is your old man.

When McGraw did get to see his father, it wasn't a visit but an ambush. Aunt Ruth would send McGraw inside some bar to demand money from his father or to have him sign some papers. I could always tell when McGraw had come back from one of these bar ambushes. His chubby cheeks would be flushed, his eyes glassy. He'd look traumatized, but also excited, because he'd just seen his father. He'd want to play baseball in the backyard right away, to burn off the adrenaline and anger. He'd swing the bat hard, whip the ball against the target we'd chalked on the garage—hard. After one bar ambush he threw the ball so hard that Grandpa said he was sure McGraw would knock the garage down.

There was always one other surefire way to tell if McGraw was upset. Like Grandpa, he stuttered. His stutter was much subtler than Grandpa's, but the sight of McGraw fighting to form words never failed to pierce my heart and renew my awareness that he was one of the people in that house who needed my protection. In every photo from those years I have a hand on Mc-Graw's shoulder, a hold of his shirt, as if he's my charge, my ward.

One day McGraw was carted off to see his father, but it wasn't the typical bar ambush. They spent time together, ate cheeseburgers, talked. McGraw even got to steer the train. When he came back he was clutching a grocery bag. Inside was one of his father's conductor hats, big and heavy as a fruit bowl. "It's my dad's," McGraw said, removing his Mets helmet and putting on the conductor hat. The visor dropped over his eyes, the band fell below his ears.

The grocery bag also contained hundreds of railroad tickets. "Look!" McGraw said. "We can take these and go somewhere. Anywhere! Shea Stadium!"

"These tickets are punched," I said, trying to dampen his enthusiasm, because I was jealous that he'd seen his father. "They're no good, *stupid*."

"My father gave them to me."

He snatched the grocery bag away from me.

Wearing his conductor hat, and a change belt his father also gave him, McGraw appointed himself conductor of the living room. He staggered back and forth, imitating the high-wire walk of a conductor going down the aisle of a moving train, though he looked more like Uncle Charlie coming home from Dickens. "Tickets!" he said. "*All* tickets. Next stop—Penn Station!" We all had to fish in our pockets for coins, no exceptions, though Grandma bought many rides on the bicentennial sofa with cookies and glasses of cold milk.

Aunt Ruth pulled the emergency brake on McGraw's living room locomotive. She told McGraw she was suing his father for child support, and McGraw would have to testify in court. McGraw would be called to the witness stand, where he'd have to swear on the Holy Bible that Uncle Harry had left his wife and six kids to starve. McGraw moaned and put his hands over his ears and ran out the back door. I ran after him and found him behind the garage, sitting in mud. He could barely speak. "I've got to stand up and say bad things about my father!" he said. "He'll never want to see me again! I'll never see my father again!"

"No," I told him. "You don't ever have to say anything bad about your father if you don't want to." I would smuggle him to Shelter Rock before I let that happen.

The case never did go to court. Uncle Harry gave Aunt Ruth some money and the crisis passed. But there were no more visits between McGraw and his father for a long time after that. Quietly McGraw took off his conductor's hat, put on his Mets helmet, and we all went back to riding the bicentennial sofa for free.

In the spare bed we shared in a far corner of Grandpa's room, McGraw and I would lie awake at night and talk about everything except the subject that bound us, though sometimes that subject would intrude. Grandpa liked to sleep with the radio on, so every few minutes a deep-voiced announcer would make me stop and listen. And every train going by in the distance would make McGraw lift his head. After McGraw fell asleep I'd listen to the radio and the trains and watch the moonlight fall through the window in wide canary yellow stripes across McGraw's chubby face. I'd thank God for him, and I'd worry about what I'd do if he weren't there.

And then he was gone. Aunt Ruth moved the cousins to a house some miles up Plandome Road. She was determined to escape Grandpa's house too, though it had nothing to do with the conditions or the overcrowding. After a nasty fight with Grandma and Grandpa she left in a blaze of temper, staying away and keeping the cousins away. She forbade them to visit.

"Did Aunt Ruth *kidnap* the cousins?" I asked Grandpa.

"You might say that."

"Will she ever bring them back?"

"No. We're em, em, embargoed."

"What's embargoed?"

I'd heard this word many times in 1973. There was a Middle East embargo, meaning the Arabs refused to sell us gas, which was the reason you couldn't buy more than ten gallons at a time at the Mobil station next to Dickens. What did that have to do with Aunt Ruth?

"It means we're on her sh, sh, shit list," Grandpa said.

Furthermore, Aunt Ruth had barred me from her house. I was prohibited from seeing McGraw and the cousins.

"You're on her shit list too," Grandpa said.

"What did I do?"

"Guilt by association."

I remember the McGraw Embargo of 1973 as a time when I too ran out of gas. I moped through the days, listless, glum. It was October. The sugar maples throughout Manhasset turned into torches of red and orange, and from the highest hilltops the town looked as if it were on fire. Grandma was always telling me to go out and play, enjoy the autumn colors and the crisp weather, but I would just lie on Uncle Charlie's bed, watching TV. I was watching *I Dream of Jeannie* one night when I heard the front door open, followed by Sheryl's voice.

"Anybody home?"

I ran out of Uncle Charlie's bedroom.

"What's this?" Grandma cried, hugging Sheryl.

"You're behind enemy lines?" my mother said, kissing her.

Sheryl waved her hand. "Pshaw," she said.

Sheryl feared no one. Fourteen years old, she was the prettiest of Aunt Ruth's daughters, and the most defiant.

"How's McGraw?" I asked her.

"He misses you. He told me to ask what you're going to be for Halloween."

I looked down.

"I can't take him trick-or-treating," my mother said. "I'm working that night."

"I'll take him," Sheryl said.

"What about your mother?" Grandma said.

"I'll run him around the block," Sheryl said, "fill his little bag with loot, and be home before Ruth knows I'm gone." She turned to me. "I'll pick you up at five."

I was on the stoop at four, dressed as the Frito Bandito. I wore a poncho and a sombrero, and I drew a black handlebar mustache in Magic Marker below my nose. Sheryl was right on time. "Ready?" she said.

"What if we get caught?" I said.

"Be a man."

Sheryl settled my nerves by making lots of jokes, and by mocking everyone who gave us candy. As we walked away from a house she'd mutter, "Could you turn down the volume on those pants, mister?" If the porch lights came on as we approached a front door, she'd call out, "Don't put on the coffee—we're not staying!" I was cackling, having a wonderful time, though every now and then I checked over my shoulder to see if anyone was following us.

"Jeez," Sheryl said. "You're making *me* jumpy. *Relax.*"

"Sorry."

We were holding hands and rounding Chester Drive when Aunt Ruth's station wagon pulled up alongside us. Glaring at Sheryl, ignoring me, Aunt Ruth hissed, "Get. In. This. *Car.*"

Sheryl hugged me good-bye and told me not to worry. I walked to Grandpa's, but stopped halfway. What would Hiawatha do? I had to make sure Sheryl was all right. She needed my protection. I circled back up Plandome Road and as I got close to Aunt Ruth's house I crept through alleys and backyards until I reached her back fence. Standing on a trash can I saw shadows in a window and heard Aunt Ruth screaming. I heard Sheryl say something, then more screaming, then glass shattering. I wanted to rush the house and save Sheryl, but I was too scared to move. I wondered if McGraw would come to his sister's defense, and if he'd then be in trouble. It would all be my fault.

I walked slowly to Grandpa's, rubbing off my mustache, stopping now and then to peer in the windows of houses. Happy families. Glowing fireplaces. Children dressed as pirates and witches, sorting and counting their candy. I was willing to lay heavy timber that not one of those kids knew anything about ambushes or embargoes.

nine | DICKENS

MY MOTHER LANDED A BETTER JOB AS A SECRETARY AT NORTH Shore Hospital, and her salary was just enough for us to rent a one-bedroom apartment in Great Neck, a few miles from Grandpa's. I would still attend fifth grade at Shelter Rock, she explained, and after school the bus would still drop me at Grandpa's, but when my mother finished work each night we'd go to our new—*home*. I noticed that she didn't trip over the word, but emphasized it.

More than any previous apartment to which we'd escaped, my mother adored that place in Great Neck. Its hardwood floors, its high-ceilinged living room, its tree-lined street—every detail was precious to her. She furnished the apartment the best she could, with castoff items from the hospital's recently redecorated waiting rooms, junk the hospital had been ready to throw out. Sitting in those hard plastic chairs, we'd wear the same tight faces as the people who had previously occupied them. We too were braced for bad news, but in our case it would be an unexpected car repair or an increase in rent. I worried that when it came, when my mother realized we would have to give up the Great Neck apartment and return to Grandpa's, this disappointment would be different. This one might destroy her.

I was becoming a chronic, constant worrier, unlike my mother, who still fended off worry by singing and speaking in positive affirmations ("Everything's going to be fine, babe!"). Sometimes I'd let her lull me into thinking that nothing frightened her, until I'd hear a scream from the kitchen and run to find her standing on a chair, pointing at a spider. As I killed the spider and carried it down the hall to the trash chute I'd remind myself that my mother wasn't so brave, that I was the man of the house, and thereafter I'd redouble my worrying.

Roughly once a year my mother would drop all pretense of optimism,

lovely colors, her roses-and-milk complexion wreathed by auburn hair. I loved the look of those words, the shapes of them, the subliminal association of their typeface with the pretty face of my mother, but it may have been their functionality that won my heart. Like nothing else, words organized my world, put order to chaos, divided things neatly into black and white. Words even helped me organize my parents. My mother was the printed word—tangible, present, real—while my father was the spoken word—invisible, ephemeral, instantly part of memory. There was something comforting about this rigid symmetry.

Now, in the basement, I felt as if I were standing up to my chest in a tidal pool of words. I opened the largest and heaviest book I could find, a history of the Lindbergh kidnapping. Given my mother's warnings about my father I felt a connection with this Lindbergh baby. I stared at photos of his little corpse. I learned the word "ransom," which I thought must be something like child support.

Many of the basement books were too advanced for me, but I didn't care. I was content to revere them before I could read them. Stacked in one cardboard box was a magnificent leather-bound set, the complete Dickens, and because of the bar I valued these books above all the others, and hungered to know what they said. I gazed longingly at the sketches, especially one of David Copperfield, my age, in a bar. The caption read: "My first purchase in the Public House."

"What's this about?" I asked Grandpa, handing him *Great Expectations*.

We were eating breakfast with Grandma.

"A boy who has great ex, ex, expectations," he said.

"What are—expectations?"

"They're a cur, cur, *curse*."

I ate a spoonful of oatmeal, confused.

"For instance," he said. "When I mar, mar, married your grandmother, I had great ex, ex, expectations."

"Fine way to talk to your grandson," Grandma said.

Grandpa laughed bitterly. "Never marry for sex," he said to me.

I ate another spoonful of oatmeal, sorry I'd asked.

Two books from the basement became my constant companions. The first was Rudyard Kipling's *The Jungle Book,* in which I met Mowgli, my cousin as much as McGraw. I spent hours with Mowgli and his adopted fathers, Baloo, the kindly bear, and Bagheera, the wise panther, both of whom wanted Mowgli to become a lawyer. At least that's how I read it. They were always nagging Mowgli to learn the Law of the Jungle. The second book was a crumbling old volume from the 1930s called *Minute Biographies*. Its butterscotch pages were filled with thumbnail life stories and pen-and-ink portraits of great men through history. I loved its lavish use of exclamation marks. *Rembrandt—Painter Who Played with Shadows! Thomas Carlyle—The Man Who Dignified Work! Lord Byron—The Playboy of Europe!* I cherished its reassuring formula: Every life began in hardship and led inexorably to glory. For hours I would look deeply into the eyes of Caesar and Machiavelli, Hannibal and Napoleon, Longfellow and Voltaire, and I committed to memory the page devoted to Dickens, patron saint of abandoned boys. His portrait in the book was the same silhouette Steve had nailed above the bar.

I was so engrossed in *Minute Biographies* one day that I failed to notice Grandma standing above me, holding a dollar. "I've been looking all over for you," she said. "Uncle Charlie's having a nicotine fit. Run down to the bar and get him a box of Marlboro Reds."

Go to Dickens? Go *inside* Dickens? I grabbed the money, tucked *Minute Biographies* under my arm and ran to the corner.

When I reached the bar, however, I stopped. With one hand on the doorknob I felt my heart racing, and I didn't know why. I was drawn to the bar, but the draw was so powerful, so irresistible, I thought it might be dangerous, like the ocean. Grandma was always reading me articles from the *Daily News* about swimmers being dragged out to sea by riptides. *This must be what a riptide feels like.* I took a deep breath, opened the door, and dove in. The door slammed behind me and I was engulfed in darkness. An alcove. Ahead was a second door. I pulled its handle and the rusty hinges squeaked. Stepping forward again I found myself in a long narrow cave.

As my eyes adjusted I saw that the air was actually a beautiful pale yellow, though I couldn't see any lamps or other possible source of light. The air was the color of beer, and smelled of beer, and each breath tasted like beer—malted, foamy, thick. Cutting through the beer smell was an odor of corruption and decay, though not unpleasant, more like that of an old forest, in which rotting leaves and mold refresh your faith in life's endless cycle. There were also faint notes of perfumes and colognes, hair tonics and shoe creams, lemons and steaks and cigars and newspapers, and an undertone of brine from Manhasset Bay. My eyes watered, as they did at the circus, where the air had a similar animal musk.

Also reminiscent of the circus were all the white-faced men with orange hair and red noses. There was the man who owned the clock-repair shop, who always gave me chocolate cigarettes. There was the cigar-chawing owner of the stationery store, who gaped at my mother in a way that made me want to kick his shin. There were dozens of men I didn't recognize, who looked as if they had just stepped off the train from the city, and several I did recognize, who wore orange Dickens softball jerseys. Many of the men sat in captain's chairs along the bar, a brick wall topped with a slab of golden blond oak, but they weren't confined to the bar area. There were men in the corners, men in the shadows, men in and around the phone booth, men in the back room—a vast mingling herd of the rare beast I'd been stalking.

There were also women in Dickens, astonishing women. The one nearest to me had long yellow hair and frosted pink lips. I watched her run a painted fingernail along the neck of a man and lean against the pillar of his arm. I shivered. The first time I ever witnessed physical affection between a man and a woman. As if feeling my shiver, she turned. "Uh-oh," she said.

"What's the matter?" the man beside her said.

"A kid."

"Where?"

"Over there. By the door."

"Hey, whose kid is that?"

"Don't look at me."

From the shadows Steve stepped forward.

"Help you, son?"

I recognized him from the softball game. He was easily the biggest man in the place. His hair was tightly curled, his face was a dark red, almost mahogany, and his eyes were blue slits. He smiled at me with teeth that were big and crooked and the barroom seemed to grow brighter. Now I knew the secret source of its light.

"Hey Steve!" said a man down the bar. "Get that kid a drink on me ha ha."

"Okay," Steve said. "Kid, you're backed up on Bobo."

Pink Lips said, "Shut up you assholes, can't you see how scared he is?"

"What do you need, son?"

"Box of Marlboro Red."

"Damn."

"Kid smokes the real shit."

"How old are you?"

"Nine. I'll be ten on—"

"Stunt your growth."

"They're for my uncle."

"Who's your uncle?"

"Uncle Charlie."

Gales of laughter.

"Get a load of that!" a man screamed. "Uncle Charlie! Oh that's rich!"

More laughter. So much laughter. If you combined all the laughter in the world, I thought, this is how it would sound.

"Sure," Steve said. "This is Chas's nephew!"

"Ruth's kid?"

"Naw, the other sister," Steve said. "Your mother is Dorothy, right?"

I nodded.

"What's your name, son?"

He had a gorgeous voice. Warm and gravelly.

"JR," I said.

"JR?" He squinted. "What's that stand for?"

"Nothing. It's just my name."

"Is that so?" He cocked an eyebrow at the bartender. "Everybody's name stands for something."

My eyes opened wider. I'd never thought of it that way.

"Got to have a nickname if you're going to come into Dickens," Steve said. "Next time you come in, either have a nickname or we'll have to give you one."

"Whatcha reading?" Pink Lips said.

I handed her my book.

"MY-noot Biographies," she said.

"It's all about famous men," I said.

"I thought *you* wrote the book on men," Steve said to the woman. She cackled.

The bartender reached under the bar for a box of Marlboros. He held them out and I stepped forward. Everyone watched me set the dollar on the bar, take the cigarettes, then back away slowly.

"Come again, kid," Bobo said.

Laughter, laughter. The laughter was so loud that no one heard my answer.

"I will."

ten | PINCH RUNNER

AUNT RUTH LIFTED HER EMBARGO AROUND THE TIME THE Arabs lifted theirs. Once again I was allowed to visit McGraw and Sheryl and the cousins. After school I'd run up Plandome Road to call for McGraw and we'd race off to Memorial Field to play catch, or to the duck pond to fish, delirious about being reunited. A few weeks later we were hit with something worse than an embargo. It was a combination embargo-ambush-kidnapping. Aunt Ruth and the cousins were moving to Arizona. Aunt Ruth dropped the news offhandedly, while having coffee with Grandma in the kitchen. "Out west" was where the cousins needed to be, she said. Mountains. Blue skies. The air was like wine, and the winters were like spring.

I never understood why adults did any of the things they did, but even I knew that the real reason for Aunt Ruth's move to Arizona must be Uncle Harry. My suspicions were confirmed days later, when Grandma told me that Aunt Ruth and Uncle Harry were going to try a reconciliation, and Aunt Ruth hoped a change of scenery would make Uncle Harry mend his ways and be a father to the cousins.

It was all a sick joke. No sooner had McGraw and I been reunited than he was loaded in the back of Aunt Ruth's Ford station wagon with all the suitcases and hauled away to a place so far and unknown that I couldn't picture it. As Aunt Ruth steered the station wagon onto Plandome Road, the last thing I saw was McGraw in his Mets helmet waving to me through the back window.

My response to the loss of McGraw was to hurl myself deeper into my three hobbies—baseball, the basement, and the bar—and combine them into one three-headed obsession. After an hour throwing the ball against the garage, pretending to be Tom Seaver, I'd go down to the basement and read about Mowgli or great men. (*Dante—He Glorified Hell!*) Then, with *The Jungle Book* and *Minute Biographies* in my basket, my mitt slung on the handlebar, I'd ride my bike to Dickens and do figure eights across the street, observing who came and went, particularly the men. Rich and poor, natty and decrepit, all manner of men stopped at Dickens, and each walked through the door with a heavy tread, as though laboring under an invisible weight. They walked as I walked when my backpack was full of schoolbooks. But when they walked out, they floated.

After a while I'd pedal from the bar to the field down the street, where boys played pickup games of baseball every afternoon. If the game went late we'd invariably have a visitor. Twilight was that witching hour when drinkers at Dickens checked their watches, drained their cocktails and hurried home. Leaving the bar they would often spot our game and undergo powerful flashbacks to their childhoods. Salesmen and lawyers would toss aside their briefcases and beg for one swing of the bat. I was pitching when such a man appeared, grinning, shooting his cuffs. He marched toward me like a manager intending to pull me for a reliever. A foot away he stopped. "The fuck are you supposed to be?" he said.

"Tom Seaver."

"Why's it say 'P I' on your shirt?"

I looked down at my white undershirt, on which I'd drawn "41" with a Magic Marker. "That's forty-one," I said. "Tom Seaver's number."

"Says P I. Wha's that—Fi? You a math whiz or sumpin'?"

"That's a four, that's a one. See? Tom Terrific."

"Nice to meet you, Tom T'rific, I'm Dead Drunk."

He explained that he needed to "sweat off the booze" before going home to "the lil' missus." Therefore he'd be our pinch runner. All the boys looked at each other. "You dopes," he said. "Haven't you ever hurr of a pinch runner? The pinch runner stands nex home plate and runsa bases erry time a batter makes contact!"

"What if nobody makes contact?" I said.

"Ho!" he said. "Cocky! I like that. Just throw the fucking ball, Tom."

I waited for the pinch runner to get set. Then I fired a speedball at the batter, who hit a slow dribbler to third. The pinch runner sprinted toward first, his limbs spastic, his necktie streaming behind him like a ribbon tied to a car antenna. He was out by a mile. He kept running. He headed for second. Out again. He ran to third. Out. No matter how many times we threw him out or tagged him out, the pinch runner wouldn't stop. He sprinted for home. Head lowered, he dove through the air, belly-flopping onto the plate, where he lay motionless as we all gathered around him, Lilliputians gathering around Gulliver. We discussed whether or not he was dead. At last he rolled onto his back and started to laugh like a maniac. "Safe," he said.

All the boys laughed with him, none more than I. I was a serious boy—my mother was serious, our situation was serious—but this man at my feet was the opposite of serious, and I noted that he'd come from Dickens. I couldn't wait to join him. I couldn't wait to become him.

Instead I became more serious. Everything became more serious.

I'd assumed that sixth grade would be a cinch, like all grades before it, but for some reason the workload doubled and turned dramatically harder. Also, my schoolmates all at once seemed much smarter than I, and more aware of how the world worked. My friend Peter told me that when you applied to college, you had to present a list of all the books you'd ever read. He already had fifty books on his list, he bragged. I don't remember all the books I've read, I told him, panicking. In that case, Peter said, you probably won't be allowed into college.

"What about law school?" I asked.

He shook his head slowly from side to side.

In Mrs. Williams's sixth-grade science class we had to sign a contract, binding us to do our best. What Mrs. Williams intended as a clever motivational device, I saw as a death warrant. I scrutinized that contract, wishing I were a lawyer already, so I could find a loophole. Each morning, the contract in my backpack, I would board the bus for school as if headed for labor camp. Shortly after I got on, the bus would pass a retirement home. I'd press my face against the window and envy those old people, sitting in their rockers, free to watch TV and read all day. When I mentioned this to my mother, she said very quietly, "Get in the T-Bird."

Steering us around Manhasset my mother told me that I needed to stop worrying. "Just try your *best*, babe," she said.

"That's the same thing Mrs. Williams's contract says," I complained. "How do I know what my best is?"

"Your best is whatever you can do comfortably without having a breakdown."

She didn't understand. According to my black-or-white view of the world, it wasn't enough to do my best. I had to be perfect. To take care of my mother, to send her to college, I needed to eliminate all mistakes. Mistakes had led to our predicament—Grandma marrying Grandpa, Grandpa denying my mother's wish to go to college, my mother marrying my father—and they continued to cost us. I needed to correct those mistakes by avoiding new ones, and by getting perfect grades, then getting into a perfect college, then a perfect law school, then suing my imperfect father. But with school getting harder, I couldn't see how I was going to be perfect, and if I were imperfect, then my mother and Grandma would be disappointed with me, and I'd be no better than my father, and then my mother would sing and cry and peck at her calculator—this was how my mind raced on the playground as I watched the other kids playing tetherball.

My mother sat me down one night in the dining room, Grandma by her side. "Mrs. Williams phoned me at work today," she said. "Mrs. Williams tells me that at recess you sit on the playground, staring off into space, and when she asked what you were doing, you told her you were—*worrying*?"

Grandma made her tsk-tsk sound.

"Now look," my mother said. "When I feel myself starting to worry, I just tell myself, *I will not worry about something that will not happen,* and that always calms me, because most of the things we worry about will never happen. Why don't you give that a try?"

Like Mrs. Williams with her contract, my mother thought her affirmation would motivate me. Instead it hypnotized me. I converted it into an incantation, a mantra, and chanted it on the playground until I induced a trancelike state. I used my mantra as both a spell, to ward off disasters, and a club, to beat back the onslaught of worrisome thoughts about disasters. I'm going to be left back and have to repeat sixth grade. *I will not worry about something that will not happen.* I'm going to fail out of school and then I won't be able to take care of my mother. *I will not worry about something that will not happen.* I'm just like my father. *I will not worry . . .*

It worked. After I'd repeated my mantra a few thousand times Mrs. Williams announced that we'd be taking a break from our many assignments. All the kids cheered, and I cheered the loudest. "Instead," Mrs. Williams said, "we'll be planning the annual Sixth-Grade Father-Son Breakfast!" I stopped cheering. "Today," she continued, holding up construction paper and glue, "we're going to design and make our own invitations, which you'll bring home to your fathers after school. Saturday morning we'll cook our fathers breakfast and read to them from our schoolwork and everyone will get a chance to know each other better."

When class ended Mrs. Williams called me to her desk. "What is it?" she asked.

"Nothing."

"I saw your face."

"I don't have a father."

"Oh. Is he—did he—pass on?"

"No. I mean, maybe. I don't know. I just don't have one."

She stared out the window beside her desk, then turned back to me.

"Is there an uncle?" she said.

I frowned.

"A brother?"

I thought of McGraw.

"Anyone who can fill in?"

Now it was my turn to look out the window.

"Can't I please just not come to the breakfast?"

Mrs. Williams phoned my mother, which prompted another dining room summit. "How can they be so asinine?" Grandma said. "Don't they know what the world is like nowadays?"

My mother stirred milk into a cup of coffee while I sat by her side. "I should've told the school about JR's father," she said. "But I didn't want them to treat him—I don't know."

"I'm going to say something to you both," Grandma said. "Now don't jump down my throat. But, well, okay, what about Grandpa?"

"Oh not that," I said. "Can't we just embargo the breakfast?"

Grandpa came into the dining room. He was wearing stained chinos, a flannel shirt crusted with oatmeal drippings, and black shoes with holes in the toes big enough to see his socks, which also had holes. As always, his fly was open.

"Where's that crumb cake you've been bragging about?" he asked Grandma.

"We have something to ask you," Grandma said.

"Speak, Stupid Woman. Speak."

My mother tried. "Would you be able to fill in for JR's father at his school's Father-Son Breakfast?" she asked. "This Saturday?"

"You'd have to put on clean pants," Grandma said. "And comb that hair. You can't go looking like this."

"Shut your goddamned mouth!" He closed his eyes and scratched his ear. "I'll do it," he said. "Now get the goddamned cake. Stupid Woman."

Grandma went into the kitchen with Grandpa. My mother gave me a blank face. I knew she was imagining what would happen if Grandpa referred to Mrs. Williams as Stupid Woman.

On Saturday morning my mother and I left our apartment in Great Neck at dawn. I wore a corduroy blazer and corduroy pants. At Grandpa's my mother and Grandma fumbled with my necktie, which was brown and wider than the runner on the dining room table. Neither of them knew how to make a Windsor knot.

"Maybe he can skip the tie," Grandma said.

"No!" I said.

We heard footfalls on the stairs. The three of us turned to see Grandpa descending slowly. His hair was slicked back, his jaws were shaved so smooth they were blue, his eyebrows and nose hairs and ear hairs were plucked and trimmed. He wore a pearl gray suit, set off by a black necktie and an Irish linen handkerchief. He looked finer than he'd ever looked for any secret Saturday rendezvous.

"The hell's the mat, mat, matter?" he said.

"Nothing," Grandma and my mother said.

"We can't tie my tie," I said.

He sat on the bicentennial couch and motioned for me to come near. I walked to him and stood between his knees. "Stupid women," I whispered.

He winked. Then he yanked my tie. "This tie is shit," he said. He went upstairs and selected a tie from his closet, which he wrapped around my neck and knotted swiftly, expertly. I smelled lilac aftershave on his cheeks as he worked under my Adam's apple, and I wanted to hug him. But we were rushing out the door, Grandma and my mother waving to us as though we were embarking on a long sea voyage.

As the Pinto went putt-putting up Plandome Road, I looked at Grandpa. He didn't say a word. By the time we reached Shelter Rock he still hadn't said anything, and I realized this had been a terrible mistake. Either Grandpa was tense about meeting new people, or he was irked about sacrificing his Saturday. Whatever the reason, he was miffed, and when miffed Grandpa was likely to say or do something that people in Manhasset would talk about for fifty years. I wanted to jump out of the car and make a run for it, hide under Shelter Rock.

The moment we pulled into the school parking lot, however, Grandpa changed. He wasn't on his best behavior, he was on someone's else's behavior. He got out of the Pinto as though stepping from a limousine at the Academy Awards, and walked into the school as if he'd endowed the joint. I fell in alongside him and as we met the first wave of teachers and fathers, Grandpa put a hand lightly on my shoulder and turned into Clark Gable. His stutter disappeared, his manner softened. By turns he was gracious, funny, self-deprecating—and sane. I introduced him to Mrs. Williams and thought within minutes that she might have a crush on the old gent. "We're expecting big things from JR," she gushed.

"He's got his mother's brains," Grandpa said, clasping his hands behind his back, standing ramrod straight, as if a medal were about to be pinned on his chest. "I'd rather see him concentrate on the baseball. You know, this boy has a rifle for an arm. He could play third base for the Mets someday. That was my position. Hot corner."

"He's lucky to have a grandfather who takes such an interest."

The students served the fathers scrambled eggs and orange juice, then joined them at long tables set up in the middle of the classroom. Grandpa's manners were impeccable. He didn't dribble crumbs down his shirtfront, didn't make any of the explosive noises that normally indicated he was full and digestion was under way. Sipping his coffee he educated the other fathers

on a variety of subjects—American history, etymology, the stock market—
and gave a sensational account of the day he saw Ty Cobb go five for five.
The fathers stared, like boys listening to a ghost story around a campfire, as
Grandpa described Cobb sliding into second base, "screaming like a ban-
shee," the blades of his sharpened cleats aimed at his opponent's shins.

When I brought Grandpa his fedora and helped him into his topcoat,
everyone was sorry to see him go. In the Pinto I let my head fall back against
the seat and said, "Grandpa—you were amazing."

"It's a free country."

"Thank you so much."

"Don't tell anyone—they'll all want one."

At home Grandpa went straight upstairs while Grandma and my mother
sat me down in the dining room and debriefed me. They wanted every detail,
but I didn't want to break the spell. And anyway, I didn't think they would
believe me. I told them everything went fine and left it at that.

Grandpa didn't reappear until later that afternoon when the Jets game
started. He sat down in front of the TV wearing his stained chinos and
oatmeal-crusted shirt. I sat beside him. Every time something interesting
happened I looked his way, pointedly, but he didn't flinch. I said something
about Joe Namath. He grunted. I went to find Grandma, to discuss my
Jekyll-Hyde grandfather, but she was busy making dinner. I went to find my
mother. She was taking a nap. I woke her, but she said she was tired, and
asked me to let her sleep a little while longer.

My mother had good reason to be tired. She was slaving to pay for our
Great Neck apartment. But in early 1975 we discovered another reason. She
had a tumor on her thyroid.

In the weeks before her surgery Grandpa's house was actually quiet,
everyone filled with dread. I alone remained calm, thanks to my mantra. I
wore out my mantra. When I overheard Grandma and Uncle Charlie whispering about my mother, and the risks of her surgery, and the chance that her
tumor would be malignant, I shut my eyes and took a deep breath. *I will not
worry about something that will not happen.*

On the day of the surgery I sat under the pine tree in Grandpa's backyard, saying my mantra to the pinecones, which Sheryl once told me were the
"pine tree's babies." I wondered if the pine tree was the mother or the father.

I placed the pinecones closer to the tree, reuniting them with their mother-father. Grandma appeared. A miracle, she said. My mother was out of surgery and everything was fine. What she didn't say, what she didn't know, was that I'd done it. I'd used my mantra to save my mother.

Bandaged around her neck, my mother left the hospital a week later, and our first night in Great Neck she went straight to bed. I ate a bowl of noodles and watched her sleep, saying my mantra under my breath, wafting it over her like a blanket.

Grandma and Grandpa congratulated my mother on how quickly she recovered after the surgery. Good as new, they said. But I noticed something different. My mother was given to more blank faces than ever. She would touch her bandage and look at me, blankly, and though she shed the bandage eventually, the blank faces didn't stop. Sitting with her, doing my homework, I'd look up and catch her staring at me, and I'd have to say her name three times to bring her out of it. I knew what she was thinking. While she'd been sick and out of work, our bills had piled up. We were going to lose that Great Neck apartment. We were going to have to return to Grandpa's. Any day now I would wake to find my mother pecking at the calculator, talking to her calculator. Any night now she would cover her face and sob.

When the inevitable moment came, my mother took me by surprise. "We're a family, you and I," she said, sitting me down at the kitchen table. "But we're also a democracy. And I'd like to put something to a vote. Do you miss the cousins?"

"Yes."

"I know. And I've been thinking a lot about that. I've been thinking about a lot of things. So here it is, babe. How would you feel about moving to Arizona?"

Images flooded my mind. Riding horses with McGraw. Climbing mountains with McGraw. Trick-or-treating with Sheryl.

"When can we leave?" I asked.

"Don't you want to think about it?"

"No. When can we leave?"

"Whenever we want." She smiled, a fragile smile, but fierce. "It's a free country."

eleven | STRANGERS IN PARADISE

J UST EIGHTEEN MONTHS IN THE DESERT HAD TURNED THE COUSINS
into precious metals. Their hair was gold, their skin copper, their faces a
stunning bronze. As they ran toward us at Sky Harbor Airport, my mother
and I took a half step back. Bundled in our dark coats and woolen mufflers,
we looked and felt like refugees from another century. "How white you are!"
Sheryl shouted, holding her forearm next to mine. "Look! It's chocolate—
vanilla! Chocolate—*vanilla!*"

Only the oldest three girls met us at the airport. It was late at night. Driving to Aunt Ruth's house, where my mother and I were to stay until we could
find our own place, Sheryl promised that we'd love Arizona. "We live in paradise," Sheryl said. "Literally! Says so on all the signs. 'Welcome to *Paradise—
Valley.*' It's a ritzy suburb of Scottsdale. Kind of like the Manhasset of
Arizona."

I peered out into the darkness, which was twice as dark as nighttime in
New York. All I saw were vague outlines of ominous mountains, a shade
blacker than the night itself. I'd read that there were mountains in Arizona,
but I'd expected something different, something on the order of the mountains in *Heidi* and *The Sound of Music,* lush and green, with sun-dappled
meadows where aproned women and cherubic kids gathered daffodils. These
mountains were barren, pointy triangles rising abruptly from the flat desert,
like the pyramids. I stared at the biggest, which Sheryl said was called Camelback. "How come?" I asked. "Because it looks like a *camel's back,*" she said, as
though I were a dope. I turned to look at the mountain again. I couldn't see
any camel. To me it looked like the pinch runner from Dickens sprawled on
his back, and the two humps were his knees and paunch.

My mother found a job immediately, as a secretary at a local hospital.
Finding an apartment proved more difficult. With so many senior citizens in
Arizona, most apartment complexes, especially affordable ones, didn't allow
children. Finally she lied to a landlord, saying she was a divorced woman,
alone. After we moved in she told the landlord that her ex-husband had cus-

tody of me, but he'd been transferred out of state and she was taking care of me until he got settled. The landlord didn't like it, but he didn't want to go to the trouble of evicting us.

With the money we got from selling our waiting-room furniture and the T-Bird, my mother and I rented two beds, a dresser, a kitchen table and two dinette chairs. For the living room we bought two folding beach chairs at a drugstore. After buying a junky 1968 Volkswagen Bug we had $750 left, which my mother kept in the freezer.

Not long after our arrival Aunt Ruth and the cousins took us to Rawhide, a pretend town in the middle of the desert, which featured a pretend gold mine, a pretend jail, even pretend people. At the front gate, within a circle of authentic Conestoga wagons, was a group of huge mechanical mannequin cowboys gathered around a campfire. Their hushed voices crackled from speakers in the cacti. They were worried about Apaches. And snakes. And weather. And the Great Unknown, which lay beyond the Rio Grande. "If we don't get across the Rio Grande by August," the head mannequin said, "we're goners fer sure." The others nodded gravely. McGraw and I nodded too. Far from home, surrounded by desert—the difference between a Conestoga wagon and Aunt Ruth's station wagon seemed slight.

We walked through the pretend town, down its one main road, which started at the saloon. The smoke from the mannequins' campfire followed us down the street. I'd thought the woodsmoke in Manhasset was intoxicating, but Arizona woodsmoke was even more fragrant, more magical, with flavors I couldn't identify, which Sheryl said were hickory, sagebrush, pinion, and mesquite. The stars in the desert were better too. Closer. Each one was a pen-light held before my face. I looked up, filled my lungs with clean desert air, and decided Sheryl was right. This was paradise. The mountains and cacti and roadrunners, everything that had seemed so strange at first, now gave me hope. My mother and I had needed something new, and this was as new as we could get. I felt the difference already. My mind was clearer, my heart lighter. My habitual worry was lessening. Best of all I could see the difference in my mother. She hadn't given me a blank face in weeks, and she seemed to have twice the energy.

Shortly after our trip to Rawhide my mother phoned Aunt Ruth to see if

McGraw wanted to play with me. "No answer—again," my mother said, setting down the phone. "How can there be no answer in a house with eight people?"

We drove to Aunt Ruth's house and knocked at the door. We put our faces against the window. No sign of anybody. When we got back to our apartment my mother phoned Manhasset, an unprecedented extravagance. It may have been the first long-distance call in the history of our family. After speaking briefly with Grandma, my mother hung up. She was white. "They're gone," she said.

"What?"

"Aunt Ruth and the cousins are on their way back to Manhasset."

"For good?"

"I think so."

"When did they leave?"

"I don't know."

"*Why* did they?"

Blank face.

We never did find out. Our best guess was that Aunt Ruth and Uncle Harry had fought, he went back to New York, and she went after him. But we could never be sure, and Aunt Ruth wasn't the type to explain.

Without the cousins Arizona changed overnight from paradise to purgatory. It started to get hot, scary hot, and summer was still months off. The Volkswagen had no air conditioning, and when my mother and I drove to the store for cold drinks, in every direction would be wavy heat, nothing moving along the sere horizon except dust devils and tumbleweeds. In a photo of me then, waiting for the school bus, I look like the first boy on Mars.

To take our minds off things, my mother and I would go for long drives at sunset. In Arizona, however, there were no waterfront houses for distraction, no Shelter Rocks. Just flat desert and more flat desert. "Let's go back to Manhasset," I said.

"We can't," she said. "We sold everything. I quit my job. We're *here*." She looked around and shook her head. "This is—home."

One Saturday, helping my mother unpack the last boxes of our belongings sent by Grandma, I found a two-foot blue device that looked like a piston with a handle at each end. It was a Miracle Chest Enhancer, according to the package in which it came. I gave it a try. "What the heck are you doing?" my mother said when she saw me, shirtless, squeezing the device in front of a mirror.

"Enhancing my chest."

"That's for ladies," she said. "It doesn't give you the kind of *enhancement* you want. Hand it over." She took the device and frowned. I saw in her face that I could occasionally be as much a mystery to my mother as she was to me.

"You're bored, aren't you?" she said.

I looked away.

"Let's go to that pretend town," she said.

At the entrance to Rawhide we said hello to the mechanical mannequin cowboys. "If we don't get across the Rio Grande by August . . ." We stopped into the saloon and my mother bought two sarsaparillas and a bag of popcorn. The barroom smell of beer and cigars made me think of Dickens. I wondered if there had been any more pie fights. We sat on a bench in the shade outside the saloon and passed the popcorn back and forth. A gunfight broke out in front of us, in the middle of the street. Four men told the sheriff they were taking over this here town. They drew. The sheriff drew. Bang. The sheriff fell. "Outnumbered," my mother said, "and outgunned."

As the dead sheriff got up and dusted himself off, my mother turned to face me. She had an idea, she said. I should go back to Manhasset for the summer. "It's our only option," she said. "I can't leave you alone in the apartment all summer. A few hours after school is one thing, but I can't have you alone by yourself, all day, every day, for three months. And with you in Manhasset I can work overtime, take a second job, maybe save up for furniture."

"How will you get along without me?" I asked.

She laughed, until she realized I wasn't kidding.

"I'll be fine," she said. "The time will fly by, because you'll be having fun, and I'll know you're having fun, and that you're with people you love."

"How will we afford a plane ticket?" I asked.

"I'll put it on a credit card and think about it later."

We'd never been apart for three days, and now my mother was proposing three months? I started to argue but the subject wasn't open to debate. Our two-person democracy had reverted to a benevolent dictatorship. It was just as well. I couldn't convince my mother that the prospect of seeing McGraw and the cousins didn't excite me. I wasn't that good a liar yet.

The night before I left, while I slept, my mother wrote me a letter, which she gave me to read on the plane. She wrote that I should take good care of Grandma, and play nice with the cousins, and that she would miss me terribly, but that she knew Manhasset was the place for me. "I can't afford summer camp for you," she wrote. "So Manhasset will be your summer camp."

Neither of us dreamed that she was sending me to Camp Dickens.

twelve | COLT, BOBO, AND JOEY D

I'D BEEN BACK IN MANHASSET ABOUT TWO WEEKS WHEN IT HAP-pened. I was throwing my rubber ball at the garage, Tom Seaver snapping another slider on the outside corner to win Game Seven, when above the roar of the crowd—the wind whooshing in the branches of the trees—I heard my name. I looked up.

"Don't you hear me calling you?" Uncle Charlie said. "Christ."

"Sorry," I said.

"Gilgamesh."

"Excuse me?"

He sighed and spoke with exaggerated slowness, enunciating each syllable more precisely than usual. "Gilgo. Beach. Do you want to go to Gilgo Beach?"

"Who?"

"You."

"With who?"

"With your uncle. What's the matter with you?"

"Nothing."

"How soon can you be ready?"

"Five minutes."

"False."

"Two?"

He nodded.

The house was empty. Grandma was shopping, Grandpa had gone for a walk, and the cousins, though they lived nearby, were never around, due to another fight between Aunt Ruth and Grandma. Could I possibly go to the beach without telling anyone? My mother had warned me several times before I left Arizona: Don't go anywhere without permission. Kidnapping still concerned her, and Grandma frequently underscored her warnings. I didn't know that my mother and Grandma had *asked* Uncle Charlie to "do something" with me, because I'd been spending too much time alone, and because I'd complained about missing my mother. They had turned to Uncle Charlie for help, assuming he'd explain it all to me. They didn't understand that Uncle Charlie, like Aunt Ruth, never explained.

I put on my swim trunks under my dungarees and packed a grocery bag with a towel and a banana, then sat on the stoop to think. There was no time to think. Uncle Charlie was crossing the lawn, dressed in his version of beachwear: Bing Crosby golf hat, Foster Grants, jeans. He was sliding behind the wheel of his massive old black Cadillac, which he'd just bought from a friend of Steve's. He adored that car. I watched him straighten the rearview, tenderly, as if pushing a lock of hair from the face of someone he loved. Then he adjusted the brim of his hat, lit a Marlboro, and started the engine. The Caddy lurched as he put it into drive. Time was up. I held my breath and ran. As I opened the door on the passenger side and dove in, Uncle Charlie jumped, startled to see me there. "Oh," he said. "Right." We stared at each other. "Better hop in the back."

"How come?" I asked.

"We're going to have passengers."

I sat on the high middle bump of the backseat, like a prince being pulled in a rickshaw, as we cruised down Plandome Road, past Dickens, past Memorial Field. On the south side of town we came to a stop outside a house with all the drapes and shutters closed. Uncle Charlie tapped the horn. From a side door emerged a man about ten years younger than Uncle Charlie, with shiny black hair and droopy black eyes. Solidly built, with broad shoulders and a deep chest, he looked like a young Dean Martin. I thought he might be one of the softball players I'd seen years before, though he was acting different now. He wasn't laughing, and he wasn't being silly. He was in pain, shielding his eyes like a prisoner being released from solitary confinement. Bending down at Uncle Charlie's window he rasped, "Hey, Chas, what do you say?" His voice was weak, like mine the morning after my tonsils were removed, but this wasn't nearly the most notable thing about how he talked. He sounded exactly like Yogi Bear.

"Morning," Uncle Charlie said.

The man nodded, as if that were all the conversation he felt up to. He walked around the car and got in on the passenger side. "Mother of God," he said, letting his head fall back against the seat. "The hell did I drink last night?"

"Your usual," Uncle Charlie said.

Uncle Charlie glanced in the rearview. Again he was startled to see me. "Oh," he said. "Colt, meet my nephew. He's coming with us today."

Colt turned and peered at me over the seat.

Within minutes the Cadillac was crammed with a half ton of men. I thought we were going to the beach, but we had enough muscle to pull a bank job. Uncle Charlie introduced me formally, stiffly, to each man. Pleased to meet you, kid, said Joey D, a giant with a tuft of gingery hair atop his spongy orange head, and features glued to the head at odd angles. He seemed to be made of spare parts from different Muppets, like a Sesame Street Frankenstein—head of Grover, face of Oscar, thorax of Big Bird. Like Colt he was ten years younger than Uncle Charlie, and treated my uncle with extreme deference, like an irreproachable older brother. Though hulking and slouch-shouldered, Joey D had the manic energy of a small man. He speed-walked, fluttered his hands, spoke in word spasms that left him winded. Like hayfever sneezes, whole sentences exploded from his mouth in one burst: *Ocean'sgoingtoberoughtoday!* Most often Joey D aimed these word spasms at himself, more precisely at the breast pocket of his tennis shirt. He was so absorbed and animated with his breast pocket that I thought he must be keeping a pet mouse in there.

Next I met Bobo, whose age was impossible to guess, though I put him closer to my uncle—mid-thirties. Bobo was the handsomest member of the group, with a surfer's thatch of corn-yellow hair and arms that popped out of his shirtsleeves, but he gave the impression that he could be a lot handsomer if he would get a good night's sleep. He oozed the smell of last night's whiskey, a scent I liked, though Bobo tried to cover it up with a quart of drugstore aftershave. Whereas Colt and Joey D deferred to my uncle, Bobo deferred to no one but his companion, Wilbur, a black mutt with wide disdainful eyes.

I listened to the conversations of the men, my head whipping back and forth as though I were watching four tennis matches at once. Reading between the lines I gathered that they all worked at Dickens, as bartenders and cooks and bouncers, and therefore Steve was The Boss. They revered Steve. When speaking of him they sounded less like employees than apostles. It wasn't always clear that they were speaking about Steve, however, because he had a number of nicknames, including Chief and Rio and Feinblatt. Each of the men also went by a nickname Steve had bestowed, except Uncle Charlie, who had two—Chas and Goose. After ten minutes I was juggling so many nicknames that I felt as if there were a dozen men in the car instead of the four I counted. The men then confused me further by rattling off a list of other nicknames, people who had stopped into Dickens the night before, like Sooty and Sledge and Rifleman and Skeezix and Tank and Fuckembabe.

"Who's Fuckembabe?" I asked. I knew I wasn't supposed to talk, but the question flew out of my mouth.

The men looked at each other.

"Fuckembabe's the porter," Uncle Charlie said. "Sweeps up the joint. Does odd jobs."

"How come you call him Fuckembabe?"

"That's all he ever says," Colt explained. "Or I should say, it's the only thing he says that anyone can understand. How'd the Yankees do today? *Ah, fuck 'em, babe.* How's the world treating you? *Ah, fuck 'em, babe, fuck 'em.*"

I didn't hear the rest of what Colt said. I was too spellbound by his Yogi Bear impression. Every singsong sentence sounded to my ear like, "Hey, Boo Boo, let's go find us some pic-a-nic baskets."

Joey D recalled for everyone the time Fuckembabe lived behind Dickens, in his car. Steve put a stop to that, Joey D said, when Fuckembabe started doing his laundry in the Dickens dishwasher. It wasn't the washing Steve minded so much, Colt interjected, as the fact that Fuckembabe hung his clothes to dry in the trees out back. The men chuckled at the memory, and Bobo told a related Steve story. Everything reminded the men of another Steve story. The time Steve stole a police car and drove around Manhasset, lights flashing, siren blaring, pulling over his friends and giving them heart attacks. The time Steve went up and down the aisle of an airplane with a carry-on full of champagne bottles, getting all the passengers roaring drunk. The time Steve took a crew of Dickens regulars out to Montauk in his boat, *Dipsomania,* but drank too much and got lost in the fog and wound up halfway to "Nova Fucking Scotia."

Uncle Charlie talked about meeting Steve for the first time when they were seniors at Manhasset High School. Steve had just been kicked out of the Cheshire Academy, in Connecticut, a school where all the boys wore blue blazers and smirks. Cheshire's loss was Manhasset's gain, Uncle Charlie said. I wanted to ask if the Cheshire Academy was where Steve learned to smile like that. In my memory Steve looked something like the Cheshire Cat from *Alice in Wonderland.*

The men hotly debated the renovation Steve was threatening to launch at Dickens, an elaborate and expensive undertaking. Besides remodeling the barroom and fancying up the menu, Steve was considering doing away with the rock bands that performed on weekends. More shocking, he was talking about possibly renaming the place—Publicans. The men didn't approve. Not one bit. They didn't like change, ever, but especially when it came to the bar.

"The fuck's a publican anyway?"

"Bird with a double chin."

"That's a pelican, dipshit."

"A publican's a bartender."

"Then why don't Chief just call the place Bartenders?"

"Who the hell's going to drink in a place called Bartenders?"

"Me, that's who."

"Publicans are bartenders and bar owners in England," Uncle Charlie said. "And in ancient Rome a publican was a tax collector."

"Makes sense. Only three sure things in life. Death. Taxes. And bartenders."

"Hey Bobo," Uncle Charlie said. "How'd you happen to get home from Dickens slash Publicans last night?"

"Search me," Bobo said.

Uncle Charlie smiled and Bobo wrapped his arms around his dog's neck. "Wilbur, boy, did you drive us home again? Huh?" He buried his face in the dog's fur, and the dog turned away, as if embarrassed by public displays of affection.

Joey D jumped in and explained to me—though mainly he was explaining to that pet mouse in his breast pocket—that Wilbur was a human trapped in a dog's body. *Humantrappedinadog'sbody!* I looked at Wilbur to see if this was true, and the dog looked at me with a face that said—*What of it?* The proof of Wilbur's extracanine intelligence, Joey D said, was the dog's adamant refusal to ride in Bobo's car if Bobo had been drinking.

"He also takes the train," Bobo chimed in. "Name me another dog that goes to the station every morning and catches the same goddamned train."

"Really?" I said.

"God's truth. This mutt commutes, kid. Catches the eight-sixteen every morning. A conductor came into Dickens one night and told me. Wilbur must have himself some girl dog over in Great Neck."

Bobo continued to stroke Wilbur's fur. I stared at them both. I knew staring was impolite, but I couldn't stop. Besides handsome, Bobo was also ursine. Not only did he have a name like Baloo, but he looked like the bear from *The Jungle Book*—shaggy, growly, with a large wet snout. It was enough to have one bear in the car—Colt, aka Yogi. Two bears made the Cadillac feel like a circus van. Also, if Bobo's connection to *The Jungle Book* weren't eerie enough, Wilbur was black and sleek, a miniature panther. Bobo resembled Baloo, but Wilbur *was* Bagheera. My head was swimming.

As we hit the expressway Uncle Charlie pushed the Cadillac up to ninety and out came the Zippos. Cigars and cigarettes were lit, stories went flying. I listened closely and learned that the men were fighting a war of nerves with the local police, whom Uncle Charlie called the gendarmes. At least one of the men had been formally "detained." I learned that on a busy night the bartenders at Dickens could clear a thousand dollars, and the bar raked in so much money that Steve was becoming one of the richest men in Manhasset. I learned that the bar fielded five separate men's softball teams, and one women's team, Dickens Chickens, which boasted not only the league's best players, but the most "stone-cold foxes." I learned that half the bartenders were fooling around with half the waitresses; that one woman at the bar was a "poor man's Cher," while another woman with facial hair was a "poor man's Sonny"; that tending bar was also known as being "behind the stick"; that

Steve hired only male bartenders, in case of brawls and holdups, and for this same reason wanted two bartenders on duty at all times; that bartenders who worked side by side developed a bond like a pitcher and a catcher; that during a barroom brawl, a bartender leaping into the fray must leap over the bar feet-first, to avoid being "cold-cocked"; that the greatest danger at Dickens, more than brawls and broads and holdups, was the hangover, which was like a cold you caught from alcohol; that there was an endless number of words for cocktails, even more than there were for sex, including snaps, belts, pops, snorts, shooters and stiffies.

I closed my eyes, let my head fall back against the seat, and felt the voices and the smoke swirling around me. Anyone happen to see Mahoney last Friday night? Question is, did Mahoney see anyone? The man was blind. Tight as a tick. He must have had some hangover the next morning. He should take the cure. I hear his old lady's had it with his shit. Where'd you hear that? His old lady, heh heh. You slut. *You* calling *me* a slut? If I read one more fucking word about America's goddamned two hundredth birthday I'm gonna puke. Real patriot, this guy. His girlfriend thinks he's a patriot—because he's a minuteman, heh heh. I'm patriotic, I just don't want to hear anything more about Ben Franklin and Bunker Hill and Paul Revere. One if by land, two if by sea. Speaking of which, Chas, I need to do number one in the sea—can't this thing go any faster?

Gradually the voices converged into one male voice, until I felt as if I were listening to The Voice. But this was better, because when I opened my eyes, the source of this voice was right there.

Bobo, who had dropped out of the conversation to scan the sports pages, looked up and addressed Uncle Charlie. "Goose," he said, "what're you doing on the Mets tonight? Koosman's on the hill and I'm always on the wrong side with that prick. I can't afford another setback. What do you think?"

Uncle Charlie removed the dashboard lighter and touched it delicately to a Marlboro. Smoke escaped in wisps from his mouth as he answered. "Chas's Rule," he said. "Bet Koos, You Lose."

Bobo nodded appreciatively.

Gilgo wasn't the prettiest beach on Long Island, or the most secluded, but I gathered that the men wouldn't think of going anywhere else—not even the topless beach nearby—because Gilgo was the only beach on Long

Island with a liquor license. Hard stuff, right on the sand. The Gilgo Bar was nothing but a flyblown bait shack with a gritty floor and one long conga line of dusty bottles, but the men strode through the front door as though it were the Waldorf. They had a deep and abiding respect for bars, all bars, and for the decorum of bars. The first thing they did was buy a round for the house—three old fishermen and a leather-faced lady with a cleft palate. Then they bought a round for themselves. With the first taste of cold beer and Bloody Marys the men began to behave differently. Their limbs seemed looser, their laughter more lively. The bait shack shook with their guffaws and I could see the hangovers lifting from them like the morning fog lifting off the ocean. I laughed too, though I didn't know what the joke was. It didn't matter. The men didn't know either. Life was the joke. "It is time!" Bobo said with a volcanic belch. "I've wet my whistle. Now I must wet my pants. To the sea!"

Marching across the sand I kept several paces behind the men, noting how they fanned out into a preordained formation. Uncle Charlie, the shortest, stepped to the fore, a flamingo leading two bears, one Muppet and a panting panther. I couldn't help seeing the men as exotic animals, when I wasn't seeing them as different archetypes of dangerous men. When they carried their beach chairs under their arms, I saw gangsters carrying violin cases. When flashes of light went off around their heads, the sun glinting off the ocean, I saw a platoon of soldiers walking into a burst of artillery. I knew that morning that I'd follow the men anywhere. Into battle. Into the jaws of hell.

But not into the ocean. I stopped at the edge of the cold green water while the men walked straight into the surf. They barely broke stride as they dropped their folding chairs and shed their clothes. Once in the water they kept walking, holding their beers and cups aloft like Statues of Liberty, until they were up to their guts, their nipples, their necks. Bobo went the farthest. He reached a sandbar far from shore, Wilbur paddling furiously alongside him.

I wasn't a strong swimmer, and I couldn't forget Grandma's dread-inducing stories of riptides that carried off whole families, but the men wouldn't let me stay on the sand. They ordered me to join them in the water, and when I did they threw me to the waves. Remembering my mother's story about the day Grandpa took her out deep and then abandoned her, I went stiff. Joey D ordered me to "unstiffen." Relax, kid, just fucking relax.

Relaxkidjustfuckingrelax. Though on dry land Joey D seemed as if he were on the verge of a nervous breakdown, at sea he was an expert relaxer. On cue he could release all the tension in his muscles and bob along like a jellyfish—a 260-pound Irish jellyfish. I watched his face as he floated, a mask of pure serenity I'd never witnessed on any man. Then his face became still more serene, and I realized that he must be peeing.

If Joey D spotted a wave that looked promising he'd angle his big body toward it, letting the wave lift him up and waft him to shore. It's called body-surfing, he said. After much cajoling and coaxing I let him show me how. I let myself go slack, unclenched myself for what felt like the first time in my life, and floated on my back. Though my ears were underwater I could hear Joey D saying, "Atta boy, kid, atta boy!" He pushed me into the path of a wave. I felt my body hoisted suddenly, high, cradled for a moment, and thrown end over end. I went spinning through the air like a human boomerang, an exhilarating out-of-control feeling that I would forever associate with Joey D and the men. Landing on the sand, I scrambled to my feet, covered with seaweed and scrapes, and turned to see the men whistling and applauding, Joey D loudest of all.

We hiked back to the chairs, our tongues hanging out like Wilbur's. None of the men had a towel, and I felt like a sissy swaddled in mine. The men flopped onto their beach chairs and let the sun dry their enormous bodies. With wet fingers they lit cigarettes and cigars and gasped with pleasure as the smoke filled their chests. I smoked too, using a crab leg as a White Owl.

Refreshed from their swim the men arranged their chairs in a circle, opened their newspapers and commenced a spirited colloquium on the news of the day, the talk going around and around me like a carousel. How about this Patty Hearst? That is one screwy broad. Maybe so but I'd still do her. If she was holding a machine gun you'd do her? *Especially* if she was holding a machine gun ha ha. You're sick. Speaking of do, I might do the Mets ten times tonight. Koos has to win eventually right? Fucking bum. Bet Koos, You Lose. Put me in your little book there for five times on the punchless Mets. How the hell did Foreman stop Frazier, will somebody please tell me that? Best fighter I ever saw was Benny Bass. Yeah my old man saw him lose the title to Kid Chocolate. Holy shit Beirut's a bloody mess. Reagan says he's the answer. Jesus—in that case what's the fucking question? What a right hook that Foreman has. He could stop a train. Did you read where the great-grandson of Nathan Hale got married this weekend? Give me liberty or give me death. That's what the groom will be saying in about one month. Check this out: Two men found in trunk of car at Kennedy Airport—cops suspect foul play. Gotta get up pretty early to fool New York's finest. Rave review of this new novel about Ireland by Leon Uris. Potato eaters meets Lotus Eaters. Whatever the fuck that means. Maybe I'll make that my beach reading this summer, I don't know enough about my ancestral homeland. Your ancestral homeland is Queens, fuckface. Hey, *Jaws* is playing in Roslyn tonight, let's all go. I can't see *Jaws* again, it took me a month to get back in the water after we saw it last summer. You don't have to worry about sharks, dipshit, your blood's ninety proof. His nuts are like cocktail olives—one bite and that shark'll be shitfaced. How do you know so much about my nuts is what I'd like to know. I'll tell you who's shitfaced—you, if you'd do Patty Hearst.

"Who's Patty Hearst?" I asked Uncle Charlie.

"Broad who got kidnapped," he said. "Fell in love with her kidnappers."

I looked at him. I looked at the men. I thought I knew how Patty Hearst felt.

The men built a sundial in the center of their circle and instructed me to wake them when the shadow reached the stick of driftwood they jabbed in the sand. I studied the shadow as it crept along. I listened to the men snore and watched the seagulls fish the shallows and thought about removing the stick. *If I knock the stick out of the sundial, time will stop and this day will never end.* When the shadow crossed the stick I woke each man as gently as I could.

No one spoke on the way home. The men were woozy from too much beer and sun. And yet they were still communicating through an elaborate code of gestures and facial expressions. They had whole conversations with shrugs and frowns. Joey D was a better shrugger than a relaxer.

Our first stop in Manhasset was Dickens. The men paused at the back door, looking at me, shrugging at each other, until Uncle Charlie nodded and they let me follow. We walked into the restaurant area. To the left I saw a long row of booths, which someone referred to as The Lounge. Beyond was the barroom, where a group of men stood along the bar. Their faces were redder than ours, though they didn't seem sunburned and their noses were like a row of fresh produce—plum, tomato, apple, dirty carrot. Uncle Charlie introduced me to each man, and lastly he singled out the smallest and toughest, the redoubtable Fuckembabe, who stepped away from the bar and toward me. His head was small, its dark brown skin stretched tight and seemingly lit from within by some combination of childlike joy and beakers of vodka. His face looked like a brown paper sack with a guttering candle inside. "This must be the migwag with the wugga mugsy," he said, shaking my hand and smiling, a becoming smile despite his dry lips and cardboard teeth. "Chas," he said, "I ain't gonna let him legweg my nugga fugga smack jack, I'll tell you that, fuck 'em, babe, fuck 'em, haw haw haw." I looked to Uncle Charlie for help, but he was laughing, telling Fuckembabe that this was true, so true. Fuckembabe then turned to me and asked me a question. "What's the biggerish thing you and your fucking muncle ever did wip the nee nonny moniker doody flipper?"

My heart beat faster. "I'm not sure," I said.

Fuckembabe laughed and patted me on the head. "Chip off the old fooking blocker blick," he said.

Uncle Charlie poured himself a drink, fixed me a Roy Rogers and told me to occupy myself while he and the men made some phone calls. I hopped on a barstool and spun in slow circles, taking in every detail of the barroom. Hanging upside down from wooden slats above the bar were hundreds of cocktail glasses, which caught and reflected the light of the barroom like a vast chandelier. Along a forty-foot shelf behind the bar were scores of liquor bottles, in a rainbow of colors, also reflecting the light and being reflected by the glasses overhead. The overall effect was like being inside a kaleidoscope. I ran my hand along the bar top. Solid oak. Three inches thick. I heard one of the men say the wood had recently been given several dozen fresh coats of varnish, and it showed. The surface was a tawny orange-yellow, like the skin of a lion. I petted it tentatively. I admired the tongue-and-groove floors, buffed smooth by a million footsteps. I studied my reflection in the old-fashioned silver cash registers, which looked as if they'd come from a general store on the prairie. With that same rapture and transport I normally experienced while pretending I was Tom Seaver, I now pretended I was The Most Popular Person in Dickens. The place was jam-packed. It was late at night. I was telling a story and everyone was listening. *Quiet, everybody—the kid's telling a story!* I was holding their attention with only my voice, my story. I wished I knew a story good enough to hold someone's attention. I wondered how Grandma would do at Dickens.

The back bar was two large panels of stained glass. Bobo appeared at my side and said I shouldn't stare at them too closely. "How come?" I asked.

"Notice anything about them?" he asked, popping a maraschino cherry into his mouth.

I leaned forward, squinting. I didn't notice a thing.

"Crazy Jane designed those panels," Bobo said. "She's a friend of Steve's. See anything in that design right there?"

I stared at the panel on the left. Could it be? "Is that a—?"

"Penis?" he said. "You betcha. And that would make the other panel . . ."

I didn't know what one looked like, but based on logic, it could only be one thing. "That's a lady's—?"

"Yup."

Embarrassed, I asked what was in the back room.

"That's where we hold special events," he said. "Bachelor parties, family reunions, high school reunions, office Christmas parties, pizza parties after all the Little League games. And the fish fights."

"Fistfights?" I said.

"*Fish* fights," Colt said, appearing on my other side.

The bartenders, Colt said, often put two Siamese fighting fish in a bowl and bet on the outcome. "But the fish," Colt said sadly, "they get tired, and we usually call it a draw."

Uncle Charlie emerged from the basement and flicked on the stereo.

"Ah," Bobo said. " 'Summer Wind.' "

"Great song," Uncle Charlie said, raising the volume.

"I like Sinatra," I told Uncle Charlie.

"Everyone likes Sinatra," he said. "He's The Voice."

He didn't notice my shocked expression.

Soon it was time for Uncle Charlie and me to go home. I fought back tears, knowing that Uncle Charlie would shower and return to the bar, while I'd eat a tense, inedible dinner with Grandpa and Grandma. I was being pulled from the men and the bar by the riptide of Grandpa's house.

"It was a real pleasure having you with us at the beach today," Joey D said. "You'll have to come again, kid."

You'llhavetocomeagainkid.

"I will," I said as Uncle Charlie led me out the back door. "I will."

I went to the beach every day that summer, weather and hangovers permitting. Upon opening my eyes in the morning I'd first check the sky, then consult with Grandma about what time Uncle Charlie had come home from Dickens. Fair skies and an early night for Uncle Charlie meant I'd be body-surfing with Joey D by noon. Clouds or a late night meant I'd be on the bicentennial sofa, reading *Minute Biographies.*

The more time I spent with Uncle Charlie, the more I talked like him, walked like him, aped his mannerisms. I put a hand to my temple when deep in thought. I leaned on my elbows while I chewed. I also sought him out, tried to engage him in conversations. I thought it would be easy. *Spending time together at Gilgo means we're friends, right?* But Uncle Charlie was his father's son.

One night I found him alone at the dinner table, reading the newspaper and eating a T-bone. I sat beside him. "Too bad about the rain," I said.

He jumped and pressed a hand over his heart. "Jesus!" he said. "Where did you come from?"

"Arizona. Ha."

Nothing.

He shook his head and turned back to his newspaper.

"Too bad about the rain," I said again.

"I like it," he said, not looking away from the newspaper. "Suits my mood."

I rubbed my hands together nervously.

"Bobo going to be at Dickens tonight?" I asked.

"False." Still looking at his newspaper. "Bobo is on the disabled list."

"What does Bobo do at the bar?"

"Cook."

"Wilbur going to be there?"

"Wilbur's on the wagon."

"I like Wilbur."

No answer.

"Colt going to be there?"

"False. Colt's going to the Yankee game."

Silence.

"Colt is funny," I said.

"Yes," Uncle Charlie said solemnly. "Colt is funny."

"Uncle Charlie, could I watch the next demolition derby on Plandome Road?"

"Every night is a demolition derby on Plandome Road," he said. "Whole town's inebriated. You don't mind if I say 'inebriated,' do you?"

I thought. I tried to decide how best to answer. After a full minute I said, "No."

He turned away from the newspaper and looked at me. "What?" he asked.

"I don't mind if you say 'inebriated.'"

"Oh." He turned back to his newspaper.

"Uncle Charlie?" I said. "How come Steve named the bar Dickens?"

"Because Dickens was a great writer. Steve must like writers."

"Why's he so great?"

"He wrote about people."

"Don't they all write about people?"

"Dickens wrote about eccentric people."

"What's eccentric?"

"Unique. One of a kind."

"Isn't everyone unique?"

"God no, kid! That's the whole goddamned problem."

He turned to me again. He looked at me hard. "How old are you?"

"Eleven."

"Sure ask a lot of questions for an eleven-year-old."

"My teacher says I'm like Joe Friday. Ha."

"Hm."

"Uncle Charlie?"

"Yeah?"

"Who's Joe Friday?"

"A cop."

Long silence.

"Eleven," Uncle Charlie said. "Ach, that's a great age." He poured ketchup on his T-bone. "Stay right there. Whatever you do, stay eleven. Don't budge. Follow?"

"I follow."

If Uncle Charlie had told me to run and fetch him something from the moon, I'd have done it, no questions asked, but how was I supposed to stay eleven? I rubbed my hands together harder.

"The Mets going to win tonight?" he asked, looking over his betting sheet.

"Koosman is pitching," I said.

"So?"

"Bet Koos, you lose."

He stopped chewing his steak and stared at me. "You don't miss a trick, do you?" He swallowed, folded his newspaper in half, and rose from the table, looking at me the whole time. Then he walked down the hall to his bedroom. I gulped the beer in his glass just before Grandma came into the dining room.

"How about a nice piece of gushy cake?" she asked.

"False. Cookies. You follow?"

Her mouth fell open.

If Uncle Charlie was too hungover for Gilgo, Grandma wouldn't say he was hungover. She'd say he'd eaten too many potato chips at the bar and his stomach was upset. One morning she didn't even bother with the potato-chip story, because Uncle Charlie was in a bad way, and the smell of whiskey from his bedroom was overpowering. I rocked in the backyard hammock, sulking.

"What's shakin', kid?"

I sat up. Bobo stood in the breezeway, Wilbur at his side. They had come to "rescue" me, he announced. "Why should Uncle Goose spoil everyone's fun?" he said. "Screw Goose. Today it's just you, me and Wilbur. The three amigos."

I couldn't imagine why Bobo would make such an offer, unless he didn't know the way to Gilgo and needed my help finding it. Or maybe he actually liked having me around. Or maybe Wilbur did? Grandma was more mystified than I. She came outside and looked at Bobo and seemed on the verge of calling the cops. Only because Bobo was a friend of Uncle Charlie, and because Wilbur gazed at her so imploringly, did she say yes.

As we pulled onto Plandome Road I thought Bobo must be very sleepy. I didn't understand that he was drunk and stoned. He finished a Heineken in three gulps and sent me into the backseat to fetch him another from a Styrofoam ice chest. I found Wilbur hiding in the well back there and remembered what Joey D had said about Wilbur knowing when Bobo was over his limit.

About two miles from Gilgo, as I was climbing into the front seat with yet another Heineken, Bobo's car went into a tailspin. We flew sideways, helicoptered across three lanes, and Wilbur and I slammed against a back door. Beer went everywhere. Ice cubes rattled around the car like beads in a maraca. I heard tires squealing, glass shattering, Wilbur whimpering. When the car came to a rest I opened my eyes. Wilbur and I were bruised, and soaked with beer, but grateful, because we both knew we should have been dead. We'd been saved by a large, soft dune, which absorbed the impact of the crash.

That night I had a dream. (Or a nightmare, I couldn't decide.) I was at the beach. Darkness was coming on and I needed to get home. Bobo, however, was in no condition to drive. Wilbur will have to drive, he told me. While Bobo slept in the backseat I rode shotgun and watched Wilbur steering us down the expressway. Every now and then the dog would fiddle with the radio, then turn to me with a toothy, demonic grin, his expression saying— *What of it?*

Aunt Ruth got wind of my Gilgo excursions and decided McGraw should go too. She dropped him off at Grandpa's one morning and I'd never seen him so excited. As the morning wore on and Uncle Charlie didn't stir, he lost heart. "Guess we're not going," he said, picking up a bat and walking out to the backyard. I followed.

Just then we heard Uncle Charlie slamming doors, coughing, demanding Coke and aspirin. Grandma hurried down the hall and asked Uncle Charlie if he was going to the beach. "No," he snapped. "Maybe. I don't know. Why?"

She dropped her voice. McGraw and I could hear only a few muttered words. *"Ruth wondered . . . take McGraw . . . good for the boys . . ."*

Then we heard Uncle Charlie. *"Bartenders, not baby-sitters . . . enough room in the Cadillac . . . responsible for two little . . ."*

After a few more exchanges we couldn't hear, Uncle Charlie came into the backyard and found McGraw and me on the stoop, each of us wearing our swim trunks under our dungarees and holding an A&P bag with our version of travel provisions—one sports magazine, one banana, one towel. Uncle Charlie, wearing just boxers, stood in the middle of the yard. "You two mopes want to go to Gilgo?"

"Sure," I said casually.

McGraw nodded.

Uncle Charlie looked at the treetops, as he often did when irritated. I sometimes thought he dreamed about living up there, in a tree house high atop Grandpa's tallest pine, a fortress more remote and secure than his bedroom. "Two minutes," he said.

McGraw and I sat in the backseat as Uncle Charlie drove around town. We stopped first for Bobo. When Bobo and Wilbur got into the front seat they looked at McGraw, then turned and looked at Uncle Charlie. "Goose," Bobo said, "our little family is growing."

"Yeah," Uncle Charlie said, clearing his throat. "That's my other nephew. McGraw, say hello to Bobo and Wilbur."

"Exactly how many nephews you got, Goose?" Bobo said.

No answer.

"Goose," Bobo said, "one of these days, I think you're going to pick me up in a freaking school bus."

As we pulled into Joey D's driveway Bobo was still giving Uncle Charlie the business. "Goose," he said, "I think I'm going to call you *Mother* Goose. Lived in a shoe, had so many nephews he didn't know what to do."

"Mother Goose," McGraw said, giggling. I shoved him. No giggling at Uncle Charlie.

"Who's that?" Joey D said, sliding into the backseat and pointing at McGraw.

"My nephew," Uncle Charlie said.

"Ruthy's kid?"

"Mm-hm."

Only Colt seemed happy to see us. "What?" he said, squeezing into the backseat, forcing McGraw halfway onto my lap. "Another kid? More the merrier, huh, fellas?"

McGraw opened and closed his mouth, and I knew why. Yogi Bear.

Uncle Charlie drove extra fast, maybe because the car was cramped and he felt everyone was eager to get out. At Gilgo he bought McGraw and me hamburgers. He'd never bought me a hamburger, in all my times at Gilgo, but McGraw always looked so hungry. Wolfing down his burger in three bites, McGraw asked if they had any milk behind that bar. I shook my head. Then Bobo belched and I told McGraw that was the signal. To the sea.

McGraw and I followed the men across the sand, and like them we dropped our stuff and stripped to our bathing suits as we walked, hitting the surf in stride. McGraw, however, kept going. He swam past me, past the men, even past Bobo's sandbar. Only Joey D noticed. As McGraw's head grew smaller and smaller in the distance, Joey D yelled, "Bring it in, McGraw!"

McGraw ignored him.

"Believe this kid?" Joey D said as I treaded water beside him. He was speaking to me, ostensibly, but I didn't answer, because I knew he was talking to his pet mouse. I wondered where he was hiding the mouse, since he was bare-chested. "Kid thinks he's Johnny Weismuller. Mile from shore. Keep going, kid—next stop, Madrid. Get a cramp now and you're fish food." Joey D turned and saw Uncle Charlie on the beach, stretched out in his chair, calmly reading the newspaper. "Great," he told his mouse. "Goose don't give a shit." *Goosedon'tgiveashit.* "I gotta keep an eye on his fucking nephew while he reads the paper. Fucking great. I'm not going to get any fucking relaxation today."

I was furious with McGraw for irritating Joey D. If any of the men complained about our going to Gilgo—really complained, not like Bobo's teasing—we'd never be welcome again. There were rules of conduct with the men, and when McGraw didn't follow those rules to the letter I wanted to punch him. At the same time I found myself envying him. He was swimming to Madrid, while I was still heeding Grandma's warnings and staying close to shore. It wasn't just that McGraw had no fear. He seemed to want that riptide, to seek it, as if he longed to be carried away. He had a touch of crazy, which made him more like the men.

When McGraw came out of the water I gave him the evil eye and he pretended not to notice. He joined me in the center of the men's circle and started to build a sand castle. I told him we shouldn't do anything that might annoy the men, but Joey D said to go ahead, "knock yourselves out." He turned to the other men and added, "Anything to keep Flipper out of the fucking water."

Alongside the sand castle McGraw and I built a sundial, which he helped me monitor after the men passed out. The jet-engine whine of their snores—and the sight of Joey D talking to his pet mouse in his sleep—made McGraw roll onto his back and giggle, which made me giggle, and we had to clap our hands over our mouths to avoid waking the men.

It was later than usual when we returned to Manhasset. There was no time for a stop at the bar. Everybody needed to get home. McGraw hung his head as we walked to Grandpa's. I gloated silently. *Ha! Serves you right. You went to the sandbar, but I got to go to the bar that matters.* Then I remembered the many bars McGraw had seen, the bars he'd been sent inside to ambush his father, and I knew he didn't feel cheated about not seeing one more. He just felt sad about saying good-bye to the men.

McGraw and I sat on the bicentennial sofa that night, playing cards, watching *The Odd Couple,* and he couldn't stop talking about Gilgo. He wanted to go every day. He wanted to live at Gilgo. He said Jack Klugman looked like Bobo. I warned him against getting his hopes up. There were variables, I explained. Weather and hangovers. You never knew from one day to the next which might flare up. In McGraw's case there was a third variable. Some days Aunt Ruth wouldn't let him go. Either he had to practice his baseball or else he was being punished. Sometimes Aunt Ruth didn't give a reason.

When McGraw couldn't go to Gilgo I found myself sitting in the men's circle and missing him, wishing he'd never gone in the first place, because now the whole experience felt diminished without him. Everything was more fun with McGraw. He was someone I could share the men with, and giggle with at the astonishing things they said and did. A horsefly bit Bobo's thigh, then flew away in drunken loops, plummeting to its death, and I wished McGraw were there to see it.

Though the men were unfailingly kind to me, they tended to ignore me, and in McGraw's absence I went hours without hearing my own voice. When the men did speak to me directly, it could be awkward. One typical exchange went like this: Joey D looked at me. I looked at him. He looked harder at me. I continued looking at him. Finally he said, "Who the White Sox play tonight?" "Rangers," I said. He nodded. I nodded. End of discussion.

Missing McGraw made me think of my mother, whom I also missed, more all the time. I stared out across the ocean one day, wondering what she was doing. Since we couldn't afford long-distance phone calls, we exchanged audio letters, recorded on cassettes. I would play her tapes over and over, analyzing her voice for signs of stress or fatigue. In her most recent tape she sounded happy. Too happy. She said she'd rented a sofa, with a pretty brown and gold pattern—no faces of Founding Fathers. "We've never had a sofa before!" she said proudly. But I worried. What if we couldn't afford the sofa? What if she couldn't make the payments? What if she started to peck at her calculator and cry? What if I wasn't there to distract her with some jokes? *I will not worry about something that will not happen.* My mantra didn't seem to work at Gilgo. The worrisome thoughts came too fast. *Why am I here? I should be in Arizona, helping my mother. She's probably driving through the desert right now, alone, singing.* With each wave that slapped the shore another unhappy thought crashed in my head.

To distract myself I turned to the men. Uncle Charlie was upset. "Can't think straight today," he said, putting his hand to his temple. "Goddamned Wordy Gurdy has me stumped."

"The fuck is a Wordy Gurdy?" Bobo said.

"Puzzle in the newspaper," Uncle Charlie said. "They give you a half-assed clue, and the answer is two words that rhyme. Like Hot Spot. Or Hell's Bells. It's child's play. The first one I got right off. Jane's Vehicles. Answer? Fonda's Hondas. But the others, I don't know. I must be suffering from Acute Sambuca Brain."

"With a touch of vodka-itis."

"That's a chronic condition."

"Give us one."

"Okay," Uncle Charlie said. "Let's see how smart you dopes are. Richard's Ingredients."

Bobo closed his eyes. Joey D poked the sand with a stick. Colt rubbed his chin.

"Fucking puzzles," Bobo said. "Life's confusing enough as it is."

"Nixon's Fixin's," I said.

Silence fell over me like a shadow. I looked up from the sand and the men were staring, frozen. They couldn't have looked more surprised if Wilbur had spoken. Even Wilbur looked surprised.

"The kid," Colt said.

"Holy shit," Bobo said.

"Give him another," Joey D said to his mouse. *Givehimanother!*

Uncle Charlie looked at me, then back at the newspaper. He read: "Terrific Gary."

I thought. "Super Cooper?" I said.

The men threw their hands in the air and cheered.

That was the day everything changed. I'd always thought there had to be a secret password into the men's circle. *Words* were the password. Language legitimized me in the men's eyes. After decoding the Wordy Gurdy I was no longer the group mascot. The men didn't include me in every conversation, certainly, but they no longer treated me as a seagull that had wandered into their midst. I went from being a vague presence to a real person. Uncle Charlie no longer jumped a foot in the air every time he found me standing beside him, and the other men took more careful notice of me, talked to me, taught me things. They taught me how to grip a curveball, how to swing a nine iron, how to throw a spiral, how to play seven-card stud. They taught me how to shrug, how to frown, how to take it like a man. They taught me how to stand and promised me that a man's posture *is* his philosophy. They taught me to say the word "fuck," gave me this word as if it were a pocketknife or a good suit of clothes, something every boy should have. They showed me the many ways "fuck" could release anger, scare off enemies, rally allies, make people laugh in spite of themselves. They taught me to pronounce it forcefully, gutturally, even gracefully, to get my money's worth from the word. Why inquire meekly what's going on, they said, when you can demand, "What the fuck?" They demonstrated the many verbal recipes in which "fuck" was the main ingredient. A burger at Gilgo, for instance, was twice as tasty when it was a "Gilgo fucking burger."

Everything the men taught me that summer fell under the loose catchall of confidence. They taught me the importance of confidence. That was all. But that was enough. That, I later realized, was everything.

Besides the random lessons the men also gave me specific tasks. They would send me to the Gilgo bar for drinks and cigarettes, or have me read them Jimmy Breslin's column, or dispatch me as their emissary to a blanket of attractive girls. I relished these tasks as a show of their trust, and threw myself into accomplishing them. When the men played poker at Gilgo, for instance, the wind whipping off the water was always a problem, and it was my responsibility to hold the face cards and the pot onto the blanket. It was a job for an octopus, but I managed, and when a card flew away I flew after it. I still remember with fierce pride the looks on the men's faces when I chased the jack of diamonds fifty yards and snared it just before it flipped into the ocean.

thirteen | PAT

I WOKE TO DARK SKIES, AN UNSEASONABLY COOL JULY DAY. NO Gilgo. I lay on the bicentennial sofa and opened *Minute Biographies.* When Uncle Charlie woke, however, he told me to get dressed. "Gilgo?" I said.

"False. Mets, Phillies. Doubleheader."

I'd been promoted.

As if going to Shea Stadium weren't astounding enough, Uncle Charlie said I could wear one of his hats. I picked a lime green number with a plaid hatband and stood at the mirror, admiring myself, tilting the brim this way and that, until Uncle Charlie told me to get a move on.

We picked up Joey D first. He complimented me on my new "chapeau." Then we picked up a bruiser named Tommy. He was large like Joey D, and while he didn't look as much like a Muppet, his features did have that same quality of haphazard and temporary attachment to his face. It was a fleshier face than Joey D's, more elastic, and when Tommy frowned, which was every two minutes, his lips would fall and the features would follow—nose, mouth, eyes and cheeks plunging toward his chin as if being sucked down a drain. Tommy complimented my hat also, then said with a frown that he too was "wearing a new hat." He had a new job, he said.

"Tommy just got hired at Shea," Uncle Charlie explained, looking at me in the rearview. "Head of security. Runs the joint. Hence today's outing. Tommy's getting us in gratis."

We stopped at Manhasset Deli for iced tea and cigarettes. Then, instead of steering toward the expressway, we circled back to Dickens.

"Who else is coming?" I asked as we all took stools at the bar.

Uncle Charlie looked off. "Pat," he said.

"Who's he?" I asked.

"She," Uncle Charlie said.

"Pat's your uncle's girlfriend," Tommy whispered.

We sat around the barroom, waiting for this Pat person. I didn't like the idea of a woman joining the group, and I certainly didn't like that she was late. At last she entered with a whoosh, as if a gust of wind had opened the door and she'd been blown through in its wake. She had hair the color of scotch, bright green eyes, and freckles that looked like tiny wet leaves stuck to the bridge of her nose. She was lanky like Uncle Charlie, a fellow flamingo, though more high-strung. "Hiya gents!" she cried, slamming her purse on the bar.

"Hey Pat!"

"Sorry I'm late. Traffic was a bear." She lit a cigarette and looked me up and down. "You must be JR."

"Yes ma'am." I hopped down from the barstool, took my hat off and shook her hand.

"My, my, my. A real gentleman. What're you doing with these bums?" She said she only wished her son, who was my age, had such nice manners. "You must be the apple of your mother's eye."

In ten seconds she'd found the quickest route to my heart.

Our seats at Shea were three rows behind home plate. Uncle Charlie and the men spread out, stretched their legs, made friends with everyone around us. Uncle Charlie told me if I needed to go to the bathroom, I should feel free, "but take note of where we're sitting and don't stay away too long." He spotted the beer man and waved him over. "Take note of where we're sitting," he told the beer man, "and don't stay away too long."

"Who do you like today?" Joey D asked Uncle Charlie.

"I'm torn. My head says Mets, my bankroll says the Philadelphia Brotherly Lovers. Who do you like, JR?"

"Um. Mets?"

Uncle Charlie pursed his lips and squinted at me as if I'd just said something very sensible. He went to phone in his bet and Pat turned in her seat to face me. "So how's your mom?" she said.

"Good."

"She's in New Mexico?"

"Arizona."

"Oh she must be so lonely without you."

"Gosh I hope not."

"Trust me. I'm a single mother. She's miserable."

"Really?"

"You don't have any brothers or sisters, am I right?"

I shook my head.

"Oh she's all alone out there! But she's making the sacrifice, because she understands how much your cousins and your grandma and Uncle Charlie mean to you! Do you talk on the phone?"

"No." I looked out at centerfield and felt a lump in my throat. "It's too expensive, so we make cassette tapes and send them back and forth."

"Oh! She must be so lonely!"

I will not worry about something that will not happen.

Uncle Charlie returned. "What did you do?" Joey D asked him.

"I did the Mets ten times," Uncle Charlie said. "Kid sounded like he had a premonition."

Joey looked at me with saucer eyes.

"What's ten times mean?" I asked.

"Depends on the bookie," Uncle Charlie said. "Sometimes a time is ten dollars, sometimes it's a hundred. Follow?"

"Follow."

Uncle Charlie looked at Tommy and asked if everything was "set."

"All set," Tommy said, standing, hitching up his pants. "On your feet, kid."

I hopped off my seat.

"Don't forget," Uncle Charlie told Tommy. "His idol is Seaver."

"Chas, like I said, Seaver can be kind of standoffish."

"Tommy," Uncle Charlie said.

"Chas," Tommy said, frowning.

"Tommy."

"Chas."

"Tommy."

"Chas!"

"It's his idol, Tommy."

"It's my ass, Chas."

"Just try."

Tommy gave his most magnificent frown yet, then motioned for me to follow. We walked down a ramp, rode an elevator, passed through a gate, jogged down some stairs. A cop waved us through a metal door, and into a dark tunnel, like a sewer. Up ahead I saw a pinpoint of light, which grew larger as we walked forward. Tommy, his voice echoing, reminded me not to leave his side, no matter what. We stepped through a portal into glaring sunshine, and there, all around us, were the 1976 New York Mets. The blue of their uniforms was blinding. The orange in their caps was like fire. They weren't real. They couldn't be real. They were like the mechanical mannequin cowboys at Rawhide.

"Willie Mays," Tommy said, nudging me. "Say hello to the Say Hey Kid." He picked up a baseball lying in the grass and handed it to me. I stepped toward Mays and extended the ball. He signed it.

"You should see his Cadillac," Tommy said as we walked away. "It's hot pink. Real big shot."

"Like Uncle Charlie?"

Tommy guffawed. "Yeah. Just like."

He brought me to Bud Harrelson and John Matlack and Jerry Koosman, all standing together, leaning on bats as if they were Irish walking canes. I almost told Koosman about Uncle Charlie's Rule, but Tommy turned me away just in time and introduced me to the Mets announcer, Bob Murphy, who wore a sports coat that looked like one of Grandma's afghans. Murphy laughed with Tommy about a dive bar they had both visited. His familiar voice came out of the same box as my father's, which gave me a confusing feeling of closeness to him.

Tommy led me to the dugout and told me to sit down, he'd be right back. I perched on the edge of the bench, beside some players. I said hello. The players didn't answer. I said I was allowed to be there, because my uncle's friend was in charge of security. The players said nothing. Tommy returned and sat beside me. I told him those players were mad at me. "Them?" he said.

"They're from Puerto Rico. *No habla inglés,* kid. Now listen. I looked everywhere. High and low. Someone saw Seaver shagging flies earlier, but he's not around anymore. So we're going to have to let that one go, okay? I'll show you the Jets' locker room, then bring you back."

He walked me through a door in the corner of the dugout. We turned down a hall and into a locker room that smelled something like Dickens—menthol and hair tonic and Brut—and as I looked for Namath's locker I felt Tommy grab my upper arm. I looked up. "Someone I'd like you to meet," he said, jerking his head toward the door. I turned.

Seaver.

"What have you got there?" Seaver said.

"Baseball."

He took it. Tommy pushed me closer to him. I watched the muscles twitch and bulge in Seaver's big forearm, level with my eye, as he worked the pen across the ball. I stared at the number 41 on his chest, just above my head. When he handed me back the ball I tried to raise my eyes but couldn't. "Thank you," I mumbled to the ground.

He walked away, down the tunnel.

"I'm such an idiot," I said to Tommy. "I didn't even look at him."

"What are you saying? You were extremely polite. A perfect gentleman. I was *very proud* to present you."

I carried my ball like a bird's egg back to our seats.

"So?" Uncle Charlie said.

"Mission accomplished," Tommy said.

A look of enormous affection flew between them.

Joey D studied my baseball, taking care to hold it by the seams. I wanted to hug him for being so careful, unlike Pat, who spun it and patted it like a snowball. "Who the heck's Jason Gorey?" she said, squinting at the signatures.

"That's Jerry Grote. He's Tom Seaver's favorite catcher."

"Who's Wanda Marx?"

"That's Willie Mays."

"He's still playing? I thought he retired."

"He did. He's a coach. He drives a pink Cadillac."

"Is he Willie Mays or Mary Kay?"

The game started. The Mets were dreadful that day, and every time they did something wrong Uncle Charlie flagged down the beer man. He also kept close tabs on the scoreboard, checking all the games from around the country, none of which was going his way either. Pat grew tired of his tension and bored with the Mets. She said she was going to look at souvenirs for her son. When she'd been gone three innings Uncle Charlie went to find her. He came back alone. "Vanished," he said dejectedly.

"She'll come home when she's hungry," Tommy said.

"Or thirsty," Joey D said.

Uncle Charlie was having a bad day, and I felt guilty, because it was already one of the best days of my life, and because it was I who had persuaded him to bet the Mets. To take his mind off his losses, and Pat's disappearance, I peppered him with questions. This seemed to work. Cheerfully he explained to me the nuances of baseball—hit-and-runs, double switches, sacrifice bunts, how to calculate batting averages and ERAs. Also, he introduced me to the covert language of baseball. Instead of saying the bases are loaded, he instructed me to say, "The sacks are drunk." Instead of extra innings he said "bonus cantos." Pitchers were "twirlers," runners were "ducks on the pond," and catchers wore "the tools of ignorance." At one point he commended my choice of idol. "Seaver's a goddamned Rembrandt," he said, and I was pleased with myself for catching the reference, thanks to *Minute Biographies*. "Grote asks for the ball on the outside corner—Seaver puts it there. Like a little dab of white paint. And Seaver's got a sixty-foot paintbrush. Follow?"

"Follow."

Even Rembrandt couldn't save Uncle Charlie from the corner he'd painted himself into that day. When the Mets rallied, Uncle Charlie's mood lifted briefly, but then the Phillies rallied, loading the bases. "Sacks are drunk," I said, trying to cheer him up, to no avail. Philadelphia's slugger, Greg "The Bull" Luzinski, sauntered to the plate, looking like Steve at a softball game, a man among boys.

"Goose," Joey D said, "I don't know how to tell you this but I feel a moon shot coming on."

"Bite your goddamned tongue."

Luzinski swatted a high-inside fastball toward left field. We jumped to our feet and watched the ball strike the distant stands with a resounding smack.

"I don't live right," Uncle Charlie said.

"I just had a feeling," Joey D said, shrugging.

"Son of a bitch," Uncle Charlie said to Joey D. "If it didn't cost me so much timber, I'd celebrate your psychic powers. You must be prescient. You don't mind if I say 'prescient,' do you?"

The Mets looked sharper in the nightcap. They took an early lead and Uncle Charlie perked up again. But again the Phillies rallied, taking the lead for good on a Mike Schmidt homer. Uncle Charlie chain-smoked and waved to the beer man and I imagined the piles of fifties and hundreds on his dresser growing smaller. After the second game ended we set off in search of Pat, whom we hadn't seen in three hours. We found her on the mezzanine, drinking beer and laughing with a group of cops. Walking to the car she leaned against me, praising my manners, saying how proud my mother must be. I knew she hadn't behaved well. At the start of the day I'd thought I was being promoted, but Pat was the one being promoted, and she hadn't made the most of her opportunity. Still, I liked her, and wished I were doing a better job of supporting her. The problem was, she was heavier than she looked, and I was cradling my autographed baseball at the same time I was carrying her. Uncle Charlie took her from me. He slung her arm around his neck and led her to the car like a soldier guiding a wounded comrade to an aid station.

When we learned a short time later that Pat had cancer, the first thing I thought of was how tender and patient Uncle Charlie had been with her in that moment. I hadn't appreciated how deeply Uncle Charlie cared about Pat—none of the men had—until she got sick. He moved into her house, fed her, bathed her, read to her, injected her with morphine, and when she died he sat in Grandpa's kitchen, his body convulsing with sobs, as Grandma held and rocked him.

I went to the funeral with Grandma. I stood over Pat's open casket, looking at her face, her cheeks scooped out by the cancer. Though there was no trace of her zany smile, I felt as if I could hear her voice, exhorting me to take care of my uncle. I turned from the casket and saw the men from Dickens gathered around Uncle Charlie, like jockeys and stable boys around a racehorse that's come up lame. I told Pat that we could both relax. Uncle Charlie will turn to the bar, I said. He'll hide there, as he did when he lost his hair. I told her that the men at Dickens would take good care of Uncle Charlie. I promised her that I could see it all. That I was prescient.

fourteen | JEDD AND WINSTON

STEPPING OFF THE PLANE AT SKY HARBOR I SAW MY MOTHER leaning against a pole, her face expectant. When she saw me her eyes filled with tears.

"How big you've gotten!" she cried. "How wide your shoulders are!"

She'd undergone some changes of her own. Her hair was different. More pouffy. She exuded energy, as if she'd had too much coffee. And she laughed—a lot. Making her laugh had always required some effort, but driving home she was giggling at everything I said, like McGraw.

"Something different about you," I said.

"Well." Her voice was quivering. "I have a new friend."

His name was Winston, she said in a tone that spelled trouble. He was tall, he was handsome, he was sweet. And funny? Oh he was terribly funny. Like a comedian, she said. But shy, she added quickly.

"How did you meet?" I asked.

"At a Howard Johnson," she said. "I was eating by myself at the counter and—"

"What were you eating?"

"An ice cream sundae and a cup of tea."

"How can you drink hot tea in this heat?"

"That's just it. The tea was cold. So I complained to the waitress, and she was very rude, and Winston, who was also eating at the counter, made a sympathetic face. Then he came over and we started talking and he walked me out to my car and asked if he could call me."

"Doesn't sound shy to me."

Neither of us spoke for several miles.

"Are you in love?" I asked.

"No! I don't know. Maybe."

"What does *Winston* do?"

"He's in sales. He sells tape. Industrial tape, packing tape, all kinds of tape."

"Duct tape?"

"I don't know. I guess so."

"Grandma will love him. He can redo her living room."

I had mixed feelings about Winston. I liked seeing my mother happy, but I couldn't help feeling I'd failed her. I was supposed to make her happy. I was supposed to make her laugh. Instead I'd gone to Manhasset and hung out with the men from the bar. And, though I could scarcely admit it to myself, I'd enjoyed being with a group of men I didn't have to worry about or take care of. Now, as punishment for shirking my responsibility, for *relaxing*, some tape salesman from Howard Johnson had taken over my job.

More worrisome was the fact that my mother had found something to like about Arizona, which meant we were staying. I thought it was time to admit that Arizona hadn't panned out. We were still struggling, still worrying about money, only now we didn't have Grandma and the cousins to compensate. Then there was the heat. "How can it be this hot in September?" I asked, fanning myself with my plane ticket. "What happened to autumn? What happened to the seasons?"

"Just one season here," she said. "Think of the money we'll save on calendars."

Yeah—she's definitely in love.

Instead of the ivy-covered junior high school set on a bluff overlooking Manhasset Valley, I enrolled that fall in the nearby middle school, which sat in the middle of the desert. I wondered if that was why they called it a middle school, because it sat in the middle of nowhere. Much of the school, like much of Arizona, was still under construction, and classes were held in temporary trailers set on cinder blocks. Under the desert sun the trailers turned to kilns by noon, and we were barely able to breathe, let alone learn.

But the trailers were the least of my troubles. After a summer with the men my Long Island accent was noticeably thicker. ("Ahm dyin' uh thoist! Wud I wouldn't give frah glass-uh wadduh!") I made Sylvester Stallone sound like Prince Charles, which meant I sounded tough, and every schoolyard hooligan wanted to prove himself by trading punches with me. Walking to class I'd hear, "Well, well, here comes Rocky Balboa-ringer," and the fight would be on. I held my own, preserving my teeth and the plane of my nose, because I fought not with anger but confusion. I couldn't understand why

Arizona kids made such a fuss about the way I said certain words. Words, which had helped me break into the men's circle at Gilgo, kept me from fitting in at my new school. Example: Arizona kids said "water" to rhyme with "otter," and mocked me when I said the word to rhyme with "oughta." What was the big deal? There wasn't any water in Arizona anyway.

It didn't help that my mother and I had no money for clothes, and I was starting to grow. My shirts were too small, my pants were suddenly capris. Floods, the kids called them, pointing, snickering. Hey, Noah-ringer, when's the Flood? Again, the preoccupation with water.

What made school especially difficult was my name. JR Moehringer was a handle that begged to be ridiculed. "What's the matter, JR," kids would say, "your mom can't afford more than two letters?" Then they would go to town on Moehringer. They would conjugate my surname like a verb in Spanish class. Homo-ringer. Geronimo-ringer. Lawn-mower-ringer. Remember-the-Alamo-ringer. Each nickname led to another schoolyard fight, though the bloodiest was when a boy simply called me Junior.

After school I'd hurry home to our latest apartment, which my mother found while I was in Manhasset. It was cheap—$125 a month—because it sat beside a raised canal that ran swift and loud with runoff from the Salt River. I'd lie on our rented sofa, icing my bruises and waiting for my mother to come home. I never did schoolwork. If I felt ambitious I'd work on an endless short story about a boy kidnapped by mutant roadrunners and held captive inside a giant cactus. Mostly I just watched reruns of *Adam-12*. I could feel myself turning into someone I didn't recognize, someone I hadn't expected that I would become. I knew I was barreling toward a cliff, and some days the only thing standing between me and the abyss was Jedd.

Jedd had been Sheryl's high-school sweetheart while she lived in Arizona, and it shattered him when she and the cousins bolted back to Manhasset. He still wrote to her and spoke to her on the phone, and he planned to move east and marry her as soon as he graduated from Arizona State. Meanwhile he considered me, her next of kin, the next-best thing, and dropped by the apartment every few days to talk about her.

I thought Jedd might just be the coolest man alive. He drove an MG convertible, burnt orange, with tan leather seats and a walnut gearshift pocked from his gold signet ring. The MG was shaped like a surfboard, and not much bigger, so when Jedd came flying down the street he looked as though he were shooting a curl above the desert. He was thin, sarcastic, tough, and he smoked Marlboro Reds just like Uncle Charlie. Holding his cigarette rigidly between the second and third fingers of his right hand, Jedd gave the Churchill V sign every time he took a puff. He had a reptilian calm, which he maintained with an intravenous drip of Coors and a regimen of strange stretching exercises. While watching TV Jedd would tug each finger until the knuckle gave a sharp pop. Then he'd twist his head to one side until his neck crackled. After this self-realignment his entire body would go slack, as if he'd released its inner torque.

As a boy Jedd had done all the standard things with his father—camping, hunting, fishing—and he must have noticed the look on my face when he talked about his adventures, because one day he suggested we go off into the great outdoors.

"Who?" I asked.

"You and me. You're always bitching about how you miss the changing seasons, falling leaves and all that crap. Let's go north this weekend and look at some snow."

When Jedd proposed the trip to my mother, she asked him questions that made me want to dive under our rented sofa. How cold will it get? Should JR bring mittens?

"Mittens?" I cried.

She stopped, a look of self-reproach on her face. "Sounds like fun," she said. "Bring me back a snowball."

We left at dawn, in Jedd's father's pickup, since the MG wouldn't hold all our gear and the cooler full of food. Within an hour the flat desert gave way to rugged hills. The air turned cool. Patches of snow appeared along the side of the road, then fields of pure white. Jedd slapped in a cassette of Billy Joel, who reminded him of New York, which reminded him of Sheryl, which gave him cow eyes. "Oh brother," I said. "Everyone around me is in *looove.*"

Jedd slugged me on the shoulder.

"You miss her too," he said. "And McGraw. The whole gang. Right?"

He asked me about Manhasset, his second-favorite subject, after Sheryl. I told him a story I'd heard at Gilgo, about Bobo tending bar wearing nothing but his bathrobe, exposing himself to customers. When someone took offense, a fight broke out, and Fuckembabe got thrown through the window of the Mobil station. I must have had a nostalgic look on my face as I pictured the scene, because Jedd said, "You'll be back before you know it. We'll all be in Manhasset soon and we'll have a big party to celebrate. At Dickens."

"It'll be called Publicans by then," I said. "Steve is going to renovate. You'll love it. It's the greatest bar in the world."

"How do you know?"

"I hang out there all the time."

"A shaver like you? In a bar?"

"Uncle Charlie and the men take me to the beach and to Mets games and afterward I hang out with them at the bar. They let me drink beers and smoke cigarettes and bet on the fish fights they have in the back room. One night my fish won."

Jedd grinned at the creativity of my lies.

We were just south of the Grand Canyon when Jedd threw the wheel hard to the right and bounced the truck onto the shoulder. He yanked the parking brake. It made a crackling sound like his neck. "This looks like a good spot," he said.

"For what?"

"Build a snowman."

"How?"

"How! How and who, that's all you say. It's like being with Geronimo and his pet owl. You take a snowball and roll it along the ground until it gets big. It ain't complicated."

In no time we stood face-to-face with a seven-foot man of snow. Jedd gave it quarters for eyes and a hot dog from the cooler for a nose. It looked like Joey D, I told him. Jedd poked a Marlboro into its mouth. "Should we light it?" I asked.

"Nah. It'll stunt his growth."

I stared at the snowman. The sun bounced off the quarters and made its eyes seem as if they were flashing. I thought Jedd a genius. No—a god. Wasn't this the first prerequisite of being a god, making a man from nothing?

"Let's set up camp here beside Frosty," Jedd said.

He pulled the truck into the woods. Beside the truck he spread a blanket, onto which he spilled a bag of screws and stakes and rods, and in minutes a tent billowed up from the ground. Inside he spread sleeping bags, pillows, and a radio. "Chow time," he said, glancing at the lowering sun. He showed me how to gather wood, how to build a fire, how to cook hot dogs on a stick. We ate on a stump as the woods filled with darkness. I washed down dinner with several Dr Peppers, while Jedd worked his way through a six of Coors. "Beer is amazing," he said, holding the bottle to my eyes. "Nutritional. Medicinal. A beverage, but also a meal."

"Bobo says cold beer on a hot day is reason enough not to commit suicide."

"Bobo sounds like a very wise man."

After a dessert of roasted marshmallows Jedd taught me how to douse the fire, how to hang leftover food so bears wouldn't come. He zipped me into my sleeping bag, then sealed up the tent and turned on a radio. "Out here in the middle of nowhere," he said, "you can pick up stations and ball games from all over the country." My heart pounded as he turned the dial and we heard voices from Los Angeles and Salt Lake City and Denver. I nearly told him about The Voice, but thought better of it. Instead I told him more about Manhasset. I told him about Steve stealing the cop car and trying to arrest the whole town, and Wilbur riding the trains. I avoided certain topics, like Grandpa's house. I didn't want to say anything to discourage Jedd from joining my family. In the middle of my monologue he started to snore. I pulled the radio into my sleeping bag. I couldn't pass up this opportunity to check for The Voice—but there were too many voices, too many cities. It was frightening and exhilarating at the same time. The sky was full of voices, more voices than stars, and like the stars they always hovered overhead, even when you couldn't see them.

Jedd woke me at dawn with a mug of coffee, my first ever. Though I loaded it with sugar and cream, I felt like a true woodsman, drinking a mug of cowboy coffee by the ashes of our campfire. Jedd fried up a pan of eggs and bacon, and after breakfast he said it was time to head back. As we pulled onto the highway I glanced behind us. The melting snowman looked as if it were slouching, sad to see us go.

The drive home seemed to take ten minutes. As we descended into the hot desert I felt a lump in my throat. "I hate cactus," I grumbled.

"I like them," Jedd said. "Know why they grow those big arms?"

"No."

He lit a Marlboro. "When a cactus starts leaning to one side," he said, "it grows an arm on the *other* side, to right itself. Then, when it starts tipping that way, it grows an arm on the opposite side. And so on. That's why you see them with eighteen arms. A cactus is always trying to stand up straight. You've got to admire anything that tries that hard to keep its balance."

I wanted to tell Jedd about my fights in school, my crush on a girl named Helen, my hatred of my name and how no one would talk to me or eat lunch with me because I was new and sounded like a member of the Gambino crime family. I didn't know why I hadn't told him these things on the way north or around the campfire. Maybe I hadn't wanted to remind myself. Maybe I hadn't wanted to be a drag. Now it was too late. He was pulling up to the canal.

I invited him in for a Coors. Rain check, he said. He had studying to do. In fact, he said, with finals coming up, he wouldn't be around for a while. I thanked him for everything and we shook hands. He threw me Billy Joel, saluted, then sped away. Standing in the street, watching his truck spin around the corner, I felt rooted to the ground.

Over dinner my mother asked me about the trip. I couldn't speak, and I couldn't understand why I felt so unbearably sad after having such a good time, and I still couldn't swallow the lump in my throat. I'd always been prone to a lump in my throat when sad, but nothing like this. I felt as though a pinecone were stuck halfway down. As I continued trying to swallow, as I balled my mashed potatoes into a snowman, my mother got up and sat beside me. "Where's my snowball?" she asked. Tears flowed down my cheeks. My mother held me while I cried myself out, which I later regretted, because I had nothing left when Sheryl broke up with Jedd soon after that day and he stopped coming around altogether.

My mother and I were spending several nights each week at Winston's house, a dress rehearsal for when we became a family. The idea of Winston as my stepfather was daunting. He was no Jedd. He was the opposite of Jedd. Instead of cool, Winston was ice cold. It wasn't that he disliked me. That might have been fixable. The problem seemed to be that Winston was bored by me.

At my mother's urging he tried. He sought me out, engaged me in conversations, looked for places where our interests and personalities might meet. But it was always obvious that he would rather be somewhere else, and inevitably his boredom evolved into resentment, then rivalry. Driving through the desert one day I mentioned to Winston how much I disliked cactuses. I wasn't sure if I believed Jedd's defense of the cactus, and I thought it would be interesting to get Winston's opinion on the same question.

"Cacti," he said. "The plural is cacti."

"Whatever they're called," I said, "I'm sick of them." Even the high school I was preparing to attend, Saguaro, was named after a cactus.

"Bet you don't know how to spell Saguaro," he said.

I spelled it for him.

"Wrong," he said. "It's with an *h*, not a *g*."

I disagreed. Winston insisted. We bet a dollar. When we got to his house he looked up my high school in the phone book, then sulked for an hour.

Things went rapidly downhill after Winston brought home the sheet from his office football pool. "I never win this thing," he said.

"Let me try?"

"Well! If it isn't Jimmy the Greek. Think you can do better?"

He shoved the sheet at me. I looked it over and remembered Uncle Charlie's many rules. Green Bay never loses at home in December. Kansas City can't cover a double-digit spread on the road. Washington's quarterback likes to drink and usually isn't at his best if the kickoff is early. I filled out the sheet and when my picks won Winston threw the fifty-dollar prize money at me. "Beginner's luck," he said, and I heard him say something nastier under his breath as I lateraled the money to my mother.

Tension ultimately ran so high between me and Winston that I would flee his house, take refuge at a playground up the street, where I would shoot baskets for hours. Invariably Winston would come find me, trailing an air of martyrdom, clearly dispatched by my mother. Basketball bored him almost as much as I did. Football was his game, he said, though he considered placekicking the centerpiece of the sport. While we played H-O-R-S-E he'd regale me with stories of his days as a kicker in college, "winning games single-handedly with my foot." He considered this phrase the height of wit.

I don't remember what finally made Winston snap. He may have noticed me smothering another yawn while he talked about placekicking. He may have felt humiliated after heaving another brick against the rim and losing at H-O-R-S-E yet again. "Let's you and me play a new game," he said, bouncing the basketball so hard that it made a scary twanging noise. "Bas-*kick*-ball." He had me balance the ball on my toe while he counted ten steps backward and stuck his wet finger in the wind. Then he sprinted toward me and booted my basketball high over the fence, into the desert. "It's up!" he shouted. "And it's *good*!" We watched my basketball bouncing among the cacti like a pinball caroming off bumper cushions. When it struck one cactus flush, the ball exploded.

Shortly after that day my mother told me that Winston and she were "taking a break." Her voice was hoarse, like the men from Dickens when Uncle Charlie picked them up in the morning to go to Gilgo. Her hair, I noticed, was no longer pouffy. And she looked exhausted. I didn't say another word the rest of that morning. While my mother wandered around the apartment, listening to Burt Bacharach, I sat on the bank of the canal, trying to figure out how I felt. I was delighted that I wouldn't have to deal with Winston anymore, but I was sad, because my mother was heartbroken. I knew that my mother was searching for romantic love, and though I didn't understand what that was, I suspected it was similar to what I was searching for, a connection of some sort, and I worried that, as much as we cared for each other, loneliness was our true common bond. In the crawl space at Grandpa's house I'd once found a diary my mother kept when she was fourteen. On the first page she'd written, *"Anyone that would dare turn beyond this page, may their conscience, if they have any, bother them the rest of their lives!"* Inside was a list of forty-two qualities she hoped to find in a man. My father possessed no more than two and a half, so I understood that my mother had compromised in her first search for love, and that she was trying in her second search to be more careful, for both our sakes. I further understood that her search was hindered by me. I remembered the lightbulb salesman in New York, whom she liked a lot. After meeting me, he suggested I be sent to boarding school in Europe. Immediately. I remembered the mechanic who threw a fit when I introduced McGraw to him as my brother. "I thought you had only one kid," he told my mother angrily, and he didn't believe her explanation that I merely considered McGraw a brother. Few men were eager to help raise my father's son, which reduced my mother's chances of finding love, and this reality, becoming clearer to me that day on the canal, filled me with guilt. *I should have done more to get along with Winston. I should have made him love me.* Somehow in my cold war with Winston I'd lost sight of my number one goal—taking care of my mother. Now I was just another man who made her life harder.

When I went back down to the apartment my mother suggested a movie. "Something to take our minds off things," she said. She proposed *A Star Is Born,* and I didn't complain. I wanted her to feel better and if that meant sitting through a romantic musical I was more than willing to make the sacrifice.

A sacrifice it was. For two hours Barbra Streisand and Kris Kristofferson broke up and made up and broke up again, for no apparent reason, until Kristofferson mercifully died. In the end, unbowed, her permed hair prickly as a cactus, Streisand belted out the movie's theme song, "Evergreen," as if it were "Amazing Grace." The lights in the theater came up. I turned to my mother, rolling my eyes, but she was covering hers, and crying. People turned and stared. I tried to comfort her, but she wouldn't stop. She cried as we left the theater, and cried harder as I opened the door to the Volkswagen for her. I ran around to the other side and got in. She didn't start the car. We sat and waited for her crying to subside, as if waiting for a monsoon to pass. Handing her one Kleenex after another I remembered what Jedd had said about cacti, how they right themselves, how they are always trying to stand up straight. This was what my mother and I were doing, I decided.

If only our arms would quit falling off.

fifteen | BILL AND BUD

MY MOTHER AND I WEREN'T MAKING IT ON HER $160 A WEEK. Even with her second job selling Avon, and my paper route, we were falling short each month, sliding deeper into debt. There was always an unexpected bill, an expense at school, a problem with the Volkswagen. "The T-Bird in New York cooperated with us," my mother said, scowling at the Volkswagen. "This thing wants to break us." I'd lie in bed at night, worrying about my mother's finances, and her fatigue. Other than the short burst brought on by Winston, her energy had never rebounded after the surgery, and I feared she'd eventually grow too tired to work. Would we live in a shelter? Would I have to leave high school and take a job to support us? Getting up in the night for a glass of water I'd find my mother in the kitchen, pecking at her calculator. Just before I started high school in 1978 the calculator won. We filed for bankruptcy.

Grandma wrote me long letters, stressing the obvious. "Take care of your mother," she wrote. "Do anything you can, whatever she needs at this difficult time. Your mother tries so hard, JR, and it's up to you to see that she eats right and takes time to relax. Make sure she relaxes." Real men take care of their mothers.

I would sit on the canal after school, so tense and worried about my mother that I thought I might die. I would wish that I could relax on cue, like Joey D in the ocean, and then mentor my mother in relaxation. If I was especially tense I'd walk to a desolate shopping mall on the other side of the canal, in the shadow of Camelback Mountain. Though the mall looked condemned, though half its stores were vacant, I found its gloomy atmosphere soothing. Dark, quiet, cavelike, the mall reminded me of Grandpa's basement. And it too held a secret trove of books.

Deep in the mall's core was a bookstore with a highly eclectic selection. There was a wide array of classics—but few bestsellers. There were many works on Eastern religions—but few Bibles. There was a newsstand spilling over with newspapers and periodicals from Europe—but not one local paper. Since I had no money for books I became a prodigious browser. I taught myself to read a novel in five visits, scan a magazine in half an hour. No one ever scolded me for loitering or tried to shoo me away, because no one was ever there. The cash register was forever unmanned.

Ogling the models in a French magazine one day I looked up and saw a line of customers snaking from the cash register to the children's section. The customers were looking around for someone to take their money. When no one materialized they gave up and left. In the far back of the store I spotted a pair of birdlike eyes peering out from behind an unmarked door, which was open just a crack. I made contact with the eyes, and the door slammed shut. I walked back and knocked lightly. I heard rustling, scurrying, and the door flew open. Before me stood a man in corduroy pants and a checked shirt, his black knit tie at half-mast. His eyeglasses were covered with the same fine dust that covered everything in the store, and he was holding an unlit cigarette. "Help you?" he said.

"I just thought I should let you know that some customers were waiting to pay."

"Really?"

We turned and looked at the cash register.

"I don't see anyone," he said.

"They left."

"Okay. Thanks for letting us know."

At the mention of "us" a second man appeared. He was taller than the first, thinner, and his glasses were much cleaner. They were thick black Buddy Holly glasses, and their lenses sparkled under the fluorescent lights. He wore a tennis shirt with a tie wider and more outdated than the first man's. I'd never seen anyone wear a tie with a tennis shirt. "Who's that?" he said, looking at me.

I stammered that I was nobody. The three of us looked at each other, having a staring contest, and then I got an idea. I asked if there might be a position open for someone to stand at the cash register and take money in the afternoons.

"How old are you?" the first man said.

"Thirteen. I'll be fourteen next—"

"Ever work in a bookstore?" the second man said.

"That doesn't matter," the first man said. "Hold on."

He shut the door and I heard them whispering furiously. When the door opened again they were smiling. "Can you be here by two o'clock?" the first man said.

"School lets out at three."

"Fine. We'll work out your schedule later."

We all shook hands and the first man introduced himself as Bill, the manager, the second as Bud, the assistant manager. Bill said he could give me twenty hours each week, at $2.65 an hour—a fortune. I thanked him profusely and shook his hand again, then went to shake Bud's hand, but he'd disappeared behind the door.

I raced home to tell my mother.

"My God!" she cried, hugging me. "That will make such a difference!"

I tried to temper her excitement, warning her that the men at the bookstore were "unusual." I couldn't think of another word.

"They'll love you," she said. "You're great with unusual men."

I wasn't sure what she meant.

I was nervous about getting along with Bill and Bud, but for the first few weeks of my employment I hardly ever saw them. I'd knock at the stockroom door when I arrived, to say hello, and wouldn't have any more contact with them until I knocked to say good-bye. The bookstore was part of a national chain, but I assumed that Bill and Bud had either seceded from the chain or been forgotten by the home office. They ran the store as their private library, ordering books and magazines that suited and expressed their view of the world, and seldom emerging from the stockroom, which doubled as Bill's bedroom. Some nights he would fall asleep reading on a lawn chair behind the watercooler.

Shy, reserved, Bill and Bud could not have been more different from the men at the bar, and those first weeks at the bookstore were so disorientingly quiet, and lonely, that I wanted to quit. Then, suddenly, Bill and Bud became curious about me, and when there weren't any customers in the store, which was almost always, they invited me to stand in the doorway to the stockroom and chat.

At first I had trouble following the conversation, because I was so intrigued by Bill's and Bud's many quirks. Bill, for instance, chain-smoked but wouldn't buy an ashtray. He stood his smoldering butts upright along the edges of desks and tables throughout the stockroom, and let them burn out, until he'd created a diorama of a forest fire. His eyes were burned out too, from reading so much, and his glasses were thicker than his beloved Russian novels. He adored the Russians, and spoke of Tolstoy with disarming familiarity, as if he owed the great writer a phone call. He owned exactly two ties, one black, one green, both knits, and when he removed one at the end of the workday he'd keep the knot tied and hang it from a peg in the wall, like a tool belt.

Bud, when excited, would sniff his fist, as if it were a prizewinning rose. He also had a habit of straightening his dandruff-flecked hair by bringing his left hand all the way over to the right side of his head, like an orangutan, a maneuver that exposed the perennial, sizable wet spot in his armpit. He clipped his fingernails compulsively, and the parings lay scattered everywhere. I once found myself handing a customer two quarters and a crescent of Bud's thumbnail.

Bill and Bud both seemed to fear people, all people, except each other, which was one reason they hid in the stockroom. The other reason was that they read. Constantly. They had read everything ever written and were hell-bent to read everything new published each month, which required that they cloister themselves like medieval monks. Though in their mid-thirties, both men lived with their mothers, had never been married, and seemed to have no aspirations to move on or marry. They had no aspirations beyond reading, and no interests outside the store, though their interest in me was growing daily. They questioned me about my mother, my father, Uncle Charlie and the men, and they were fascinated by my relationship with Dickens. They asked about Steve and his motivation in giving the bar such a literary name, which led to a conversation about books generally. Bill and Bud quickly gleaned that I loved books and knew nothing about them. Through a series of rapid, probing questions they ascertained that I was intimately familiar with only *The Jungle Book* and *Minute Biographies*. They were appalled, and angry with my teachers.

"What are you reading in school right now?" Bill asked.

"Scarlett's Letter," I said.

He put a hand over his eyes. Bud sniffed his fist. "It's—*The Scarlet Letter*," Bud said. "Not Scarlett's. It's not the sequel to *Gone With the Wind*."

"Do you like it?" Bill asked.

"Kind of boring," I said.

"Of course," Bud said. "You have no frame of reference. You're thirteen."

"I actually turned fourteen last—"

"You know all about lust and nothing about shame," Bud said.

"He needs a nice healthy dose of Jack London," Bill said to Bud.

"Maybe Twain?" Bud said.

"Maybe," Bill said. "But the boy's from the East Coast—he should read New York writers. Dos Passos. Wharton. Dreiser."

"Dreiser! You want to turn him into a cynic like you? And no one reads Dos Passos anymore. Dos Passos is Dos Passé. If he wants to read about the East Coast, let him read Cheever."

"Who's Cheever?" I asked.

They turned slowly toward me.

"That settles that," Bud said.

"Come with me," Bill said.

He took me to the fiction section and pulled down every title by John Cheever, including the thick collection of short stories that had just been published. He brought the books into the stockroom and quickly ripped the cover off each one. It seemed to cause him pain, like ripping off a bandage. I asked what he was doing. He said bookstores couldn't return every unsold paperback to the publishers—the publishers didn't have room for them all—so they returned only the covers. When Bill and Bud wanted a book they simply ripped off the cover and mailed it to the publisher, who reimbursed the chain, "and everyone is happy." He assured me this wasn't stealing. I couldn't have cared less.

I spent that weekend reading Cheever, swimming in Cheever, falling in love with Cheever. I didn't know sentences could be made like that. Cheever did with words what Seaver did with fastballs. He described a garden full of roses as smelling like strawberry jam. He wrote about longing for a more "peaceable world." He wrote about my world, the suburbs outside Manhattan, scented with woodsmoke (his favorite word) and peopled with men hurrying from train stations to bars and back again. Each story revolved around cocktails and the sea, and each one therefore seemed as though it were set in Manhasset. One actually was. The first story in the collection mentioned Manhasset by name.

On Friday afternoons Bill and Bud would quiz me about what I'd read that week in school. They would then cluck with disgust and take me around the bookstore, filling a shopping bag with coverless books. "Every book is a miracle," Bill said. "Every book represents a moment when someone sat quietly—and that quiet is part of the miracle, make no mistake—and tried to tell the rest of us a story." Bud could talk ceaselessly about the hope of books, the promise of books. He said it was no accident that a book opened just like a door. Also, he said, intuiting one of my neuroses, I could use books to put order to chaos. At fourteen I felt more vulnerable than ever to chaos. My body grew, sprouted hair, shuddered with urges I didn't understand. And the world beyond my body seemed equally volatile and capricious. My days were controlled by teachers, my future was in the hands of heredity and luck. Bill and Bud promised, however, that my brain was my own and always would be. They said that by choosing books, the right books, and reading them slowly, carefully, I could always retain control of at least that one thing.

Books were the main part of Bill and Bud's lesson plan, but not the only part. They tackled how I talked, teaching me to modify my Long Island accent. When I said I was going for "cawffee," they made me stop and say it again. They tried to improve how I dressed. Though hardly fashion plates themselves, they had learned a thing or two from scouring the Italian and French magazines they ordered for the store, and they often asked salesgirls from boutiques in the mall to advise me about stretching my "trousseau." They broke me of my habit of wearing nothing but jeans and white T-shirts, and Bud gave me Lacoste shirts he'd "outgrown," though I suspected the shirts were gifts from his mother and actually too big for him. They supplied me with basic information about art, architecture, and especially music. Sinatra was fine, Bud said, but there were other "immortals." Sniffing his fist he made a list of records "every cultured young man must own." Dvořák. Schubert. Debussy. Mozart. Especially Mozart. Bud was devoted to Mozart. I folded his list and put it in my pocket and saved it for years, because it was such a touching and earnest recipe for betterment. I told Bud, however, that I couldn't afford records. The next day he brought in all the records on the list from his own collection. Call it a loan, he said. We sat in the stockroom, Bud playing the records on a portable turntable, conducting with a pencil, explaining why Mozart's Piano Sonata in C Major was perfection, why Beethoven's trios were sublime, why Holst's *Planets Suite* was frightening. While Bud tutored me in music Bill made the greater sacrifice. He manned the cash register all afternoon. For me, he said, and only me, he would deal with the "madding crowd."

Not long before the end of my freshman year, Bill and Bud asked what colleges I was considering. The subject of college always depressed me, because my mother and I had no money. In that case, Bill and Bud said, you need to get into one of the best colleges, because only the best pay your tuition. I told them jokingly about my mother's bedtime lullaby when I was younger: "Harvard and Yale, babe, Harvard and Yale."

"Not Harvard," Bud said. "What do you want to be—an accountant? Ha."

"No. A lawyer."

"Dear God." He fell onto his stool and sniffed his wrist furiously. Bill lit a cigarette and stretched out on his lawn chair. "How about Yale?" he said.

"Yes," Bud said. *"Yale."*

I told them in a wounded voice that they were cruel to be kidding me like that. "Yale is for rich kids," I said. "Smart kids. Other kids."

"No," Bud said. "Yale is for all kinds of kids. That's the great thing about Yale."

They were suddenly talking over each other, rhapsodizing about Yale, recounting its history, its roll call of famous graduates, from Noah Webster to Nathan Hale to Cole Porter. They sang a few bars of the Yale fight song, praised the professors in Yale's English department—the finest in the world, they assured me. I was shocked by how much they knew. Later I realized that they must have once dreamed of attending Yale themselves.

"Yalies are smart," Bill said, "but not geniuses."

"A Yalie doesn't know everything about one thing," Bud said, holding up one finger. "A Yalie knows one thing about everything."

"A Yalie is urbane," Bill said. "You know what 'urbane' means, right?"

"Yes," I said, laughing.

They waited.

"It means you live in a city."

Bud handed me a dictionary.

"A Yalie is a man of the world," Bill said. "A Renaissance man. That's what you want to be. A Yalie can shoot a gun, dance a fox-trot, mix a martini, tie a bow tie, conjugate a French verb—though he doesn't go so far as to speak the whole language—and tell you which of Mozart's symphonies were written in Prague, and which in Vienna."

"A Yalie is so very F. Scott Fitzgerald," Bud said. "You'll remember that every character in Fitzgerald is a Yale man. Nick Carraway, for one."

I averted my eyes. With a groan Bill rose from his lawn chair and went out to the sales floor to rip the cover off *The Great Gatsby*.

Not wanting to explain to Bill and Bud that my mother and I were the kind of people who didn't *get in,* I simply said, "It's just too frightening to think about—*Yale*." It was the wrong thing to say, and the right thing.

"Then it's decided," Bud said. He rose from his stool and came toward me, sniffing his fist, adjusting his Buddy Holly glasses. "You must do everything that frightens you, JR. Everything. I'm not talking about risking your life, but everything else. Think about fear, decide right now how you're going to deal with fear, because fear is going to be the great issue of your life, I promise you. Fear will be the fuel for all your success, and the root cause of all your failures, and the underlying dilemma in every story you tell yourself about yourself. And the only chance you'll have against fear? Follow it. Steer by it. Don't think of fear as the villain. Think of fear as your guide, your pathfinder—your Natty Bumppo."

I thought this an odd speech from a man who hid in the stockroom of a bookstore in a semiabandoned mall. But it struck me that Bud might have been so passionate on the subject because he was giving me the advice no one had given him. I saw that this was a pivotal moment between us, that something profound should be said, but I couldn't think of anything, so I smiled tentatively and said, "Who's Natty Bumppo?"

He breathed loudly through his nose. "What are they teaching you in that school?"

That night over dinner I told my mother two things. I wanted to save up and buy Bill a new lawn chair for Christmas. And I'd decided to apply to Yale. I tried to make it sound like my own decision, but she got me to recount my discussion with Bill and Bud. "You charmed them," she said with a half smile.

"What do you mean?"

"I knew you would."

But it was the other way around. They had ripped the cover off me.

Somehow, months after declaring bankruptcy, my mother was able to get another credit card. She used it to buy me a plane ticket to New York that May—she was determined I spend every summer in Manhasset, because I enjoyed the men so much—and a ticket for herself that August, so that we could drive up to Yale together and have a look around before I started my sophomore year of high school. We borrowed Uncle Charlie's Cadillac, and Grandma and Sheryl came along for the ride.

As my mother drove I sat beside her and cringed at the conversation swirling around the Cadillac. Instead of Colt and Bobo talking about who was "boning" whom at Dickens, the women were clucking about fashion and cooking and hairstyles. Sacrilege. To provide a corrective to the conversation I interjected random items from the Yale brochure in my lap. "Did you know Yale was founded in 1701? That means it's almost as old as Manhasset. Did you know Yale's motto is *Lux et Veritas*? That means 'Light and Truth' in Latin. Did you know the first Ph.D. ever was awarded by Yale?"

"Does it say in your little book there how much the whole shebang costs?" Sheryl asked from the backseat.

I read aloud. "'A reasonable estimate of the total cost of a year at Yale is eleven thousand three hundred and ninety dollars.'"

Silence.

"Why don't we listen to some nice music?" Grandma said.

Before we saw Yale we heard it. As we pulled into New Haven the bells were ringing in Harkness Tower. I almost couldn't bear how beautiful they sounded. I stuck my head out of the car and thought, *Yale has a voice, and it's speaking to me.* Something inside me answered to those bells, some explosive mix of poverty and naïveté. I was already prone to see everything I admired as sacred, and the bells exploited this delusion, casting a hallowed aura over the campus. I was also prone to turn every place that barred me into a castle, and here was Yale, deliberately decorated with turrets, battlements and gargoyles. But there was also a moat—the canal outside our apartment in Arizona. As we parked the Cadillac and walked around, I began to panic.

Our first stop was Sterling Library. With its dark nave, vaulted ceilings and medieval archways the library was meant to evoke a church, a house of worship for readers, and we were appropriately pious. Our footsteps on the stone floors rang out like gunshots as we walked down a hall into a reading room, where summer-school students curled up with books in old, fat, hunter green leather chairs. We left Sterling and walked across a broad lawn to Beinecke Rare Book and Manuscript Library, home of Yale's priceless treasures. A squat building, its walls were adorned with small marble squares that turned different colors as the sun slid across the sky. We passed Commons, the freshman dining hall, with its immense marble columns and the names of World War I battles etched along its façade. By now I was overwhelmed with despair, and my mother saw. She suggested we take a break. In a sandwich shop at the edge of the campus I sat with my cheeks on my fists. Eat your hamburger, Grandma said. He needs a beer, Sheryl said. My mother asked me to speak, to put into words what was upsetting me. I didn't want to say aloud that I would give anything to go to Yale, that life wouldn't be worth living if I couldn't get in, but that I surely would not get in, because we weren't the "getting in" kind. I didn't have to say. My mother squeezed my hand. "We'll get in," she said.

I excused myself and bolted from the sandwich shop. Like an escaped lunatic I staggered around campus, staring at students, peering in windows. Every window framed a more idyllic scene. Professors talking about ideas. Students drinking coffee and thinking brilliant thoughts. I walked into the Yale bookstore and nearly fainted when I saw the walls and walls of books. I sat in a corner and listened to the silence. Bill and Bud hadn't warned me. They had told me about Yale's history, its allure, but they hadn't prepared me for its tranquillity. They didn't tell me that Yale was the more peaceable world for which I'd been longing. Again the bells started ringing. I wanted to throw myself on the ground and weep.

At New Haven Green I sat under a spreading elm and stared at the hundred-foot ramparts that rimmed the Old Campus, trying to picture myself on the other side. I couldn't. Of all the grand houses I'd admired from afar, Yale was the most impregnable. After an hour I heaved myself to my feet and walked slowly back to the sandwich shop. Sheryl and Grandma were annoyed that I'd been gone so long. My mother was concerned for my mental state. She handed me a gift she'd bought me in a souvenir shop, a letter opener with the Yale insignia. "To open your acceptance letter with," she said.

Back in Manhasset my mother and I went to the bar for dinner. Steve's renovation was complete and the bar was now officially Publicans, a different place, more sophisticated, with lobster on the menu. Uncle Charlie was tending bar, wearing khakis and a cashmere V-neck. He too had been renovated. He came by our table to say hello. "What's with him?" he asked my mother, jerking his head in my direction.

"He fell in love with Yale today," my mother said, "and assumes it's unrequited."

"Is Bobo here?" I asked him. Bobo and Wilbur could cheer me up.

"Missing in action," Uncle Charlie said.

I dropped my head.

Uncle Charlie shrugged and walked back to the barroom, diving through a curtain of smoke. Men cheered his reappearance and clamored for refills. "Keep your goddamned shirts on!" he said. "I've got phone calls to make." Everyone laughed. I laughed in spite of myself, and revised my dreams. After

Yale rejected me, I decided, I'd attend some tiny, anonymous college. I'd get decent grades, finagle my way into some law school, then con some half-assed law firm into hiring me. I'd earn less than I hoped—*be* less than I hoped— but if I lived frugally I might still be able to take care of my mother and send her to college and sue my father. And, as a consolation for my disappoint- ments, when I came home from the law firm each night I'd stop by Publicans for a few belts. I'd talk with the men, laugh off the cares of the day and the regrets of my life. Staring into the barroom, watching Uncle Charlie pour drinks, I felt suddenly at ease, knowing that as surely as Yale would reject me, Publicans would accept me. If I couldn't have the light and truth of Yale, I could always count on the dark truth of the bar. And only occasionally, when I'd had too much to drink, or not enough, would I let myself wonder how it all might have been different if Yale had let me in.

sixteen | JR

TWO SHOTS TO THE CHEST AT POINT-BLANK RANGE, AND THEN the faceless culprit ran away. My mother and I saw the whole thing, along with millions of other people. The attempted murder of J.R. Ewing was the season-ending cliffhanger of *Dallas*, the most-watched TV show on earth, and when J.R. Ewing hit the floor, clutching his wounds, JR Moehringer knew he was in for a long hot summer.

The identity of J.R.'s attacker became a national obsession, and my teenage identity crisis became a daily crucible. My first name, which I hated slightly more than my last, was suddenly a household word, emblazoned on T-shirts, bumper stickers and magazine covers. Russian tanks were overrun- ning Afghanistan, fifty-two Americans were being held hostage in Iran, but J.R. Ewing was Topic A in the summer of 1980. Everyone I met would stam- mer in their haste to blurt out The Question: Who shot you? I'd smile as if no one had thought to ask me that before, then say something inane. *Sorry— the producers swore me to secrecy.* Sometimes I'd just make my best belly-full- of-lead face. People loved that.

Manhasset was malarial with J.R. Fever by the time I arrived for my sum- mer visit. I looked forward to some mindless chatter and the Wordy Gurdy, but Uncle Charlie and the men were fixated on Ewing Doings. "Had to be Bobby," Uncle Charlie said, stretched out in his chair, sun and cocoa butter making his head shine like a conch shell. "The Cain and Abel thing. Oldest story in the book."

"No way," Colt said. "Bobby's a pussy."

"Sue Ellen offed the motherfucker," Bobo said.

"I read that Vegas is giving odds on the different suspects," Joey D said.

"Wonder how you'd get a bet down on that?" Uncle Charlie said.

"If there's a way," Joey D said, "you'll find it."

Being named JR had always been complicated. Long before J.R. Ewing was shot, my name had been an infallible Pavlovian prompt, triggering the same response every time I met someone new. *What does JR stand for?* Embarrassed to be named after a father who disappeared, I answered for years with evasions. Then, gradually, I developed more cosmetic reasons to fear being called Junior. Junior was an overgrown simpleton who wore bib overalls and played checkers on a cracker barrel outside a general store. Junior was the opposite of everything I hoped to become. To distance myself from this image, to fend off would-be nicknamers, to obscure the specter of my absent father, I switched from evasions to one whopping lie. "JR doesn't stand for anything," I'd tell people. "It's my *legal* first name."

This was partly true. JR, without dots, was how I signed my name to all legal documents. My birth certificate did bear a *J* next to an *R*. I simply didn't mention that these letters were an abbreviation at the end of my name, signifying the great void in my life.

For years the lie had worked beautifully, efficiently shutting down every questioner, until *Dallas*. People now weren't so easily put off—meeting someone named JR was too delicious, like meeting someone named FDR—and when they interrogated me, harassed me, I was forced to craft an even bigger lie. "I was conceived right after John F. Kennedy was assassinated," I would say, "and my parents couldn't decide which Kennedy to name me after— John or Robert. They were caught up in that whole Camelot thing. So they invented a name that would stand for both. JR. No dots."

As the hype around *Dallas* grew into hysteria, I went on autopilot, telling my bigger lie in the zombie monotone of a schoolchild reciting the Pledge of Allegiance. Again I found sanctuary in my lie—until Yale presented yet another challenge. After sending for the application I wrote my mother and declared to her that I intended to type JR Moehringer, no dots, at the top of the first page. She fired back a letter. "You may not apply to Yale under an assumed name." You're the one who made me assume it, I thought. But she was right. I didn't want to do anything that would hurt my chances. For Yale, for Yale only, I agreed to be John Joseph Moehringer Jr., a name that felt no more mine than Engelbert Humperdinck.

With each mention of my name that summer, with each discussion of what JR "stands for," the memory of my father resurfaced. I wondered where he might be. I wondered if he was still alive, and how I would ever know if he wasn't. Many nights, long after Grandma and Grandpa had gone to bed, I would find myself at the kitchen table, my ear to the radio. After thinking I'd conquered this old addiction, I'd fallen off the wagon, and my relapse made me feel weak and ashamed. I wanted to talk with someone about it, but there wasn't anyone. I didn't dare raise the subject with Grandma, who would scold me and then write my mother. I tried to talk with McGraw, but the older he got, the less willing he was to discuss fathers. "I'm afraid if I start," he said, "I'll never stop."

I would have liked to speak with Uncle Charlie, but he was haunted that summer by his own voices. Sitting in the kitchen late one night, listening to the radio and reading, I heard the breezeway door open, then heavy footsteps, as if someone were killing cockroaches in the dining room. With a crash Uncle Charlie appeared in the kitchen doorway. From six feet away I smelled the whiskey. "Look who's here," he said. "Look who's here, look who's here. Whatcha say, sport? Didn't 'spect anyone wake."

He pulled a chair from the table, scraping it loudly across the floor. I clicked off the radio. "How's it going?" I asked.

He sat, put a cigarette between his lips. Thinking. Lit a match. Thinking more. "JR," he said, pausing to touch the flame to the cigarette, "people are scumbags."

I laughed. He jerked up his head and stared. "Think I'm joking?"

"No sir."

"JR, JR, JR. Your uncle is a very perceptive man. You follow?"

"Yes sir."

"Who's more perceptive than me?"

"No one."

"Excuse me, poor grammar. Who is more perceptive—than I?"

"No one."

"Bet your ass. I studied psychology, buddy boy. I've read everything. Don't you forget it. No one pulls the wool over these eyes." He pointed at his eyes, which were like two drops of dried blood, then launched into a long unintelligible story about someone—he wouldn't name names—who hadn't shown the proper sympathy for how much Pat had suffered at the end. Uncle Charlie hated this person, hated everyone, hated the whole goddamned world, and he was going to give everyone a piece of his mind one of these days. He slammed the table, pointed at the window, at the unfeeling world beyond, as he described this "scumbag bastard" who had dishonored Pat's memory. I was frightened, but fascinated. I didn't know that Uncle Charlie was capable of rage, and I didn't know that Publicans was a place you could bring rage. I thought people went to the bar when sad, and got happy, period. A simple transaction. While I thought Uncle Charlie's rage might lead him to toss me into the wall at any moment, I also felt that rage was something we had in common. I was always in a rage—about my mother's health, about my name—and I'd been in a rage about my father just before Uncle Charlie walked in the door. That I couldn't *tell* anyone about my rage served to triple my rage, and some days I felt that I might burst into flames of rage. Yes, I wanted to say, yes, let's both give way to our rage! *Let's bust up this whole goddamned kitchen!*

"JR, do you hear me?"

I started. Uncle Charlie was glowering at me.

"Yes," I lied. "I hear you. I follow."

The ash on his cigarette needed flicking. He didn't notice. He took a drag and the ash fell down his chest. "Ach, no one cares," he said. He started to cry. Tears slipped from behind his dark glasses and skidded down his cheeks. I felt rotten and selfish for thinking of my own rage and not giving my full attention to Uncle Charlie's.

"*I* care," I said.

He looked up. A wan smile. Drying his tears he told me about the first time he met Pat, in a bar on Plandome Road. She walked across the barroom and reproached him for his hat and dark glasses. "You son of a bitch," she said. "You have the nerve to feel self-conscious about having no hair when boys are coming home from Vietnam with no legs?"

"Mind your own business," he told her, though he liked her style. Ballsy. A gun moll. A dame straight out of Raymond Chandler. They started talking and found a number of things in common, foremost a quasi-religious regard for barrooms. Also, Pat was an English teacher, and Uncle Charlie loved words, so they talked about books and writers. Days later she sent him a telegram. CAN'T STOP THINKING ABOUT YOU—MUST SEE YOU. She asked him to meet her at a roadhouse outside town. "I got there early," he said. "Sat at the bar. Had a cocktail. Thought about leaving. Got up to leave."

He acted it out. "I made for the door," he said, lunging toward the stove, knocking over his chair. "Can you imagine how everything would be different? JR, for Christ's sake. Do you see? How everything would be different—if I'd *left*? Do you follow? How things turn on a dime? You follow?"

"I follow," I said, picking up his chair.

"She comes sailing through the door. Herself. Beautiful. A ten. No, fuck it, an eleven point five. Summer dress. Lipstick. What a beauty." He sat again. He stubbed out his cigarette, which was already out. He closed his eyes, laughing to himself. He was there again at the roadhouse with Pat. I felt as if I were intruding. "Right behind her," he whispered, "comes her husband. She's—*married*. The husband's been following her for weeks. *Weeks*, JR. Thinks she's cheating on him. Which she isn't. Though she's about to. With me."

"Did you know him?"

"Who?"

"The husband?"

"JR, you're not listening. He was the most feared son of a bitch who ever walked the face of the earth. He's the reason you can't drink alcohol at Jones Beach anymore. But that's another story. The husband sits down next to Pat and tells the bartender, 'Get them a drink on me.' Then he says, 'Chas, if it was anybody else, they'd be dead.'" He paused. "Pat was divorced six months later. She and I have been together ever since. Excuse me. Bad grammar again. She and I *had been* together. Until . . ."

The clock above the stove sounded like someone banging a pot with a spoon. Uncle Charlie lit another cigarette. He smoked with his eyes closed and neither of us said anything until I couldn't bear the silence. "We had a good time at Shea," I said.

He opened his eyes and looked at me, no idea what I was talking about.

"We couldn't find her," I said. "Remember?"

"Oh right." He sighed. Two long plumes of smoke shot from his nose, which made me think of a dragon. "Now we'll never find her."

I'd managed to say exactly the wrong thing.

"She loved Publicans," he said. "She loved to laugh—she laughed all the time—and just when I'd think she couldn't laugh any more, she'd come into Publicans and laugh twice as much. And she loved Steve to pieces."

"What did Steve—"

"Time to turn in," he said. He stood, knocking over the chair again. I picked it up again.

"How old are you?" he said.

"Fifteen. I'll be—"

"That's a great age. Jesus, what a great age! Stay right there. Don't get any older."

I led him down the hall, his arm around my neck. Standing inside the door to his bedroom I watched him climb under the covers with all his clothes on. He lay on his back and stared at the ceiling. "JR, JR, JR," he said. He kept saying my name, as though the air were full of JRs and he were counting them.

"Good night, Uncle Charlie." As I shut the door, however, he had one more thing he needed to get off his chest.

"Who shot J.R.?" he said. "Had to be the brother-in-law. No one hated J.R. more than Cliff."

seventeen | SHERYL

"SOMEONE HAS TO MAKE A MAN OUT OF YOU," SHERYL SAID wearily. "I guess it'll have to be me."

It was 1981, the summer before my senior year, and we were riding the train into Manhattan, where Sheryl had gotten me a job as a file clerk at the law firm where she was a secretary. I looked at her, confused. I was sending my mother real money, buoying her hope that I'd soon be a lawyer—what could be more manly than that? Also, at sixteen years old I defined myself by the company I kept, and commuting to Manhattan meant I was keeping company with hundreds of men. Perforce and ergo, as they said at the firm, I was a man.

Not hardly, Sheryl said. Manhood wasn't a feeling, in her view, but a performance. Having just graduated from a small junior college with a degree in interior design, Sheryl was obsessed with surfaces. How you dressed, what you wore and smoked and drank—these externals determined a person's inner self. It didn't matter that I felt like a man—I didn't act or look like one. "That's where I come in," Sheryl said.

Sheryl had moved into Grandpa's house just before I arrived that summer. (She was saving up for an apartment of her own, and in the meantime she was trying to break free of her nomadic mother.) Living with Sheryl, commuting with her and working with her, I found myself receiving manhood lessons around the clock. As a bonus, when Sheryl wasn't talking about manhood she was attracting swarms of men eager to sit with us on the train. She looked like a young Ingrid Bergman, with dark blond hair and a pert, slender nose.

Someone else might have bridled at Sheryl's endless exhortations. Stand up straight. Tuck in your shirt. What are we going to do about getting you some muscles? But I did whatever she said, without question, because Sheryl seemed to understand how the world worked. She was the only person, for instance, who pointed out when the third rail popped three seconds before the train appeared, and she was the first to warn me never to touch that third rail, ever. "Like me," she said, "it's always—*electrified*!" No one but Sheryl could tell me the proper way to read a newspaper on a crowded train, folding the entire paper once, longwise, then peeling back one half page at a time, to avoid disturbing the men on either side. More important, Sheryl explained that the newspaper I read was a sandwich board proclaiming my social status, income, genealogy, IQ. Working stiffs read the *Daily News*. Housewives, *Newsday*. Crazies, the *Post*.

"Grandpa reads the *Post*," I protested.

She batted her eyelashes at me, as if to say, Any more stupid questions?

We were standing on the crowded platform when Sheryl pointed out a man fifteen feet away. "See that guy?" she said. Leaning against a lamppost was a businessman in a charcoal gray suit who looked like Cary Grant's better-looking older brother. I'd seen him going into Publicans many times, and I'd always marveled at his suavity. "Notice what he's reading?"

It was the *New York Times,* folded longwise.

"Bluebloods and mucky-mucks read the *Times,*" she said. "No matter how boring it might be."

I didn't tell Sheryl that I liked reading the *Times,* that one of the best things about working at the firm was having that half hour on the train to read it. I thought the *Times* a miracle, a mosaic of minute biographies, a daily masterpiece. I was starved for information about the world—I hadn't been anywhere and didn't know anyone who had—and the *Times,* like Yale, seemed expressly designed for my special brand of ignorance. Also, I loved how the *Times* made life appear containable. It satisfied my mania for order, for a world separated into black and white. It slotted all the madness into seventy pages of six skinny columns. I did everything I could to hide my love of the *Times* from Sheryl, who believed that a real man read the *Times* and only a hopeless nerd enjoyed it. But Sheryl had a sharp eye. She saw how closely I concentrated on the *Times* and took to calling me JR Muckraker.

The two critical tests of a man's mettle, Sheryl believed, were women and liquor. How you reacted to each, how you *managed* each, went a long way to determining your manliness quotient. I told her about Lana, a girl back in Arizona who was many tiers above me in the high-school hierarchy. Lana's hair was dirty blond, in both color and cleanliness. She didn't wash it every day, which gave her a tousled, greasy sex appeal. The strands flicked her shoulders as she walked down the halls, chest out, like a cadet. Her breasts, I assured Sheryl, never moved, and she wore short-shorts that revealed the taut upper parts of her long caramel thighs. "If her leg were the United States," I told Sheryl, "you could see all the way up to Michigan."

"Battle *Creek*!" Sheryl said, and I laughed, though I wasn't sure what she meant. I don't think Sheryl was sure either.

Overall Sheryl was blasé about Lana. Without meeting her, she said, it wasn't possible to know if the girl justified all my heavy breathing. On the subject of whiskey, however, Sheryl had plenty to say. She liked to drink and she took pleasure in teaching me how. After work each night we'd stop at a grungy bar in the bowels of Penn Station, where the smoke and darkness made everyone look like Charles Bronson, so the bartenders never questioned my age. Sheryl would treat me to a couple of cold mugs of beer, after which we'd buy large plastic cups of double gin and tonics for the ride home. By the time we stepped onto Plandome Road, our feet weren't quite touching the pavement.

On a steamy Friday night in the middle of August, Sheryl proposed that we stop at Publicans for a last drink before heading to Grandpa's house. I said that I didn't think Uncle Charlie would approve.

"You go to Publicans all the time," she said.

"In the day. Nighttime at Publicans is different."

"Says who?"

"It's just understood. Nighttime is different."

"Uncle Charlie won't care. He wants you to be a man. Be a man."

Reluctantly I followed her through the door.

I'd been more right than I knew. Publicans was a completely different place after dark. Racier. Everyone laughing, talking at once, and it all seemed to be about sex. People were saying things they would regret tomorrow, I could just tell.

There was such a pageant of characters, in such a variety of costumes, that I felt as if Sheryl and I had snuck backstage at a grand opera. There were priests and softball players and executives. There were men in tuxedoes and women in gowns, on their way to charity functions. There were golfers just off the links, sailors just off the water, construction workers just off the jobsite. The bar was as crowded as the rush-hour train Sheryl and I had just ridden from Manhattan, and in fact could have been an extension of the train, another car coupled to the caboose, because it was long, narrow, filled with many of the same faces, and seemingly rocking from side to side. We edged deeper into the crowd and Sheryl bummed a cigarette from a young man, touching his arm, placing a hand on his shoulder, throwing back her hair. I remembered that she had a brand-new pack of Virginia Slims in her purse, and I suddenly understood. All her talk about making me a man was a cover for her master plan. Finding herself a man. She only wanted to make me a man so she'd have an escort to Publicans, where all the eligible men were. She couldn't go alone, of course. She didn't want to look desperate.

Feeling used, I ditched her. I bored into the crowd, tunneling toward the restaurant. After ten feet, however, my progress was halted. Unable to go forward, or back, I leaned against a pole. Beside me was a girl in her mid-twenties. She had a pretty face and wore a plaid dress with darts in the side that accentuated her figure. "All right if I lean here?" I asked.

"Free country."

"Hey, my grandfather says that all the time. Have you been hanging out with Grandpa?"

She started to answer, then saw that I was joking. "What's your name?"

"JR."

"Ewing?"

"Right."

"Guess you hear that a lot."

"You're the first."

"What does JR stand for?"

"It's my legal name."

"Really? And what do you do, JR Ewing, when you're not at Southfork?"

"Work at a law firm. In the city."

"A lawyer?"

I stood up straighter. No one had ever called me a lawyer before. I couldn't wait to write and tell my mother. Plaid Dress took a cigarette from her purse and fumbled with a matchbook. I took the matches and lit her cigarette exactly as I'd seen it done in *Casablanca*. "How about you?" I asked, in Uncle Charlie's voice. "What's your story?"

Sheryl had instructed me to ask this question of women. Women like questions about themselves more than they like jewelry, Sheryl had said. So I followed up my question with another, and another, assailed Plaid Dress with questions, learning that she worked as a salesgirl, that she hated it, that she wanted to be a dancer, that she lived with a roommate in Douglaston. And that the roommate was away in Barbados. "Won't be back for a whole week," Plaid Dress said. "My apartment is sooo empty."

Grinding my jaws, I saw that her beer had a sip left. "Speaking of empty," I said, "let me buy you another." I headed for the bar. Sheryl intercepted me. "We're out of here," she said, grabbing my necktie.

"Why?"

"Uncle Charlie saw you and he's mad."

Uncle Charlie had never been mad at me in my life. I said something about wanting to run away to Alaska. "Oh Christ," Sheryl said. "Be a man."

Walking home, Sheryl had an idea. Since we were already in trouble with Uncle Charlie, we might as well go for broke. She suggested a nightcap in Roslyn. Bars there were more lax. She took the keys to Uncle Charlie's Cadillac and we went to an infamous joint, where an eight-year-old could order a Tequila Sunrise without anyone blinking. "Go get us some cocktails," she said, pushing me toward the bar. I fought my way through the crowd and when I returned with two gin and tonics Sheryl was surrounded by five marines. They looked as if they were detaining her at a checkpoint. "Here he is!" she cried as I came into view.

"You the baby-sitter?" one marine asked Sheryl.

"Cousin," Sheryl said. "I'm trying to make a man out of him."

"Looks like a mighty big job," another marine said. Seeing me flinch, he extended his hand to me. "Only kidding, man. What's your name?"

"JR."

"What! Naw! Hey, everybody, this guy's name is JR!"

His buddies wheeled away from Sheryl and gawked at me.

"Who shot him?"

"Ask who shot him."

"Who shot you?"

Sheryl wasn't about to surrender the spotlight without a fight. "Did someone say shots?" she shouted.

"Whoo!" the marines roared. "Yeah! Shots for JR! Let's shoot JR!"

A marine handed me a shot glass and ordered me to drink. I did. It burned. A different marine handed me another glass. I drank it faster. It burned more. The marines then lost interest in me and went back to scrumming over Sheryl. She lit a cigarette. I watched her hold the first puff of smoke in her open mouth like a ball of cotton before sucking it down, and I thought, Of course—smoking. Casually I lit one of Sheryl's cigarettes, as if it were my twentieth that day, not the first of my life. I took a drag. Nothing. I looked at the cigarette and smirked. Is that all you got? I took another drag. Deeper. The smoke hit my sternum like a short, hard right. After an initial burst of euphoria came hysteria, then nausea, then classic symptoms of malaria. Sweating.

Shaking. Delirium. I levitated above the marines. Looking down on the bald spots in their crew cuts I thought, Fresh air now. *Freshairnow.*

I did a Frankenstein walk to the rear exit. Jammed. I pushed. The door gave and I fell into a narrow alley. A brick wall. I pressed my back against the wall. Oh wall. Dependable wall. Hold me, wall. I slid down. Sitting against the wall I tipped my head back and tried to breathe. The air felt refreshing. Like a waterfall. I held my face to the air a long time before realizing that I was directly beneath a pipe spurting some kind of greenish liquid. I rolled onto my side. The streetlights made multicolored pinwheels on the oily surfaces of the puddles in the alley. I don't know how much time passed as I watched the pinwheels—an hour? five minutes?—but when I summoned the strength to stand and go back inside Sheryl was not pleased. "I've been looking all over for you," she said.

"Alley."

"You do not look good."

"Don't feel good. Where's Bravo Company?"

"They retreated when they realized I wasn't Iwo Jima."

On the way back to Manhasset I noticed for the first time that Sheryl was a horrible driver. She sped up, slowed down, switched lanes, came to lurching stops at red lights. By the time we reached Grandpa's house I felt seasick. I didn't wait for Sheryl to come to a complete stop in the driveway. I leaped from the moving car, ran inside and vomited in the bathroom. Crawling into bed I clung to the mattress, which was rising slowly like a soufflé. Sheryl came and somehow sat on the edge of the mattress, even though it was ten feet off the ground. She told me I was going to wake the whole house. Stop groaning, she said. I didn't know I was groaning.

"Well, congratulations!" she said, or tried to. It came out: Congratchama-lations! "Snuck into Publicans. Got thrown out of Publicans. Drank with m'reens. Smoked your fersh smigarette. I'm s'proud of you. S'proud."

"Are you the devil?"

She left the room.

"Hey," I called. "Why did you break up with Jedd?"

If she answered, I didn't hear.

Somewhere in the house a radio was playing. Count Basie's "One O'Clock Jump." Beautiful song, I thought. Then the bouncy rhythm started to make me more nauseous. Would I ever be well enough to enjoy music again? I tried to fall asleep, but words and ideas leaped around in my head. I thought I was experiencing penetrating flashes of insight, and I wanted to write them down. I couldn't get out of bed, however, because the mattress was still rising. How much farther could it go before my back would be pressed against the ceiling? I felt like a car on a hydraulic lift. Sprawled on my stomach, my head hanging over the side of the bed, I committed my flashes of insight to memory. I thought, My mother is the printed word, my father is the spoken word, Sheryl is the slurred word. Then all was blackness.

In the morning I woke from a nightmare in which marines were storming Grandpa's house and using the chevrons from their sleeves to retape the bicentennial sofa. I took a long hot shower and sat on the stoop with a cup of black coffee. Uncle Charlie came outside and glared at me. I braced myself, but he saw my bloodshot eyes and must have concluded that I'd suffered enough. He shook his head and looked at the treetops.

"Now I can drive us home from the bars in Roslyn," I said to Sheryl, showing her my new driver's license, which my mother had forwarded to me. We were on the early-morning train, near the end of August, and Sheryl held the license up to the light from the window, to get a better look. She read: " 'Height, five-ten. Weight, one-forty. Hair, auburn. Eyes, hazel.' " She laughed. "Nice photo," she said. "You look about twelve. No. Strike that. Eleven. What does your mother say in her letter?"

I read: " 'I'm attaching your insurance card, sweetheart, because if you're ever in an accident, you must show that you have insurance.' " I looked down, embarrassed. "My mom's kind of a worrywart," I mumbled.

In the same letter my mother reported that she'd gotten a new job at an insurance company, which she was enjoying. "I don't have such pressure at work or such a workload that I come home dead tired," she wrote. "I think you will see a big change in me when you come home in that even though I am tired at the end of a day, when I come home now I do have something left of me."

Folding the letter and tucking it into my pocket I told Sheryl about the clunker my mother had bought for me, a 1974 AMC Hornet with an orange racing stripe, which cost four hundred dollars. I didn't tell Sheryl how the letter made me miss my mother, or how I looked forward to seeing her in two weeks, or how I worried about her all the time. I didn't confess that while riding the train some mornings I couldn't stop imagining something bad happening to my mother, that I'd try to replace these fears with my old mantra, then berate myself for adhering to my boyhood superstitions, then tell myself that it was better to be safe than sorry, because maybe the mantra still had some magic left in it, and if I abandoned the mantra I might cause something bad to befall my mother. I knew Sheryl would say that real men don't think that way. Real men don't have mantras, and real men certainly don't miss their moms.

Sheryl came searching for me in the file room later that morning. She had a cross look on her face, and I assumed it was because I didn't have any money for lunch and I'd asked her to float me a loan. "It's your mom," she said. "There's been an accident. They're waiting for us at home."

We ran to Penn Station. Sheryl bought a six-pack and we drank them all before we reached Bayside. "I'm sure it will be fine," she said. But already it wasn't fine. My mantra had failed, and I had failed my mother.

Walking past Publicans I looked in the window, heard the laughter, saw the happy faces along the bar. I almost suggested to Sheryl that we stop for a quick one. Uncle Charlie would understand. I hated myself for this impulse, for letting my thoughts stray one second from my mother, but I was frightened and I regarded Publicans as the best available antidote to fear. I longed for the bar in a new and desperate way, a portentous way.

At Grandpa's house I threw some things into a bag and Sheryl kissed me good-bye. "Be a man," she said, not in her typical way, but in a tender, encouraging way, as if she believed I would be.

Grandpa bought me a plane ticket and Uncle Charlie drove me to the airport. Along the way he told me what he knew. My mother had been returning home from work when a drunk driver going the wrong way, with no headlights, hit her head-on. She had a broken arm and a concussion. The doctors were concerned that she might have suffered brain damage. "She has amnesia," Uncle Charlie said.

I asked Uncle Charlie what would happen if my mother couldn't remember me. He said he wasn't sure what I meant. I wasn't sure either. I think I was asking him who I would be if my mother didn't know me.

eighteen | LANA

THERE WERE JAGGED CUTS ON HER FACE AND CLUMPS OF MATTED blood in her hair. Her eyes were half open, a new and terrible kind of blank face. I leaned over her. "Mom?" I said. From somewhere behind me a nurse said my mother was on powerful pain medication and would be in "limbo" for some time.

"You're pretty big for a ten-year-old," the doctor said.

"Excuse me?"

"Your mom told me she had a ten-year-old son."

"Oh."

"And when I asked if she knew where she was, she said New York."

"We moved here from New York."

"I thought as much. I even took her to the window and showed her the palm trees and cacti, but she insisted. New York."

When visiting hours ended I left the hospital and went back to our apartment. I tried to calm down by reading a book. No chance. I turned on all the lights, then turned them all off. I sat in the dark, thinking. I sat on the bank of the canal, watching the water. I was exhausted, but couldn't go to bed, because whenever I closed my eyes I pictured the moment of impact. Frightened, lonely, I thought about what my mother had told the doctor. She was right, in a way. I was ten years old.

There was no planning, no premeditation, no thought whatsoever: My hand was reaching for the phone and my finger was dialing Lana, the high-school glamour girl I'd described to Sheryl. Before I'd left for the summer Lana and I had talked briefly at a party, and even made vague promises to get together. I didn't think she was serious, and I'd never expected to work up the courage to phone her. But now, with my mother in limbo and my psyche in freefall, I felt an urge that transcended teenage lust, if anything can be said to transcend teenage lust. I felt a longing for Lana that was like the longing for Publicans, and I knew dimly that it had something to do with the need for protection and distraction.

We met at a Mexican restaurant near her house. Lana wore her shortest shorts and a flowery blouse, the shirttails knotted at her waist. A summer in the sun had given her skin an astonishing luster, while lightening her hair with streaks of honey and buttermilk. I told her about my mother. She was very sweet and sympathetic. I ordered a bottle of wine, almost as a lark, and we both smirked when the waiter didn't ask for identification. After dinner Lana seemed tipsy as we walked to the parking lot. "Is this your new car?" she asked.

"Yes. It's a Hornet."

"I see that. Nice racing stripe."

"It's orange."

"Yes. Orange."

I asked if she needed to be home early.

"Not really," she said. "What did you have in mind?"

"We've got two options. We can go to a movie. Or we can get some Löwenbräu and drive to the top of Camelback?"

"Camelback. Definitely."

A buddy had once shown me the many lovers' lanes that honeycombed the first hump of Camelback Mountain. He liked to go up there and spy on couples when he was bored and horny. But that had been months ago, and it had been broad daylight, and now it was a dark moonless night. Nothing looked familiar as I drove up and down and around the hump, searching, hoping that Lana wouldn't sober up or grow restless. She fiddled with the radio while I told her that I was determined to find one special spot, which afforded a breathtaking view and total privacy, neglecting to mention that it sat on a cliff atop a steep slope of rock. At last, after forty-five minutes, I found the familiar dirt road that ran up the side of the hump and dead-ended at the slope that led to the special spot.

"Ready to climb?" I said, shutting off the Hornet.

"Climb?"

I held the bag of Löwenbräu in one hand and Lana's arm in the other. The slope grew steeper with every step. Lana, panting, asked how much farther. "Not much," I said, though I had no idea. I hadn't actually climbed with my buddy. I'd simply taken his word for what was up there. Eventually the slope became a wall, a nearly perfect vertical. "Ouch!" Lana said. She'd brushed a cactus and scraped her thigh. She was bleeding. At the top the wall curved back toward us. I threw the bag of Löwenbräu up, pulled myself over with a chin-up, then reached back for Lana. When we had both reached the summit we lay on our backs, gasping, laughing, inspecting her injury. We then crawled forward to the far edge of the cliff and there was the view my buddy had described, a million lights shimmering below us, as if the valley were a still lake reflecting the stars.

"Damn," Lana said.

I opened two beers and handed one to her. A breeze blew her dirty blond hair into her eyes and I pushed it back. She leaned forward to kiss me. I closed my eyes. Her bottom lip was plump, like a marshmallow. She pushed her tongue inside my mouth. I opened my eyes. She opened hers. I could discern the edges of her contact lenses, the clots of mascara at the tips of her eyelashes. She closed her eyes again and kissed me harder, forcing my mouth open wider. I undid the top button of her shirt. No bra. Impossibly firm. I squeezed, and tried to look without staring. I didn't want to be ungentlemanly. She pulled away and undid the knot at her waist, then opened her shirt, inviting me to stare. She reached into my pants. I took off her shorts.

"Are we going to do this?" she said.

"I hope so."

"You need to wear something."

"I'll keep my shirt on."

"No. Like a condom."

"I don't have a condom."

"Then we can't."

"Right, right. Of course not." Pause. "Why not?"

"Do you want a little JR Junior running around?"

I stood. I took a long swig of Löwenbräu and stared at the stars, chastising myself. *Why didn't I think of birth control?* Simple. Because I didn't know anything about birth control.

Lana lay at my feet, her shorts off, stretched out in the starlight like a sunbather. Her legs were apart and she was glistening between them. No star overhead glistened more brightly, and suddenly no star seemed as far away. If I let this moment pass, I thought, if I let Lana put on her clothes and then walked her down the slope to the Hornet, this night would haunt me forever and possibly determine the course of my life. At the very least I'd have to move. I wouldn't be able to face Lana, or my schoolmates, or drive each day past Camelback Mountain. Thereafter, for me, Camelback would be Mount Virgin, mocking me and my inability to reach the top. I had to do something, and fast, because Lana looked as if she were seconds from standing and putting her shorts back on.

"Wait here," I said.

"Wait—where?"

Before she could say another word I dove over the side of the cliff and went sprinting down the slope. Racing to reach the bottom before she could protest, or follow, I miscalculated the angle and severity of the incline. I tripped, then rolled. A cactus stopped me, its stickers sinking like knitting needles into my knee. I screamed.

"What happened!" Lana yelled.

"Nothing!"

She must have assumed I had condoms in the car. She certainly couldn't have foreseen what I was about to do. She would have screamed if she'd known that I was going to start up the Hornet and peel away, leaving her on that windblown mountain.

In Scottsdale, in 1981, nothing was open after midnight. The desert was dark, desolate, closed until morning. My only hope was an all-night convenience store. I sped down the hump and swerved onto Scottsdale Road. With every shuttered store and darkened strip mall I thought about giving up. But fifteen miles from Camelback I spotted a neon sign. Circle K.

I didn't have the vaguest idea what a condom looked like. I'd never held one, seen one, or talked to anyone about one. I went up and down the aisles, looking for the Condom Section. I checked the toiletries aisle. I checked the office-supplies aisle. I checked the cooler. *Maybe condoms are perishable and need to be kept fresh.* Ice cream, soda, milk—no condoms.

Eventually I realized that condoms, like skin magazines and cigarettes, were naughty, and therefore must be kept behind the counter. I looked up and there they were, on pegs above the clerk, small boxes with pictures of silhouetted couples preparing to engage in the physical act of love. I slouched with relief, then tensed up. *If condoms are tools of vice there must be some age requirement. Better do something to make myself look older.* I grabbed a copy of the *New York Times*.

"That all?" the clerk asked.

"Yes. Um, no, actually. Throw in a box of them condoms there, why doncha?"

"What kind?"

"Medium, I guess."

"What *brand,* stud?"

I pointed. He set a box of Trojans atop the *Times*. I slid a twenty across the counter. "Keep the change," I said. He scowled and handed me the change.

Fifty minutes had passed since I left Lana. She was either terrified or furious. As I raced back to the mountain I pictured her up there, which made me think about the special spot where I'd left her, and I remembered then that I'd found that spot by trial and error, and that it had taken forty-five minutes of driving up and down and around the hump, in the dark. I didn't know how I'd ever find it again. Fishtailing onto the long road that led to the base of the mountain I checked the speedometer. I was doing seventy-five and both the Hornet and I were shaking. I thought the Hornet might throw a piston rod. I thought I might throw a piston rod. Nothing looked familiar. How could anything look familiar on the side of a mountain in the pitch dark? I told myself to slow down, take it easy, I was going to kill myself in a car accident on the same day my mother was nearly killed in a car accident. I imagined her coming out of limbo, the doctor giving her the bad news. Your son is dead. "What was he doing on Camelback Mountain?" she'd ask weakly.

I came to a familiar fork in the road, but couldn't remember if Lana and I had gone left or right. I turned left, mashed the accelerator and noticed that my foot had gone numb. The cactus stickers in my knee were oozing their poison into my bloodstream, which meant my leg would require amputation. I tried to pick the stickers out of my kneecap as I drove, and at the same time I began rehearsing what I would say to Lana's father. He would either kill me—I remembered he'd played defensive end for the Chicago Bears—or have me arrested.

A more ghoulish scenario took shape in my mind. Lana, deciding that I was crazy, and that I'd abandoned her, might have wandered away, gotten lost, stumbled in the dark, and fallen down a ravine filled with snakes and lizards and wild bobcats. Did they even have wild bobcats in Scottsdale? Probably. And like sharks they were probably attracted to the smell of blood. I remembered the cut on Lana's leg. When the police found Lana's mauled body, no one would believe she'd agreed to wait for me on top of the mountain while I went for condoms. Everyone would think I'd asked for sex and Lana refused, so I'd killed her. I drove faster, feeling the numb sensation in my knee spread to my hip. Not only would I go to jail for murder, not only would I lose my leg, but each day in the yard the other prisoners would ask the same question: *How'd you lose your leg?* It would be poetic justice, divine retribution for all my whining about people asking what JR stood for, just as this night was divine retribution for trying to get laid while my mother lay in a hospital bed, bandaged and broken and adrift in some heavily medicated limbo.

I was passing the same houses, the same cacti, over and over. I was driving in circles, going around and around the hump. I couldn't even say for sure if I was on the right hump. Was it the first or second hump? I turned on the radio to steady my nerves and thought of my father. I cursed him. I punched the radio. *If my father had been around when I was growing up I'd know about condoms and none of this would be happening! If he'd used a condom none of this would be happening!* I pulled to the side of the road, put my head on the steering wheel and wept. From someplace deep inside me I brought up great shuddering sobs for my mother, for myself, and for Lana, who at that moment was being eaten alive by wild bobcats.

I thought of the Hemingway story Bill and Bud had made me read, "The Snows of Kilimanjaro," and the opening line about the summit of the mountain, called the House of God, where lay the dried and frozen carcass of a leopard. "No one has explained what the leopard was seeking at that altitude," Hemingway wrote. What was the point of that goddamned story? Was it that curiosity had killed the cat? Was the leopard trying to get laid? Did leopards look anything like bobcats? Why read stories unless they could provide some practical help in emergencies like this? I considered phoning Bill and Bud, but I didn't know their home numbers. Then I thought of phoning Publicans. Of course! Publicans! Surely Uncle Charlie or Steve would know what to do. Then I heard them asking me why I was on top of Camelback Mountain when my mother was in the hospital, and I also heard them laughing. *The kid tried to lose his virginity—but instead he lost the girl!* I would take my chances with Lana's father and the homicide detectives before I'd face the men at Publicans.

Ahead was a mailbox that looked like a red barn. *Lana commented on that red mailbox when we drove past it.* How cute, she'd said, pointing, and I remembered turning left. Now I turned left again and saw a familiar house with a wagon wheel in the front yard. Then a cactus with more than the usual number of arms, which had made me think of Jedd—and then the dirt road that dead-ended at the slope beside the special spot.

Leaping out of the car I yelled up at the stars. "Lana!" No answer. "Lannnaaa!" I tried to sound like Tarzan. I tried to sound like Brando yelling, "Stelllaaa," but I sounded more like Costello yelling, "Hey Abbott!" Maybe she was refusing to answer. It was my only hope. *Please God let her be angry but alive.* Before beginning to climb I had another thought, one I would always remember with equal parts astonishment and shame. *If Lana is still there, still alive, I might be able to explain and apologize and maybe we can still—do it. In which case I'd better put on the condom now.* Since I'd never seen a condom I'd need light to slip it on, and the only light on that dark mountaintop was in the Hornet. I got back in the car, turned on the dome light and opened the box of condoms. No instructions. I placed one condom on my finger. How could such a little cap stay put during sex? I didn't know and I didn't have time to figure it out. I placed the rolled-up condom on my flaccid penis, like a beret, then struck out for the summit.

"Lana!"

My voice echoed across the mountain.

"Lana!"

Nearly two hours had passed since I left her.

"Laaaaaana!"

The pain in my leg was blinding, and my knee wouldn't bend, which made the climb take longer. At the top I chinned myself up and peered forward. I saw Lana at the far edge of the cliff, curled in the fetal position, asleep. I crawled toward her. She woke, reached for me. Her breath smelled like Juicy Fruit and Löwenbräu. "Have you been crying?" she asked, kissing me. She pulled me on top of her. I could barely support myself on my numb leg, but she helped me, guided me. "It's right—here," she whispered. Inside. Then deeper. She rocked me back and forth, showed me how, until I understood. I looked out across the valley, all those lights, all those houses, all those windows I'd peered into as a boy. Finally someone was letting me in.

After, Lana and I lay on our backs, shoulder to shoulder. "Your first time?" she said.

We both laughed.

"Sorry," I said.

"Don't be. It's exciting when it's someone else's first time."

I told her about my hunt for condoms. "I never had anyone go to such— lengths," she said.

She fell asleep with her head on my chest while I counted stars. Turning my head I saw, in the dirt nearby, gleaming in the moonlight like a clam, the unused and rolled-up condom. Had I become a man and a father in the same heedless moment? I didn't care. Either way I was no longer a boy.

My best guess was that I was neither boy nor man, but something in between. In limbo. Even Sheryl would have to admit that much. I wondered if shedding boyhood was something like amnesia, if you forgot yourself and your old life, forgot all the familiar things you thought you would never forget, and started fresh. I hoped so. I wished it were so on the brightest star I could see. And I wished there were someone I could ask.

nineteen | FUTURE ME

MY MOTHER CAME HOME FROM THE HOSPITAL AFTER A WEEK, her arm in a large cast. Upon waking each morning she would move from her bed to the couch and sleep on and off throughout the day, because of the pain medication. The good news was, her doctors had concluded that she'd suffered no brain damage. And her memory had returned. But she didn't speak much, and when she did her voice was a faint, far-away rasp, without any inflections. Her voice, it seemed, like her face, had gone blank. After school, after my shift at the bookstore, I would sit in the chair opposite the couch, alternating between watching my mother sleep and filling out my Yale application.

The first page was a minefield, full of loaded questions, like *Father's*

Legal Name. I thought about typing "Johnny Michaels." I typed "John Joseph Moehringer." Next question: *Father's Address.* I mulled several possibilities. "Not sure." "Unknown." "Missing." I typed "Not Applicable" and stared hopelessly at the words.

Bill and Bud had been crazy, or callous, persuading me to apply to Yale. The finest school in the nation wasn't about to let its students be contaminated by the likes of me, a low-rent loser, a gypsy who didn't know his father's whereabouts. Undoubtedly the admissions committee dropped applications like mine into a special basket with a little sign: WHITE TRASH.

Yale doesn't care if you know where your father is, Bill and Bud said when I confronted them.

I snorted.

"But if it bothers you so much," Bill said, "find him."

As if it were that simple. Then I thought, Maybe it is.

Time had passed. I was almost seventeen, a different person—my father probably was too. Maybe he was curious about me. Maybe he'd phoned Grandpa's house, looking for me, only to have someone hang up on him. What if my father would be pleased to hear *my* voice? It was possible, especially since I didn't want anything from him anymore. Though I was ashamed to admit it, I no longer hoped to sue my father. That plan had fallen away and in its place was an aching desire to meet him, to find out who he was, so I could start deciding who I might be.

Finding him would be easy, I figured. After all, I was taking journalism classes in school, writing for the school newspaper—my first story was a transparently fawning profile of a local disc jockey—and I was delighted to learn that one of the primary things reporters did was find people. My search for my father would be my first try at investigative journalism. And if I found that he was dead, so be it. There would be peace in knowing, and I would be able to type "Deceased" under *Father's Address,* an improvement over "Not Applicable."

I couldn't tell my mother about my search. She'd feel betrayed that I wanted to meet the man who had tried to kill her, especially after a drunk driver had nearly killed her. So I conducted my search in secret, after school, using the phone in the journalism office to call radio stations and comedy clubs across the nation. No one knew where my father was living, or if he was living. I went to the library and checked phone books from scores of cities, but there were always too many Johnny Michaelses and no John Moehringers. After a month I hadn't turned up a single lead.

While my mother was at the market one day I quickly dialed a former colleague of my father's at WNBC in New York City. I'd spent weeks trying to coax the colleague to the phone, and this was the only time his secretary said he'd be available. As he checked to see if he had a number for my father, my mother returned. She'd forgotten her grocery list. "Who are you talking to?" she asked. I shrugged. The man came on the line and said my father had left specific instructions that his whereabouts were not to be given out. I argued, but he hung up. My mother sat beside me and we both stared at the phone. She asked if I wanted her help. "No," I said. She touched her arm, the one that had been broken in the car accident. The cast had only recently been removed, and the arm had atrophied. It gave her frequent pain, and now I was giving her more pain. Also, while recovering, my mother hadn't been able to work, and our bills had piled up. She was stressed about money, more stressed than usual, and I was adding to her stress.

"I'm sorry," I said.

"Don't apologize. A boy needs a father." She smiled sadly. "Everyone needs a father."

My mother went through her papers and pulled out an old address book. She thought she might have a number for my father's sister in Florida. She put on her glasses and reached for the phone with her atrophied arm. Not wanting to listen I went to my bedroom and worked on my Yale essay.

My mother did reach my father's sister, though it might have been better if she hadn't. The sister said my father didn't want to be found. That was that. "Anyway," my mother said, standing at the stove, making dinner, "I left a message for her to give to him. We'll see."

The phone rang early the next morning. I recognized The Voice right away.

"Dad?" I said.

"How are you feeling?" he asked. He sounded sad.

"Fine," I said.

"Fine?"

"Yes."

"But when—how—?"

My mother grabbed the phone. With her hand cupped over the receiver and her back to me, she whispered to my father. Later she confessed to me the message she'd left with my father's sister: *JR is very sick and he would like to meet his father—before it's too late.* One of her finest lies.

When my mother gave me back the phone my father sounded amused. He asked what was new, and seemed interested to hear that I was applying to Yale. I was flattered, because I was a sap. He wasn't interested, he was suspicious. He knew that Yale was expensive and thought I was calling to put the touch on him for tuition. After I mentioned the financial-aid forms scattered across our kitchen table, he changed his tone, and even said he'd consider coming to Arizona to see me, so long as my mother promised not to have him thrown in jail. She had to promise several times, with me relaying each promise, before he believed her. Fine, fine, he said at last. He was living in Los Angeles, working at a rock station—he would fly to Phoenix that weekend.

I asked my mother how I would spot my father at the airport. I had no memory of him.

"It's been a long time," she said. "He used to look a bit like—I don't know."

"Like what?"

"You."

"Oh."

She was having a cup of coffee. She looked into the cup and pondered. "He liked to eat," she said. "He was a chef once."

"He was?"

"So I'll bet he's heavier. He liked to drink too, which can affect how a person looks. And he was starting to lose his hair. I imagine he's lost more."

"You're saying I should look for a fat, drunk, bald version of me?"

She put her hand over her mouth and laughed. "Oh JR," she said. "You're the only one who can make me laugh." Then abruptly she stopped laughing. "Yes," she said. "Yes, I think that probably is about right."

I stood near the gate, gazing into every man's face as if it were a crystal ball. Is that me in thirty years? Could *that* be me? Is that—Future Me? Each man stared back, though none showed any recognition. When I saw the flight attendants walk off the plane I kicked the ground. He'd done it again. I thought my father had changed, but no one changes.

Off the plane came one last passenger. A pugnacious fireplug of a man, he was three inches shorter than I, but with my nose and chin. He looked like me with an extra thirty years and another seventy-five pounds, plus several more layers of muscle. Our eyes met. I felt his gaze connect as if he'd hurled a baseball across the terminal and hit me in the middle of the forehead. He strode toward me and I took a step back, thinking he might strike me, but he folded me carefully into a hug, as though I were breakable, which I was.

The feel of my father, the thrilling width of him, the scent of his hair spray and cigarettes and the whiskey he drank on the plane, made me weak. More than his feel and smell, the fact of him staggered me. I was hugging The Voice. I'd forgotten that my father was flesh and bone. Over time I'd grouped him with all my imaginary fathers, and now, struggling to reach around his shoulders, I felt as if I were hugging Baloo or Bagheera.

At a coffee shop near Sky Harbor we sat across from each other at a wobbly table, each of us staring, seeing the resemblance. He told me about his life, or the life he wanted me to think he'd led, full of adventure and danger and glamour. He made his past sound romantic, to distract us both from his present, which was grim. He'd squandered his talent, blown through his money, and was at the start of a long decline. He told story after story, a Scheherazade in dark shades and a leather jacket, and I said nothing. I listened intently and believed every word, every lie, even while I knew they were lies, and believed that he noticed and appreciated my rapt attention and credulity, that this was why he was telling me so many stories. Later I realized he noticed nothing. My father was nervous also, more nervous than I, and telling stories was how he steadied his nerves. I thought he was there before me at last, but as always he was hiding behind that voice.

I remember few details of my father's oral autobiography. I remember him telling me about famous beauties he'd bedded, but I don't remember who, and celebrities he'd known, though I can't recall which. What I remember best is what neither of us said. My father offered no explanation or apology for disappearing, and I didn't ask for one. Maybe we felt that the time wasn't right. Maybe we didn't know where to begin. Most likely neither of us had the guts. Whatever the reason, we fell into a conspiracy of silence, each of us pretending that the fact of my father's abandonment of me and his mistreatment of my mother wasn't sitting there on the table between us, like a dead rat.

It was easier for me to pretend. My father—as a grown man, as a father—understood better than I what he'd done. I saw this in his face, and heard it in his voice, without recognizing it for what it was. I would recognize it years later, when I knew much more about guilt and self-loathing, and how they make a man look and sound.

Of the many stories my father told that night, one did manage to lodge itself in my memory. When I asked where he got his radio alias, and why he used one, he said that Moehringer wasn't our real name. His late father was a Sicilian immigrant named Hugh Attanasio, who couldn't find work because all the factories on the Lower East Side were run by "Italian-hating Krauts." To fool the Krauts, Hugh took the name of his recently deceased German neighbor, Franz Moehringer. My father never liked the name Moehringer, and he didn't like his old man, so when he broke into show business he became Johnny Michaels.

"Wait," I said, pointing to my chest. "I'm named after your father's dead German neighbor?"

He laughed and shifted into a German accent. "Yah vell," he said, "eet zounds funny ven you put eet like zat."

We met for coffee the next morning at my father's hotel. He had a gray complexion and his eyes were pink. Apparently he'd stopped into the hotel bar after I left him. His hangover rendered him unable to resume his monologue of the night before, and therefore I could no longer sit back and listen. Someone had to talk. I sputtered about Bill and Bud, Uncle Charlie, Publicans, Lana, Sheryl, my life's ambitions.

"Still with the lawyer thing?" my father said, lighting one cigarette with the dying end of another.

"Why not?"

He frowned.

"How do you rate your chances of getting into Yale?" he said.

"Heavy underdog," I said.

"I think you're going to get in," he said.

"Really?"

"They can't get many applications from this wasteland," he said. "You'll give them geographical diversity."

His flight back to Los Angeles left at noon. Driving him to the airport I tried to think of something profound to say. Before we parted I thought we should address the topic we'd been avoiding. But how? My father turned up the volume on the car stereo and sang along with my Sinatra cassette as I ran through different speeches in my head. I thought I might confront him. Why did you leave my mother and me without a penny? Or I might take a forgiving tone, suggest we start over. Look, the past is past, and I hope we can put it all behind us. Whatever I said needed to be clever, but also serious, and struggling to find the right words, to strike the exact tone, I stopped paying attention to the road. I ran yellow lights, swerved in and out of lanes, narrowly dodged a truck backing out of a driveway. Squealing up to the airport curb I threw the Hornet into park and turned to my father. Looking him straight in the eye I said—nothing. He reached into the backseat for his garment bag, hugged me, then climbed out and slammed the door. Disgusted with myself, ashamed of my cowardice, I gripped the steering wheel and stared straight ahead. I thought how disappointed Bud would be when I told him I'd let fear get the best of me.

That night I would realize exactly what I'd wanted to say to my father, and I would write it down. I'd wanted to tell him that I understood he hadn't been cut out for fatherhood, hadn't ever wanted the job in the first place, so there was no point in my regretting his not being around while I was growing up. What I regretted was my own lost opportunity. I felt that I would have enjoyed being a father's son.

I heard a knock on the window. My father was peering in, making a motion for me to roll down the window. Obviously he too felt something profound should be said. I leaned over and cranked the handle.

"JR," he said, as the glass lowered, "I just need to tell you one thing."

"Yes?"

"You drive like nuns fuck."

twenty | MY MOTHER

I T HAD TO BE SIMPLE BUT COMPLEX, SPARSE BUT LYRICAL, HEM-
ingwayesque and Jamesian at the same time. It had to be careful and con-
servative, but also fresh and bold, evidence of a young mind teeming with
insights. It would determine the course of my life, and my mother's life, and
either make up for the mistakes of all the men in my family or perpetuate
their tradition of failure. And it could be no longer than three-quarters of a
page.

Before beginning my essay for Yale I made a list of big words. Only the
biggest words, I felt, would force the Admissions Committee to overlook my
many deficiencies. At seventeen years old, I'd developed a philosophy on big
words that was no different than my philosophy on cologne. The more the
better.

My word list:

Provisional
Strident
Bucolic
Fulcrum
Inimical
Behemoth
Jesuitical
Minion
Eclectic
Marquis de Sod
Esthetic

I loved words—their sound, their power—without understanding or ap-
preciating their precision, and this led to one jaw-dropping sentence after another. "Try as I might," I wrote, addressing the Admissions Committee
directly, "I feel unable to truly convey the emphatic pangs of hungry ignorance that attend this my seventeenth year, for I fear that my audience is well
fed!"

As my fingers flew across the keys of the secondhand typewriter my mother had bought me, I could hear the Dean of Admissions summoning everyone into his office. "I think we've got something here," he'd say, before reading a few choice passages aloud.

My mother, however, after reading my essay, chose three small words to express her opinion. "You sound—insane."

I ripped the essay from her hands and stormed into my bedroom to try again.

I began a new essay, a *wordier* essay, about my "ambition" to attend Yale. I was quite taken with this word. "I have ambition," I proclaimed, "in the sense that one would describe the man who wishes to outrun a speeding train as ambitious. And the behemoth bearing down on me? Ignorance!" I thought it sounded brilliant, but again my mother flatly rejected my effort.

Over the next few weeks, between Thanksgiving and Christmas, my mother and I shouted and slammed doors and shoved my notebook back and forth, arguing about words. She would stare at me and I could almost hear her wishing she'd never taught me to love words, had never shown me those flash cards when I was a boy. I would stare back at her and wonder if her car accident had caused some brain damage the doctors hadn't detected—or was the woman simply unable to appreciate topflight writing? I brought my many drafts to Bill and Bud, who told me that my mother had been far too kind in her appraisal.

With the December 31 deadline just days away I walked out of my bedroom, brandishing another essay. "Worse than the last," my mother said, handing it back.

"That essay will get me accepted!"

"That essay will get you committed."

To spite her, I went back into my bedroom and batted out a slapdash essay with not one big word, just a plain and simple description of working at the bookstore with Bill and Bud, how they taught me to read by giving me bagfuls of books and talking with me patiently about literature and language. I wrote about how they transmitted their enthusiasm for books, and how I saw Yale as an enlargement of this experience. Dull as yesterday's dishwater. I thrust it at my mother. "Perfect," she said. I was never so confused.

On New Year's Eve my mother and I drove to the post office. The day was windy and bright. She kissed her fingertips and touched the envelope before I dropped it into the mailbox. At home we ate a pizza and when my mother went to bed I climbed up to the canal and looked at the water and listened to some drunken Arizonans across the way singing "Auld Lang Syne."

Every day thereafter I watched the mail, though of course I knew that the Admissions Committee wouldn't make its decision for months. The only letter that arrived was from Sheryl. I was touched, because I thought she'd decorated the page with Yale's logo, that majestic-looking *Y*, but on closer inspection I saw that Sheryl had drawn martini glasses at the end of every sentence, a pictograph of how she'd been spending her time. She was dating So-and-So, who liked to (martini glass), and she'd bumped into What's His Name, and they stayed out very late (martini glasses), and the gang at Publicans (martini glasses) sent me their love. In closing she signed off, "Have a cocktail. I am! XOXO, Sheryl."

Spring came. I spent every warm night on the canal, wondering if the Admissions Committee had decided about me that day, or if they would decide in the morning, or perhaps the following afternoon. I looked at the stars reflected on the water's surface and wished on each one. Please. *Please.* I didn't know what I would do if I didn't get in. As a backup I'd applied to Arizona State, but I couldn't muster any enthusiasm for going there. If Yale rejected me, I thought, I'd probably just light out for Alaska. Sometimes I let my mind run with this fantasy, pretending the canal was a wild river in the Yukon, where I lived in a log cabin, fishing and reading, subsisting on grizzly-bear meat, hardly ever thinking about Yale, except on snowy nights, sitting by the fire, combing the lice out of my beard and petting my dog—Eli.

Whenever I climbed down from the bank of the canal and returned to the apartment I'd find my mother awake, working at the kitchen table. We would talk awhile, about everything but Yale, and then I'd go to bed and listen to Sinatra until I fell asleep.

On April 15 a letter arrived. My mother put it in the middle of the kitchen table. We might have stared at it all day if she hadn't begged me to open it. I took the letter opener she'd bought me when we visited Yale and slit the envelope. I removed the one sheet of onionskin, unfolded it, read silently.

"Dear Mr. Moehringer: It is a great pleasure to inform you that the Admissions Committee has voted to offer you a place in the Yale Class of 1986."

"What is it?" my mother said.

I continued to read in silence. "I am also pleased to notify you that your financial need has been met."

"Tell me," my mother said.

I handed her the letter. Oh dear God, she said, reading, tears filling her eyes. She held the letter against her heart. I grabbed her and danced her around the living room, in and out of the kitchen, and then we sat side by side at the table and read the letter over and over. I shouted the letter, she sang the letter, and finally we fell silent. We couldn't say anything else. We didn't dare, and we didn't need to. We both believed in words, but there were only three words for this day, this feeling. We got in.

I phoned Grandpa's house and told them. Then the phone call that counted. Publicans. I'd never phoned Uncle Charlie at the bar before, so he assumed the worst. "Who died?" he said.

"Just thought you might be interested to know that your nephew got accepted to Yale."

Pause. I heard fifty voices in the background, a baseball game on TV, glasses clinking. "No shit," he said. "Hey everyone! My nephew got into Yale!" He held up the phone and I heard cheers, followed by a riotous, boozy chorus of "Boola Boola."

At the bookstore I walked calmly into the stockroom, as though I were there to pick up my paycheck. Bill and Bud were reading. I remember—I will always remember—that Bud was sitting on his stool, listening to Mahler's Symphony no. 1. "Any word?" he said.

"About what?" I said.

"You know," Bill said.

"What? Oh. Yale? I got in."

Both men were weepier than my mother.

"He's got to get cracking now," Bill said to Bud, who was wiping his eyes, blowing his nose, sniffing his fist. "Boy oh boy he's got a hell of a lot of reading to do this summer."

"Plato," Bud said. "He should read *The Republic* right away."

"Yes, yes," Bud said, "they'll start him on the Greeks, to be sure. But maybe he should read some plays. Aeschylus? *Antigone? The Birds?*"

"What about Thoreau and Emerson? How can he go wrong with Emerson?"

They took me around the store, filling a shopping bag with coverless books.

On my last day of work at the bookstore Bill and Bud and I stood in the back room, eating bagels and drinking champagne. A going-away party, though it felt like a funeral. "Listen," Bill said to me, "Bud and I have been talking."

They stared at me as though I were a caged bird they were getting ready to release into the wild.

"It might be wise," Bud said, "to lower your expectations."

"You seem—afraid for me," I said.

Bill cleared his throat. "We just think there are some things you're not—"

"Ready for," Bud said.

"Like?"

"Disillusionment," Bud said without hesitation.

Bill nodded.

Champagne nearly came through my nose.

"I thought you were going to say booze and drugs," I said. "Or girls. Or rich kids. Or mean professors. But—*disillusionment?*"

"Disillusionment is more dangerous than all those things put together," Bud said.

He explained, but I wasn't listening. I was laughing too hard. "Okay," I said. "I'll be sure to watch out for—disillusionment! Ha ha ha!" Bud gave his fist a vehement sniff. Bill smoothed his knit tie. Poor dopes, I thought. Hiding in the back room all this time had warped their minds. Disillusionment. *How can I be disillusioned when everything from here on is going to be perfect?*

We turned off the lights and left the store. I shook their hands and went one way, they went the other, and that was the last I ever saw of Bill and Bud. When I returned to Arizona that Christmas and visited the store, a man at the cash register told me they had been fired. He wouldn't say why, and I could only hope it had nothing to do with all those coverless books.

. . .

"How are you going to get along without me?" I asked my mother at the airport.

She laughed, until she realized I wasn't kidding. "Just take care of *yourself*," she said. "And always know I'm happy thinking of the marvelous experiences you're having."

I wanted to stay in Arizona that summer, spend time with my mother. Absolutely not, she said. Sheryl had arranged for me to return to the law firm, to earn some spending money for college, and my mother wanted me to have as many days as possible going to Gilgo with Uncle Charlie and the men.

We sat, waiting for my flight to be called, looking at the screen listing the departures and arrivals. I said something about all the departures and arrivals in our life together. My mother hooked her arm through mine. "You'll have lots of vacations," she said. "Before you know it you'll be coming—home."

She still tripped over that word.

My flight began to board.

"You'd better go," my mother said.

We stood.

"I should stay. A few weeks more."

"Go."

"But—"

"Go JR," she said. "Go."

We looked at each other, not as if we wouldn't see each other for a long time, but as if we hadn't seen each other in a long time. We'd been concentrating so intently on getting by, and getting in, that we hadn't taken a good look at each other for years. I looked at her now, her green-brown eyes wet, her lip trembling. I threw my arms around her and felt her hugging me back tighter than ever. "Go," she said. "Please just go."

Sitting on the plane, waiting to pull away from the gate, I looked out the window and berated myself for letting my mother down. At the pivotal moment of our good-bye I hadn't said anything profound. If ever a moment called for profundity, that was it, and I'd muffed it. I felt even more ashamed about the reason. I wasn't sufficiently traumatized. I was excited to be starting my life, which meant that I was an ingrate and a bad son. I was abandoning my mother without the slightest guilt, blithely waving good-bye over my shoulder.

Sometime after my plane took off I realized why I wasn't traumatized about saying good-bye. I'd been saying good-bye to my mother since I was eleven. Sending me to Manhasset, urging me to bond with Uncle Charlie and the men, my mother had been weaning me from her, and herself from me, by imperceptible degrees. It might have been the fleecy clouds streaming by the window of the plane that made me understand. My mother had subtly, secretly snipped away a sliver of herself every summer.

Thereafter, I'd have to contend with all security blankets by myself. And none would be more secure, or more smothering, than Steve's bar.

PART II

⌘

They say best men are molded out of faults,
And, for the most, become much more the better
For being a little bad

—William Shakespeare, *Measure for Measure*

twenty-one | THE DEVIL AND
MERRIAM WEBSTER

THE CABDRIVER SET MY SUITCASES ON THE CURB OUTSIDE PHELPS Gate. There were families everywhere and he looked left and right for mine, as if I'd had a family when he picked me up at Union Station and they must have fallen out of the cab on the way to the campus.

"You alone?" he asked.

"Yes."

"Need some help with your stuff?"

I nodded.

He hoisted one of my suitcases and we walked side by side under a tall archway, through a long dark tunnel, into the bright spacious green of Old Campus. Even Yale's front door, I thought, is designed to reenact and symbolize the whole promise of the place—darkness yielding dramatically to light.

We asked for directions to Wright Hall, which turned out to be a century-old dormitory building not much sturdier than Grandpa's house. My room was at the top of a five-flight staircase, and there were people already in it. One of my three new roommates was unpacking his underwear with the help of his parents and sisters. He and I shook hands while his mother lunged at the cabbie. "You must be so proud!" she cried. "Isn't this a fabulous day to be a parent?"

Flustered, the cabdriver doffed his hat and shook the mother's hand. She introduced herself and her husband, and before she could ask the cabdriver if he preferred to summer on the Vineyard or the Cape, I handed him his money and thanked him.

"Oh," the mother said. "I didn't—"

"Good luck," the cabdriver said to me, doffing his hat again as he backed out the door.

Everyone looked at me. "Flying solo today," I said.

The mother gave a fake smile. My son is living with this vagabond? The sisters went back to folding jockey shorts. "So," my new roommate said, trying to break the tension, "what does JR stand for?"

A second roommate came through the door with his parents and his limousine driver right behind, toting a matching set of designer luggage. Introductions were made. The second roommate's father, an elegant man with an ominous glare, cornered me and began bombarding me with questions. Where was I from? What high school did I attend? He then asked what I'd been doing with myself all summer. "Working at a law firm in Manhattan," I said proudly.

"What firm?"

I told him the name. He didn't react. "It's a small firm," I said. "I'm sure you've never heard of it." He frowned. I'd lost him. I tried to recover. "Though the partners did break away from a much larger and more prestigious firm several years ago."

This was true. And yet when the father asked which larger firm that was, I drew a blank. I blurted the first three lawyerly names that came to mind— Hart, Schaffner and Marx. As luck would have it the father was in the clothing business. He knew Hart Schaffner Marx, makers of men's suits, knew them well. I saw the father conclude that I was a liar and a fool and turn from me in disgust.

Time to get some air.

I hurried off to the same spreading elm where I'd retreated when I first visited Yale with my mother. Sitting with my back against the elm I watched my schoolmates arrive, a flotilla of families sailing with the wind up College

Street, in cars that cost three times what my mother earned in one year. I never thought until that moment how odd I might appear, showing up at Yale alone, and I never anticipated how different my schoolmates would be from me. Aside from the tangibles—clothes, shoes, parents—what I noticed that first day was their self-confidence. I could almost see their self-confidence rising off the campus in shimmering waves, like the August heat, and like the heat it sapped my strength. I wondered if self-confidence could be acquired, or if, like fathers and flawless skin, it was just something you were born with.

One confident boy stood out from all the rest. He reminded me of a photo Bud had once shown me of a marble bust from antiquity. Caesar, I thought. His eyes gleamed with that same imperial confidence. They were the eyes of his father, or uncle, or whoever that man was helping him lug his stereo to his room, and they bedazzled everyone who walked by. This was the first day of the school year, and yet this boy gave all indication that he was about to graduate. He had Yale wired. He knew everyone, and those he didn't know he stopped, eager to know them. He held up his chin slightly, as though each person he addressed were standing on a stepladder, a pose that accentuated his regal bearing, as well as his beaky nose and jutting jaw. He smiled as if he had a winning lottery ticket in his pocket, and I supposed he did. His success was that assured. He looked like someone to whom nothing bad would ever happen.

How could I attend the same school with such a boy? How could we occupy the same planet? He wasn't a boy at all, but a full-grown man. If I were ever to stand beside him—an unlikely prospect—I'd feel as though I were wearing velvet shorts and holding a giant lollipop. He existed on another plane of reality, worlds removed from me, though there was also something gnawingly familiar about him. I stared and stared until I had it. He looked like Jedd.

Jedd. I wished I could phone him and ask his advice. Jedd would know what to do. But I hadn't spoken to Jedd in years. I thought of phoning my mother, but that was out of the question. She'd hear the panic in my voice, and I couldn't let her know I was losing heart on the first day.

Later that night I put Sinatra on my roommate's turntable and stretched out on the window seat in our common room, leafing through the catalog of classes, which ran four hundred pages. This is why I came to Yale, I thought, cheering up. This would be my salvation. I'd tune out everything else and focus on Anthropology 370b, "The Study of American Culture," or English 433b, "The Craft of the Writer," or Psychology 242a, "Human Learning and Memory." I'd learn Chinese! Or Greek! I'd read Dante in the original Italian! I'd take up fencing!

Then I spotted something called Directed Studies. A program open to a "select" number of freshmen, Directed Studies was a yearlong exhaustive survey of Western civilization, an intense immersion in the canon. I ran my finger along the list of writers and thinkers covered. Aeschylus, Sophocles, Herodotus, Plato, Aristotle, Thucydides, Virgil, Dante, Shakespeare, Milton, Aquinas, Goethe, Wordsworth, Augustine, Machiavelli, Hobbes, Locke, Rousseau, Tocqueville—and that was just the first semester. I looked out the window, thinking. A group of students was gathering in the courtyard below. Again I saw the supremely confident boy, Jedd Redux, holding forth. The Emperor of Yale. Directed Studies was the only way to compete with such a boy, the only way to contend with his confidence, and maybe acquire some of my own.

I phoned my mother and asked what she thought. She worried that I'd be biting off too much, too soon, but hearing in my voice the need to prove myself fast, she encouraged me to apply. And if somehow I got in, she said, I should skip taking a part-time job as we'd discussed. I should use all my spare time to study, study, study, she said, and if I needed money she would dip into the small settlement she got after her accident.

A new Yale notebook under my arm, two new pens in my pocket, I ran down Elm Street as the bells in Harkness chimed. A few leaves were already beginning to turn. I'd been accepted to Directed Studies, which I deemed an immense honor, though I found out later that the program accepted virtually every masochist willing to work four times harder than all other freshmen. Rushing to my first class, a literature seminar, I thought of all the times Uncle Charlie had told me to stop the clock, stay right there, freeze, usually at just those moments when I wanted life to hurry up. Now at last had come a time to savor.

My literature seminar was taught by a tall rawboned man in his forties, who had a Vandyke beard and eyebrows that were brown and constantly aflutter, like miller moths. He welcomed us officiously and told us about the glories we'd soon encounter, the prodigious minds, the timeless stories, the immemorial sentences so well crafted they had outlasted empires and epochs and would endure for millennia to come. He leaped from poem to play to novel, citing from memory the greatest lines and passages of *The Divine Comedy* and *The Prelude* and *The Sound and the Fury*—and his favorite, *Paradise Lost,* in which we'd soon be making the acquaintance of Satan. He spoke with particular sadness about the loss of paradise, and with peculiar admiration for Satan as a literary character, and it struck me that this professor, with his pointed beard and furry eyebrows, may have modeled himself in part on the Prince of Darkness. I drew a picture of him in my notebook, a sketch in the style of *Minute Biographies,* and beneath it I wrote: Professor Lucifer.

As one would expect of Lucifer, the professor sat magisterially at the head of the table and made a sales pitch for our souls. Everything we would be reading, he said with compelling gravitas, descended from two epic poems, the *Iliad* and the *Odyssey.* These were the seedlings, he said, from which the great oak of Western literature had grown, and continued to grow, extending branches to each new generation. He envied us, he said, because we were about to encounter these two masterpieces for the first time. Though written nearly three thousand years ago, each poem remained as fresh and relevant as a story in that morning's *New York Times.* "Why?" he asked. "Because each grapples with that timeless theme—the longing for home." In my notebook I wrote, "Grappled—good word." Then, seeing that my penmanship wasn't quite perfect, I erased the notation and wrote it again, more neatly.

I loved the way Professor Lucifer pronounced certain words, especially "poem." He didn't rhyme it with "home," as I did, but with "goyim." Each time he said the word ("The thing to remember about this *POY-um*—"), he'd rest his bony right hand on his tattered copies of the poems, like a witness swearing on a Bible. Though his copies were twice my age, though their pages were a dark mustard yellow, I could see that they had been lovingly preserved, delicately handled, and underlined with geometric precision.

Our first assignment was to read half of the *Iliad,* then write a ten-page paper. I walked directly to Sterling Library and found a leather chair in the reading room. Beside me a window opened onto an enclosed garden, where a fountain burbled and birds chirped. Within minutes I faded into my leather chair, fell back into the folds of time, and landed with a thud on the wind-scoured beach of Ilium. I read for hours without a break, discovering to my delight that aside from the longing for home, the poem was also about men, and the tinfoil armor of manhood. I held my breath as I came upon the scene between Hector, the greatest Trojan warrior, and his infant son. Hector, dressed for battle, says good-bye to the boy. Don't go, Hector's wife pleads—but Hector must. It's not his will, but his fate. The battlefield calls. He holds the boy, "beautiful as a star shining," kisses him good-bye, then says a prayer: "Some day let them say of him: he is better by far than his father."

At midnight I went back to my room, my head teeming with ideas for my paper. I sat at my desk and turned on the gooseneck lamp over my desk. While my roommate snored in the top bunk I opened my new dictionary and made a list of very big words.

Professor Lucifer handed back our papers by throwing them down the length of the table. He told us he'd put as much effort into grading them as we'd put into writing them. He was "appalled," he said, by our crude analyses of the POY-um. We were unworthy of Directed Studies. We were unworthy of Homer. He looked directly at me several times as he spoke. Everyone fished through the stack of papers and when I found mine my stomach dropped. A red "D+" was scrawled on the first page. The boy next to me found his paper and looked equally stricken. I peeked over his shoulder. He'd gotten a B-plus.

After class I took sanctuary under my spreading elm and read Professor Lucifer's margin notes, which were written with a red pen that leaked, so the pages appeared blood-spattered. Some comments made me wince, others made me scratch my head. Repeatedly he'd circled the word "somehow," and in the margin he'd written, "Intellectual laziness." I hadn't known that "somehow" was a sin. Why hadn't Bill and Bud told me? Was there a bigger word for "somehow"?

Before beginning my next paper I went to the Yale bookstore and bought a bigger dictionary, from which I culled a list of bigger words, five-syllable jobs. I vowed to astonish Professor Lucifer, to make his Vandyke stand up. He gave my second paper a D. Again I retreated to my elm.

No matter how hard I studied that fall, no matter what I tried, the result was always a C or a D. For my paper about John Keats's "Ode on a Grecian

Urn," I spent a week reading the poem backward and forward, memorizing it, saying it aloud while I brushed my teeth. Surely Professor Lucifer would see the difference. In his margin notes he said I'd written my worst paper of the semester. He said in so many words that I'd treated Keats's urn as my personal urinal. He did not relish my phrase "A poem saved is a poem urned."

By the end of the semester I'd worn a footpath between the classrooms and my elm, and I'd come to a gloomy conclusion: Getting into Yale had been a lucky break, but getting through Yale, getting a diploma, would be a miracle. I was a good student from a bad public school, meaning I was woefully unprepared. My schoolmates, meanwhile, were coasting. Nothing took them by surprise, because they had prepared for Yale all their lives, at world-famous prep schools I'd never heard of before arriving in New Haven. I'd done my prepping in the stockroom of a bookstore with two mad hermits. Some days I suspected that my schoolmates and I didn't even speak the same language. I saw two boys walking through the courtyard and overheard one proclaim to the other, "That's so very recondite!" The other boy laughed uproariously. Later that week I saw the same two boys. "Wait just a minute," said the recondite one. "Teleological arguments hold no water with me!"

Philosophy was the only class where I did well, because there were no right answers. Even there I was astonished by my schoolmates' confidence— or arrogance. While discussing Plato in seminar I looked to the right and saw that the boy beside me had scribbled rejoinders to Socrates in the margins of his text. "No!" "Wrong again, Soc!" "Ha—not likely!" In a million years I wouldn't disagree with Socrates, and if I did, I'd keep it to myself.

Just before finals, sitting under my elm and observing its spidery roots as they radiated from me in every direction, I concluded that this was what I lacked—roots. To do well at Yale you needed a foundation, some basic knowledge to draw upon, as the elm drew water through its roots. I had none. Frankly I wasn't even sure this tree was an elm.

As the first semester drew to a close, I did manage to reach one small goal. I turned eighteen. In December 1982, eighteen was the legal drinking age in New York. Which meant that at long last I could take shelter somewhere other than my spreading elm.

twenty-two | CAGER

UNCLE CHARLIE WAS BEHIND THE BAR, DRYING A HIGHBALL glass and watching the Knicks. From the way he held the glass, as though he might break it over someone's head, and the way he glared at the TV, as though he might break it over someone's head, I could tell he had heavy timber on the wrong team.

It was Friday night, dusk. The place wasn't crowded yet. Families were eating dinner in the restaurant and a crew of early drinkers stood along the bar, each in a posture of extraordinary repose, like New England farmers in a field leaning against a stone wall. Entering from the restaurant I stopped at the edge of the barroom, put a foot on the brick footrest along the base of the bar and stared at the back of Uncle Charlie's head. Feeling my stare he turned slowly.

"Look. Who's. Here," he said.

"Hello," I said.

"Hello yourself."

"What're the Knicks doing?"

"Taking years off my life. What're you doing—here?"

Like a jury the men along the bar swiveled their heads toward me. I didn't know what to say. I set down my suitcase and Uncle Charlie set down the highball glass. He plucked his cigarette from the ashtray and took a long drag, squinting at me through the cirrus clouds of smoke. He'd never looked more like Bogart, and Publicans had never felt more like Rick's Café Americain, which may have been why, placing my driver's license on the bar, I said something about the "letters of transit." Without picking up my license Uncle Charlie stared at it and pretended to count the years since my birth. Then he let out a long rolling sigh.

"So this is the day," he said. "D-Day. Or should I say B-Day? You've come to have your first legal drink." The men along the bar chortled. "My nephew," he said to them. "Is he beautiful?" There was a deeper murmur of masculine approbation, like a neighing of horses. "According to the laws of the sovereign state of New York," he continued, louder, "my nephew is a man today."

"Then the law is *fucked*," said a voice in the shadows to my right.

I turned and saw Joey D stomping down the bar. He was fighting to keep a frown on his big Muppet face, though I could see a grin behind the frown, like the sun trying to break through clouds. He snatched my driver's license from the bar and scrutinized it under the dim lights. "This can't be," Joey D said. "Chas—the kid? Isn't a kid?"

Uncle Charlie gave his head a what's-this-world-coming-to shake.

"Well, the law is the law," Joey D said. *Wellthelawisthelaw!* "I guess we have no choice. Let me buy the kid his first drink."

"Nephew, you're backed up on Joey D," Uncle Charlie said.

"Backed up?" I'd heard this expression before, but I wasn't quite sure what it meant.

"You have a drink coming on Joey D. What'll it be?"

The magic words. I shot a foot taller. "What to drink?" I said, staring at the bottles behind Uncle Charlie. "Big decision."

"The biggest," he said.

He wasn't exaggerating. Uncle Charlie believed that you are what you drink, and he classified people by their cocktail. Once you were Sea Breeze Jack or Dewars-and-Soda Jill, that was the book on you, that was what Uncle Charlie would pour as you walked through the door at Publicans, and good luck trying to "reinvent" yourself with Uncle Charlie.

Together we ran our eyes along the row of bottles.

"I think a Yale man should drink gin," he said, reaching out and tapping a bottle of Bombay. "Nice gin martini. I make the finest in New York, by the by. I add a few drops of scotch, my secret recipe. Got it from a British butler who came in the joint one night. He worked at one of the estates on Shelter Rock Road."

"For the love of Mike!" someone shouted. "A gin martini? The juice of the evil juniper berry? You just took off the kid's training wheels and you're going to strap him to a fucking Kawasaki?"

"Well put," Uncle Charlie said, pointing at this man's chest.

"Stick a nipple on a Budweiser," someone mumbled, "and shove it in his fucking mouth."

"How about a Sidecar?" a woman asked. "Sidecars are delish. And Chas, you make the best in the biz."

"That's true," Uncle Charlie said. He turned to me and cupped a hand to one side of his mouth so only I could hear. "I use cognac instead of brandy," he said, "and Cointreau instead of triple sec. The best. But we don't get much call for them anymore. It was a big drink in the thirties." He turned back to the woman. "Don't make me squeeze a lemon, sweetheart, I don't even know where the goddamned squeezer is."

A rollicking argument broke out about difficult-to-mix drinks, which led to a debate about what the passengers on the *Titanic* were drinking when the ship hit the iceberg. Uncle Charlie insisted it was Pink Squirrels and bet ten dollars with a man who insisted it was Old-Fashioneds. I asked if Bobo was around. Bobo could tell me what to drink. Uncle Charlie frowned. Bobo had a little accident, he said. Fell down the stairs to the basement of the bar. Hit his head. "If you're hungry," he said, "Smelly will make you something."

"Smelly?" I said.

"The cook."

"No," I said. "I just wanted to see Bobo. Is he all right?"

Uncle Charlie grimaced. Joey D was the first to reach Bobo at the bottom of the stairs, he said. Joey D turned Bobo's head and cleared his airway, probably saved his life. A lot of blood, Uncle Charlie said. I shot a look at Joey D, who looked away, bashful. I remembered the way Joey D had acted as self-appointed lifeguard to McGraw and me at Gilgo, and I felt a surge of love for him and his heroic nature. Seeing my loving gaze he turned red. "Fucking Bobo," he muttered to his pet mouse.

"Was Bobo drunk when he fell?" I asked.

Uncle Charlie and Joey D looked at each other, not sure how to answer. I realized how stupid the question was.

"The sad part," Uncle Charlie said, "is that the fall caused some kind of nerve damage. Bobo's face is partly paralyzed on one side."

People fall down a lot at Publicans, I said. Joey D reminded me about Uncle Charlie's recent spill. While demonstrating for everyone along the bar how to play the Green Monster at Fenway Park, Uncle Charlie had stepped awkwardly and fallen into the liquor bottles, cracking three ribs. Steve rushed him to the hospital, where the doctor asked how in God's name he'd done this to himself. Uncle Charlie—drunk, wearing a paper gown and dark glasses—moaned, "Playing the wall at Fenway," a line that raced up and down the bar the next day. It had since become a catchphrase, cited whenever someone was suffering delusions of grandeur. Or any other kinds of delusions.

Uncle Charlie was now ignoring at least a dozen thirsty customers, trying to help me decide if I was Gin-and-Tonic JR or Scotch-and-Soda Moehringer. "Maybe I should have one of those Sidecars?" I said.

He put his hand over his eyes. "False," he said. "My nephew is not fucking David Niven."

"I hope to hell he's not fucking David Niven," said a man climbing onto the stool to my left. "If he's fucking David Niven, he's got some explaining to do."

Uncle Charlie chuckled and set a Budweiser before the man. He explained that I'd just turned eighteen and we were trying to select my first legal cocktail. The man shook my hand and congratulated me. "Chas," he said, "let me buy your newly legal nephew a drink."

"JR, you're backed up on Cager," Uncle Charlie said.

While Cager lit a cigarette I looked at him closely. He had curly, carroty hair, which tumbled out of his golf visor like a houseplant that had outgrown its pot. He looked a bit like a van Gogh self-portrait—the haunted eyes, the orange coloring—though his smile was jolly, with gaps between his teeth. Despite his loose jogging suit I could make out the physique of a former athlete. Linebacker, I guessed. Maybe a power forward. His arms were massive.

From my right side a man in a tweed Irish walking cap came elbowing his way up to the bar and into the conversation. "Goose," he said, "speaking of British actors, I think your nephew looks a bit like—Anthony Newley."

Cager laughed and put a hand on my shoulder. I looked nothing like Anthony Newley, but Tweed Cap was baiting Uncle Charlie, who instantly took the bait, throwing back his head and erupting into song. Cager and Tweed Cap explained to me that whenever someone mentioned Anthony Newley, Uncle Charlie automatically belted out a chorus or two of "What Kind of Fool Am I?" My uncle couldn't help himself, they said. Some kind of crazy reflex.

"Like Pavlov meets Pavarotti," I joked.

They stared at me, uncomprehending.

"Who's Anthony Newley?" I asked.

Uncle Charlie stopped. He lifted Cager's Budweiser off the bar and slammed it down, which startled me more than his singing. "Who's Anthony Newley?" he said. "Only one of the greatest troubadours of all time."

"Like Sinatra?"

"Troubadour, not crooner. Holy Mother of—Anthony Newley! JR! 'What Kind of Fool Am I?' From the classic Broadway show, *Stop the World I Want to Get Off!*"

I stared.

"What are they teaching you at that college?"

I continued staring, not sure what to say. He threw his arms out and resumed.

What kind of fool am I,
Who never fell in love?
What kind of man is this?
An empty shell,
A lonely cell
In which an empty heart must dwell?

Applause rippled down the bar.

"Something about that song," Joey D told his mouse, "really turns Chas's crank."

"That song tears me up," Uncle Charlie said. "What kind of fool—beautiful sentiment, don't you think? *Beautiful.* And Newley. What a voice. What a life."

Uncle Charlie began to build me a gin martini. Tired of deliberating, he'd made an executive decision. He told me that I was an "autumn type," as was he, and good British gin, ice cold, tastes like autumn. Hence, I would drink gin. "Every season has its poison," he said, explaining that vodka tastes like summer, scotch tastes like winter, and bourbon tastes like spring. While measuring and mixing and stirring he circled back and told me Newley's life story. Grew up poor. Didn't know his father. Became a Broadway star. Married Joan Collins. Suffered depressions. Searched for his father. I enjoyed the story, but I was spellbound by the teller. I always thought Uncle Charlie had a narrow emotional range, which went from melancholy to surly, except for those nights when he came home from the bar full of rage. Now, at Publicans, in the early part of the evening, surrounded by friends, buzzing from his first drink, he was an entirely different man. Chatty. Charming. Capable of the kind of steady attention I'd sought from him for years. We talked a long time, more than we'd ever talked, and I marveled that even his voice was different. His customary Bogart impression veered now and then into something richer, more complex. He used more outrageous mixtures of big words and gangster slang, and he enunciated more precisely, with more flourishing rolls of the tongue. He sounded like William F. Buckley in C Block.

The only drawback to this new Uncle Charlie was that I had to share him. My pathologically self-conscious, semireclusive Uncle Charlie, I discovered that night, was a performer at heart, with a devoted following. He also had a well-honed routine, the centerpiece of which was a flamboyant rudeness. He told customers to pipe down, shut the hell up, hold their horses, keep their god-damned fucking shirts on. I thought he might take out a seltzer bottle and spray it in someone's face. When the bar got really busy Uncle Charlie would tell a customer, "The most important and beautiful thing we can do in an orderly and civilized society—*is patiently wait our turn.*" Then he would turn back to the conversation he was having with his friends, telling them why Steve McQueen was a real movie star, illuminating for them the intricacies and com-plexities in the poetry of Andrew Marvell. Sometimes, while half the customers were trying to get his attention, he would be reciting "To His Coy Mistress" to the other half. It was an act, and Uncle Charlie was an actor to the core. A method actor. Before he made a drink you could see him asking himself, "Why am I doing this—what's my *motivation?*" The more methodical he became, the more impatient some customers grew, which made him that much more me-thodical, and ruder, which made his fans in the barroom cheer and egg him on.

As an actor, Uncle Charlie would transform himself instantly, effort-lessly, into a preacher, monologist, matchmaker, bookmaker, philosopher, provocateur. He played many roles, too many to catalog, but my favorite was The Maestro, and the music he conducted was the conversation along the bar. His baton was a Marlboro Red. No less than everything else he did at Publicans, Uncle Charlie smoked with a sense of theater. He'd hold an unlit cigarette an exceedingly long time, until it became fixed in the minds of his audience, like a handgun. Then he'd make a grand production of striking a match and bringing the flame to the cigarette tip. The next rounded phrase that fell from his mouth would be encased within a dollop of smoke. Then, when he flicked his ash—tap, tap—everyone leaned forward and watched closely, as if Willie Mays were tapping his bat on home plate. Something interesting was about to happen. At last, as he dropped the burned match into the glass ashtray with a light *plink,* he delivered the punch line or came to the crucial point, and I was tempted to yell, "Bravo!"

Uncle Charlie finished his Newley story and my martini at the same time. He pushed the glass toward me. I sipped. He waited. Fantastic, I told him. He smiled, like a sommelier approving my palate, then glided away to serve three men in suits who had just walked through the front door.

Before I could take another sip I heard a voice behind me. "Junior!" I froze. Who but my father or mother knew my secret name? I wheeled and saw Steve, arms folded across his chest, face set in a frown, like the famous photo of Sitting Bull. "What's the meaning of this? Drinking? At my bar?"

"I'm eighteen, Chief."

"Since when?"

"Five days ago."

I handed him my license. He looked it over. Then he broke into that wide Cheshire smile, so vivid in my boyhood memory. "God I must be getting old," he said. "Welcome to Publicans."

He smiled still wider. I smiled too, and held it until my cheeks ached. Neither of us said anything. I rubbed my hands together, wondering if there was something I should say, some traditional thing one said upon drinking legally for the first time. I wanted to say the perfect thing, to make myself worthy of Steve. And of his smile.

Uncle Charlie came back.

"Junior's a man now," Steve told him. "I remember he'd come in here when he was this high." He held his hand at his waist.

"Time's winged fuckin' chariot," Uncle Charlie said.

"Get Junior a drink on me."

"Nephew, you're backed up on Chief," Uncle Charlie said.

Steve smacked me hard between the shoulders, as though I were choking on a crouton, then walked away. I looked at Uncle Charlie, Joey D, Cager, all the men, praying no one had heard Steve call me Junior. The only thing more permanent than your choice of cocktail in Publicans was the nickname Steve bestowed on you, and his baptisms could be brutal. Not everyone was as lucky as Joey D, who was named after one of Steve's favorite musical groups, Joey Dee and the Starliters. No-Drip hated his bar name. Sooty would have preferred to be called something else. But too bad. Sooty made the mistake of walking into Publicans right after quitting time at the garage where he was a mechanic. When Steve saw him and yelled, "Get a load of Sooty," the poor man was never called anything else. Eddie the Cop didn't mind his nickname, until he rolled his car on the expressway and became paralyzed from the waist down. Thereafter he was Wheelchair Eddie. In Publicans you were who Steve said you were, and God have mercy on those who complained. One poor guy demanded that the men at the bar stop calling him Speed, because he didn't want people thinking he had a drug habit. So the men christened him Bob Don't Call Me Speed, and called him by that nickname every chance they got.

Satisfied that no one had heard Steve—the men were already jabbering about other subjects—I relaxed against the bar. Uncle Charlie freshened my martini. I finished it. He freshened it again. He complimented me on my metabolism. Hollow leg, he said. Must run in the family. I finished what was in my glass and before I set it down the glass was full again. Glasses at Publicans magically refilled themselves, as did the barroom. Whenever five people left, ten more filed in.

Fuckembabe arrived and welcomed me home, I think. "Flopsum when you humbled me with a dropsy back in the day," he said, punching me playfully. "Remember how I flummed your peepee with a wugwop? And your uncle said he figgered you were a boyboy Johnny wonny smack jack."

"You said it, Fuckembabe," I exclaimed.

After my third martini I put a twenty on the bar to pay for my next. Uncle Charlie slid the bill back toward me. "On the house," he said.

"But—"

"Nephews of bartenders drink free. Always. Follow?"

"Follow. Thanks."

"Speaking of dough." He took a wad of cash from his pocket and peeled off five twenties. He tossed them on top of my twenty. "Happy birthday. Buy some diaphanous coed a malted. You don't mind if I say 'diaphanous,' do you?"

I made a move to take the money. Uncle Charlie waved me off. False, he said. He looked down the bar. I followed his gaze. Before each man and woman sat a pile of bills. When you walk into the joint, Uncle Charlie instructed, put up your money, all your money, and let the bartender take what he needs as the night goes on. Even if the bartender is your uncle and never takes your money. "It's tradition," he said. "Protocol."

By midnight more than one hundred people were crammed into the barroom, as tightly as the bricks in the walls. Smelly came out from the kitchen and Uncle Charlie introduced me. He was a powerful man, though short, with fiery orange hair and an orange mustache twirled at the ends. I thought he looked like a weight lifter in an old-time carnival. Uncle Charlie said he was an "artiste" in the kitchen, and that he did to steak what Picasso did to stone. A man named Fast Eddy showed up and I told him I'd been hearing his name for years. He was a nationally renowned skydiver, and when I was a boy he'd vowed publicly to parachute into Grandpa's backyard, as part of a bet he'd lost to Uncle Charlie. It was the talk of Manhasset for weeks, and I used to keep a vigil in the backyard, waiting for Fast Eddy to appear above the treetops. I noticed now that he sat on his barstool as if landing on it from a height of three thousand feet. He seemed flattered that I knew so much about him, and he asked Uncle Charlie if he could buy me a drink.

"JR," Uncle Charlie said, "you are backed up on Fast Eddy."

Fast Eddy was seated next to Cager, who seemed to be his best friend, though also his archnemesis. I gathered that the two had been trying for decades to best each other at bowling, bridge, billiards, tennis, golf, and especially Liars' Poker, which they explained to me was like Go Fish for adults, played with the serial numbers on dollar bills. Cager was said to have the advantage in their two-man tournament, because nothing rattled him. Nerves of steel, Fast Eddy said, with a kind of affection. Cager never got nervous lining up the final shot on a nine ball, Fast Eddy told me, because once you've lined up the enemy in the crosshairs of your M60, everything else is pretty easy.

"Cager?" I said. "Went to war?"

" 'Nam," Fast Eddy said.

Cager seemed too cheerful and lovable for a man who had been to war. At the first lull in the conversation I moved closer to him. "Do you mind if I ask how long you were in the army?" I asked.

"One year, seven months, five days."

"And how long were you in Vietnam?"

"Eleven months, twelve days."

He drank his beer and fixed his eyes on Crazy Jane's stained-glass genitalia panels behind the bar. He seemed to be looking straight through the glass, as if it were a window onto Southeast Asia. What he hated most, he said, was being wet all the time, slogging back and forth through the swamps. "We were never ever dry. And then there was all this elephant grass, tall shoots that cut your skin like razor blades. So you were constantly wet *and* your skin was covered with cuts."

As Cager talked about Vietnam all other voices along the bar faded. I felt as if everyone else had gone home and the lights had been turned off, except the one directly over Cager's head. He said his time in 'Nam started with weeks and weeks of waiting. He'd been in-country six months, mostly in the Mekong Delta, and still nothing had happened, so he let himself relax. Maybe this won't be that bad, he thought. Then, around Cu Chi, his unit walked into an open field and it felt as if the world had exploded. Ambush, they thought. But in fact the field was booby-trapped. Cager was hit in the neck and fingers. Just scrapes, he added quickly, embarrassed to mention it, because nine of the fifteen men with him were killed. "Choppers wouldn't even fly in to help us," he said. "Too dicey."

When the smoke cleared and the choppers did come, Cager helped load the wounded. One soldier asked Cager to go back and find his feet. Please, he kept saying—my feet, my feet. Cager waded into the elephant grass and found the soldier's feet, still in their blood-soaked boots. He handed them to the soldier just before the chopper lifted off.

"Nixon got me out," Cager said. "Your Uncle Chas hates Nixon because of that Watergate bullshit, but Nixon promised to get me home by Christmas, and he made good on that promise."

Promises were big with Cager, I saw. I promised myself I'd never break a promise to Cager.

Hours before shipping home, Cager said, he walked through a trip wire. He heard the click, felt the wire tight across his shin, and shut his eyes, preparing to see the face of God. But the mine hadn't been set right. After the telltale click, nothing. Terror, then relief.

"Anyway," he said, "when I finally got home I wanted two things. Just two things. A tuna fish sandwich and a cold beer on Plandome Road. I could *taste* it. But wouldn't you know—there was a taxi strike. Here I am just off the plane from hell and I can't get home from fucking La Guardia."

We both laughed.

If Cager felt any lingering bitterness about what he'd endured, he didn't show it, though he did confess to a recurring nightmare. Sitting in Publicans, drinking a cold Budweiser, he looks up and sees some officers coming through the door. Time to report, soldier. You got the wrong guy, he tells them—I did my time. One year seven months five days. They don't believe him. On your feet, grunt. Time to hump that M60 across the Mekong. Time to leave this bar.

"Did you ever think about Canada?" I asked.

He frowned. His father was regular army, a veteran of World War II, and Cager worshipped the old man. They went to Army-Navy football games together when Cager was a boy, and his father took him into the Army locker room. His father introduced him to Eisenhower and MacArthur. "You don't forget a thing like that," Cager said. So when his father died at the start of Vietnam, he added, what else could a devoted son do but go to war?

I asked Uncle Charlie if I could buy Cager a beer.

"Cager," he said, "you're backed up on the birthday boy."

Uncle Charlie slammed the bar and pointed at my chest, the first time he'd ever given me this signal of official approval, which felt like having Excalibur tapped on each shoulder. He pulled three dollars from my pile and winked at me. I understood that my drinks were free, while drinks I bought for others were not. I was glad. I wanted to pay for Cager's drink. I realized that the same rule must apply when a man offered to buy me a drink. Uncle Charlie would charge the man a dollar as a token. Money wasn't the issue. It was the gesture, the timeless gesture. Buying another man a drink. The whole barroom was an intricate system of such gestures and rituals. And habits. Cager explained it all. He told me, for instance, that Uncle Charlie always worked the west end of the bar, under the stained-glass penis, because Uncle Charlie didn't like to deal with waitresses putting in drink orders from the dining room at the east end. Joey D liked the waitresses, however, and therefore Joey D always worked the east end, under the stained-glass vagina. Somehow, Cager said, the conversation at each end of the bar reflected the stained-glass backdrop: bawdier and more aggressive at Uncle Charlie's end, mellower and less linear at Joey D's. I also noticed that everyone in the place had his or her own unique way of asking for a drink. Joey D, can you build on this concept? Goose, would you freshen up my martini once more before I go home to my miserable excuse for a husband? One man would ask for a refill by merely flicking his eyes at his empty glass, as if checking the speedometer while driving down a highway. Another would extend his hand and touch pointer fingers with Uncle Charlie, reenacting Michelangelo's *Creation of Adam*. There couldn't be too many bars in the world, I thought, where a man acted out a scene from the ceiling of the Sistine Chapel when he wanted an Amstel Light.

I bummed one of Cager's Merit Ultras and never wanted to leave his side. I wondered if he came to Publicans every night. I wished he'd been part of the Gilgo Beach crew when I was a boy, but I couldn't imagine a man like Cager lounging on the sand or bodysurfing. I couldn't imagine a man like Cager anywhere but the bar, late at night. He seemed too big, too mythic to simply be walking down the street in broad daylight. I realized that for the first time in months I felt no fear, as if Cager's courage were rubbing off. Cager was contagious. He had been through the fires of hell and come back with his mind and sense of humor intact, and just standing by his side made me confident about my own small battles. The euphoria I felt was the same I'd experienced reading the *Iliad*. In fact the bar and the poem complemented each other, like companion pieces. Each smacked of ageless verities about men. Cager was my Hector. Uncle Charlie was my Ajax. Smelly was my Achilles. Lines from Homer came back to me and I heard them in new ways. "There is a strength," Homer wrote, "in the union even of very sorry men." How could you hope to fully appreciate such a line unless you'd bought Cager a Budweiser and listened to his war story? The best part was, when Cager stopped talking, I wouldn't have to prove to some satanic professor that I'd absorbed every word and learned what I was supposed to learn.

And yet I was very much a student that night, jotting notes of what Cager and others said, their stories and snappy remarks. I took more notes than in Professor Lucifer's class, because I didn't want to forget. Curiously, the men didn't think twice about my note taking. They acted as though they had been wondering when someone was going to start recording their hard-won wisdom.

At three in the morning the bar "closed," though no one made any move to leave. Uncle Charlie locked the doors, poured himself a Sambuca and leaned. He looked beat. He asked how I was doing at school. He saw that something was wrong. Spill it, he said. Throughout the night I'd noticed that, besides the many jocular roles Uncle Charlie played behind the bar, there was one serious role. He was the Chief Justice of Publicans. He was Goose, the Lawgiver. People presented him with problems and questions, and he issued verdicts all night long. There might be an appeal. Then he'd issue his final ruling, slamming a bottle like a gavel, pointing a finger at the appellant's chest. Case closed. So I presented my brief, or started to. A man with a mullet—a huge mullet, almost a double mullet—interrupted. He draped himself across the bar and mewled to Uncle Charlie, "One for the road, Goose?"

"Hold the phone," Uncle Charlie snarled. "I'm talking to my nephew who's having problems in school."

Mullet turned to me. He looked concerned for my welfare. I wasn't eager to bare my soul to Mullet, but I didn't see that I had any choice. I didn't want to be rude. I told him and Uncle Charlie about feeling inadequate compared to my schoolmates, especially my roommates, one of whom had already published his first book. Another had spent his summer working at Memorial Sloan-Kettering Cancer Center. "They named a kind of leukemia after him," I said. "You can die from something named after my roommate." Then there was the boy who'd memorized most of Shakespeare's tragedies. He had a pithy line from the Bard for every occasion, whereas I was lucky if I could remember that Hamlet was from Denmark. Lastly there was Jedd Redux, who seemed to grow more confident as the year went on.

"I get it," Uncle Charlie said. "You feel intimidated because you started life with a seven-two, different suits."

"A what?"

"A seven and a two, different suits, worst poker hand possible."

"I don't know about that," I said. "I just feel like—a fish out of water."

"Me too," Mullet said. We both looked at him. "I feel like a man out of beer. Goose—please."

Uncle Charlie puffed out his cheeks and stared at Mullet. Slowly he reached into the ice and removed a bottle of beer. "On the house," he said, slamming the bottle in front of Mullet. "Now kick the bricks."

Mullet disappeared into the crowd, his hair reminding me of the fluke of a whale as it submerges.

Uncle Charlie leaned close to me and asked, "What did you expect? You're at the best school in the country. You think they let dummies into Yale?"

"Just one."

"Ach. What do you have to read this weekend?"

"Aquinas."

"Medieval philosopher. What's the problem?"

How to boil it down into a few words? It was more than being intimidated, more than poor grades. I read and read, worked as hard as I could, but without Bill and Bud to translate, I was lost. *Henry IV, Part One?* I didn't know what the fuck they were saying. And what made it really frustrating— they were all standing around in a bar. How could I fail to understand a bunch of bar talk? Then there was Thucydides. Christ. I wanted to crawl inside the book and slap the old bastard around. I wanted to scream at him, *Just give me the bottom line, man!* I'd memorized one sentence from Thucydides' history of the Peloponnesian War, a sentence that dragged on longer than the war itself. "For the true author of the subjugation of a people is not so much the immediate agent as the power which permits it having the means to prevent it." No matter how many times I read that sentence it didn't make any sense, and now I just walked around chewing on it, muttering it to myself, like Joey D. Now there was Aquinas! He changed the world with his logical proof of the existence of God, but no matter how closely I followed his step-by-step argument I couldn't see any proof. Where was the proof? I believed in God, but I couldn't see the proof, or the point of trying to offer proof. Such a thing seemed the quintessential article of faith.

And the worst part, the most galling thing of all, was that I always had twice as much work as my schoolmates, because I'd signed up for Directed Goddamned Studies.

I must have been lost in these thoughts for quite a while, because Uncle Charlie was snapping his fingers in front of my face. I blinked and remembered he'd asked me a question. What's the problem? I wanted to tell him, but couldn't, not because I was embarrassed, but because I was drunk. Righteously, irredeemably drunk, and yet fully aware of the wonderful redundancy of being young and drunk. Though it was one of the drunkest moments of my life, I would always remember it vividly, that complete absence of fear and worry. I was talking about my problems, but I had no problems. Except one. I couldn't form words. Uncle Charlie was still staring at me—*What's the problem?*—so I said something about Aquinas, which came out, "Equine asses is hard." Uncle Charlie grunted, I grunted, and each of us pretended, or honestly believed, we'd had a real man-to-man. "Closing time," he said.

I scooped up my money, retrieved my suitcase and made for the door. I was leaving with pockets full of notes about Cager and others, plus ninety-seven dollars more than when I'd arrived, and I'd been declared a man by the men of the bar, including Steve. A birthday to remember. Someone shadow-boxed me toward the door. It might have been Cager. It might have been Cager's shadow. As I walked out into the rosy-fingered dawn everyone said, "Come back soon, kid." They didn't hear—or didn't understand—my answer.

"Owl ill," I said. "Owl ill."

twenty-three | TROUBLE

SOPHOMORE YEAR WILL BE EASIER, MY MOTHER PROMISED. BEAR down, she said. Keep trying. Try, try again. With Directed Studies and Professor Lucifer behind me, she predicted, I'd surely bring up my grades.

I didn't have the heart to tell my mother that trying was futile, because my brain was broken. Trying only emphasized and exacerbated the problem, like pumping the gas pedal when the engine is flooded. I couldn't tell my mother that I was probably going to fail out of Yale, that I would soon bungle this golden opportunity for which she'd have given her atrophied right arm.

The classroom, I'd concluded, was not my arena. The barroom was. After turning eighteen I decided that barrooms were the only places I was as clever as my classmates, and my classmates thought so too. When we went out drinking I could feel myself rise in their estimation. Though I'd been admitted to Yale, *acceptance* was something more elusive, and it seemed to happen only while my new friends and I were having cocktails.

Unlike Publicans, however, New Haven bars charged for drinks. I needed a source of income, fast, or I'd lose my new friends as quickly as I'd made them, an idea that frightened me more than the prospect of failing out. I considered taking a job in one of the dining halls, but the pay wasn't good and I didn't want to wear what one friend called the Paper Hat of Poverty. I applied to the libraries, but those jobs were the most coveted and the first to be filled. Then, a bolt of inspiration. I would start my own laundry service. (I still remembered what Grandma had taught me about handling a steam iron.) I would let it be known that a new entrepreneurial venture was opening on campus, offering same-day service and charging just fifty cents per shirt. I nearly called my business Moehringer 'Round the Collar, but a friend wisely dissuaded me.

Response was overwhelming. Boys dropped off Santa Claus sacks bulging with shirts, and soon I was ironing several hours a day, a great deal of work for a little bit of money, but the alternative was to lose my friends, stay home while they were trotting off to nightclubs and bars, and this I couldn't do.

My best customer was Bayard, a fellow sophomore whose superiority to me in every way was expressed in his melodically Waspy name. I'd heard of only one other Bayard—Bayard Swope, whose estate had been the model for the Buchanan mansion in *The Great Gatsby*. Tall, blond, unflappable, the Yale Bayard played polo and owned his own tuxedo and was said to trace his roots back to the Huguenots. He'd come to Yale from one of those famous prep schools, and he dressed as if he'd leaped off the drawing boards of Ralph Lauren. He owned a shocking collection of shirts—paisley, broadcloth, candy-striped, button-down, spread-collared, silk—and seemed to own exactly two of every style, as though he were preparing to ship off on some Noah's Ark of Garments. He also owned several custom-made white dress shirts with British collars and paper-thin French cuffs, each a work of art. Dropping them off at my room he fanned them across my bed and we stood before them in mutual admiration. "It makes me sad," I said, "because I've never seen such—such beautiful shirts before." I assumed he'd recognize the quotation from *Gatsby*. He didn't.

I promised Bayard I'd have his shirts washed and pressed in two days, but time got away from me. I had papers to write, bars to haunt, and by the end of the week Bayard was miffed. He had nothing to wear. He left four progressively angrier messages with my roommates, and I didn't dare return his calls. I pledged to wake up at dawn and fill his order. Meanwhile it was Friday night. My friends were getting together at a bar near campus. I put Sinatra on the stereo and stood before my closet. I'd cycled countless times through all my jeans and Bud's Lacostes. *If only I had something new to wear.* I glanced at Bayard's laundry bag. I was going to do his shirts in the morning anyway—what was the harm? I ironed a pale pink button-down and slipped it on.

It was autumn. It was always autumn at Yale, as if Yale were the birthplace of autumn, as if autumn had been invented in one of the labs on Science Hill and escaped. The air was heady, bracing, like a slap of aftershave on each cheek, and I told my friends we should drink gin, quoting Uncle Charlie's theory that each season has its poison. Great idea, my friends said. After two rounds we were drunk. And starved. We ordered steaks, and more martinis, and when the bill came I was heartsick. I'd blown two weeks of laundry profits in three hours.

We headed for a house party off campus. Students were dancing on the lawn and the porch when we arrived. We pushed up to the front door, into the dense swaying crowd inside. I saw Jedd Redux leaning against a wall, smoking. I asked if he had an extra cigarette. From the breast pocket of his ultracool blazer he pulled a pack of Vantages. I admired the bull's-eye on the wrapper, the hollowed-out filters. Each cigarette looked like a rifle shell. I introduced myself. His name was Dave. He said he needed another drink. I followed him like a puppy toward the kitchen and squeezing through the crowd we bumped smack into Bayard. "There you are," Bayard said.

"Heyyy," I said.

"Need my shirts, man." He was wearing a wrinkled flannel, the kind of shirt I'd normally be wearing.

"I'm so sorry," I said. "I had two papers due and fell behind. I'll get to your shirts first thing in the morning. Promise. Scout's honor." I put my hand over my heart. Bayard looked down and noticed the monogram on my cuff. His cuff. His monogram.

"Is that my—shirt?" he said.

"I'll let you two work this out," Jedd Redux said, backing away.

I started to explain, but Bayard stopped me. With a half smile of pity on his face, he took a step sideways and walked on past me, delivering a swift and forceful lesson in class.

I went back to my room and stayed up all night, washing and ironing Bayard's shirts. At dawn, starching the last of his cuffs, I made a string of promises to myself.

I will never drink gin again.

I will learn to smoke Vantages.

I will apologize to Bayard and then avoid him for the rest of my time at Yale.

I will try, try again.

She was with a friend of mine, whom she was dating, and we all reached the door of the lecture hall at the same moment as class let out. She had thick yellow hair, almond-shaped brown eyes, and an exquisite nose—a perfect isosceles triangle in the center of her oval face. There was such geometry about her face, such symmetry, that I did what the art-history professor advised when encountering great portraits. I saw her in sections. First the full lips. Then the white teeth. Then the high cheekbones and exquisite nose. Lastly those brown eyes, soulful and scornful at the same time, as if she could love you or hate you, depending on the very next thing you said.

"Sidney," she said, offering her hand.

"JR," I said.

She wasn't wearing the androgynous Yale uniform of sweatshirt, torn jeans and sneakers. Instead she wore black wool pants, a gray cashmere turtleneck, and a leather driving coat. She had the kind of figure molded by years of competitive ice skating, I could just tell. That high hard bottom, like Dorothy Hamill. She even had a version of the Dorothy Hamill haircut. It was an effort not to stare.

"Don't you love this class?" she asked. "Isn't it so fascinating?"

"Not really," I said, laughing.

"Then why are you taking it?"

"I'm thinking about law school."

"Uck. I wouldn't be a lawyer for all the money in the world."

I thought, That's because you already have all the money in the world.

My friend put a proprietary arm around Sidney and pulled her away. I went back to my room and listened to Sinatra and tried not to see her face in sections, floating before me, while I read the decision in Dred Scott.

We bumped into each other days later. A chance meeting on the street. I made a motion to hurry away, not wanting to waste the time of the campus goddess, but she forced me to stop, asking me questions, touching my arm lightly, tossing her hair. I didn't flirt back, because she was dating my friend, and my reticence seemed to confuse and arouse her. She touched my arm more.

"Are you ready for the final in Con Law?" she asked.

"Oh right," I said sarcastically. "When is that? Tomorrow?"

"Would you like to study together?"

"Together?" I said. "Tonight?"

"Yes." She smiled. Flawless teeth. "Together. Tonight."

She lived in an apartment off campus. When I arrived she had a bottle of red wine opened, so we spent ten minutes studying the Supreme Court before we set the books aside and studied each other. I wanted to give her the Sheryl Treatment, ask her lots of questions, but she beat me to the punch, barraging me with questions, and I found myself telling her about my mother, my father, Publicans, everything. I felt the wine and her brown eyes cracking me open. I told her the truth. I made my father sound more like a rogue than a villain, and built up the men of the bar into gods, but these exaggerations weren't false. They were what I believed, just as I believed myself authentic when imitating the men of the bar, using their language and gestures. The impression fooled me as much as it did Sidney.

Opening a second bottle of wine, she told me about herself. The youngest of four, she grew up in southern Connecticut, on the water, directly across the sound from Manhasset. She was two years older than I, a junior, and hoped to become a film director or an architect. The next Frank Capra or the next Frank Lloyd Wright, I said. She liked that. Her parents were powerful, brilliant, thoroughly involved in the lives of their children. They owned a construction company and lived in a large house her father had built with his own hands. She admired her mother but idolized her father, a real Hemingway type, she said, down to the white beard and fisherman's sweater. Her naturally husky voice dropped an octave when she mentioned a brother who had died and how her parents had never been the same since. She had a way of talking intimately that felt as if she were drawing a curtain around us.

Just after midnight it started to snow. "Look," she said, pointing to the window. "Let's go for a walk."

Swaddled in hats and mufflers, we roved around campus, holding our faces to the sky, catching snowflakes on our tongues.

"Do you realize we've been talking for hours?" she asked.

"We haven't done any studying," I said.

"I know."

We looked at each other uncertainly.

"So what does JR stand for?" she said.

"I'll tell you when I know you better."

It was a reflex—I didn't want to tell her my standard lie, and yet I didn't want to divulge the truth—but somehow it sounded flirtatious. Before I could retract or soften it Sidney pressed against me. We walked on through the snow, hips touching, looking at our footprints side by side.

Back at her apartment we drank hot chocolate and smoked cigarettes and talked about every subject but *Brown v. Board of Education*. At dawn she fixed us eggs and coffee. I left her apartment an hour before the exam, totally unprepared, and totally unconcerned. I pushed the pencil along the pages of the blue exam booklet for four hours, writing nonsense about the Constitution, knowing I'd fail and yet feeling ecstatic, because I also knew I'd see Sidney minutes after the exam ended. I knew she'd come through my door without knocking, and she did. "How'd you do?" she asked.

"Not good. You?"

"Aced it."

I asked if she'd like to go for a cup of coffee, but she was in a hurry. She was driving home and wanted to get there before the roads were bad.

"What are you doing?" she asked.

"I'm leaving for Arizona in the morning."

"Well. Merry Christmas. Thanks again for a lovely evening."

She gave my cheek a peck and waved over her shoulder as she sailed out the door.

I bought a six-pack and sat on the window seat, drinking, listening to Sinatra, watching students in the courtyard below. They were saying good-bye, hugging, rushing off to Union Station. I felt the campus emptying like a balloon losing air. The phone rang. My mother calling to see how I did on the exam. No. Sidney, calling from the car. A phone in the car? I'd never heard of such a thing. "Hey you," she said. "Come have dinner."

"Together? Tonight?"

"Together. Tonight. Call me back and let me know what train you're getting. I'll meet you at the station."

I hung up, took a swig of beer, and burst into tears. The first time in my life I ever wept with joy.

Standing on the platform as my train pulled in, she was wearing a white overcoat and her hair and eyelashes were sprinkled with snowflakes. She'd made reservations at a waterfront restaurant, where neither of us touched our food. Plates came and went, unnoticed as our breath. Then we were speeding through deep woods in her sports car. We roared up to her parents' house and sat in the car, the heater blasting, Phil Collins playing on the radio, each of us waiting for the other to speak. Through the falling snow, through the trees, I saw a silver river flashing in the moonlight. I thought with a wince of the canal in Arizona.

She took me inside. All the lights were off, everyone asleep. She led me upstairs to a guestroom. "What about your parents?" I whispered as she shut the door. "Won't we wake them?"

"They're very liberal," she whispered.

The lamp beside the bed gave off a harsh light, like a lamp at Grandpa's, but I didn't want to turn it off. I wanted to see Sidney. I slipped one of my argyle socks over the bulb and turned just as Sidney was unhooking her bra and dropping it to the floor. She stepped out of her pants, and her panties, and came forward, suffused in an argyle glow. She took off my clothes, put a hand on my chest and pushed, once. I fell onto the bed. She slid on top of me, under me. Ooh, she said softly, then again, louder. Then much louder. Your parents, I said. They're cool, she said. Ooh, she said again, then yes, then ooh and yes in breathless combinations. I didn't think there could be so many combinations. I concentrated on the combinations, numbering them, using them to block out all other thoughts, including any thought of enjoying myself, because I was determined to hold on, to perform, to last. The feel of Sidney beneath me, the sight of her body, was a dream, and if I enjoyed it, paused for one half second to take any pleasure in it, the dream would end. Yes, Sidney said, through clenched teeth, yes, yes, until the word lost all meaning, becoming a sound on which we both concentrated, then a soft whoosh of contentment that was a counterpoint to the wind outside.

Lying together we said nothing for so long that I thought she was asleep. At last she said, "Do you smell something burning?" I looked at the lamp. My sock on the bulb was smoking. I grabbed it, knocking the lamp over, making a tremendous racket. Sidney laughed. I then made the burned sock into a hand puppet, "Sockrates," who offered a philosophical commentary on the shocking behavior he'd just witnessed.

"You're trouble," she said, laughing into her pillow.

"Why?"

"You just are." She hugged me. "I'm not sure I need your kind of trouble."

I woke to find her standing over me with a mug of coffee. "Morning, Trouble," she said.

She wore a billowy white satin robe that was falling open. I took the mug from her and as she turned away I grabbed her and pulled her onto the bed.

"My parents," she said.

"They're liberal."

"Yes, well, the liberals are awake, and they have expressed some interest in meeting the man in the upstairs guestroom."

Since my suitcase was still in Sidney's car, I put on my clothes from the night before and followed her downstairs. Her parents, though white-haired and a good deal older than my mother, were liberal as advertised. They didn't seem at all scandalized. They poured me a cup of coffee and invited me to join them at the breakfast table.

Each had Sidney's husky voice, and like her they fired questions at me. I wasn't sure they would find my stories as entertaining as Sidney had, so I deflected their questions with questions of my own. I asked about their interests. They were passionate about Italian opera, hothouse orchids, and cross-country skiing. I knew nothing about these subjects, and felt as if I'd failed my second exam in twenty-four hours. I asked about the family construction business.

"Some companies build houses," Sidney's mother said. "We build *dwellings*." She said this word, "dwellings," in the same rapturous tone Professor Lucifer used when he said "POY-um." Her voice rose and her cheeks pinkened as she spoke about the human need for shelter. I told her about Manhasset's mansions and Shelter Rock and what they symbolized to me as a boy. I could see that she liked this story.

Sidney's father stood, put his hands in the pockets of his chinos and asked casually about my family. I bragged about my mother. He smiled. "And your father?" he said.

"I didn't really meet him until recently."

He frowned. I couldn't tell if it was a frown of sympathy or disapproval. Sidney's mother changed the subject and asked what I was studying at Yale. What do you hope to be? I mentioned law school, and both parents looked relieved.

"We'd better be going," Sidney said. "I have to drive JR to the airport."

Along the way, however, Sidney had a change of heart. She said she'd decided to drop me in Darien, where I could catch the shuttle the rest of the way.

"Why?" I asked. "What's going on?"

"I just think it's for the best."

"Tell me why."

"Look. I'm seeing someone else."

"I know." I mentioned my friend, the one who had introduced us in Constitutional Law. No, Sidney said. Someone else besides. My stomach dropped, and I felt a lump in my throat.

She spun off the highway at Darien and when we reached the shuttle stop she jumped out. I sat motionless while she grabbed my suitcase from the trunk and ordered me out of the car. I refused. She set my suitcase on the pavement and waited. I didn't budge. The standoff lasted five minutes. Finally she put my suitcase back in the trunk and got back in the car. Neither of us said a word as she raced south on I-95, weaving in and out of traffic like an Indy-car driver. By the time we reached the airport, however, she wasn't angry anymore. I even sensed some grudging admiration on her part when we kissed good-bye.

"Merry Christmas," she said. "Trouble."

The first nickname I ever liked.

. . .

I knew less about love than about constitutional law, but on the flight to Arizona I decided I was in love. Or else I was having a stroke. I was sweating, shaking, suffering pains in my chest. It didn't help that I could still smell Sidney on my hand, and in my pocket I found a crumpled napkin that bore her lip print. I held my hand to my nose, pressed the napkin to my mouth, and the flight attendant asked if I was ill.

My mother asked the same thing as I stepped off the plane.

"I think I'm in love," I said.

"Wonderful!" she said, throwing her arm around me as we walked out of Sky Harbor. "Who's the lucky girl?"

In the car, over dinner, late into the night, I tried to talk with my mother about Sidney, but I found the conversation unexpectedly complicated. I wanted to question my mother about love, but I felt the need to be careful, because I didn't want to stir unpleasant memories of her romantic disappointments. I wanted to ask if our apartment by the canal disqualified me for a goddess who lived beside a silver river, but I didn't want to disparage the home my mother had done her best to make for us. Finally I just said, "Sidney's so up here." I held my hand above my head. "And I'm so down here." I dropped my hand to my knees.

"Don't say that. You have so much to offer."

"Yeah. No money, no clue what I want to do with my life—"

"No clue?"

"I mean, besides becoming a lawyer."

"Look," she said. "It's not the worst thing in a relationship if the man puts the woman on a slight pedestal." She smiled and gave my shoulder an encouraging rub, but I couldn't force a smile in return. "JR, falling in love is a blessing. Try to enjoy it."

"What if I get my heart broken?" I asked.

She stared over my head.

"Mom?"

Blank.

"Mom?"

She lowered her gaze and looked at me.

"You'll live," she said.

· · ·

Sidney met me at the airport with a bottle of champagne, which we passed back and forth as she sped north on I-95. It was a Sunday night, the temperature below zero. There wasn't another car on the highway. We had the world to ourselves.

We reached Yale around midnight. Frozen trees clicked in the wind. Streets were solid chutes of ice. We stopped by my room, picked up my Sinatra albums, then went to her apartment and locked ourselves inside. Sidney laughed slyly when I moved a big chair against the door.

We didn't leave for days. Snow fell, melted, fell again—we scarcely noticed. We never turned on the TV or the radio. The only sounds in the apartment were Sinatra's voice and ours, his moans and ours, and the wind. When starved we ordered food from a restaurant on the corner. The phone rang off the hook, but Sidney never answered it, and she didn't own an answering machine. If boyfriends were looking for her, she didn't seem to care, and I took her indifference to mean that she was done with all men but me.

Time passed imperceptibly, then stopped altogether, lost its grip on us. We would lie on our sides for an hour, staring at each other, smiling, touching fingertips, saying nothing. We would fall asleep. We would wake, make love, then fall asleep again, fingers interlocked. I had no idea if it was morning, night, what day of the week, and I didn't want to know.

At one point, while Sidney slept, I sat in a chair at the foot of the bed, drinking a beer, trying to organize my feelings. I'd been awed at first by Sidney's beauty, I was honest with myself about that, but now it went deeper. This was more than sex, more than love. I'd experienced the power of sex with Lana, and puppy love with a girl or two since, but those were hasty rehearsals for this. This was big, this was going to change me forever, and this might just kill me if I wasn't careful, because I was already desperate. Already I felt that I'd give anything to hold on to this feeling, this primal energizing force I'd been lacking for nineteen years. I'd always believed that sex and love were the great catalysts, the things that converted a boy into a man, and plenty of people I trusted had intimated as much, but until now it was all in the realm of theory. I'd never really believed how explosive those catalysts could be, how magical it might feel if sex and love occurred in one moment, one person. I'd been a cynic, I realized, but now, as Sidney opened her eyes, as I looked into those bottomless pools of brown, down to the taproots of her soul, I believed that she was capable of effecting a metamorphosis in me, and maybe pulling off a miracle. She could make me a man; more remarkably, she might make me happy.

When we did get out of bed I would mix a pitcher of martinis and we'd lie on the living room couch, talking. A boyhood spent listening for The Voice was paying dividends at last. I could hear things in Sidney's voice—her hopes, her fears, the subtexts and master plots of her life. To show her how carefully I was listening, I would tell her story back to her, in my own words, and venture what I thought the meaning might be. She loved this.

Talking to Sidney about myself, I detected things in my own voice as well. All my life I'd censored myself. Now I said exactly what I felt, blurted it all out to this beautiful woman who listened as ardently as she made love. Caught up in this uncensored spirit, I told Sidney on our fourth or fifth day together that I intended to marry her. We were eating bagels in her kitchen. She stopped chewing and stared.

"Marry?" she said.

"Yes," I said. "I'd like to give you a diamond ring and marry you. Someday."

Her eyes widened and she left the room.

A short while later she said it was time for us to go back into the world. "I'm getting agita," she said, pulling on a pair of tight jeans.

"What? Agita?"

"I need fresh air, Trouble. We have to sign up for classes. Yale? Life? Remember?"

"Because of what I said? About getting—?"

"I'll call you later."

I caught the next Amtrak train to New York, then switched at Penn Station to the Long Island Railroad, the local to Manhasset. Uncle Charlie was startled to see me walk through the door at Publicans a week after I'd left for Yale. "Who's dead?" he said.

"No one. I just needed to see some friendly faces."

He pointed at my chest. I felt better instantly. Then he reached for the gin. I frowned. "No," I said. "I'm off gin. Please. How about scotch?"

He looked appalled. Changing my drink? An unthinkable breach of Publicans protocol. But he saw that I was hurting and didn't press the point. "What's the pitch?" he asked, pouring.

"Girl trouble."

"Lay it on me."

He slid the glass in my direction, as if moving a bishop across a chessboard. I gave him the quick overview, omitting the precipitating event—my gaffe about marriage. "She just threw me out," I said. "Claimed she had agita."

"What the hell is that?"

"I think it's Yiddish for nerves."

"She Jewish?"

"No. She just likes words."

A man in a red-and-black hunting jacket and an orange hunting cap sat down beside me. "Hey punk," he said. "How goes the war?"

"His girlfriend has agita," Uncle Charlie said.

"Sorry to hear that."

I told Deer Hunter my story, from meeting Sidney to getting the heave-ho. When Uncle Charlie was busy helping other customers I also told Deer Hunter about my clumsy marriage proposal.

"Whoa," he said. "Whoa, whoa, *whoa*. What about your buddy?"

"Who?"

"Your friend who was dating this broad. Does he know you fucked her?"

Uncle Charlie came back and leaned his elbows on the bar, listening.

"Oh," I said. "My friend. Yeah, well, he didn't even like her that much. They were just dating. You know. Casual."

"No," Deer Hunter said. "That's your problem right there. Broads come, broads go, everyone gets angina. But you backdoored your buddy. You violated the code. You need to make that right."

"I think you're missing the point," I said.

I looked to Uncle Charlie for moral support, but he was pointing at Deer Hunter's chest.

twenty-four | FATHER AMTRAK

SIDNEY'S AGITA PASSED AND I LEARNED MY LESSON. I ADOPTED A policy of speaking less, listening more. I went on loving her uncontrollably, desperately, but I tried to be quieter about it.

I also tried to attack my schoolwork, but it was harder than ever, because of Sidney. I couldn't concentrate. In lectures and seminars, while the professor nattered on about Berkeley and Hume, I'd stare into the distance, picturing Sidney's face. When I heard applause I knew that the lecture was over and it was time to go back to my room and sit on the window seat and think about Sidney.

She created a tricky paradox. If I could win her love, then I could become the man I'd hoped to become when I'd first applied to Yale. But I couldn't hope to win her love unless I graduated, and to do that I'd have to stop obsessing about her and do my schoolwork, which didn't seem remotely possible. Sitting in the library, trying with all my might to focus on Nietzsche's *Beyond Good and Evil,* I looked up and saw Jedd Redux. We hadn't met since he'd witnessed Bayard catch me at shirt poaching. He offered me a Vantage.

"Was that you and Sidney walking down York Street the other day?" he said.

"Yes."

"Are you two—?"

"Yes."

He threw back his head and opened his mouth, as if he were going to scream, but he made no sound.

"You're one lucky son of a bitch."

He lit my cigarette with a silver lighter that looked as if his great-grandfather had carried it in the trenches of World War I. We smoked. "Seriously," he said. "Lucky." Pause. "Lucky lucky lucky."

We looked at the book-lined walls. He blew a smoke ring that dangled over my head like a noose.

"Lucky," he said.

At the end of sophomore year my luck was holding. I passed all my classes, barely, and Sidney and I were still together. Better than together. She told me she'd broken things off with all the men in her life and she was seeing only me.

I went to Arizona to spend the summer, and Sidney went to Los Angeles to attend a program for aspiring filmmakers. I wrote her long love letters. Her replies were neither long nor loving. Quick roundups of her social schedule. She was attending cocktail parties with movie stars, working out with the USC men's swim team, tooling around Hollywood in a convertible Mercedes. She did visit me one weekend, and managed to bewitch my mother. The first time Sidney left the room my mother stared into her dinner plate.

"That," she said, smiling as if she knew a secret, "is the most beautiful girl I've ever set eyes on."

"I know," I said glumly. "I know."

I brought Sidney to my other home when we returned to Yale that fall. I made sure it was a Saturday night, mid-November, the most festive time of year at Publicans. Standing just inside the door I gave Sidney a quick primer on the major players, pointing out Uncle Charlie, Joey D, Cager, Colt, Tommy, Fast Eddy, Smelly.

"What does Smelly do?" she asked.

"He cooks."

"The cook is named Smelly. I see."

The bar was filled with familiar faces, and family faces. One of the cousins had married and moved away, but McGraw and his four remaining sisters, including Sheryl, were living nearby with Aunt Ruth, who was seated at the center of the bar that night, nursing a cognac. I introduced her to Sidney. "Upper or middle?" Aunt Ruth asked, giving Sidney the once-over.

"Pardon?" Sidney said.

"Upper or middle class?" Aunt Ruth asked.

I covered my face with my hands.

"Upper," Sidney said. "I guess."

"Good. We need a better class of people in this family."

Sheryl was at the bar that night also, and she rushed to Sidney's side, pulling her from Aunt Ruth, like a rodeo clown saving a cowboy from a charging bull. I pushed down the bar to get us some drinks. Uncle Charlie was working and he'd already seen Sidney. "Hubba-hubba," he said.

"And," I said, "she's smarter than she is beautiful."

He grabbed a scotch bottle by the neck as if it were a chicken he was going to strangle. "Then you know what?" he said. "You're in deep shit, my friend."

As Sidney and I drove back to Yale she stared hard at the road. I asked what was on her mind. She said she could see why the bar had been "special" to me. She turned and showed me her blinding smile, the one that made state troopers give her warnings instead of speeding tickets, but there was something behind it. She saw why the bar had been special to me as a boy, but she couldn't see the wisdom in continuing to cherish the place as a young man. She may also have been imagining her parents' faces as they met Joey D and Uncle Charlie.

Sidney had given up her apartment and was living her senior year in a dorm room. We sat on her bed and talked some more about the evening. "Why does that Dolt guy sound like Yogi Bear?" she asked.

"Colt? I don't know. That's just his voice."

"And why's he called Colt?"

"Everyone in the bar has a nickname, but Steve never got around to nick-naming Colt, so Colt felt left out, and one night he announced that hence-forth he wanted to be called Colt."

"Uh-huh. And why does that one guy who looks like a Muppet—"

"Joey D."

"—talk to himself?"

"When I was a kid I thought he was talking to a pet mouse in his breast pocket."

"Hm."

Shortly after our trip to the bar Sidney said she needed "time." Time to catch up on schoolwork, time to plan what she was going to do after graduation. It wasn't agita, she promised, taking my hand between hers. "Time," she said. "Just give me a little time to get organized."

"Of course," I said. "Time."

Without Sidney, I had nothing but time. I might have done the smart thing and attended class, caught up on schoolwork. Instead I wrote for the *Yale Daily News,* and haunted Beinecke Library, sifting through collections of letters by Hemingway and Gertrude Stein and Abraham Lincoln. Often I'd spend the whole day in one of Yale's museums, especially the Center for British Art, where I'd sit and look at the John Singleton Copley portraits of people in colonial America. Their faces, lit by a certain innocence and purity, but also by mischief, reminded me of the faces along the bar at Publicans. It couldn't be coincidence, I thought, that Copley posed some of his subjects in taverns, or so it appeared to me. I'd sit for long stretches in front of an eighteenth-century Hogarth, *A Midnight Modern Conversation,* which showed a table in an alehouse and a dozen drinkers laughing and pirouetting and falling to the floor. The painting sometimes made me laugh out loud, and it always made me homesick.

I left the museum one night and stopped in a corner bar. I drank a scotch. I had with me a copy of the poems of Dylan Thomas. I read some, drank another scotch. On the way back to my room I decided to check out a party I'd heard about. It was in a basement. Fifty students were hovering around a keg while a boy in the corner played a spinet piano. I leaned on the piano and watched.

He looked at me as he swayed up and down the keyboard.

"I know you," he said. "JC, right? Mo, Moo—"

"Moehringer."

"Right. You and Sidney."

I nodded.

"Must be rough," he said. "She and that grad student. That's got to suck." He stopped playing when he saw my face. "Uh-oh," he said.

I ran to Sidney's room. Sleet was falling, the sidewalks were slick, and I was drunk, so I fell. Twice. Wet, bruised, out of breath, I crashed through her door and hit the light switch. She shot upright in bed. She was alone.

"JR?"

"Is it true?"

"JR."

"Don't. Please, please, don't lie. Just tell me if it's true."

She pulled her knees to her chest and didn't say anything. I wanted to slap her, interrogate her, force her to give me every detail. How long? How often? Why? But there was no point. I saw the uselessness of it all, the futility of questions. I walked out, leaving her door wide open.

The train to New York was full and the only seat to be had was in the bar car. I wasn't complaining. Curled against the window I sipped my scotch and watched Connecticut fly by. In the seat across from me sat a priest. His head was bald, except for a few pipe-cleaner strands on top. His blue eyes were close-set, roofed by fluffy white eyebrows, and fixed on me. I prayed he wouldn't speak to me.

"Where you headed?" he asked.

I turned slowly, as if I had a sprained neck. "Manhasset," I said. I turned back to the window.

"Manhasset?" he said. "Where's that?"

"Long Island," I mumbled

"Manhasset, Long Island. Has a nice lilt about it. Man-*hass*-et. Sounds made up."

"It is." This sounded ruder than I intended. I turned to him again. "It's the home of that lying shrew, Daisy Buchanan."

"And her cretinous husband, Tom." He raised his drink in a silent toast, to me or the Buchanans, I wasn't sure. "Home for the holidays?"

"Unscheduled hiatus."

"You sound troubled, son."

"I just found out Daisy has been two-timing me."

"Ah."

"Sorry. Bad form, I guess, talking to a priest about a girl."

"Nonsense. That's all I hear about. Love and death."

"Oh. Right. Priests and bartenders."

"And hairdressers." He ran his hand across his scalp. "Or so I'm told. Let me guess. First love?"

"Yes."

" 'First love or last love,—which of these two passions is more omnipotent? Which is more fair?' Longfellow."

I smiled. "My grandmother used to recite his poems to me."

The priest continued reciting. " 'The star of morning, or the evening star? The sunrise or the sunset of the heart? The hour when we look forth to the unknown and the advancing day consumes the shadows—or that when all the landscape of our lives lies stretched behind us, and familiar places gleam in the distance—And sweet memories'—um—'and sweet memories'—what's the line—I'm getting old. Anyway, you get the idea."

The priest reached out and gave my knee an affectionate slap.

"Let me buy you a drink," he said. "What are you drinking, my boy?"

He shook the ice cubes in his empty cup like a backgammon player rattling the dice.

"Scotch," I said.

"Of course. What else is there?"

When he returned I thanked him and asked where he was headed. Religious conference, he said. He was representing his church, which was in some rural New England town I'd never heard of. We talked about religion, and he was delighted to discover I'd recently read Saint Augustine's *Confessions*.

"You must be a Yalie," he said.

"For the moment."

"You're not thinking of dropping out!"

"I think Yale is going to drop *me*. My grades."

"Grades can be brought up. Bright boy like you."

"It's hard, Father. Harder than I expected."

" 'The fascination of what's difficult has dried the sap out of my veins and rent spontaneous joy and natural content out of my heart.' Yeats."

"Yeats must have gone to Yale."

"If he had, he'd have found it hard too. Creative minds, you know."

"You're kind. But I'm an idiot. At my high school I felt like Einstein—now I realize why. Half the kids were stupid and the other half were stoned. At Yale I'm the stupid one. And the stupider I feel the less I go to class, which makes me fall more behind, which makes me feel stupider." I leaned back in my seat. "I was going to go to law school," I said quietly. "Fat chance. And I don't know how I'm going to break that news to my mother."

"Your mother's bent on you going to law school?"

"Very bent."

"What would you like to do?"

"I don't know."

"You must have some idea."

"I'd just like to—write." The first time I'd ever said it aloud.

"Bravo! The noblest calling! Poetry?"

"Newspapers."

"No. You look like a poet. You pout like a poet. Maybe a novelist?"

I shook my head. "I'd just like to be a newspaper reporter."

"Ah well." He slumped, disappointed. "That's fine too."

"I'd rather write other people's stories."

"Why not your own?"

"I wouldn't know where to start."

"Well there is something to that. And there is a magic about newspapers, I'll grant you. I do love picking up the *Times* each morning and seeing all that teeming life."

"Tell that to my mother."

"She'll be happy if you follow your heart. And if you *graduate*."

The word made my stomach clench. I swallowed half my scotch in one gulp.

"Make yourself happy," the priest said. "That's the way to make Mother happy."

"I'll bet you're not the only son of a single mother."

"Fifth son in a family of ten. But my mother had her heart set on my becoming a priest—so I'm not unsympathetic to your plight."

"You'd love Manhasset. Nothing but big Catholic families."

"Sounds like paradise."

"There's one main road, with lots of bars. At the top is the most popular church, St. Mary's, and at the bottom is the most sacred bar."

"A cosmology worthy of Dante. Shall we?" He rattled the ice in his empty cup again. I pulled my wallet from my pocket. He waved me off. My treat, he said, going to the bar.

I was starting to feel the scotch warming my extremities. My toes were full of scotch. My fingernails, hair, eyelashes—scotch. I wondered if Father Amtrak was slipping something into my drink, but I put the thought from my mind. "You know," I told him when he returned with the next round, "you talk a lot of sense for a priest."

He slapped his thigh and yelped with laughter. "I'll have to remember that!" he said. "Oh I'll have to tell that one to the other priests at the conference."

He locked his fingers behind his neck and stared at me. "I think we've reached some very important decisions here tonight, JD."

"JR."

"First, you're going to bring up those grades."

"I guess so."

" 'The indefatigable pursuit of an unattainable perfection, even though it consist in nothing more than in the pounding of an old piano, is what alone gives a meaning to our life on this unavailing star.' Logan Pearsall Smith."

"Who?"

"Very wise man. Essayist. Book lover. Born eons before you."

"You know a lot about books, Father."

"I spent a lot of time alone as a boy."

"I thought you came from a big family."

"Being alone has nothing to do with how many people are around. Now, I was making another point. Oh yes. Second, you're going to be a writer. I'm going to enjoy looking for your stories in the newspaper. You're going to write about real people and the things they do on this unavailing star."

"I don't know. Sometimes I try to say what's on my mind and it comes out sounding like I ate a dictionary and I'm shitting the pages. Sorry."

"Can I tell you something?" the priest asked. "Do you know why God invented writers? Because He loves a good story. And He doesn't give a damn about *words*. Words are the curtain we've hung between Him and our true selves. Try not to think about the words. Don't strain for the perfect sentence. There's no such thing. Writing is guesswork. Every sentence is an educated guess, the reader's as much as yours. Think about that the next time you curl a piece of paper into your typewriter."

I took my Yale notebook from my backpack. "Would you mind if I write that down, Father? I'm trying to get in the habit of writing down things smart people say to me."

He pointed to my Yale notebook, which was three-quarters filled.

"Looks like you've run across a great many smart people."

"These are mostly things I've overheard in Publicans. That's the name of my uncle's bar."

"It's true what you say about bartenders and priests." He looked out the window. "Two consonant callings. We both hear confessions, we both serve wine. There's a fair bit in the Bible about publicans too, though the word meant something different in the time of Jesus. 'Publicans and sinners,' that's the phrase, I think. They were synonymous."

"I was practically raised by publicans. My uncle and the men at the bar kept an eye on me when my mother wasn't around."

"And your father?"

I fanned the pages of my notebook and didn't answer.

"Well," the priest said. "Well. You were lucky to have so many men pitch in."

"Yes, Father. I was."

"People just don't understand how many men it takes to build one good man. Next time you're in Manhattan and you see one of those mighty sky-scrapers going up, pay attention to how many men are engaged in the enter-prise. It takes just as many men to build a sturdy man, son, as it does to build a tower."

twenty-five | SINATRA

THE INSPIRATION I TOOK FROM MY TALK WITH FATHER AMTRAK wore off as quickly as the scotch. I went into a tailspin that winter of 1984. I stopped studying, stopped going to classes. Most dangerous of all, I stopped worrying. Each morning I stretched out on the window seat, reading novels, smoking cigarettes, thinking about Sidney, and when the weekend came I rose, put on my overcoat and took the train to New York, then on to Publicans, where I would visit with the men for two days straight, returning to Yale late Sunday. The men seldom asked why I was home from school so much, why I was majoring and minoring in Publicans. When they asked in a general way how things were going, I mumbled about Sidney, but I never let on that I was courting disaster, that expulsion was now more than a possibil-ity. It was a certainty. I didn't know what their reaction would be, and I didn't want to know. I was afraid they might be pleased, which might force me to reconsider my feelings for them and the bar. Also, I was afraid that I might be pleased, that I might take pride in describing the mess I was making of my life. For the first time I suspected a self-destructive streak in myself, a suspicion bolstered when I read a biography of F. Scott Fitzgerald and greedily highlighted passages about his landing on academic probation at Princeton and dropping out. I caught myself thinking that maybe failing out of college was a prerequisite to becoming a writer.

On the first warm day of March I sat on the ledge outside my second-floor bedroom window. The air was soft, the students passing on the street below were in shirtsleeves. They looked brisk and cheerful. They were off to classes and practices, and I wanted to join them, but I couldn't. I'd dug too deep a hole for myself. I wondered what would happen if I just fell off the ledge. Would I die or merely break my collarbone and make a scene? It wasn't a suicidal impulse, more a bleak fantasy, but I recognized it as a new and alarming turn in my thoughts.

Then I saw Sidney. She was coming down Elm Street, in my direction, wearing a white blouse and a short suede skirt, her hair in a barrette. On the sidewalk below a group of boys saw her too. They elbowed each other and grinned. "Check this out," one muttered. "Damn," said another. One of the boys was polishing an apple against his shirt. As Sidney approached he stopped midpolish. His lips formed a small startled O. He extended the apple toward Sidney, and she reached out and grabbed it, without slowing her pace. She reminded me of the men from the bar, hitting the ocean in full stride. She took a bite of the apple and kept walking, never looking back, as if there were nothing remarkable about strangers offering her tributes as she passed. I heard in my head Uncle Charlie's voice the night he first saw Sidney. *You're in deep shit, my friend.*

Days later a highly placed dean, the dean of deans, called me to his office. The case of John Joseph Moehringer Jr. had been referred to him by my professors, many of whom, he said wryly, were feeling "neglected." The dean was "alarmed" to hear of my poor attendance, "distressed" by my plummeting grades. He waved a hand over his desk, across which he'd spread my transcript. If "matters" didn't improve, he said, he'd have no choice but to phone my "parents" and discuss my leaving school.

"John," he said, looking at my legal name across the top of my transcript, "is anything wrong? Anything you'd care to share with me?"

I wanted to share it all, every detail, from Professor Lucifer to Sidney.

The dean looked so kind, with his round rimless eyeglasses, his distinguished crow's-feet, and the dashing spray of gray at each temple. He looked like Franklin Delano Roosevelt, and I yearned for a man to tell me I had nothing to fear but fear itself. Rather than Roosevelt's cigarette in a holder, the dean clenched in his teeth a black pipe that pumped out a delicious aroma— brandy, coffee, vanilla, woodsmoke—the distilled essence of paternal concern. The rope of blue smoke from his pipe fooled me for a second into thinking Franklin Dean Roosevelt and I were enjoying a fireside chat. Then I remembered that we weren't father and son but dean and student, that we weren't speaking heart-to-heart, but sitting knee-to-knee in his cramped office above the school that was about to give me the boot. "It's complicated," I mumbled.

I couldn't talk with so fine a man about madness and lust. I couldn't confess to Franklin Dean Roosevelt that I was hounded by mental images of Sidney with other men. You see, Dean, I can't concentrate on Kant because I keep picturing a certain grad student caressing my ex-girlfriend while she straddles him, her blond hair spilling across his—No. For this dean, Kant was the ultimate turn-on. Kant was his *Penthouse*. I looked at his floor-to-ceiling bookshelves and knew he wouldn't understand my not finding all the excitement I needed in books. I didn't understand it myself. He'd lose whatever sympathy he had for me, and if I couldn't have his respect, at least I could have his pity. I sat, letting the seconds explode on a mantel clock somewhere behind me, savoring his pipe smoke and looking everywhere but his eyes. I would let him break the silence.

But he had nothing to say. What was there to say about such a boy? He puffed his pipe and watched me as though he were at a zoo and I were an interesting, if sluggish, creature.

"Well," I said, leaning forward in my chair, as if to go.

"Maybe a tutor?" he suggested.

Of course a tutor would help, but I barely had money for books, and whatever I had left over was reserved for the train to Publicans, which my roommate called the Disorient Express. I told Franklin Dean Roosevelt I would consider a tutor, that I would try harder, but as I left his office I thought the best thing to do would be to go back to my room and start packing. I couldn't imagine I had more than a month left at Yale.

Instead, improbably, I got on with it. Shortly after my meeting with the dean I broke my habit of running off to Publicans every weekend. I scraped and clawed my way through the semester, passing all but one class, a turn-around made possible by two encouraging voices always in my ear. One was my mother, who wrote beautiful letters in which she promised there would be other Sidneys, but never another Yale. If I believed in love, she wrote, and she knew that I did, then I shouldn't abandon my first love, Yale, to mourn my second, Sidney. I would look back on this time, my mother wrote, and re-member remarkably little of it, except the extent to which I tried or did not try.

If I'd read my mother's latest letter a dozen times and still couldn't get Sidney out of my mind, I'd turn up the volume on that other soothing voice—Sinatra. He gave my heartbreak musical accompaniment and, more important, intellectual justification. Memorizing dates for a history exam, or theories for a philosophy exam, I'd also be memorizing Sinatra, whose lyrics became my new mantras. Rather than tell myself, *I will not worry about something that will not happen,* I chanted, *Guess I'll hang my tears out to dry.* It helped. After committing his lyrics to memory, I explicated them, looked for meaning beneath the words, as Professor Lucifer once hoped I'd do with Keats. I typed the best lyrics on index cards and pinned them above my desk. They read like one long misogynist monologue, the kind of thing you might hear any night of the week in Publicans, but the way Sinatra said it, with bravado and pathos and without the Long Island accent, made it sound more sophisticated, more tenable. Sinatra told me that women were dangerous, even lethal. Sidney was just a beautiful woman, he said, and being betrayed by a beautiful woman was a rite of passage for any young man. He'd walked through the same fire. You'll live, he promised. The pain will put hair on your chest. My love for Sinatra was already deep, but that spring I developed a physical dependence on his voice.

I also heard my father's voice toward the end of that semester. He phoned me out of the blue to suggest another visit, and promised that this one would be better, more meaningful, because he'd quit drinking. He was on "the straight and narrow," he said, and if I ever needed to talk, I should phone him, collect. I told him about Sidney, and my struggle to stay afloat at Yale. He rec-ommended I consider dropping out. College isn't for everyone, my father said.

When school let out in May I went to Manhasset to spend the summer. I told my mother I'd have a better chance of finding a summer job in New York than in Arizona. But of course the truth was that I wanted to catch up on lost time at Publicans. My first night at the bar I celebrated two milestones—my academic survival and Sidney's graduation. In my mind the latter was the greater cause for rejoicing, because from now on I'd have Yale to myself. Never again, I told Uncle Charlie, would I have to hear rumors about Sidney, or witness her biting other boys' apples.

As senior year began I was myself again. Going to class, writing for the *News,* close to the number of credits needed for a diploma. I sat at my desk, typing a paper, listening to Sinatra, feeling strong. All at once, out of nowhere, my happiness got the best of me. I heard new meanings in Sinatra's lyrics. If Sidney is no different than other women, I reasoned, maybe I should forgive her. If beautiful women lie and cheat, such is the price of loving a beautiful woman. I wondered where Sidney was at that moment. Had she broken up with the grad student? Did she think of me? Did she ever want to hear my voice?

She answered on the second ring. She cried, said she missed me, and we made plans to meet for dinner the next night.

We sat at a table in a dark corner of the restaurant, and the waiter knew to leave us alone. Sidney explained carefully, in detail, why she'd done what she'd done. She'd been unhappy at Yale, she said. Depressed, homesick, she'd behaved in ways that she now couldn't believe, and she placed most of the blame on her first love. She'd been sixteen, and he was a much older man, who misused her, and cheated on her. The experience left her disillusioned and cynical, with warped ideas about fidelity.

She was older and wiser now, she promised, touching my arm. As was I, she added. She saw it in my eyes, she said—a new strength and self-assurance, which she found "insanely attractive." By the time our waiter brought the check Sidney was on my lap. "So," she whispered in my ear, "would you like to take me back to your place and show me your etchings?"

Standing in the middle of my bedroom, undoing her blouse, Sidney glanced at my desk. "What's all this?" she asked, pointing to a stack of papers.

"Stories."

"About?"

"A dumb rube and the beautiful girl who crushes his heart."

"Fiction or non?"

"I'm not sure."

She took a pen from the desk and wrote a giant heart on one of the pages, and inside she wrote, in her perfect architect handwriting, "The End." Then she turned off my gooseneck lamp. In the dark I heard the antique buttons of her blouse hit the floor.

This time, I told myself, everything would be different. Success with both Sidney and Yale depended on balancing the two, devoting myself to neither. I had to do a better job of managing my time and emotions, especially the latter. In the past I'd led with my heart, displayed my desperation like a badge of honor. I'd thought I was being honest, but I'd been a sucker. This time around, I vowed, I'd be cool.

Sidney noticed the difference, and it made her act different as well. Though I no longer talked about the future, Sidney wouldn't shut up about it. Many nights we sat in bars, long after last call, after the other barstools had been turned upside down and the bartender wanted to go home, and she would make lists of names for our future children. On Friday afternoons she would insist that I take the train south to spend the weekend with her and her parents. (She was living with them until she decided what she wanted to do with her life.) Her parents were different too. They didn't frown at things I said. They smiled encouragingly when Sidney and I discussed living together. After dinner we'd all move into the living room to drink cocktails, read the *Times,* watch public television, as if we were already a family. When Sidney's parents went up to bed, Sidney and I would stoke the fire and she'd read Proust while I studied. Sometimes I would look out the window and imagine some little boy watching from across the street. Once or twice I felt that part of me was still out there, in the woods, peering in.

On my twentieth birthday Sidney and I drove to Boston, which Sidney thought would be a good place to live together after I graduated. The city was close to her family, so she wouldn't be homesick, but far enough that we could blaze our own trail and be independent. "Won't this be a lovely place to start our new life?" she said, speeding up and down the narrow streets of the North End. "We'll have a cute little apartment. And every night we'll build a great big fire and drink coffee and read to each other from *Remembrance of Things Past*."

"And there are several good law schools in the area," I said.

"I thought you were going to be a newspaperman?"

"Lawyers make more money than newspapermen."

"We don't need money," she said. "We have love."

But we needed money too. Since the laundry disaster sophomore year I'd held a series of part-time jobs, always earning just enough to pay for booze and books, but senior year I found full-time work at a bookstore-café next to the Center for British Art. The store would have been Bill and Bud's idea of paradise. Its front wall was plate glass from floor to ceiling, so the sales floor was always flooded with natural light, and a horseshoe-shaped bar in the middle of the fiction section served gourmet coffee and pastries. My job was to sit on a stool at the cash register and ring up the occasional sale. Since the place catered almost exclusively to homeless people and grad students—who took advantage of the free-refill policy, guzzling coffee until they were jittery as crackheads—sales were few, and I had plenty of time to read and eavesdrop on conversations about art and literature. The atmosphere was invigoratingly, absurdly intellectual. I once watched a fistfight break out between two busboys over who would get to keep Jacques Derrida's silver pipe cleaner, which the famous literature professor had left beside his plate after eating a sandwich.

I was also in charge of the bookstore stereo, which meant Sinatra all the time. Grad students would clap their hands over their ears and plead for something else. Even the homeless complained. "Jeez kid," a homeless man shouted at me, "a little Crosby would be nice for a change." I relented one winter day and played Mozart. Bud's favorite—the Quintet for Piano and Winds in E-flat. I opened my copy of Chekhov and my eye fell on the line "We shall find peace. We shall hear the angels, we shall see the sky sparkling with diamonds." I snapped the book shut and felt the words hit my bloodstream like an Uncle Charlie martini. I'd found peace, I'd heard angels, and the sky *was* full of diamonds—it was snowing, thick feathery flakes, making the glass-walled store feel like a snow globe. I watched the snow sprinkle the campus, sipped my coffee, listened to Mozart, and told myself—warned myself—this might be it. I might never be happier. I was going to graduate, I was applying to law schools, I was reunited with the love of my life. Even my mother was feeling better. She was having some success selling insurance, and dating again.

A customer approached the counter. I rang up his book and as I handed him his change I heard something smash against the front window. I turned, the customer turned, everyone turned. A huge snowball was flattened against the glass. Outside, in the middle of the street, Sidney stood with a hand on her hip, beaming. I ran outside, picked her up and twirled her in circles. I told her that one minute ago I thought I'd never be happier, and now I was twice as happy, and it was all her doing. "I love you," she said, over and over.

In my memory it seems like five minutes later that I was walking out of Sterling Library, a rough draft of my senior thesis in my backpack, and it was spring again. I bumped into Franklin Dean Roosevelt. He congratulated me on how well I looked. He added pointedly—with some emotion—that he was looking forward to seeing me, above all people, in a mortarboard and gown on commencement day.

Sidney and I went skinny-dipping in a secluded cove that she knew of in Long Island Sound. We swam to a wooden float far from shore and lay on our backs in the sun, holding hands, talking in low voices, for some reason, though there was no one near us. In fact the world seemed to have been covered in a second Great Flood, of which we were the only survivors.

"Tell me the truth," I said.

"Always," she said.

"Have you ever been this happy?"

"Never," she said. "I never dared to hope that I would be this happy."

My mother wrote to say she'd bought an airplane ticket and a new blue suit for my graduation. I read her letter under my spreading elm, then looked up at the high branches, bursting with new green buds, and fell peacefully asleep. When I woke it was twilight. Walking back to my room I spotted a handbill announcing guest lecturers coming to speak on various topics. *Who has time to sit in a stuffy lecture hall and listen to these drones, particularly at the start of spring?* The name of one drone caught my eye. Frank Sinatra. Poor bastard. A geeky economics professor at MIT, and he's named after the coolest man on the planet.

I read more closely. The handbill seemed to suggest that this Frank Sinatra coming to Yale was Frank Sinatra, singer. He'd been invited to speak

THE TENDER BAR | 211

about his "art." I read the words over and over. A joke, obviously. Then I realized the date. April 1. Very funny.

My schoolmates, however, swore it was no joke. Sinatra was coming, they said, though they didn't care. I went by the lecture hall on the appointed day. No crowd, no commotion. I sat on the steps and watched cars go by. Some joke. Standing to go I saw a student hurrying up the steps with a huge ring of keys. "You here for Sinatra?" he asked.

"He's really coming?"

"Four o'clock."

"Where is everybody?"

"It's only two o'clock."

"I thought there would be a line, people hoping to get a good seat?"

"It's not like George Michael is coming."

He let me in. I picked a good seat and waited while the hall filled around me. There were still empty seats when Sinatra stepped quietly through a side door, no entourage, no bodyguards, flanked only by his wife and a frowzy dean. He sat calmly beside the lectern and crossed his legs, waiting.

He didn't look the way I'd pictured him. He was thicker and more avuncular than I'd expected. He seemed no more exceptional than the dean who fluttered about the podium, adjusting the microphone, maybe because Sinatra was dressed like the dean. In every photo I'd ever seen, Sinatra wore a tux, or a sharkskin suit with a thin tie. That day he wore a tweed blazer, charcoal slacks, a golden necktie, and polished cordovan loafers. Sinatra was trying to look collegiate, to fit in. My heart went out to him.

I watched his eyes. I'd seen those blue eyes so many times, on album covers, in movies, but no camera could convey their full blueness from a few feet away. They darted left and right, sweeping the room like blue searchlights, and I noticed that they turned different shades of blue as they moved—indigo, royal, navy. Behind the blueness I saw something more striking. Fear. Frank Sinatra was afraid. Eating a plate of pasta with hit men didn't scare him, but speaking to a roomful of nerds made him sweat. His hands shook as he fumbled with note cards and slipped them into his breast pocket. He glanced at his wife, down front, who sent him a you-can-do-it smile. Watching him writhe, seeing him suffer the same desire to be liked that I'd suffered for four years at Yale, I wanted to shout, *Relax, Frank! You're worth the whole damn bunch put together!*

The dean said a few introductory words and Sinatra stood and walked to the lectern. He coughed into his fist several times, to clear his throat, and began. The Voice was scratchy. It sounded like my oldest vinyls. He thanked us for inviting him to speak on the subject of his "art," and though he was an artist, he said, he wanted us to know first and foremost that he was a saloon singer. He loved *saloons,* and clearly loved the word. Every time he said "saloon" his vocal cords relaxed and his streetwise Hoboken accent reemerged, overtaking his valiant attempt at Ivy League elocution. A saloon was the birthplace of his voice, he said. A saloon was the launch pad of his identity. A saloon was where his mother took him as a boy and sat him on the bar and told him to sing for all the men. I looked around. Was everyone getting this? *Frank Sinatra grew up in a bar!* No one seemed all that surprised, but I was pounding my fist on my thigh.

I hadn't thought it possible to feel more grateful to Sinatra. I already gave him half the credit for getting me over Sidney, getting me back together with Sidney, and helping me graduate. But when he made me feel there was nothing wrong with loving saloons, that growing up in a saloon didn't disqualify a young man for success, or happiness, or the love of someone like Sidney, I wanted to rush the podium and wrap my arms around him. I wanted to thank Sinatra for seeing me through a dark time, for singing me through. I wanted to invite him to Publicans, and I almost did. I raised my hand to speak during the question-and-answer session. *If you love saloons, Frank, have I got a saloon for you!* But before The Voice could call on me, the dean stepped forward and said it was time for our honored guest to leave.

Sinatra thanked us for our time and, looking relieved, slide-stepped out the door.

twenty-six | JR MAGUIRE

IN THE DAYS BEFORE GRADUATION, I HAD ONE LAST ASSIGNMENT, one last requirement to fulfill, though this one was self-imposed. I needed to legally change my name. I needed to jettison JR, and Junior, and Moehringer, to sweep aside those burdensome symbols and replace them with something normal, some name that didn't come from the German neighbor of my father's pseudonymous father. I wanted to deny my father and refuse my name, and I wanted a name that Sidney wouldn't be able to deny or refuse when I asked her to take it in marriage.

But I had to hurry. Yale was days away from printing diplomas for the Class of 1986, and I resolved that whatever name appeared on my diploma would be my name for keeps. I'd worked too hard for that diploma, vested it with too much meaning to have it bear any name other than my legal name. I would not let my identity fork. I would not go through life with two different names, the second coming of Johnny Michaels, aka John Moehringer.

I spent hours and hours in Sterling Library, compiling lists of potential names. I looked through novels, poetry anthologies, baseball encyclopedias, volumes of *Who's Who*, collecting lyrical names, unusual names, ultramasculine names. I imagined myself for five minutes at a time as Chip Oakwood, Jake McGunnigle, Clinton Vandemere. I practiced my new signature as Bennett Silverthorne, Hamilton Gold, and William Featherstone. I went to sleep as Morgan Rivers and woke as Brock Manchester. I gave serious consideration to becoming Bayard Something or Other, but after stealing the man's shirt I couldn't justify stealing his name. I experimented with the names of nineteenth-century baseball players, like Red Conkright and Jocko Fields, and went around campus for an afternoon thinking of myself as Grover Lowdermilk. I tried medleys of terribly British names I found in the annals of Parliament, like Hamden Lloyd Cadwallader. Eventually I realized that every name I liked, all the names on my short list, were just as prone to mockery as JR Moehringer.

In the end I settled on Charles Mallard. Plain. Simple. Charles in honor of Uncle Charlie, Mallard because it sounded moneyed and Old World. Charles Mallard was a man who wore neckties adorned with pictures of pheasants, and knew how to clean a twelve-gauge, and bedded all the best-looking girls at the club. Charles Mallard was who I thought I wanted to be. Charles Mallard I was. For one weekend. At the last minute a buddy saved me from formalizing this fantastic mistake by pointing out that I was letting myself in for a lifetime of being called Chuck Duck.

I decided to remain JR, but I would make JR my legal first name. Then I'd no longer be lying when I told people it didn't stand for anything. For my last name I'd take my mother's maiden name, Maguire. JR Maguire. Sidney wrote it in her architect handwriting on the front of my Yale notebook. Very handsome, she said. Below it she wrote, "Sidney Maguire." We both agreed it had a certain ring to it.

The clerk at New Haven Superior Court said changing your identity was a breeze. "Fill out this form," she said, sliding a sheet of paper toward me, "and you can be anyone you want."

"I want to change my first name to JR. Just JR. That's okay?"

"Just JR? It wouldn't stand for anything?"

"No. That's the whole point. Is that legal?"

"Change your name to R2D2 for all the state of Connecticut cares."

"Great."

"What will the last name be?"

"Maguire."

"JR Maguire," she said. "What's your name right now?"

"John Joseph Moehringer Jr."

She hooted. "Oh boy," she said. "Definitely an improvement."

I took the form to my room and phoned my mother to tell her what I was doing. She wasn't thrilled—Grandpa's name had its own unhappy associations for her—but she understood. The change would cost seventy-five dollars, I told her, which I didn't have. Courting Sidney had left me a little short. My mother said she would wire me the money right away.

Counting my seventy-five dollars as I left Western Union, I decided to give John Joseph Moehringer Jr. a proper sendoff. I walked into town and stopped into a bar. I saw my friend Bebe, the only other student at Yale who delighted in barrooms as much as I. Hey, I told her, guess who died. Junior! That's right, Junior Moehringer is dead! Long live JR Maguire! She laughed nervously, no idea what I was talking about. Let me buy my friend Bebe a drink, I told the bartender, and then I explained myself, giving them both a brief history of my name and how much I hated it and why I was shaking it off at last.

"Bon voyage, Junior!" I said, raising my beer.

"See ya, Junior!" Bebe said, clinking her bottle against mine.

"Sayonara, asshole!" the bartender shouted.

I woke the next morning with a throbbing head. I lay on my back, eyes closed, trying to piece together what happened after I left Western Union. I remembered making a toast. I remembered Bebe and the bartender laughing and saying something like, "JR Maguire is *on fire*. What's your *desire*, JR *Maguire*!" The rest was a void. I thought about phoning Bebe, asking her what happened—then it all came roaring back to me. I jumped out of bed and rifled through the pockets of my jeans. The seventy-five dollars was gone. All of it. Junior, that sneak, that rat, had gotten me drunk and rolled me.

I sat at my desk and looked at the form. JR Maguire. Such a handsome name—and I'd screwed it up. Worse, I'd drunk it up. I went to the bathroom and looked in the mirror and told myself that I didn't deserve a name so handsome. I deserved to go through life as JR Moehringer. A cross between an alias and a lie.

Sidney kissed me and said she didn't care about my name. Days later I discovered that what she didn't care about was me. Once again she was seeing someone on the side.

I learned the truth in her bathroom. An envelope on the counter was addressed to Sidney in a man's blocky handwriting. I read it several times. "Is Junior still in the picture? If so, why? I can't wait to [illegible] when I see you again."

When I handed Sidney the letter she asked, "Where did you get that?" She took it from me and told me about him, a few facts I would rather not have known. He was a trust-fund kid with a fast yacht and a much better name. He was from her hometown, he was funny, he was smart—but he was just a friend, she pleaded. I wanted to believe her, or forgive her, but even Sidney didn't expect me to. I tried to think of something to do besides break up, but I couldn't, and Sidney couldn't either. Days before graduation we said good-bye, forever.

I yearned to hit Publicans for my traditional post-Sidney binge, but there wasn't time. It was graduation day. My mother was there, standing in my room, wearing her new blue suit, smiling into space, thinking back, I knew, on all the days when such a moment was unimaginable.

As I marched across Old Campus in my black gown and mortarboard, I heard the bells in Harkness and remembered the first time I'd heard them, seven years earlier. I recalled how they had tormented me, but now, as I took my seat among my fellow graduates, all torments fell away, and in their place was a radiant gratitude, which I ranked as the day's true achievement, more than the diploma I was about to receive.

Only one sad moment marred that splendid afternoon. It all happened so fast, I wondered later if I'd imagined it. Just after the ceremony Sidney stepped out from the crowd, holding a large bouquet of lilies. She thrust them at me and kissed my cheek. She whispered that she was sorry, that she would always love me, then turned—short skirt, tanned legs, heels—and walked across New Haven Green. I watched her disappear in the shadow of my spreading elm, one sanctuary dissolving into another.

I felt no anger. Instead I felt with unusual clarity how young we were, Sidney no less than I. Maybe it was the tassel hanging in my eyes, making me think with self-conscious maturity, but for a brief moment I recognized and appreciated how much, despite her sophistication, Sidney was a girl. We both pretended to be adults, but that's all it was, pretending. We craved the same things—safety, sanctuary, financial security—and Sidney may have craved them more than I, because she'd enjoyed them growing up and knew how important they were. In her desperation to obtain them, she had acted out of panic, not malice.

Driving my mother to Manhasset I refused to think of Sidney. I concentrated on the good things about the day while my mother studied my diploma. "It's all in Latin," she said.

"Except for my name—a mix of German and gibberish."

"*Primi Honoris Academici?* What does that mean?"

I shook my head. "No clue."

A diploma I couldn't read, a name I couldn't abide. I didn't care. I prized that diploma, considered it a second birth certificate. My mother ran her finger over the name. "JR Moehringer," she said. "You got Yale to print JR? And with no dots?"

"Some last-minute negotiating."

"What happened to JR Maguire?"

"I had—a change of heart."

She looked at my hand on the steering wheel. "And the Yale ring?" she asked.

"Let's talk about that over dinner."

Yale had recently mailed my mother a catalog of rings, which for some reason captured her imagination. She'd become strangely obsessed with buying me a ring as a graduation present. She said I must have a ring. A ring, she said, was part of the Yale experience. Like a diploma, she believed, a ring would be proof that I'd gone to Yale. "Sparkling proof," she said.

I didn't want a ring. I told my mother about my aversion to men's jewelry, and I pointed out that Yale rings were expensive. She wouldn't listen. You must have a ring, she insisted. Fine, I said, send me the catalog, I'll order a ring. But I would pay for it myself, by working extra hours at the bookstore-café.

Over dinner at Publicans my mother knew I hadn't kept my word, that the money for the ring had gone the way of the money for the name change. "You promised you were going to order a ring," she said in a disappointed voice.

"And I did."

From the breast pocket of my blazer I removed a velvet box and slid it across the table. She cracked the box open. Inside was a Yale ring. A woman's ring. I explained that Yale had been our dream, and our accomplishment. I told my mother that I couldn't have gotten into Yale without her, and certainly couldn't have gotten through without her. "As far as I'm concerned," I said, "you graduated from Yale today too. And you should have some proof. Sparkling proof."

Her eyes welled with tears, and she tried to speak, but her voice caught in her throat.

After dinner we moved into the barroom. Uncle Charlie was behind the stick and in my honor he played Sinatra all night. "This is your 'Pomp and Circumstance,' " he said, cranking the volume on "My Way." When a young hippie wannabe in a suede coat with fringes along the sleeves asked Uncle Charlie to please play something else, Uncle Charlie glared at him and slowly raised the volume.

Steve gave my mother a big hello. He complimented her ring and flashed a chivalrous variation of the Cheshire smile. Cager tipped his visor to my mother and told Uncle Charlie he wanted to buy her a drink. "Dorothy," Uncle Charlie said, "you're backed up on The Cage."

I tried to whisper something to my mother about Cager's time in Vietnam. I wanted her to know what an honor it was to have Cager buy her a drink. But Fuckembabe interrupted. "Your son," he said to my mother, "splitches the sploozah like nobody else in this casbah, especially when he walla wallas the umpty boodles, I wanna tell you!"

"Oh?" she said, looking to me for help. "Thank you."

While my mother was talking to Uncle Charlie and Fuckembabe, Cager tapped me on the shoulder. He asked what subject I'd chosen for a major. History, I said. He asked why. I told him one of my professors had said that history is the narrative of people searching for a place to go, and I liked that idea.

"So how much do they get for a Yale education these days anyway?" he asked.

"About sixty thousand," I said. "But most of that was paid for by grants and loans and scholar—"

"And what year was the Magna Carta signed?"

"Magna—? I don't know."

"Just as I thought. Sixty thou, down the drain." He lit a Merit Ultra and took a swallow of Budweiser. "Magna Carta—1215. Foundation of English law. Bulwark against tyranny. They let you out of fucking Yale without knowing that?"

He sounded as though my graduation had set his teeth on edge. And he wasn't the only one. Colt sounded standoffish too, like Yogi Bear stealing a picnic basket that turns out to be empty. Were the men, like Sinatra, somehow intimidated by Yale? I couldn't stand to think Yale might be a barrier to the bar, so I downplayed my diploma, talked up my shitty grades and my emasculation by Sidney, and sure enough their mood improved.

When the kitchen closed, people in the restaurant drifted into the barroom for nightcaps, followed by the waiters and waitresses, now off duty, ready for their first cocktails of the night. Everyone congratulated me and flattered my mother and reminisced about their own graduations. My cousin Linda arrived and presented me with two gifts. The first was news that McGraw would be home next week. He'd just finished his first year at Nebraska, where he'd earned a baseball scholarship, and I was dying to see him. Her second gift was a silver pen from Tiffany. Linda knew I harbored indistinct notions of becoming a writer. My mother didn't know, however, or didn't want to know, so Linda's pen pointed the way to the conversation we'd been dodging for years. At long last—nestled in Publicans, brazen with scotch—I admitted to my mother that I wasn't going to be a lawyer. Law school wasn't for me. School of any kind wasn't for me. I'm sorry, I said. I'm so sorry.

My mother held up her hand. Wait, she said. Slow down. Her heart wasn't set on my being a lawyer. She only pushed me in that direction, she said, because she wanted me to make a contribution to the world, and to build a career, instead of just punching a clock. She'd be happy if I was happy, no matter what career I chose. "What is it you think you might like to do instead of law school?" she asked sweetly.

The question swirled above our heads like the blue smoke. I averted my eyes. How to tell my mother that what I wanted to do next was pick out a barstool at Publicans and get comfortable? I wanted to play Liars' Poker, watch baseball, gamble—read. I wanted to settle in at the bar and have a cocktail and enjoy the books I'd felt too intimidated and rushed to enjoy at Yale. At long last I wanted to sit on a chair and look up at the sky. . . .

My mother was waiting, calmly holding her glass of zinfandel. What is it you think you might like to do? I contemplated opening with something blunt and direct. *Mom, I just don't see the point of this whole work-ethic thing.* But I feared that this would knock her right off her barstool. I considered quoting Whitman. *I want to "lean and loaf at my ease observing a spear of summer grass."* But my mother didn't give a damn about Whitman and she would find my song of myself off key.

Of course I didn't know what to say because I didn't know what I wanted. My inability to see life in anything but black or white prevented me from understanding my contradictory self. Yes, I wanted to loaf and lean against the bar, but I also wanted to strive and succeed, to make lots of money, to be able at last to take care of my mother. Failure was so painful to me, so frightening, that I was trying to appease it, make an accommodation with it, rather than fight it head-on. Shuttling back and forth all those summers between my mother and the men, I'd developed a dual personality. Half of me wanted to conquer the world, half of me wanted to hide from it. Unable to fathom my conflicting impulses, let alone explain them, and seeking an answer that would satisfy my mother, mollify my ambition, and still leave me free to lean against that bar, I announced loudly, impulsively, to myself as well as to her, that I was going to write a sprawling roman à clef about Publicans. I was going to be a novelist.

"A novelist," my mother said in her flattest monotone, as if I'd said I wanted to sell cheese sandwiches outside Grateful Dead concerts. "I see. And where will you live?"

"Grandpa's."

She recoiled. Aunt Ruth and the cousins were living at Grandpa's again. Conditions at the house were wretched.

"Until I can figure something out," I added quickly. "Eventually I'll get a room somewhere."

I felt quite proud. I thought I'd hit on a plan that meshed my mother's dreams and mine. In fact my plan synthesized her worst fears. She twisted her new ring on her finger as though preparing to give it back, and she looked around the barroom, possibly rethinking her decision to send me there every summer. She'd always had a fixed idea of Publicans, based largely on my romanticized reports, and now I could see that she feared she'd misjudged the place, that it might not have been wise to let me become so enamored of it. She looked at the faces along the bar, the men and women who would have thought that writing a novel about them was a fine idea, and her expression was like Sidney's when she first walked into Publicans.

I looked around too. Down at the other end of the bar was a group of young men about my age, all of whom, I'd heard, had recently landed their first jobs on Wall Street. They were knocking down $150,000 a year, at least, and each looked like the kind of son who would make a mother proud. I wondered if my mother saw them too, if she was thinking she'd like to trade me for one of them.

"This is your plan?" my mother said. "You want to be a starving writer living in a garret?"

I wasn't altogether sure what a garret was, but it sounded cool, maybe just the kind of starter apartment I needed.

"You have to have a job," my mother said. "End of story."

"I will have a job. Writing my novel."

I smiled. She didn't.

"A job job," she said. "You have to earn a salary so you can pay for health insurance, and clothes, and if you're determined to live at Grandpa's, you need to give something to Grandma for meals."

"Since when?"

"Since you turned twenty-one. Since you graduated from Yale University. You need money, JR. Money to live. Money for, for—if nothing else—your bar tab."

I didn't explain that there was no bar tab, that nephews of bartenders drank free. I knew that this argument wouldn't help my cause, or put my mother's mind at ease. I drank my scotch and kept my mouth shut, the last wise decision I would make for a very long time.

twenty-seven | RJ MOHINGER

I WENT UP AND DOWN PLANDOME ROAD, FILLING OUT APPLICATIONS, introducing myself to every store owner and manager. By the time I reached the top of Plandome Road I was beat. The day was scorching and I needed a drink. I checked my watch. Almost happy hour. I looked up. The next store was Lord & Taylor. I'll fill out one more application, I told myself, and then head to Publicans for a beer and a Smelly Burger with Uncle Charlie.

The personnel woman at Lord & Taylor said there were no openings in Men's Fashions. I could taste that beer as I stood and thanked her for her time. "Wait now," she said. "We do have something in *Home* Fashions."

"Home Fashions?"

"Towels. Soaps. Candles. It's a lovely department. And the position is full-time."

"I don't know." I thought of my diploma. I thought of my pride. Then I thought of the look on my mother's face at Publicans. "When would I have to—When could I start?"

"Right away."

The personnel woman and I rode the escalator down to Home Fashions, which was housed in the store's subbasement. She introduced me to the staff of the department, four ladies who must have been among the original suffragettes. The manager of Home Fashions took me into a back room and guided me through orientation, which lasted ten minutes, since there wasn't much to be oriented about. Lord & Taylor had no computers, no cash registers, no visible sign that the twentieth century was drawing to a close. Every sale was written on an order pad, receipts were made with carbon paper, and in the rare event of a cash sale, change was made from a metal strongbox. Customers found it quaint, she said, that Lord & Taylor hewed to the old ways. She handed me an apron, made me a name tag—RJ Mohinger—and sent me onto the sales floor. "You can start," she said, "by dusting."

In one of the mirrored music boxes for sale in Home Fashions I caught a glimpse of myself. *That looks like me, but it can't be me, because I'm wearing an apron and holding a feather duster and standing in the subbasement of Lord & Taylor.* Yale in May, Home Fashions in June. I thought of my fellow Yalies, like Jedd Redux and Bayard. I imagined the careers they were launching, the exciting lives they were beginning to build. The way my luck was going one of them was bound to get a flat on Shelter Rock Road and stop into Lord & Taylor to use the phone, and there I'd be, aproned, gelded, up to my neck in scented soaps.

"Excuse me."

I turned. A customer.

"RJ," she said, peering at my name tag, "could you help me with the Waterford?"

The woman pointed to various pieces of crystal she wanted to examine. I took them from a case and set them before her on a soft cloth. Lifting them to the light she asked me detailed questions, and though I didn't know the answers, I realized that at Lord & Taylor there were no grades. I told her that the methods used by the Waterford factory in Ireland dated to the time of the Druids. I told her about the bells that chimed each day at the Waterford Castle (I was describing Harkness Tower) and assured her that each piece of Waterford was unique, like a snowflake, like a human soul. I didn't know what would come out of my mouth next, and I was just as anxious as the customer to find out. I lied eloquently, profligately, shamelessly. I lied my ass off, lied my apron off, and through lying I felt that I reclaimed some portion of my dignity.

The customer bought six hundred dollars' worth of Waterford, making me high seller for the day in Home Fashions. Apparently this was a feat without precedent. No employee in the history of Home Fashions had ever been high seller on his or her first day, the manager said as she handed me a candy dish. "What's this?" I asked.

"High seller for the day wins a prize. Today's prize is a silver candy dish."

"Congratulations," said one of the suffragettes, a woman named Dora, who wore eyeglasses as big as TV screens. From her insincere tone I could tell that she'd been the second-highest seller, and that she'd had her eye on that candy dish.

Next day, same thing. I sold about eight hundred dollars' worth of merchandise, and was rewarded with a set of steak knives. All that first week I outsold the suffragettes by a wide margin, and Sunday I shattered some long-standing Home Fashions record, the store equivalent of Roger Maris's sixty-one home runs. I was moving merchandise faster than Lord & Taylor could restock it, and not only Waterford. I was selling enough candles to light Shea Stadium for a night game, enough bath towels to soak up Manhasset Bay.

The suffragettes in Home Fashions gave me dirty looks all day, as if I opposed their right to vote. I was their worst nightmare: young, full of energy, free of the foot maladies that plagued them after decades on the sales floor, and hogging the daily prize they counted on to augment their pay. I gave myself dirty looks too, every time I caught sight of myself in one of the mirrored music boxes. Things were bad enough when I believed I'd taken a job that was beneath me. Now I faced the possibility that I'd found my true calling. Like water I'd sought my own level. Was this why I'd bombed at Yale? Why Sidney had rejected me? Because I'd been aiming too high? Was it my destiny to be the best clerk in the history of Home Fashions? At different times I'd been worried about harboring some dark attraction to failure. Now I worried about my inexorable success in Home Fashions, and what it foretold.

But there was something more worrisome about Home Fashions, more horrible. More shameful. I liked it. All those nights peering into windows around Manhasset, all that pining after fine homes and nice things, had turned me into some kind of Home Fashions savant. In the deepest recesses of my subconscious I'd developed a fetish for Home Fashions, a nauseating innate talent. Even when I didn't try I sold the stuff like no one else. In fact, not trying was the key. The less I tried, the better I did, and the more sick pleasure I got from it. I took to that apron like a dirt mule to a plow.

Tortured, confused, toting the latest prize I'd won for being the day's top seller, I retreated each night to Publicans with two other salesclerks, women my age. One worked in cosmetics, the other in lingerie. They thought I was funny, and an audacious liar, not because they heard me bullshitting customers but because I kept insisting I'd graduated from Yale.

"I always thought if I had a soul-killing job it would be as a lawyer," I told them. "But maybe Home Fashions is what I'm supposed to do. I can't ignore the fact that this is the first thing I've ever done well."

"Don't worry," Cosmetics said. "I'm sure this is just a phase."

"Really?" I said hopefully.

"If everything you've told us about yourself is actually *true*," Lingerie said, "then you're bound to start fucking up again real soon."

Autumn arrived. I spent my days at Lord & Taylor, smashing sales records, my nights at Publicans, learning from Cager and Fast Eddy how to play Liars' Poker. In my free time I outlined my Publicans novel, watched *Oprah* with Grandma, and sat on the stoop, reading. I was there on a crisp, classic October afternoon when the mailman came up the drive with the fateful pink envelope. I recognized the architect handwriting from twenty feet away. Taking the envelope from the mailman's hand I tore it into a half dozen pieces. A minute later I taped the pieces together. She missed me, loved me, wanted to meet me in the city for dinner.

I vowed not to go. I read a few more pages of my book, made myself a cup of tea, phoned Sidney and told her I'd come that night. I spent the rest of the afternoon primping and rehearsing different facial expressions in the bathroom mirror. Cool. Calm. Collected.

On my way to the train station I stopped into Publicans for some encouragement. The only person I knew at the bar was Fuckembabe. He asked where I was going all fancy.

"Dinner with my ex-girlfriend," I said, rolling my eyes.

"Ah, fuck 'em, babe."

"You said it, Fuckembabe."

"Fuck 'em, babe. *Fuck* 'em."

"Did you ever have a girl break your heart?" I asked.

Fuckembabe put his face an inch from mine. He gave me a nine-beer smile and the smell of liquor on his breath almost made my necktie go up and down. Still, I didn't back away, and he seemed touched, as if my steadiness were a show of loyalty. Then he imparted some fatherly advice I never forgot. "I once hooded a young wicky dixie," he said. "And when she wugged my hookah I told her I wouldn't fuggin' stand for that, no sir, and I rama lama whipsawed her the whole livelong diggledy doo. See wahm come from?"

Sidney was no longer living with her parents. She had an apartment on the top floor of a town house on the East Side. When she opened the door I felt weak. She was more beautiful than I remembered. The brown eyes, the autumnal yellow hair—it had been only two months, but I'd forgotten. I told myself that beauty can't be remembered any more than it can be described.

At the restaurant I ordered a scotch. Sidney ordered a vodka and tonic and came straight to the point. She apologized for hurting me again. But this apology was different. It didn't sound like the standard prelude to reconciliation that I was expecting. She talked about Trust-Funder—his family, his yacht, his sense of humor—as if he was more than a friend, more than a fling. She cared about him, she said, though she cared about me too. She was torn.

I couldn't bear to hear so many details about Trust-Funder. All the scotch at Publicans wouldn't be enough to erase the details Sidney was putting into my head. To change the subject I asked what she was doing. Working for a small ad agency, she said, and loving it. Apparently she'd abandoned her dreams of architecture and filmmaking. She asked what I was doing. I told her about my novel, the working title of which was *Tales of a Wayside Gin Mill.* I'd written eighteen pages so far. I told her about Smelly heaving a meat cleaver at someone in the bar, how the blade stuck in the wall like a tomahawk. I thought I might open the book with that. I knew that Publicans made Sidney uneasy, but I didn't have anything else to talk about, and I was trying to avoid the subject I knew would make her sick. Sensing that I was hiding something, she bore down.

"What are you doing for money?" she asked.

"I've got a job."

"Where?"

"Nowhere. It's hardly worth mentioning, just a stopgap kind of thing."

"JR. Sweetheart. Where are you working?"

"The Home Fashions department of Lord & Taylor."

"What fashions?"

"Ho-home."

The waiter came to take our order and Sidney waved him away. "We're going to need more time," she told him. "A lot more time." She straightened her silverware, refolded her napkin and stared at the white tablecloth as though it were the first page of a speech she was about to give. Then she delivered not so much a speech as a lamentation. Where's your ambition? What became of your hopes and goals? What was the point of going to Yale? Why in the hell are you selling candles and crystal?

"Because," I said miserably, "I'm good at it."

"Have you applied to newspapers? Have you sent out your articles from the *Yale Daily News*? Have you contacted the *New York Times*?"

"*New York*—? Please. You're cut off. No more vodka for you."

"You've always talked about the *Times*. You've always said the *Times* was your dream."

"I have?" I wasn't aware. "Look. The *Times* is way out of my league. The *Times* is like—you. It was a miracle I got into Yale, a miracle I met you. Lightning doesn't strike three times."

"You have to stick your neck out in this life, Trouble."

"I stuck my neck out. With you. Look where that got me." I scrunched my head into my shoulders. She laughed.

After dinner we went for a walk on Madison Avenue, looking in the windows of the shops. Sidney took my hand, pressed herself against me. I hated myself for how much I wanted her.

Back at her apartment we lay on the floor of her living room, talking, mostly about books. She was reading more than she had at Yale, she said, and discovering a whole new group of exciting young writers. I envied every writer she named, less because they were talented and published than because they had impressed Sidney. I also suspected they weren't her discoveries but Trust-Funder recommendations. I rolled across the floor toward Sidney and kissed her. Her lips were softer than I remembered. I undid her blouse. I cupped her breast, nudged her knees apart with my leg. She undid my belt and ground against me and started to say ooh and yes. Abruptly she stopped and pulled away. "Wait," she said. "Tonight's been lovely. Let's not ruin it."

"How will this ruin it?"

"I need to go slow."

A voice in my head told me Sidney wanted to go slow because I was hanging out at Publicans and working at Lord & Taylor. *If I'd walked in the door talking about my new job on Wall Street, we'd already be naked.* I jumped to my feet. Dizzy. The room was spinning. I'd had too much to drink. And yet not nearly enough. Sidney jumped up, caught me by the arm, asked me to stay so she could explain. I pulled my arm free. If I left right then I could salvage some pride. More important, I could catch the 1:19 and be at Publicans before last call.

twenty-eight | TIM

T HE BAR WAS PACKED. I SQUEEZED BETWEEN A QUARTET OF salesmen complaining about their bosses, or their bonuses, I couldn't tell, and a man whose wife had recently left him for another woman. Uncle Charlie had his hands full, advising them all at once. When he saw me, saw the look on my face, he snapped his head back as if someone had waved smelling salts under his nose.

"Who's dead?"

"Me. I just had dinner with Sidney."

"Bitches," he said, slamming a Dewars bottle on the bar. "They're all bitches."

The salesmen and the cuckold grunted in solidarity.

Uncle Charlie poured, and poured, and set before me a glass brimming with scotch. A Trevi Fountain of scotch. He then started opening bottles of beer for the salesmen and lost track of me. I looked around the barroom. Someone else might have seen nothing more than a random crowd of drinkers, but I saw my people. Kith and kin. Fellow travelers. Every sort of person was there—stockbrokers and safecrackers, athletes and invalids, mothers and supermodels—but we were as one. We'd all been hurt by something, or somebody, and so we'd all come to Publicans, because misery loves company, but what it really craves is a crowd.

Uncle Charlie turned again to me. "Okay," he said, "let's hear it."

I took a deep breath. Bad idea. Oxygen, combined with the scotch, made me sad again—and mumbly. Uncle Charlie told me later that I said something like, "Whenever someone dies, people talk about life being fragile, but fuck that, seems to me love is the fragile thing, it's hard to kill someone but love dies faster than fresh-cut flowers, is what I think, mumble mumble, fucking mumble." Uncle Charlie didn't know how to reply, but he didn't have a chance to reply, because I'd inadvertently set off a free-for-all. Men began voicing their opinions about love and women from every direction.

A man wearing a snazzy seersucker suit said love was no different than other intoxications. "All euphoria is followed by depression," he said. "What goes up—down. The measure of how drunk you are is how much pain you're in the next day—am I right? Same goes for love. You pay through the nose for every orgasm."

"Thanks," Uncle Charlie said. "It's going to take me a week to get that image out of my head."

A man beside Seersucker, whose hair looked like a large tobacco leaf spread across his scalp, stepped forward. "Okay, here's the deal on beautiful women," Tobacco Leaf said. "Beautiful women are often lonely, but never alone. See, they *always* have a boyfriend, so even if they're vulnerable, they're never available. It's one of life's conundrums."

Uncle Charlie nodded. "Conundrums," he said.

I heard a voice behind me. When I turned no one was there. I looked down. Level with my navel was a large aquiline nose. Attached to the nose was a man with piercing blue eyes and cheeks dented by deep Shirley Temple dimples. In an incongruous basso this dimpled imp asserted that women were more "evolved" than men, therefore more capable of contradictory emotions. They could hate you and love you at the same time, he said. With men, he said, it's all or nothing at all.

Uncle Charlie hummed a few bars of "All or Nothing at All." "Half a love never was dear to me," he said to Dimpled Imp.

A fourth man, with a forehead so large and blank that I felt an urge to write something on it, chimed in that if women were more evolved, it was only in the sense that extraterrestrials were more evolved. "Ever notice the peripheral vision broads have?" he said. "A man sees a woman, say, on the train, he stares like a bird dog staring at a dead duck. He can't help himself. But a woman can size you up without turning her head. When you're staring at a woman, she knows, pal, she knows, and she's staring right back, even if it looks like she's reading her paper. They're aliens, I tell you."

Uncle Charlie grumbled his agreement and pointed at Forehead's chest.

"The other thing about women that no one likes to talk about," Seersucker said to Tobacco Leaf, Dimpled Imp and Forehead, "is how they disappear. Like phantoms." Sometimes, Seersucker confessed, when he saw a beautiful woman, he followed her for a block or two, just to see where she was going. Was she married? Was she meeting a lover for an afternoon tryst? Was she shopping for underwear? Invariably the woman ducked into a doorway or a store, and when Seersucker followed, zap, she was gone.

"You sick fuck," said an off-duty cop drinking a Spanish coffee. "Do you have any idea how many creeps like you I collar every day?"

Seersucker, Tobacco Leaf, Dimpled Imp and Forehead all looked at their feet, ashamed.

"Know who's a very unattractive woman?" Uncle Charlie said. "Sigourney Weaver."

"I love her!" Seersucker said. "I'd leave my wife and kids for her."

"You'd leave your wife and kids for *Earl* Weaver," Tobacco Leaf said.

"You're not serious about Sigourney Weaver," Uncle Charlie said.

"Dead serious," Seersucker said.

"He looks serious," Dimpled Imp said.

Uncle Charlie lifted his hands off the bar as though it were a hot stove. He studied the cocktail glasses hanging over the bar, trying to choose the right glass to break over Seersucker's head. "In that case," he said to Seersucker, "there can be only one ineluctable conclusion. You don't mind if I say 'ineluctable,' do you? If you think Sigourney Weaver is sexy then you are a homosexual."

I too thought Sigourney Weaver was sexy, and I liked her name, a stage name chosen from a guest list in *The Great Gatsby*. Uncle Charlie was so indignant, however, that I didn't make a sound. He railed on about the "unfuckability" of Sigourney Weaver, then whammed his hand on the bar. Case closed. None of us was allowed to date Sigourney Weaver. And if we disobeyed, if any of us did date Sigourney Weaver, ever, we wouldn't be served in Publicans. We then debated who was the quintessence of womanhood. Which siren could there be no disagreement about, among any group of men? A straw poll was held, Elisabeth Shue won, though an old-timer with ears like apricots kept insisting that we were shortchanging Myrna Loy.

"Enough about broads," Uncle Charlie said. "It's depressing. I haven't had sex since the Cuban Missile Crisis."

The conversation shifted from women to baseball, a frequent segue at Publicans. Uncle Charlie began an impassioned disquisition on the subject of "those other fickle bitches—the Metropolitans." The Mets had clinched the National League East, and Uncle Charlie analyzed for us their chances in the playoffs and the Series. As Mets fans we were eager for his predictions, but just as he was getting warmed up a rowdy gaggle of college girls at the end of the bar held their empty glasses over their heads and shouted, "Can we get some service?"

"The aliens are thirsty," Seersucker muttered.

Uncle Charlie went to help the girls. I turned to my right, where a man about ten years older than I was leaning against the bar, reading a book. He had large black eyes, a bushy black moustache, and wore a smart black leather coat, very fashionable, very expensive. Handsome in a hard-to-believe, almost preposterous way, he held a martini glass as if it were a thorn-covered rose.

"Hey there," I said. "What are you reading?"

"Rilke."

I introduced myself. His name was Dalton. He was a lawyer—or said he was. He'd just gotten back from a 'round-the-world trip—or said he had. He wrote poetry—or said he did. Nothing he said seemed true, because he flatly refused to give any details, like what kind of law he practiced, where he'd traveled, or what kind of verse he wrote. All kinds of law, he said impatiently. Somewhere in the Far East, he said, waving his hand. Just your basic poetry, he said, adding, "Asshole." I thought his boldness, his vagueness, his black leather jacket, and his James Bond handsomeness, meant he must be a spy.

For someone so guarded Dalton turned out to be quite a talker. As long as the subject wasn't himself, he had a wide range of opinions he wished to share. Better than anyone at Publicans he understood how to keep the conversational shuttlecock from hitting the ground. We talked about art, movies, poetry, food, and we talked about talking. We agreed that Publicans was paradise for talkers. At most bars, Dalton said, people talk to justify drinking—at Publicans they drink to justify talking. I told him that Thomas Jefferson and Montaigne and Cicero all thought conversation the manliest art. I said that I thought conversation was still the best way we had of knowing each other. He seized my hand and shook it. "You said it!" he cried. "You said a mouthful, Asshole."

When Dalton asked why I was so dressed up, I told him I'd gone into the city to have my ex-girlfriend remove my heart from my chest and eat it in front of me. He shoved his book into my sternum. "You need to meet my friend Mr. Rilke," he said. "Rilke says, 'We are not to know why this and that masters us.' Rilke says, 'Sex is difficult; yes. But they are difficult things with which we have been charged. . . .'"

I wrote these and other lines on a napkin, along with the random and certifiable observations of Seersucker & Co. At closing time I felt fine. Sidney was a blur, like something that had happened decades before. I drank the last of my scotch, slammed the glass on the bar and pointed at Uncle Charlie's chest.

"What the?" Uncle Charlie said.

I looked down. I'd shattered my glass.

"Leave it, sport," he said, seeing the look on my face. "Go home."

"Yes," Dalton said, looking down at his leather coat, which I'd splashed with scotch. "By all means, Asshole. Go home."

I reeled down the sidewalk to Grandpa's house and passed out on the bicentennial sofa. Waking at dawn I did an impetuous thing. I gathered all my articles from Yale and put them, along with a hastily typed résumé, into an envelope addressed to the *New York Times*. I'd show Sidney. And when the *Times* turned me down I'd forward the rejection letter to her. Dropping the envelope into the mailbox outside Publicans, I continued on to Lord & Taylor, where I sold more than one thousand dollars' worth of merchandise, winning a silver letter opener, which I contemplated plunging into my heart.

A few days later I was shaving, getting ready for my shift at Lord & Taylor. Grandma came to the bathroom door. "Pat died," she said.

Pat? Pat died years ago. I squinted at Grandma's reflection in the mirror.

"Uncle Pat," she said. "Pat Byrne."

She meant the father of my other cousins, the boys Grandma had always held up as "perfect gentlemen."

"Those poor boys," she said, wiping her eyes with the towel I handed her. "Nine boys without a father. Imagine."

. . .

The church was hot, airless, overflowing with people. Grandma and I sat pressed together in a back pew and watched the Byrne sons carrying their father's casket. Each son had slicked-back hair, pinkish cheeks, and great wads of muscle under his suit. They were all from the same mold, they all looked like their father, though one son seemed to stand apart. He even seemed to shoulder most of the weight of the casket. My heart ached for him, for all the Byrnes, and yet I wanted to leave. I wanted to run to Publicans, talk with Dalton about Montaigne, drink away all thoughts of fathers and death. But after the service Grandma insisted I drive her to the Byrne house.

We sat in the living room with Uncle Pat's widow, Aunt Charlene. She was my mother's first cousin, my first cousin once removed, but I addressed her as Aunt Charlene, as I always had. When I was a boy Aunt Charlene seemed to sense the storm of thoughts blowing through my head, and she spoke to me with a kindness that made me instantly calmer. She was no different that day. We talked for a long time, but I remember only one subject we covered. Fathers. She confided in me that she worried how her sons would cope without their father. I sensed that she wanted me to tell her something helpful, impart some wisdom about being a fatherless son, but I had none to give.

Just then Aunt Charlene's son Tim, the strongest pallbearer, stepped forward. He apologized for interrupting. He shook my hand, accepted my condolences. His hand dwarfed mine. He was exactly my age but twice my size. He'd just graduated from Syracuse, where he'd played football, and his arms were the width of my legs. He spoke with the kind of blunt Long Island accent I'd worked hard to lose, but listening to him I wished I could get it back. His accent made him sound tough.

He asked if Aunt Charlene needed anything. Drink? Food? He held her hand as he asked. He was so sweet with his mother that Grandma looked at him with a mix of disbelief and adoration. Tim bent down and gave Aunt Charlene a kiss, then went off to get her a drink, fix her a sandwich, make sure the guests were comfortable. Grandma stared after him, then turned to me, her eye twitching, as if batting out a message in Morse code.

She didn't need to say it.

Real men take care of their mothers.

twenty-nine | TIMESMAN

DORA ANSWERED THE PHONE AT THE SALES DESK WHILE I WAS with a customer. Above my fraudulent spiel about the candles and soaps I heard Dora telling the caller I was busy and couldn't possibly be disturbed. "Who?" she shouted into the phone. "*New York Times*?"

I sprinted to the sales desk and ripped the phone from Dora.

"Hello?" I said. *"Hello?"*

It was a woman from the personnel department at the *Times*. Her name was Marie. In the weeks since I'd sent my clips to the *Times,* I'd forgotten putting the number for Lord & Taylor on my résumé. It had seemed safer than the number at Grandpa's, where someone might think a caller was trying to get down a bet. Marie said my clips had been read by an editor, who liked them. Half of me wanted to scream. The other half wondered which wise guy from Publicans was doing a pretty fair falsetto and pranking me. Smelly—is that you? But this Marie person kept using words Smelly wouldn't know, so I decided she was the real thing. The *Times* offered a training program for recent college graduates, she said. You started as a copyboy, but you could work your way up to a position as a full-fledged reporter. Was I interested? I tried to think of the perfect way to say that I was. I wanted to sound casual, but not too casual. Eager, but not overeager. I gripped the phone tighter and looked at Dora. No help. I looked at the customer I'd just abandoned. Less help. She was tapping her foot, checking her watch. I decided to keep it simple. "I'm interested," I said to Marie.

"Good. How soon can you get me some more samples of your work?"

"More? I sent you everything I wrote for my college paper."

"Huh, that is a problem. The editors feel they need to see more before they can make a decision."

"I suppose I could go to New Haven and look through the microfilms at the library. Maybe I missed something."

"Why don't you do that. And if you find anything, let me know."

After hanging up the phone I was delirious with adrenaline. I danced back to the customer and sold her a box of jasmine-scented candles, eight or twelve hand towels, and a Waterford cigarette lighter, which helped me edge out

Dora for high seller that day. The prize was dinner for two at an Italian restaurant. When I gave Dora the gift certificate she put her hand on my cheek. "Such a good boy," she said. "I don't know why all the other ladies hate you."

Waiting to pull out of Grand Central, leaning my head against the window, I saw her walk through my reflection. She wore a tan linen skirt and a sheer ivory short-sleeved top, and she was carrying a slice of pizza on a paper plate. Trying to find a car that wasn't crowded, she stooped to peer into my window, then continued down the platform. Moments later she came back. This time I waved. She jumped, then smiled. She came into the train car and sat beside me. "Hello, Trouble," she said. "Where you heading?"

"Yale. To get some more clips to show the *New York Times*."

"No!"

"I sent them my stuff and they want to see more."

She squeezed my knee.

"You?" I said.

"Home to see my parents."

As the train clacked north I talked about fate. Fate kept throwing us together, I argued. From Constitutional Law to Grand Central our paths were forever crossing. Obviously fate was trying to tell us something. How else to explain this chance encounter? Especially when I was going back to Yale on an errand inspired by her. The universe, I said, wants us together.

She let me plead my case while she ate her pizza. When she finished she patted her hands together, to get rid of the crumbs, and said, "Maybe I was wrong."

"Really?"

"Yes. Maybe you should have gone to law school after all."

I frowned. She stroked my arm. She said that she agreed with everything I said, but she didn't want to risk hurting me again. "That's what I was trying to tell you when we had dinner last month," she said. "I'm confused. I'm fucked up. I need—"

"I know. Time."

"You're always so sure about people," she said. "Everything is so black or white with you. You don't have any trouble letting people in."

"I wish I knew how to let people out."

She patted her lips with a paper napkin. "My stop," she said. "Good luck with the *Times*. Let me know how it goes."

She kissed me and hurried off the train.

When I reached New Haven all I wanted to do was find a bar and call my mother. I had to force myself to sit in Sterling Library and look through microfilms of old newspapers, which did not improve my mood. Though there were indeed articles I'd forgotten, there had been good reason for forgetting them. They were insignificant briefs about nothing, a few hundred words here and there about this speaker or that event. Marie at the *Times* wouldn't deign to use them to wrap up her unfinished sandwich after lunch.

Now I really needed a drink. I phoned my former roommate, who had stayed in New Haven to attend law school. We met another friend and two women at a bar. After a few drinks we all piled into the friend's car and headed for a restaurant. Along the way my friend accidentally cut off a car full of young men our age. They were wearing muscle shirts and gold chains and they were not appeased by our apologetic wave. At the next red light they rushed our car and threw open the doors. I was in the front passenger seat with a woman on my lap. I leaned across her, to shield her from the blows, which made me a stationary target. One man, wearing rings or brass knuckles, punched me six times, rapidly, in the side of my face, saying something like, "Yalie dick," while another man exchanged punches with my friend, the driver. When the light turned green my friend managed to get the car into gear and sped away.

My lip was gushing blood. A bump on my forehead felt like a budding antler. Something was wrong with my eye. We went to a hospital but the wait was several hours. "We'll self-medicate," my friend said, leading me to a bar around the corner. I wondered why the bells in Harkness were ringing so late. I asked the bartender. "They're only ringing in your personal belfry there, ace," he said. "You prolly got some kinda concussion. Tequila's the best thing for that." I looked at him. He was familiar. The bar was familiar. Was this the bar where I drank up the seventy-five dollars my mother had sent me to become JR Maguire? I told my friends that JR Maguire wouldn't have gotten mugged. JR Maguire was too smart to let something like this happen to him. They had no idea what I was talking about.

I slept a few hours on my roommate's sofa and at dawn I caught the first train to New York. From Grand Central I took a cab to the *Times*. Standing across the street from the newspaper I marveled at how grand and august the building looked, the globe lights along its front wall with their Old English lettering: 𝔗𝔦𝔪𝔢𝔰. The same typeface as the sign above Publicans. I wanted to sneak closer and peer through the windows, but there were no windows. I thought of the great reporters who passed through that front door each day, then thought of my pathetic clips in the folder under my arm. I wished those muscle-shirted thugs in New Haven had beaten me to death.

A man stood ten feet from me. He wore a checked blazer, white shirt, regimental necktie, and his thick shock of white hair reminded me of Robert Frost. Though he had no teeth he was eating what appeared to be a baloney sandwich, and beaming at me, as if he were about to offer me a bite, as if he knew me. I smiled back, trying to place him, before noticing that he was wearing nothing from the waist down. His "personal" baloney, in the glaring early-morning sunlight, was white as scrimshaw. When I looked at it, he looked at it, then looked up, smiling still wider, delighted that I'd noticed.

Now there could be no doubt. Clearly the universe was speaking to me, and it was saying that I was not meant to work at the *Times*. The signs were everywhere, from my encounter with Sidney to my assault in New Haven. Now this. The universe was telling me that I would have been to the *Times* what Naked Frost was to Times Square—an obscene intruder. As cops descended on Naked Frost and dragged him off, I wanted to rush to his defense, to tell the cops that Naked Frost wasn't to blame, he was only an unwitting messenger of the universe. I felt more kinship with the man than pity or contempt for him. Between the two of us, I probably had more alcohol in my bloodstream.

In a way, I was relieved. Had I landed the job at the *Times* I couldn't have summoned the courage to walk into that building each day. It was all I could do now to walk across the street and push my way through the revolving doors, into the marble lobby, up to the security guard. I told him my name and handed him my folder and asked him to give it to Marie in personnel. Hold on, he said. He picked up a phone, spoke to someone, hung up. "Thoid flaw," he said to me.

"Excuse me?"

"Thoid flaw."

"Third—me? No, no, I just came to drop off this folder. I don't need to see her. I don't *want* to see her."

"What can I tell you? She's waitin' fawya."

The only sensible thing to do was run. Catch the next train to Manhasset, hide in Publicans, never look back. But how could I disappear now that I'd been announced? Marie would think I was a kook, and that was something I could not abide. Better that she see me disheveled and half drunk than that she think me unstable.

Rising to the third floor I studied my reflection in the brass doors of the elevator. I'd always imagined striding into the newsroom of the *New York Times* in a brand-new suit, with polished black lace-ups, an English spread collar, a gold necktie, and matching suspenders. Instead I was wearing torn jeans, scuffed loafers, a T-shirt flecked with blood. And my right eye was swollen shut.

Heads turned as I stepped off the elevator. I looked like a deranged reader come to settle a score with a reporter. An editor near the mailboxes chewed an unlit cigar and gawked. His cigar made me think of my breath, which must have been Fuckembabe-esque. I'd have traded ten years of my life for a mint.

The newsroom was one whole city block long, a fluorescent prairie of metal desks and men. Presumably there were women working at the *Times* in 1986, but I didn't see any. I saw nothing but men stretching to the horizon, dapper men, bookish men, distinguished men, wizened men, all milling about beneath rain clouds of smoke. *I've been here before.* One man I recognized from TV. He had been in the news recently for going to jail to protect a source, and he was known for his ubiquitous pipe, which he was puffing that morning. I wanted to approach him and tell him how much I admired him for going to jail in defense of the First Amendment, but I couldn't because I looked as if I'd been in jail also, and not for defending any amendments.

At the far end of the newsroom, at last, I saw a woman, one lone woman, sitting at a tiny desk. Marie, no doubt. The walk toward her took a week. Everyone I passed was on the phone, and I was certain they were all talking with one another about me. I wanted to apologize to each of them for profaning this place. I wanted to apologize to Marie, who now rose and received me with such a look of distress that I wondered if she'd have the guard in the lobby fired five minutes after I left. "Jay?" she said.

"JR."

"Right."

We shook hands.

She pointed me to a chair and seated herself behind her desk. She straightened a few envelopes, put a pencil in a pencil cup and a sheaf of papers in an out-basket. I felt sure she was equally quick when judging people, putting them into their proper places. She then turned to me and waited for me to explain myself. I considered lying, but didn't have the energy. I considered simply smiling, but I didn't want to cause my split lip to start bleeding again. Also, I thought a tooth might be loose. There was nothing to do but tell her about the mugging, concisely. I almost made the case that I'd actually been mugged twice, if you counted Sidney, but decided against trying to be clever. When I finished Marie tapped a long fingernail on her desk. "You *can* tell a story," she said. "I'll give you that."

I assured her that I meant no disrespect, showing up in this condition. I explained the mix-up with the guard. I told her that I loved the *Times,* worshipped the *Times,* read every book I could get my hands on about the history of the *Times,* including out-of-print memoirs by fusty old editors. In trying to explain my feelings for the *Times* I suddenly understood them better myself. It dawned on me why I'd been fascinated with the *Times* since I was a teenager. Yes, the newspaper offered a clearly delineated, black-and-white vision of the world, but what it also offered was that elusive bridge between my mother's dreams and mine. Journalism was just the right blend of respectability and rebelliousness. Like lawyers, *Times* reporters wore Brooks Brothers suits and read books and crusaded for the downtrodden—but they also drank hard and told stories and hung out in bars.

This wasn't the opportune moment for an epiphany. The exertion of explaining myself, understanding myself, and profusely apologizing for myself—and all the while trying to aim my tequila breath wide of Marie's nose—made me pale. And my lip was bleeding again. Marie handed me a tissue and asked if I'd like a glass of water. She told me to relax. Just relax. A young man so obviously unconcerned with appearances, she said, so open to adventure, so enamored of the *Times* and knowledgeable about its traditions, would make a very fine reporter indeed. In fact, she added, I looked as though I had the makings of a war correspondent. She saw in that chair beside her desk something more than a twenty-one-year-old screwup from Long Island with a black eye and a hangover and a folder full of dreadful writing. Whatever else I might be, she said, I was "refreshing."

A long time passed while Marie stared at me, thinking. I could see that she was weighing two options. She blinked her eyes, twice, and clearly chose Option B. She said there was a protocol to hiring people. She didn't have the power to offer me the job right then. Editors would have to be consulted. Procedure would have to be followed. "However," she said, "I do like the cut of your jib."

I'd never heard this expression. I thought she'd said, "I'd like to cut off your jib." I tried to think how to respond but Marie was on her feet, offering her hand again. Barring something unforeseen, she said, she'd soon be able to welcome me to the *New York Times*.

When I barreled into Publicans two hours later with my news, the place went berserk. Finally, the men said, I was *doing* something with my life. Getting into college, that was fine. Graduating, that was all well and good. But this was a real accomplishment. Newspapermen—Jimmy Cannon, Jimmy Breslin, A. J. Liebling, Grantland Rice—were barroom gods, and my being admitted to their ranks merited booming hurrahs and bear hugs.

Uncle Charlie gave my hand a bone-crushing pump, then decided that wasn't enough. He came around from behind the bar and kissed my cheek. "The *New York Motherfucking Times*," he said. The last time I'd seen him that proud was when he explained the over and under to me, when I was eleven, and I got it right away. Colt bowed at the waist and said the same thing he'd said when I got into Yale, the same thing he said whenever I did anything right. "Must have been all those Wordy Gurdys."

Steve roared. He made me retell certain parts of the interview, describe again and again Naked Frost, and the security guard, and the horrified faces as I walked through the newsroom. He examined my shiner under the bar light, and I thought he might produce a jeweler's eyepiece for a better look. I couldn't decide which impressed him more, my black eye or my new job. But he was more than impressed. He was vindicated. His innate optimism was confirmed. Steve believed that everything works out in the end, that comedy always follows tragedy, that good things happened to all bad boys from Publicans, and now something very good had happened to the nephew of his senior bartender.

"Extra! Extra!" he said. "Junior is a *Times*man!"

Then it was enough already about me. Steve and the men turned back to the TV, where the Mets were locked in a sixteen-inning nail-biter with the Houston Astros in the National League Championship Series. While everyone drank and watched the game I ducked into the phone booth and dialed my mother.

The Mets won Game Six of the World Series a few days before I started at the *Times*. Down to their last strike, given up for dead, they came storming back and stunned the Boston Red Sox in the bottom of the tenth. Now the Mets were going to win the whole thing, everyone at Publicans knew. "Those poor bastards in Boston," Uncle Charlie said to me, just after Ray Knight crossed home plate with the winning run. "Think of the bars like this one across New England. Ach. My heart breaks for them." Uncle Charlie loved underdogs, and no underdog was more tragic than the Sox. For a moment he made me ashamed of my unalloyed happiness about the Mets winning.

By my calculations the Mets' victory parade would march through Manhattan on the same morning, at the same moment, I was marching into the *Times* for my first day of work. Of all the signs I'd ever gotten from the universe, this was the loudest and clearest. Against all odds, my team and I were no longer losers. My new life, my real life, my life as a winner, was under way at last. I was moving beyond all previous failure, beyond the dangerous lure of failure, outgrowing my boyish indecision about whether to try or not to try.

There was only one slender thread connecting me to my old life, to my sense of myself as a lost cause. Sidney. I'd received another letter from her that week. Still loved me, still missed me, still needed time. Enclosed was a photo of herself. I stood at Publicans just after Game Six ended, rereading her letter and gazing at her photo as the celebration raged all around me. The bar was bedlam. We were all full of whiskey, full of an unreasonable faith in ourselves and the future, inferred from the good fortunes of our Mets, and I got an idea. I asked Fuckembabe to bring me a pen and a stamp from Steve's basement office. He either told me to check the lower shelf or go fuck myself. I got the pen and stamp from Uncle Charlie, then scratched out my address on Sidney's envelope and readdressed it back to her. I resealed the envelope, her letter and photo inside, and pushed my way through the crowd, through the front door, to the mailbox just outside. My lucky mailbox. The same mailbox from which I'd sent my clips to the *Times*.

It was vividly clear to me. If I wrote Sidney to take all the time she needed, I'd win her in the end. I would outlast Trust-Funder, and whoever else came along, and Sidney and I would marry. We would live in a house near her parents and have two towheaded children, and every time she yawned or took a phone call in the other room my stomach would lurch. That life waited for me, meticulously planned, prearranged. I could see it towering before me like a drive-in movie screen. But there was another life waiting, a Sidneyless life, also prearranged. I couldn't see it yet, but I could sense it, believe in it, thanks to the *Times* and the Mets and Publicans. I could hear the voices of that other life as distinctly as the voices at my back, inside the bar. I remembered Professor Lucifer lecturing us about free will versus fate, the riddle that had vexed great minds through the ages, and I wished I'd paid more attention, because leaning against my lucky mailbox, dangling Sidney's letter above the slot, I didn't know why fate and free will needed to be mutually exclusive. Maybe, I thought, when we come to our crossroads, we choose freely, but the choice is between two fated lives.

I let the envelope go. I'd never rebuffed Sidney before. No one had ever rebuffed Sidney before. I knew that when she received her own letter and photo—return to sender, no comment—she'd never contact me again. I walked back inside Publicans, asked Uncle Charlie for another scotch and told him what I'd done. He pointed at my chest and we drank a toast. To me. To the Mets. On October 25, 1986, after I'd lost the great love of my life, Uncle Charlie declared to the bar—no one was listening, but it was nice to hear him declare it—that his nephew was a winner.

thirty | MR. SALTY

B EING A COPYBOY WASN'T MUCH MORE COMPLICATED THAN BEING a clerk in Home Fashions. A copygirl explained the whole job to me in five minutes. I was responsible for "fetching sandwiches" and "separating carbons." Since the editors didn't have time to get their own meals, she said, I'd go around the newsroom throughout the day, taking orders, and then run across the street to Al's All-Night Deli. The rest of my time I'd spend gathering and sorting paper from the wire room. The *Times* had computers, but the editors, especially the older editors, refused to use them. Thus, paper still flooded the newsroom. Articles, essays, bulletins, wires, memos, stories, and summaries of stories being offered for tomorrow's front page—it all came spluttering and chattering off big printers, in thick sets of twelve carbon copies, which had to be pulled apart, folded a certain way, and distributed—fast. Many editors wouldn't know about a breaking news event until they saw the bulletin land in their wire baskets, so copykids were a disproportionately critical link in the chain of information. Even more critical: Top editors got top copies, on which the ink was most legible, and bottom editors got bottom copies, which were faintest, and in some cases illegible. "It's a status thing," the copygirl said. "You'll get yelled at if a bottom editor gets a top copy—but God help you if a top editor gets a bottom copy."

She rolled her eyes and expected me to roll mine. I was so glad for the job, however, so awed by the *Times*, that I couldn't wipe the look of exuberant joy off my face. *You mean it's my responsibility to feed all these talented journalists? And to let these famous editors know what's going on in the world?* "Sounds great!" I said.

From then on the copygirl avoided me, and I overheard her talking with another copygirl, referring to me as "that twit from Long Island."

Friendlier copykids explained the big picture of the training program. It was, they said, a series of small indignities followed by exponentially larger rewards. You fetched sandwiches, you separated carbons, you worked nights, holidays, weekends, until an editor noticed you. Maybe he'd like the way you always remembered that he wanted spicy mustard on his pastrami. Maybe he'd appreciate the tight fold you gave his carbons. Suddenly you were his protégé, and whenever possible he'd pass you an author interview for the book review, or a roundup for the real estate section. If you handled these assignments reasonably well he'd give you better ones. A shooting, a train derailment, a gas leak in the Bronx. One of these would be your big chance, the story that would make or break your newsroom reputation. If you made the most of your big chance you'd get a tryout on the city desk. Thirty days straight, no time off, writing, writing, a test of endurance as much as talent. The tryout was the grail. The tryout was the whole point of being a copykid. If you survived the tryout, physically and mentally, without any mistakes—above all, without causing the newspaper to run a dreaded correction—then a secret committee would convene and decide once and for all if you were *Times* material. If so, you'd be promoted to full-time reporter and given a desk and a living wage. If not, you could stick around as long as you liked, fetching sandwiches and separating carbons until you turned sixty-five, but you'd always be a copykid, a drone, a newsroom nonperson.

Given these conditions, and the cutthroat competition, it was to be expected that the two dozen copykids in the training program scuttled around the newsroom like rats in a maze. And yet we were calm compared to the editors, several of whom seemed moments away from a full-on psychotic episode. Some drank beer while they worked. Others ran to a bar across the street between editions for a blast of something stronger. And everyone smoked. Smoking was not only permitted but required, and most days the newsroom was more fogbound than Manhasset Bay. One notorious editor started his day with a pipe, switched to cigars as the afternoon wore on, then chain-smoked unfiltered Camels in the hour before deadline. He looked 150 years old and snacked on the entrails of copykids. His nickname was Smoky the Bastard, and several copykids warned me to stay as far from him as possible.

Though the *Times* reminded me of Yale—too many smart people in a confined space—I didn't feel intimidated. I felt right at home, and I thought the reason must be the junky furniture and the stained orange carpet and the backed-up toilets. My years at Grandpa's house had been ideal preparation. But of course the real reason for my relative calm was Publicans. No matter what happened in the newsroom during the day, I knew that the barroom was waiting for me at night. I could always count on the men at Publicans to give me a pep talk, and the women to give me fashion tips. All *Times*men wore smart suspenders, matching neckties, and cap-toed shoes as big and seamlessly constructed as canoes, and though I didn't have money for such things, my former coworkers from Lord & Taylor sat with me at Publicans and gave me pointers on augmenting my wardrobe. They taught me to "borrow" things from department stores. Suspenders and neckties, they said, could be "tried out," then returned. And I could always "smell successful," they said, by stopping into a store on my way to work and giving myself a few squirts from the testers.

I was madly happy. I put in long hours in the newsroom and volunteered to work overtime. I even dropped by the newspaper on days off, acting as if I belonged, pretending to be busy. If I couldn't find anything else to do, I would hang out in the morgue, where the *Times* archived every article dating back to the Civil War. I would read byline folders of star reporters, studying their style. On a whim one day I asked the woman who ran the morgue if she had a file on my father. She did indeed. The file was thin, but fascinating. I brought it out to the newsroom and sat reading it as though it were the Pentagon Papers. One article, just after the Beatles had appeared on Ed Sullivan, quoted my father as an expert on rock 'n' roll. While reading I started to whistle "I Want to Hold Your Hand."

"Who the fuck is—whistling!" Smoky the Bastard shrieked.

Scores of reporters and editors stopped and turned.

"Me?" I said.

"Whistling in a newsroom is bad luck—asshole!"

Everyone was staring. I couldn't think of anything to say. When everyone turned back to their work, smirking, I checked the clock on the wall. Five-thirty. If I left right then I could make happy hour at Publicans.

Hangdog, walking down to Penn Station, I came upon a commotion outside the Penta Hotel. Fire engines. Cops. Swarms of onlookers. "What's going on?" I asked a woman.

"Hotel's on fire."

My big chance. I ducked into a phone booth and dialed the city desk. An editor answered. "Hi, this is JR Moehringer!" I said. "I'm down here at the Penta and it looks like the hotel is going up in flames!"

"*Who* is this?"

"JR Moehringer. New copyboy. *I can smell the smoke.*"

"The Penta is—on fire? You smell *smoke*?"

"Yes sir. Burning my nose. Thick."

"Jesus H. Christ. Okay, let me patch you to rewrite. Tell him what you see. Give him some color. Then go find someone in charge out there. Bob, can you take dictation from someone named Guillermo Winger?"

I'm being patched to rewrite. What a break for me that the Penta was burning to the ground. My days of fetching sandwiches and separating carbons were numbered. The editors would arrange my tryout immediately. I couldn't wait to tell Uncle Charlie and Steve about my coup, my scoop, my personal

"Penta Gone" Papers—that would get a big laugh in the barroom. Knowing that the men at the bar would want to hear all about the fire, in full detail, I turned to watch. The firefighters seemed remarkably calm. They were standing around, laughing, chatting. The cops too. Nobody seemed all that concerned. I looked at the hotel. No flames. No broken windows. No smoke. But I still smelled the smoke. I turned again. On the other side of the phone booth was a pretzel cart. The vendor was gabbing with the firefighters and forgetting about his pretzels, which were turning black and giving off sulfurous clouds of smoke that blew directly into my face. Uh-oh. I hung up the phone and sprinted toward the firefighter wearing the biggest hat. He had such a boiled ham of a face that he could have been the mayor of Manhasset. "What's the story here, Chief?" I said. "I mean, Officer? I mean, what gives? I'm JR Moehringer. From the *Times*."

"Relax, kid, relax. Everything is okeydokey. It's a drill. We do this once a month."

"The hotel's not on fire?"

"Nah."

"Are you sure?"

Hearing the disappointment in my voice the firefighter inclined toward me, to see if I were an aspiring arsonist. I walked dejectedly back to the pay phone and dialed the city desk. The same editor answered. "Winger!" he said. "Sorry I lost you. Must have cut you off when I tried to transfer the call. Hold on now, the next voice you hear will be Bob. He's going to take your feed."

"That won't be necessary."

"What?"

"The Penta doesn't actually seem to be—on fire. Per se."

"What?"

"It's just a drill."

"A what?"

"A drill."

"Winger, for chrissakes, you said you smelled smoke."

"Right. When I spoke to you—it's a funny thing, actually—I was standing next to a pretzel cart. And the pretzels were burning."

I heard the editor wheezing, as if maybe he'd breathed in some pretzel smoke too. He caught his breath and yelled at Bob to stand down. "False alarm," I heard him say. "Some copyboy . . . pay phone outside the Penta . . . burning pretzels . . ." I couldn't hear what Bob said, but his tone didn't sound pleasant. The editor came back on the phone. "Thanks for calling," he said. "Thanks for making me go into the Page One meeting, like a schmuck, with a false alarm. Why don't you knock off for the day. Go get yourself a pretzel, okay, Mr. Salty?"

Dial tone.

Mr. Salty? I hoped that nickname wasn't going to stick. Even Guillermo Winger would have been better than Mr. Salty.

The train to Manhasset broke down in the freight yards just outside Penn Station. The lights died and we didn't move again for two hours. Sitting in the dark I replayed my day over and over. *Whistling in a newsroom is bad luck—asshole! Go get yourself a pretzel, okay, Mr. Salty?* When the train finally got under way, when I reached the front door to Publicans, it was about eight-thirty, and I didn't walk through the door—I dove.

Joey D's cousin Michael was tending bar, and I was glad. Michael was the right man for the job, the perfect bartender for my mood. I needed distraction, new topics to fill my head, and Michael was a wholesale supplier of new topics. As the only sober person in Publicans—he'd been off booze for years—Michael was always lucid and bursting with interesting facts and ideas he'd culled from his reading. He was also famously cranky, and I craved his crankiness too. He looked like a recently commissioned Ulysses Grant: fearsome, bearded, bristle-headed, dying for a cigar. Now more than ever I needed to sit with General Grant, to commiserate about the whole bloody campaign. Before I was all the way onto the stool, General Grant was out of the blocks like a shot, talking about Donald Trump and Caspar Weinberger and Babe Ruth and Marla Hanson and John Gotti and Carlo Gambino and the Archduke Franz Ferdinand and the *Achille Lauro* and gridlock and quarks and ozone depletion and what the W. B. stood for in Yeats's name. The acrid odor of burned pretzels began to subside.

Working the other end of the bar was Joey D. I waved to him, but he looked right through me, as if hypnotized. He was talking, though no one was within two feet of him. A full-on conversation with his pet mouse, only this time it looked as if his mouse were talking back. I asked General Grant what the hell was wrong with his cousin. "There's been a Josie sighting," he said, wiping the bar with a rag.

"Oh no," I said. "She's here? Tonight?"

He gave an annoyed nod.

Joey D and Josie had recently divorced, and since their parting was not amicable the scheduler took pains to make sure they never worked together. Some nights, however, due to illness or vacations, it couldn't be helped—Josie and Joey D were forced to work side by side. On those nights Joey D would look more like an undertaker than a bartender. Watching Josie as she moved among the tables, he'd tell customers under his breath how she'd done him wrong. One memorably uncomfortable Josie Night, the men dubbed Joey D's end of the bar the Beer-muda Triangle. People wandered down for a drink and were never heard from again—sucked into the vortex of Joey D's sad tale of woe.

Uncle Charlie blamed himself. It was he and Pat who'd originally brought Joey D and Josie together. Worst bet of my life, Uncle Charlie said whenever Joey D was mooning and whining about Josie. Other bartenders rolled their eyes behind Joey D's back and joked about "Josie and the Pussy-Whipped." Even Steve, who loved Joey D, lost patience now and then. At least once he'd summoned Joey D to the basement and told him to grow up. "You can't be acting this way in a barroom," Steve said. "It *depresses* people. Time to be a man, Joey D. Be a man." When I heard about Steve calling Joey D on the carpet, I shuddered. I'd rather be put on the rack, I thought, than summoned to the basement by Steve and lectured on manhood.

I couldn't tell Steve or any of the men that Joey D had my full sympathy and support. If I'd been forced to work with Sidney I'd have behaved no better. Besides, I couldn't think ill of Joey D, no matter what he did. I'd always feel grateful to him for being kind to me and McGraw when we were boys, for teaching me to bodysurf and scanning the waves for McGraw's head. Also, I knew that Joey D continued to watch Uncle Charlie, making sure *his* head didn't go under. Joey D considered himself Uncle Charlie's lifeguard, bodyguard and rear guard. He fretted over Uncle Charlie's gambling. He defended Uncle Charlie in every barroom brawl. And after Uncle Charlie had put in a night behind the bar, Joey D would sponge up his stains and spills. "Fucking Chas," Joey D would say, rubbing. "When will he realize—a clean bar is a happy bar." Then Joey D would take a wire brush and buff out the indents in the wood where Uncle Charlie had slammed bottles in anger or enthusiasm. For my money, that was love.

Subconsciously I also liked, and slightly envied, the way Joey D worked out his rage. If he felt brokenhearted, he broke a few heads. He unapologetically took out his frustrations about Josie on drunks who made trouble at Publicans, and he did it with style. The barroom brawl was Joey D's art form. He was to bar fighting what Hemingway was to bullfighting—a practitioner, a connoisseur, an apologist. I once asked Joey D how many fights he'd been in over the years and he counted slowly, rapturously, like Casanova recalling how many women he'd had. "At least three hundred," he said. "And I only lost one." He paused, reflected. "Actually," he said, "never mind, that one was a draw."

Joey D believed that his finest hour came about when some hardass, after being thrown out of Publicans, ripped a post from the back fence and began swinging it at the crowd. Joey D caught the fencepost in midair, snatched it away and broke it over his knee, then knocked the guy cold. "I'm not bragging—don't get me wrong—but that was the coolest fucking thing I ever did." *CoolestfuckingthingIeverdid.*

The secret to fighting, Joey D told me, was relaxing. To kick the ass of another, you must unclench your own ass. Soft fist, he said, hard punch. It was all very Zen, and hard to believe from a meat-and-potatoes palooka like Joey D. But it was true. The most relaxed look I'd ever seen on his Muppet face was while saving me from the beating of a lifetime. It happened when a loudmouth got into a beef with Uncle Charlie. There was a long list of names no one was allowed to call Uncle Charlie—Baldy, Kojak, Egg Head, Penis Top, Chrome Dome, Mr. Clean—and the loudmouth used them all in one shocking taboo diatribe. I stepped forward to defend my uncle and the loudmouth grabbed my shirt and cocked his fist. I was a half second from a busted nose and a flight through the front window when Joey D bounded over the bar like the winner of the U.S. Open hurdling the net. I'll never forget his face—that same serene expression he wore while floating on his back at Gilgo—as he served the loudmouth down the length of the barroom floor, an ace worthy of McEnroe.

I left General Grant and took my drink to Joey D's end. I sat with him while he watched Josie and complained to his mouse. Soon we were inter-rupted by the Publicans softball team tromping through the back door. They had beaten Kilmeade's behind the sterling play of Cager. Though his visor was pulled low I saw the victorious grin on Cager's dirt-streaked face. He looked as if he were just back from a successful mission. Something in me, more than in Cager, always made me see his visor as a netted helmet, and the softball bat he carried over his shoulder as an M60. I shook his hand and felt a bolt of testosterone shoot up my arm. "Buy you a beer?" I said.

"That what you Ivy Leaguers call a *rhetorical* question?" he said.

He asked how I was doing at the new job, and I heard myself telling him about phoning in the pretzel fire. I didn't know why I was telling him. Maybe I wanted sympathy. I should have known Cager wasn't in the sympa-thy business. "Guillermo Winger?" he shouted, laughing, rapping his bat on the ground. "Mr. Salty? Oh that's rich! Oh that's fucking priceless!" He laughed so hard that I thought he would have an asthma attack. "Oh you must have been—*tied in knots*—about that pretzel fire!" I started laughing too. *So I phoned in a pretzel fire! So what?* It wasn't a total loss if it could pro-vide a prince of a guy like Cager with such a belly laugh. Now we were both stooped over, laughing, smacking the bar, smacking each other, and when I smacked Cager's back it was no different than smacking the bar. Solid oak. No give.

When Cager was able to catch his breath, when he'd dried his eyes and taken a swig of cold beer, he told me to relax. Relax, kid, just fucking relax. There are mistakes, he said, and then there are mistakes. In the army he once accidentally blew up a chopper. Come on, I said. God's truth, he said. He was firing mortar rounds, target practice, and something went wrong. A mortar jammed. He jimmied the thing and there was a fizzing noise—the gun fired. An unmanned Chinook was sitting on a helipad nearby. "Boom," Cager said. "Still owe Uncle Sam about six mil for that one."

The time had come to set aside all these irrelevant topics and talk about the only thing that mattered, the evening's main event, the softball game. Other players gathered 'round and we all hung on Cager like ornaments on a Christmas tree as he recounted the victory. Someone complimented his nifty glove work at third base. Second coming of Brooks Robinson, someone said. Shucks, Cager said, feigning modesty. More than his play in the field he was proud of one moment of horseplay with Steve. Several home runs had been hit, Cager said, and each one splashed down in the pond beyond the fence. Cager shouted to Steve, "We're running out of balls, we're going to have to fish some out of that pond—did you bring the pole?" "Naw," Steve said, "she's coming down later with the kids." Steve was referring to his wife, Georgette, née Zaleski. Cager had to call time-out until he and Steve could compose themselves.

I left Cager and drifted back up the bar to General Grant. He was now engrossed in conversation with an investment banker in a blue pinstripe suit, a prosperous-looking man in his fifties, whose pepper-and-salt mustache seemed grown specifically to match his black-and-white tie. They were both smoking cigars, discussing the Civil War, and I thought the conversation must have been prompted by how much General Grant looked like General Grant. But it turned out that Banker was a hard-core Civil War buff. He told me and General Grant a few little-known facts about Shiloh, Antietam, Gettysburg. He also told us that Lincoln ran a bar as a young man and slept in the back room.

"Did you know that?" I asked General Grant.

"Who doesn't know that?" General Grant said. "Lincoln also was in the distillery business. Made a very smooth Kentucky bourbon."

Colt spun me away. "You think you're so smart," he said. "Suck on this. How many Batman villains can you name? There are supposedly three dozen and I can only come up with ten." He thrust a sheet of paper at me.

I almost said something about the absurdity of Yogi Bear making a list of Batman villains, but Colt was so earnest, so solicitous of my help, that I held my tongue and looked over what he had so far. Joker, Riddler, Puzzler, King Tut. It reminded me of the list of names no one was allowed to call Uncle Charlie. "How about Bookworm?" I said.

"Bookworm!" Colt said, slapping his forehead. "Forgot about Bookworm."

Uncle Charlie arrived. Unwrapping a new box of Marlboros, he asked General Grant for a vodka with a cranberry splash, then put a hand to his temple. "JR," he said, "I was reading today and came across the word 'nidifugous.' What does it mean?"

I shrugged.

Uncle Charlie asked for the Book of Words. General Grant reached behind the bar and brought down from a shelf a beautiful old volume, which
everyone called the Book of Words, often with a whispery reverence, as though
it were the Book of Kells. General Grant set the book before Uncle Charlie,
who leafed through the pages and announced that "nidifugous" meant "leaving the nest shortly after hatching." He was delighted by this definition. Now
I was wedged between Uncle Charlie and Banker, the beer was cold, the subject was words, and I was so happy that I didn't ever want to move. But I
needed to pee.

In the men's room I thought I might be hallucinating. Both urinals were
overflowing with cash. Fives singles, quarters. Returning to the barroom I
asked Uncle Charlie about it He frowned. "Don started that nonsense," he
said.

Don, a Princeton-educated lawyer in town, was one of Uncle Charlie's
oldest friends. A few nights earlier, Uncle Charlie said, Don decided it would
be good karma to pay tribute every time he went to the head. "Something
about appeasing the pee gods," Uncle Charlie said, sighing. "Anyway, now
everybody's doing it. New tradition."

"Do people make a wish when they throw money in? Like coins in a
fountain?"

"Do I know what people do in the head? Christ, what a question. But I'll
tell you this. Don keeps careful track, a written record, of how much money
accumulates before some sicko reaches in and scoops it out. And someone always reaches in, eventually. Human nature, you know. Talk about your 'filthy
lucre.'"

Bartenders weren't happy about the Don Fund, Uncle Charlie added.
They were all paranoid about getting paid with urinal money, and since
everyone knew that the bartenders were wary of wet cash, cheapskates and
con men were running fivers under the faucet before setting them on the bar.
"Pay with a wet five," Uncle Charlie said out of the side of his mouth, "and
the chances are good your drink will be on the house."

I laughed and threw an arm around Uncle Charlie's neck and told him I
felt great. No, better than great. *Grrreat.* I told him I had not been feeling
great a short while ago, but now I felt—great. Why? Because Publicans had
distracted me. Distraction, I said. We all need it, and Publicans provides it,

like no place else. But Uncle Charlie didn't hear, because suddenly standing before us was Don. Jesus Christ, Uncle Charlie said, speak of the goddamned devil. We were just *talking* about you. He introduced me to Don, who was Uncle Charlie's age and height. The resemblance ended there. Uncle Charlie had mentioned that Don was a wrestler when younger, and it still showed. He had that solidity, that thickness, that permanently low center of gravity. He also had the most open and friendly face in the bar, with upswept eyebrows and a bright pat of red veins on each cheek, like a toy wooden soldier. He was immediately likable, lovable, and I could see why he rated so high in Uncle Charlie's book.

I told Don what I'd just been telling Uncle Charlie, about Publicans satisfying that underrated human need—distraction. Distraction was the name of the game, I told Don, and he said that he couldn't agree more. He told me how the bar had helped him through many a bad time in his life, how it had become particularly important to him a few years earlier, just after he got divorced, when distraction was the best hedge against depression. Then suddenly we were all distracted by Banker, who was giving a very interesting talk about Lincoln's obsession with *Macbeth*. "The play spoke to his sense of foreboding," Banker said.

"Lincoln believed in omens," General Grant said.

"Who doesn't?" Uncle Charlie said.

"Lincoln read *Macbeth* days before he was assassinated," Banker said. "Did you know that? Can't you just picture him in his stovepipe, reading about 'murder most foul,' right before he's going to be murdered?"

"You think he wore his hat when he read?" Don said. "No way Lincoln wore that big stovepipe hat when he read."

"You'd look good in a stovepipe," Banker said to Uncle Charlie.

The image of Uncle Charlie in a stovepipe got a huge laugh.

"God I miss my hair," Uncle Charlie said to Don, apropos of nothing. Don patted him on the arm.

"Hey Colt!" someone yelled from across the bar. "Just thought of another Batman villain! Clock King!"

"Nice work," Colt said, adding the name to his list.

"How about Mr. Salty?" I said.

"False," Uncle Charlie said. "There was no Mr. Salty."

Exactly, I said. Exactly.

thirty-one | ALADDIN

I WORKED A DOUBLE SHIFT THAT THANKSGIVING, AND BY THE TIME
I got to Grandpa's there wasn't a crumb left from dinner. The house was
dark, the cousins asleep. I walked down to Publicans and found it mobbed.
Thanksgiving was always the best and busiest night at the bar, when everyone
in town stopped by after dinner, and everyone who ever lived in town returned, looking to reunite with former flames and old friends.

Just inside the door I ran into DePietro, a schoolmate from Shelter Rock.
I hadn't seen him in years. He was working at the World Trade Center, he
said, brokering treasury bonds He asked about my Thanksgiving.

"What Thanksgiving?" I said.

"No turkey?" he said.

I shook my head.

"You look bad, pal. You look like a man who could use some Silk Panties."

Colt was behind the stick, and DePietro asked him to whip up a batch of
Silk Panties. When I asked what Silk Panties were, both DePietro and Colt
waved their hands as if I shouldn't concern myself with such trifling details.
"*Salud*," Colt said, draining a pitcher of clear liquid into a shot glass. Though
clear, the liquid poured slowly, like syrup.

"Tastes like frozen peaches," I said, sipping.

"It'll freeze your peaches all right," Colt said.

"I need to eat something," I said. "Is it too late to have Smelly make me a
burger?"

DePietro insisted I go with him to his parents' house, right now. He had a
surprise for me. I didn't have the energy to argue. The Silk Panties were hitting
me like a Valium smoothie. He drove at dangerous speeds through Manhasset
Woods, lurching to a stop outside a tall Tudor house that looked familiar. I
thought I might have peered in its front window when I was a kid. He brought
me through a back door into a spotless kitchen and piled a plate high with
leftovers—turkey, walnut stuffing, a slab of pumpkin chiffon pie. As I inhaled
the food DePietro told me stories, unforgettable stories, including one about
a kid he knew who broke the course record at Plandome Country Club when

he was one week shy of his eighteenth birthday. Puffing out his chest, the kid presented his scorecard to the pro, who told him to piss off—you had to be eighteen to set the course record. One week later, the morning of his eighteenth birthday, the kid returned at dawn, hired a caddie, then went out and broke the course record again. Submitting his scorecard, he told the pro to shove it up his water hazard. "His blade work on the back nine was a thing of beauty," DePietro said. "Someone told me he jarred the last putt from about forty, cocky motherfucker."

I told DePietro I'd give anything—except the plate of leftovers before me—to have that kind of confidence.

Stuffed, happy, I returned with DePietro to Publicans, and drank more Silk Panties, and by three in the morning I was falling from DePietro's BMW convertible onto Grandpa's driveway, shouting all the things for which I was thankful, like DePietro, and Silk Panties, and Publicans, which DePietro later swore I pronounced "Pumpkin Cans."

Weeks later I sat at the bar with Cager and told him I was working up a new theory about Publicans. I was hungry and lonely on Thanksgiving? Publicans fed me. I was depressed about being Mr. Salty? Publicans distracted me. I'd always thought of Publicans as a sanctuary, but now I believed it was something else altogether. "Publicans is the Aladdin's Lamp of Long Island," I said. "Make a wish, give the bar a rub—and presto. Aladdin, aka Publicans, provides."

"Now wait," Cager said. "Was Aladdin the guy who rubbed the lamp, or the genie *in* the lamp?"

"Either way," I said.

"Publicans grants wishes?" Cager looked up and addressed the rafters. "I want the four horse in the seventh race at Belmont."

Uncle Charlie chortled.

A man in a gorgeous camel-hair topcoat walked up to the bar and asked what we were talking about. Aladdin, Cager said. "Yes," the man said agreeably, smiling. "He was great in *Shane*."

"You're thinking of Alan Ladd," Cager said.

A woman, whose hair was a shocking police-tape yellow, overheard. "I loved that show!" she cried.

"What show is that?" Cager said.

"Password."

"That was Allen Ludden,' Cager said.

"Allen Ludden grants wishes?" the first man said.

"Sure he does," Cager said. He leaned into me and muttered, "The password is—*morons*."

I asked Uncle Charlie what he thought of my Publicans-Aladdin theory. "The only Aladdin I care about is in Vegas," he said.

As people came rolling into the bar that night I remarked to Uncle Charlie that Publicans seemed more crowded all the time. Every night was like Thanksgiving.

"You have no idea," he said. "You cannot believe how much booze we're going through per week. A Mississippi of Michelob. A Lake Huron of Heineken."

"Huron or Pontchartrain?" Cager said.

"Which is bigger?" Uncle Charlie said.

"The biggest is Pontchartrain. I think you meant to say Pontchartrain?"

"In my whole life I've never meant to say Pontchartrain."

Some of the credit for the record-setting receipts that fall went to Wall Street. The stock market was on fire, which translated into a boon for every bar within the tristate metropolitan area. But the real reason for Publicans' runaway success, according to Uncle Charlie and other sages along the bar, was Steve. Steve continued to draw people to the bar in ever greater numbers, for reasons that were hard to put into words.

"That's why Chief's expancing," Uncle Charlie said. "Between us. Sotto voce. Kapish? Deal's not done yet. He's opening a joint in the city, a second Publicans, on the South Street Seaport." He folded his arms and opened his eyes wide. "You ain't seen nothing yet," he said.

I wasn't sure where South Street Seaport was, and my ignorance played to Uncle Charlie's strength. Few things gave him more joy than drawing a map on a cocktail napkin. He was the bar cartographer, and he made for me an elaborate diagram of lower Manhattan, with the Seaport here, the financial district there, a blue *X* marking the spot where Steve's new joint—Publicans on the Pier—would be. It would sit at the end of Pier 17, with a vast wall of glass facing the Brooklyn Bridge. Spectacular view, Uncle Charlie said. Great location. Heavy foot traffic. Right next door was a popular restaurant owned by quarterback Doug Flutie, and not twenty feet away was a majestic hundred-year-old twin-masted schooner that was a floating maritime museum. "It's a half block—not even—from Wall Street," Uncle Charlie said, "and maybe half a mile from the Trade Center. If that. As far from the towers as we are right now from St. Mary's."

Not everyone thought Publicans on the Pier such a good idea. As word got out about Steve's new venture, many in Manhasset said they didn't understand why Steve wanted the headaches, the hassles. He already owned the entire block of Plandome Road where Publicans was located. He was the most popular publican in the history of Manhasset, which was saying something, given Manhasset's status as the Valhalla of Alcohol. According to these isolationists, Steve was like America—big, rich, powerful, admired. He should stay home, they said, count his money, play it safe. If the outside world had anything for Steve, let the outside world come to him.

I got the sense that what the naysayers really didn't like was the idea of sharing Steve with the outside world. They were jealous in advance of the throngs in Manhattan who would soon discover Steve, the swells and hotshots and high rollers who might turn Steve's head, woo him from us. When Steve became another Toots Shor, a world-famous restaurateur carousing with celebrities and hobnobbing with mayors, he'd have no use for the peons he'd left behind. As Publicans on the Pier became a hit, Publicans in Manhasset would be relegated to an afterthought.

In those first months of 1987, the naysayers seemed to be right. Steve wasn't around anymore. He was always dashing into the city, negotiating deals, signing contracts, overseeing the start of construction. "More and more we see less and less of Chief," Uncle Charlie said dolefully.

The barroom, without Steve's Cheshire smile, was noticeably dimmer.

In Steve's absence we talked a lot about him, eulogized him as if he'd died. But the more we talked about Steve, the less I felt that we knew him. The most beloved person in Manhasset, the most studied, Steve was the least understood. People always mentioned his effect on them, but I never heard anyone describe his essential qualities. Everyone seemed to feel that he or she had a claim on Steve—but everyone shared the same few threadbare facts about him. He loved hockey. He loved Heineken. He lived for softball. His spirits soared the second he heard doo-wop music. He'd split his sides over a good pun. We all knew—and repeated—the familiar Steve stories. The time he stayed up all night drinking and then drove his red '51 Chevy to the end of Long Island for a drag race with some punks—Manhasset's own James Dean. We laughed about his stock phrases. Whenever he was asked what he did for a living, especially at the end of a fourteen-hour work-day, he'd say wryly, "I'm independently wealthy." Whenever he was asked the secret of running a bar he'd say, "People come to a gin mill to be abused and I provide them with that service!" Whenever a bartender asked if his new girlfriend could drink free, Steve would say, "She ain't earned her wings yet."

But that was all we knew, and when we added it all up, it felt like much less than the sum of its parts.

During one discussion about Steve, I heard Uncle Charlie say what I'd al-ways suspected, that the key to Steve was his smile. Whenever Steve walked into Publicans, Uncle Charlie said, he bestowed that smile like a gift. People would wait all day, saving up stories about funny things that happened to them, dying to tell Steve, to get one of those smiles. "It's never like—Oh brother, here comes the boss," Uncle Charlie said. "It's like—hey, what took you so long?"

I put forward my theory again. When it came to the Aladdin-Publicans metaphor, I was a dog with a rag. I suggested to Uncle Charlie that everyone reacted so strongly to Steve because he was Aladdin. He gave people what they wanted.

"I don't think Aladdin was the one who granted the wishes," Uncle Char-lie said dubiously, pulling on his earlobe. "I think Aladdin was the guy who wrote the story of the lamp and the genie."

At last I went to the Manhasset library and checked out a copy of *Arabian Nights*. I sat at Uncle Charlie's end of the bar, reading, and learned that Aladdin is the name of the rootless boy who is the hero of the story; that one day a sorcerer, who the boy believes to be his uncle, sends the boy into a cave to fetch a "wonderful lamp"; that the sorcerer seals the boy in the cave with the lamp; that the boy rubs his hands together nervously and, in doing so, summons a genie who offers to provide whatever the boy needs.

I relayed all this to Uncle Charlie and we got into an intense back-and-forth about whether Steve was more like the lamp or the genie. I held firmly that Publicans was the lamp, Steve was the genie, as well as the source of the light. Without Steve we were hanging out in a lightless, genieless lamp.

Later I talked to Dalton and DePietro about my theory and told them excitedly that Aladdin might be the key to my Publicans novel. I would write a modern version of *Arabian Nights* and call it *Publican Nights*. DePietro wasn't listening, because he was trying to score with a woman known around town to be a loon. He wasn't listening to her either, just pretending to listen, a remarkable piece of acting since she was as boring as she was loony, and ended every sentence with the phrase, "like you *read* about." Dalton was only half listening, his nose buried in a collection of Emily Dickinson. On the bar was a folder of poems Dalton had written about Publicans, including several about Uncle Charlie, who was to Dalton what the blackbird was to Wallace Stevens. "Fuck Aladdin," Dalton said. "Listen to this." He read me "It might be lonelier." We talked about Dickinson, then women poets, then women in general. I told Dalton that I'd noticed his way of eyeing a beautiful woman who walked into the bar—not with lust but delight. Very observant, he said. Women don't like being leered at, but they love being looked at with delight.

"Do they?" Uncle Charlie said. "Because I find it a burden."

I mentioned Sidney, and I was shocked to learn that Dalton had his own Sidney, a woman in his past who broke his heart and now was the benchmark by which all subsequent women were judged. Every man, Dalton assured me, has a Sidney. It was the only time I'd ever heard him sound sad.

"Emily knew," he said, wagging the book. "Daffy bitch hid in the attic because she preferred loneliness to the horrors of love."

DePietro looked away from his date and considered Dickinson's picture on the book cover. "Not exactly a looker," he said.

"She's got a sourpuss like you *read* about," said his date.

"She was an angel," Dalton said. "Think of the sensitivity. Think of the pent-up passion. What I wouldn't give to go back in time and nail that little hellcat. Give her a good enjambment. Know what I mean?"

"If anyone could score with a virgin spinster hermit in nineteenth-century

New England," I said, "it would be you. And, come to think of it, if Publicans were Aladdin's lamp, I'd wish for just a little of your power with women."

"The power," Dalton said, "is realizing that we're all powerless against them, Asshole."

Besides, he added, you've got it all wrong: Most likely we tell the bar what we want, and the bar, like a magic lamp, shines a light on what we need.

"*Steve* is the lamp," I said.

"I thought Steve was the genie," DePietro said.

"Steve's the light," Dalton said.

We all looked at each other, confused. DePietro turned back to his date, Dalton turned back to Emily, and I turned to face the door, to await the bar's next gift—a woman. I prayed it would be a woman. I knew it would be a woman. The ideal woman. The woman who was going to save me. I had an unwavering faith in the bar and in my theory. And in women.

But Dalton was right. The bar didn't grant wishes, it filled needs, and what I needed at that moment was not a woman but a certain kind of friend. Days later a large man walked into Publicans, said hello to no one, and stationed himself beside the cigarette machine. He was two feet taller than the machine and his shoulders were several inches wider. I put him in his late thirties. He ordered a Screwdriver and stared straight ahead, making eye contact with no one, as if he were Secret Service and the president's motorcade was on its way. "Who's the mameluke?" I whispered to Uncle Charlie.

"Mameluke," Uncle Charlie said. "Good word."

I agreed, though I wasn't sure what it meant.

Uncle Charlie narrowed his eyes and looked toward the cigarette machine. "Oh—yeah—he's on the job." I shook my head, not familiar with the term. "Copper," Uncle Charlie said. "Fuzz. NYPD. Just bought a house at the bottom of one of the hills. He's a good man. Very good man." He lowered his voice. "There's a story there."

"What is it?"

"I'm not at liberty. But it's a doozy."

The man walked over. "Hey Chas," he said.

"Ah," Uncle Charlie said. "Bob the Cop, I'd like you to meet my nephew, JR."

We shook hands. Uncle Charlie excused himself and ducked into the phone booth.

"So," I said to Bob the Cop, noticing that my mouth was suddenly dry, "my uncle says you're a police officer?"

He nodded, an economical nod, as though telling a blackjack dealer, Hit me.

"What precinct?" I asked.

"Harbor."

Neither of us said anything for a full minute.

"What do you do?" he asked.

I cleared my throat. "I'm a copyboy."

He frowned. I'd called myself a copyboy hundreds of times, but this was the first time I heard how ridiculous it sounded. Not many job titles ended with "boy." Bellboy, paperboy, stable boy. Standing before Bob the Cop, seeing his reaction, I wished I could say I was a copy*man*. Or, at least, Carbon Separator.

But it wasn't my job title that Bob the Cop found distasteful. "I'm not too crazy about newspapers," he said.

"Oh?" I said. "Well, I'm scared of cops, so I guess we're made for each other."

No reaction. Another full minute passed. Again I cleared my throat.

"Why don't you like newspapers?" I asked.

"My name was in the papers once. Didn't enjoy the experience."

"What were you in the papers for?"

"Long story. Look me up sometime."

He went to make a donation to the Don Fund. Uncle Charlie returned. "Your friend," I said to him, "is a mite terse."

"Man of few words," Uncle Charlie said.

"Man of no words," I said.

"I like it. People talk too much."

Bob the Cop returned. I smiled. He didn't.

It took me half the night to figure out which movie star Bob the Cop looked like. (I had plenty of time to think, since the silences yawned on for minutes at a time.) With a jolt, I realized—John Wayne. It wasn't the face so much as the physique and phrenology. He had Wayne's body—that wide hipless torso—and Wayne's oversize rectangular head, which seemed made expressly for a cowboy hat. If you put a cowboy hat on Bob the Cop's head, I thought, he wouldn't flinch. He'd just reach up and touch the brim and say, "Howdy." He even held his body like Wayne, that slightly swaying stance that proclaimed, *All the Apaches in the world won't take this fort*. I half expected him to saddle up his barstool before he sat on it.

Once he'd obtained the right amounts of alcohol and undivided attention, the Quiet Man actually made some noise that night. In fact he told some of the finest stories I'd ever heard in Publicans. Bob the Cop loved stories, and he was in the right line of work for finding them. Stories floated past the prow of his police boat every day, especially in the spring, when the water turned warm and corpses bobbed to the surface like corks. Floaters, Bob the Cop called them. During those first balmy days of April, when everyone's mind was on rebirth and renewal, it was Bob the Cop's job to take a grappling hook and fish stiffs from the murky ooze. Mob hits, suicides, missing persons—the harbors and rivers were apple bobs of tragedies, and telling stories was how Bob the Cop coped.

Publicans was wall-to-wall storytellers, but none had Bob the Cop's ability to hold our attention. Part of it was fear. If we stopped listening, would he punch us? But part of it was his delivery, which worked along the same principle as Hemingway's spare style. Bob the Cop wasted no time, no energy. He painted scenes and characters with the fewest possible words, inflections and facial expressions, because like Hemingway he didn't need any frills. Unshakably confident in his story's interest, Bob the Cop spoke in a steady monotone and maintained a card sharp's deadpan, which also created a sense of uncertainty as to genre. You didn't know if Bob the Cop was doing tragedy or comedy until he wanted you to know. Then, his thick New York accent was the crowning touch. It was the right voice for describing that underworld through which he moved, peopled with hookers and grifters, sleazy politicians and contract killers, a comic book hell in which someone was always making a mistake that cost someone else dearly. Whether describing a plane crashing into the East River because of pilot error, or an undercover detective's boneheaded blunder that let a perp go free, Bob the Cop's accent always seemed to fit the accident.

My favorite stories, however, were the ones about his kids. He told me about taking his five-year-old son with him on his police boat. It was supposed to be a slow day, but a helicopter went down in the river and Bob the

Cop raced to the scene, pulling survivors from the water. Later that night, when Bob the Cop was tucking his son into bed, the boy was upset. "I don't want to go with you to work no more," his son said. "How come?" Bob the Cop asked. "Because I can't save the people." Bob the Cop thought. "How about we make a deal?" he told his son. "You come with me to work, and if anything bad happens, you let me save the big people, and you save the little people."

When Bob the Cop stopped telling stories, when he turned to listen to someone else's story, I leaned into Uncle Charlie's chest. "Bob the Cop *is* a good guy," I said. "A really good guy."

"I tell no lies," he said.

"What's his story?"

Uncle Charlie put a finger to his lips.

thirty-two | MARVELOUS

UNCLE CHARLIE OWED SOMEBODY A BUNDLE, AN AMOUNT SO large, I heard, he could barely pay the vigorish. "What's a vigorish?" I asked Cager.

He took off his visor and scratched his red hair. "The vig is like the interest on a Visa card," he said. "Except this Visa will break your fucking kneecaps if you miss a payment."

Uncle Charlie already walked like a flamingo with sore knees. I couldn't imagine how he'd walk if he got crossways with his creditors. According to Sheryl, who had been asking questions along the bar, Uncle Charlie owed the mob a hundred thousand dollars. Joey D said it was more likely half that amount, and Uncle Charlie's creditors weren't mobsters, just a local syndicate. I wondered what was the difference. I wondered if Mr. Sandman was still in the picture.

I worried about Uncle Charlie's debt, and I particularly worried about the way he refused to worry. He would strut back and forth behind the bar, singing to the doo-wop music on the bar stereo. I watched one night as he danced out from behind the bar and across the floor, a tangoing flamingo, and I thought I understood him. After losing his hair, and Pat, Uncle Charlie had given up on sustained happiness—career, wife, kids—and was trying only for short bursts of joy. Any worry, any prudent thought, which interfered with his bursts of joy, he ignored.

This strategy of joy at all costs, besides being delusional, led him to be careless. Two undercover cops, acting on a tip, sat at the bar for a week and watched Uncle Charlie transacting business more boisterously than a commodities trader. While mixing drinks Uncle Charlie was taking bets, parlaying bets, working the phones. At week's end the two cops came to Grandpa's house, this time in uniform. Uncle Charlie was lying on the bicentennial sofa. He saw them coming up the walk and met them at the screen door. "Remember us?" one cop said through the screen.

"Sure," Uncle Charlie said, calmly lighting a cigarette with his Zippo. "Scotch and soda, Seagram's and Seven. What's up?"

They took him away in handcuffs. Over the next few days they sweated Uncle Charlie for the names of his bosses and associates. When word got out that he wasn't saying anything, that he hadn't given the cops a single name, presents began to arrive at the jail. Marlboros, newspapers, goose-down pillows. A high-priced lawyer also arrived, his services paid for by someone who preferred to remain nameless. The lawyer told the cops that Uncle Charlie would die before cooperating, and he persuaded them to reduce the charges from gambling to vagrancy. When word reached Publicans we all went limp with laughter. Only Uncle Charlie could get arrested for vagrancy—*in his own living room.*

I wish I could say that Uncle Charlie's arrest jolted me, or embarrassed me, or made me worry more about his safety. If anything it made me proud. He returned to the bar a conquering hero, having shown toughness and fortitude in a tight spot, and no one hailed him more adoringly than I. The mobsters who monitored Uncle Charlie's vigorish—who "held his paper," as the men said—worried me, but the cops didn't, because I believed the barroom myth that cops and gamblers played a game of cat and mouse, which no one took seriously. On some level I knew that my thinking was warped, my pride in Uncle Charlie misplaced, and this was probably why I didn't tell my mother about Uncle Charlie's arrest. I didn't want her to worry about her younger brother, or me.

Soon after his release from jail there was a change in Uncle Charlie. He started gambling more, risking more, maybe because his narrow escape made him feel invincible. He then started losing more, so much that he had no choice but to take his losses seriously. At the bar he would complain bitterly about various athletes and coaches who had cost him money that day with their miscues and errors. He claimed he could retire to the tropics if not for Oakland manager Tony LaRussa. He could buy a Ferrari if not for Miami quarterback Dan Marino. He was compiling a mental list of athletes who had screwed him, and he included those play-by-play announcers who didn't sufficiently castigate his blacklisted athletes.

Though I couldn't learn the exact size of Uncle Charlie's debt, his individual losses were legend. Colt told me that Uncle Charlie lost fifteen thousand dollars in one night, playing Liars' Poker with Fast Eddy. Joey D said Uncle Charlie was addicted to underdogs, "the more under, the more canine, the better." Cager backed this up by telling me about the night Uncle Charlie let it slip that he was "intrigued" by the line on Saturday's Nebraska-Kansas game. Nebraska was laying sixty-nine points. "Imagine," Uncle Charlie said to Cager, "you take Kansas and at the opening kickoff you're up sixty-nine to nothing."

"No," Cager said. "I'd steer clear of that game, Goose. With a spread like that, the oddsmakers must know something, and what they probably know is that Kansas couldn't beat St. Mary's girls' lacrosse team. *Junior* varsity."

Next time Cager walked into the bar he asked the inevitable question.

"I took Kansas and the sixty-nine points," Uncle Charlie said, bowing his head.

"And?"

"Nebraska seventy, Kansas oogatz."

Cager blew air slowly through the gaps in his teeth.

"But Cager," Uncle Charlie said achingly, imploringly, *"I was in it the whole way."*

After telling me about this conversation, Cager asked me, "What can you do with a man like that?"

Cager was a savvy gambler, who won more than he lost, and actually supported himself by gambling, so he offered to help Uncle Charlie. "Only way you'll ever make a dent in your number," Cager told him, "is come with me to the track and we'll pick out some long shots."

Uncle Charlie glared at Cager. "The fuck do I know about horses?" he said.

"The fuck do you know about horses?" Cager said. "The fuck do you know about *horses*?"

In March 1987, I saw firsthand how far things had deteriorated for Uncle Charlie, when I woke to find him standing over me. "Hey," he said. "You 'wake? Hey?" The bedroom was filled with Sambuca fumes. I checked the clock: 4:30 A.M. "Come on," he said. "I wan' talk you."

Wrapping a robe around myself I followed him out to the kitchen. Normally in that condition he wanted to talk about Pat, but this time it was money. He was worried. He didn't give me a hard number, but he left no doubt that it was a number he could no longer ignore. The delusional joy was gone. His only hope, he said, his last chance, was Sugar Ray Leonard.

I was well aware of the upcoming middleweight title fight between Sugar Ray Leonard and "Marvelous" Marvin Hagler. The "Super Fight," as it was being billed, had been the main topic of conversation for weeks at Publicans. Every bar has some affinity for boxing, because drinkers and boxers sit on stools and feel woozy and measure time in rounds. But at Publicans boxing was a sacred bond that all the men shared. Old-timers still recalled fondly when Rocky Graziano was a regular, decades before the bar was Publicans, and I'd once seen two men in the back room nearly come to blows, arguing about whether or not Gerry Cooney was a legit contender or a tomato can. The imminent clash between two superb fighters like Leonard and Hagler was viewed by such men as the approach of a rare comet would be viewed by NASA scientists. Drunken NASA scientists.

Leonard, retired three years, his hair sharply receding at the temples, was an elder statesman of the sport at just thirty years old. He'd been pretty when he was a young Olympian—now he looked distinguished, like a diplomat. He'd always had a thoughtful glimmer in his eye, which made him seem deceptively demure, but now he also had a detached retina, suffered in one of his last fights, and doctors said one good blow, landed flush, could leave him blind. He was no match for the reigning champion, Hagler, who was ornery, homely, bald, in the full flower of his violent prime. Like Godzilla with a grudge Hagler had been mauling every comer. He hadn't lost in eleven years, and yet he considered all his victims, including fifty-two knockouts, mere appetizers before the main course—Leonard. Hagler hungered for Leonard. He wanted to prove himself the fighter of the decade, and to do this he needed

to lure Leonard out of retirement and humiliate him, dethrone the media dar-
ling. He also disliked Leonard personally, and so he wanted to destroy him.
He didn't care if he caused Leonard to go blind, deaf, or dead. Given Hagler's rage, and Leonard's rust, the fight wasn't so much a fight as an arranged
execution. Vegas was making Hagler the prohibitive favorite, but as the sun
peered through the window over the kitchen sink Uncle Charlie told me that
Vegas was wrong. The fight was a mismatch all right, but not the mismatch
Vegas perceived. He was betting heavy timber, more timber than in the Pa-
cific Northwest, on Sugar Ray Leonard.

I saw that Joey D was right. Uncle Charlie was addicted to underdogs.
And he didn't just bet them, he became them. All of us were guilty of giving
our hearts to athletes. Uncle Charlie gave them his soul. Seeing him foam at
the mouth about Leonard, I was struck by the danger of identifying with anyone, let alone underdogs. And yet I couldn't worry about Uncle Charlie anymore, because it was five-thirty in the morning and I had my own problems.

After nearly five months at the *Times* I was still fetching sandwiches, still
separating carbons, still the infamous and laughable Mr. Salty. I'd written a
few microscopic briefs, and I'd contributed notes for a humdrum roundup of
fan celebrations after the New York Giants won the Super Bowl. An "inauspi-
cious debut," Uncle Charlie called it. I'd expected that the *Times* would restore
my self-confidence, but it was stripping away the little I had left. And to make
everything worse the newspaper was threatening to strip me of my name.

A top editor called me into his office. He was a big man with big glasses,
a big bow tie, and a big problem with me. He'd heard from the copydesk that
I'd been insisting my byline should read JR Moehringer, without dots. A
copyboy *insisting*? It was heresy.

"Is this true?" he asked.

"Yes sir," I said.

"No dots? You want your byline to read JR Moehringer, without dots?"

"Yes sir."

"What does JR stand for?"

Easy does it, I told myself. The editor was asking me to reveal my darkest
truth, and I knew what would happen if I did. He'd decree that henceforth my
byline read as my birth certificate: John Joseph Moehringer Jr. The men at
Publicans would then know my real name, and I'd never be JR or Kid again. I'd

be Johnny, or Joey—or Junior. Whatever meager identity I'd been able to forge in Publicans would disappear. Moreover, every time I was lucky enough to earn a byline in the *Times* it would be someone else's name. It would be my father's name, a reminder of him and a credit to him. I couldn't let that happen.

"JR," I told the editor, feeling sick, "doesn't stand for anything."

"JR is not your initials?" he asked.

"No, sir."

Dodged a bullet there. It was no lie to say JR wasn't my initials.

"JR is your legal first name? Just a J and an R?"

"Yes, sir."

Why did I drink that seventy-five dollars my mother sent me to change my name?

"I need to study this," the editor said. "It just doesn't look right. JR. No dots. I'll get back to you."

Later that night at Publicans I told Uncle Charlie about my meeting with the editor.

"Why didn't you just tell him your name?" he asked.

"I don't want people knowing I'm named after my father."

"Who's named after whose father?" Colt said.

I gave Uncle Charlie a pleading look. He pursed his lips. Colt looked at Uncle Charlie. Then me. Uncle Charlie shrugged. I shrugged. Colt lost interest.

That was the great thing about Colt.

The editor scowled at me, as if I'd brought him corned beef instead of tuna salad. He'd now spent ten minutes on me and my name, twice what he'd ever spent on any copyboy. "I've done some research," he said. "It does seem there's some precedent here. Were you aware that Harry S. Truman did not use a dot after his middle initial?"

"No sir, I wasn't."

"The *S* didn't stand for anything. And e.e. cummings? Also no dots."

"I see."

"But by God we gave them dots anyway. The president, the poet, we gave them dots, whether they liked it nor not. And do you know why? Because it's *Times* style. And do you know why? Because it looks ridiculous otherwise.

And we're not about to break with precedent, or with *Times* style, for a copy-boy, are we? Hereafter you will be J dot R dot Moehringer."

The editor scratched a note in a folder, which I assumed was my personnel file. He looked up, shocked that I was still standing there.

"Good day," he said.

I went out drinking with several copyboys. We sailed around midtown, laughing, making fun of the editors, imagining different things we could do to their sandwiches. We went to Rosie O'Grady's, an Irish saloon that reminded me slightly of Publicans, then to a place across from the *Times*, a dive with peanut shells on the floor and men fast asleep at the bar, like babies in high chairs.

A groan went up as we walked in. "What's the matter?" I asked the bartender.

"Leonard just won the fourth round."

He jerked his head toward a radio atop the cash register. With all the stress and turmoil about my name, I'd completely forgotten about the Super Fight. I said good-bye to my fellow copyboys and ran to Penn Station.

I reached Publicans just as Uncle Charlie was returning from a movie theater in Syosset, where he, Colt, and Bob the Cop had watched the fight on closed circuit. "Who won?" I asked.

Uncle Charlie, face glazed with sweat, shook his head. "J.R.," he said, lighting a cigarette, "it was the fight to end all fights."

"Who won?"

"Four hundred million people tuned in to this fight," he said. "Every celebrity on the planet was ringside. Chevy Chase. Bo Derek. Billy Crystal. That bitch from *Dynasty*."

"Linda Evans?"

"The other bitch."

"Joan Collins."

"Ex-wife of—?"

"Anthony Newley."

"That's my boy. And you'll find *this* interesting. Sinatra was there."

"No."

"Trust me, J.R., no one even noticed him. This fight was too engrossing. This was a donnybrook. This was the last scene of *The Quiet Man*."

High praise. The fight at the end of *The Quiet Man* was deemed by every man in Publicans to be the finest in cinematic history, better than the fights in *Rocky, Raging Bull, Cool Hand Luke,* or *From Here to Eternity.*

Uncle Charlie sat on a barstool and ordered a vodka with a cranberry splash and a shot of Sambuca on the side.

"Who won?" I said.

"Hagler's in blue trunks," he said. "Leonard's in white, red piping down the sides and red tassels on his shoes. They both look—beautiful. Oiled up, 158 pounds of gleaming muscle, their bodies in tip-top condition. Roman gladiators. First round, Hagler stalks Leonard, and Leonard dances away. Like Astaire. No, fuck it, Astaire was clubfooted compared to Leonard. You never saw a man this light on his feet. Hagler wants to kill the son of a bitch. Small problem. He can't find him. Leonard glides around in circles, Hagler chasing, and when Hagler stops, Leonard stops and throws a feathery combo, jab, jab, uppercut, jab, then dances away. Bye-bye. I'd like to stay and chat but—jab, jab—got to run. First round Bob the Cop and I award to Leonard, though I think Colt gives it to Hagler. Colt. Fucking Colt."

"Who won?" I said.

"Second round, Leonard again, no question. He's a genius, a master. An artiste. Stick, jab, dance. By the third round Hagler is starting to come unglued. He's a madman."

Uncle Charlie slid off his stool and bent into a fighter's crouch. People paused in their conversations, put down their drinks, and turned to see what he was doing.

"Leonard is tormenting Hagler," Uncle Charlie said. "Stick and jab, stick and jab, right hand, left hook, then he bounces away from Hagler, verbally taunting him all the while."

Uncle Charlie stuck, jabbed, taunted the shadows, his cigarette dangling from his lips. The crowd in the barroom now began to collect around Uncle Charlie, forming a circle.

"Hagler is on the offensive," Uncle Charlie said, "but Leonard is on a fucking pogo stick. He's got a Buck Rogers jet pack on his back. Hagler has trained all his life for this, but Leonard has trained to render Hagler's training useless, to make him feckless. You don't mind if I say 'feckless,' do you?

"Fourth round, Leonard is controlling the fight, so calm, so relaxed, that he brings his fist all the way behind his back and twirls it in the air, the old razzle-dazzle, and socks Hagler right in the breadbasket. Humiliating. No respect for the man. Smiling at him. Still, you get the feeling Leonard is teasing a wild tiger.

"Fifth round, Leonard stops. No more dancing. Can't dance. Tired. Fatigue setting in. Hagler catches Leonard with a right. Pow. Another. Bam. Each blow enough to kill you or me. Hagler sends in a hard left to the ribs. Stiff. Again. Bracing. *Again.* Hagler's hammer has been cocked for four rounds—*now he's getting his chance to drop it!* Wham! He bangs Leonard's head and face! Leonard is hurt!"

Uncle Charlie snapped a flurry of left-right combinations. The whole barroom had now come to a halt, no one being served, no one talking, everyone part of the circle around my uncle.

"Hagler wobbles Leonard! But Leonard ducks, dives, holds, escapes. Still taunts Hagler. *I'm still pretty, you scumbag. You still can't touch me.*"

Uncle Charlie backpedaled. A moonwalking flamingo. The exertion seemed to be making him drunker. Like Leonard he should have fallen, should have been unconscious, but some supernatural force was keeping him on his feet. "Sixth, seventh, eighth rounds," he said, "both fighters so weak they can hardly stand. Leonard doesn't stop, though. If he stops he's dead. You see in his eyes what he wants to do, what he'd do if he weren't so tired. What both of them would do. You realize, J.R., how much the whole thing—everything—is about being tired. Every man sees his life as a prizefight, don't let anyone tell you different. Follow? There's nothing you can't learn from boxing. The poets knew. Who am I thinking of? Which poet was a boxer?"

"Byron? Keats?"

"Whoever. You know what I'm saying. Ninth round. One of the great rounds of all time. Hagler throws Leonard into a corner and they stand toe-to-toe. Hagler unleashes the heavy artillery. He's killing him. I'm screaming at Leonard, 'Get out! Get out!'" Uncle Charlie fluttered his fists, trying to get out of the corner. "Bob the Cop turns to me and says, 'It's over. Leonard is done.' But Leonard, don't ask me how, punches his way out. He swats Hagler sideways and dances away and the crowd comes to its feet."

The crowd in the bar also stirred, and cheered, and leaned forward for the finish.

"Tenth round. Hagler busts Leonard with an uppercut. Leonard counters—combination, right hand, left hook. Eleventh round. Hagler—left, right, left to the head. Jesus. Leonard answers—flurry, wham, flurry. Unbelievable.

"Final round," Uncle Charlie said. "The two men come out at the bell and what do they do? What do you suppose they do, J.R.?"

"I don't know."

"They beckon each other. J.R., they thump their chests and pound their heads and motion. *Come on, fucker! Come on!* Imagine that kind of courage!"

I thought I saw tears in Uncle Charlie's eyes as he reenacted the last seconds. He circled my barstool, flicking jabs at my chin, and straight rights, and left hooks, each punch coming within a half inch of landing. Beads of sweat ran down his head. I thought of the time he'd broken his ribs in Publicans, playing the imaginary wall at Fenway, and I prayed he wouldn't break any bones, his or mine, going the distance with the imaginary Hagler. "At the bell," Uncle Charlie said, gasping, "Leonard is so tired, his cornermen have to carry him back to his corner." Uncle Charlie acted as if cornermen were helping him to his barstool. "They announce the decision. The judges are split. One for Hagler, two for Leonard. Leonard wins. Biggest upset in boxing history. Don't take my word for it. The announcers are saying the same thing. Biggest upset in history. Leonard is leaning against the ropes. He can't support himself, but when they tell him he's won—the joy in his face! He's so tired—so tired, J.R.—but when you win you don't really know how tired you are."

Uncle Charlie slumped forward. The barroom shook with applause. Everyone seemed to understand what the fight meant to Uncle Charlie, and it had little to do with whittling down his vigorish. I kissed him on his head and told him congratulations.

"I felt sorry for Hagler," Uncle Charlie said a while later, after he'd toweled off and caught his breath. "He looked so sad. So unmarvelous. Is that a word? You don't mind if I say 'unmarvelous,' do you?"

"No."

"Did you know Hagler legally changed his name to Marvelous? Why would a man with all his money go to the trouble of legally changing his name? To something so silly? What would possess a man to do such a thing, J.R.? Why would he give a shit? What? Why are you looking at me like that?"

thirty-three | COPYGIRL

A S DEFTLY AS HE MIXED COCKTAILS, UNCLE CHARLIE MIXED HIS customers. He had an uncanny knack for introducing people. He would point to one person's chest, then another's, then extol them to each other, then virtually command them to be friends or lovers. He was a catalyst even when he didn't mean to be. At a dinner party in West Hampton I found myself seated next to two young newlyweds. I asked how they met, and they told me they had been at a bar, "a great old bar," and they were both trying vainly to get the bartender's attention. They started chatting about this bartender, how comically rude he was, and soon forgot all about him and focused on each other. I asked if this bartender happened to be bald, and if he was wearing dark glasses, and if he told them to keep their shirts on. Their mouths opened at the same moment, as if they were baby birds waiting to be fed.

One of Uncle Charlie's great matchmaking coups was Don and Dalton. No one but Uncle Charlie thought the urinal comptroller and the barroom poet could be pals. But Uncle Charlie made a point of introducing them because they were both offbeat geniuses, and both lawyers, and because he had a hunch. A short while later Don and Dalton decided to hang out a shingle together. Their new law firm was officially launched with a cocktail party at Publicans, where Don and Dalton intended to do much of their lawyering. A proud night for them, it was a triumph for Uncle Charlie, who presumed that by introducing Don and Dalton he was guaranteed free legal aid the rest of his life.

The offices of Don and Dalton were on Plandome Road, three blocks from the bar, just above Louie the Greek's diner, and the space came with a small apartment in the back. Don and Dalton were looking for a tenant, I heard someone along the bar say. I asked Don if they'd consider renting to me. "Don't you want to see it first?" he asked. I didn't.

Grandma begged me not to go. Her eye was twitching terribly as she laid out her case. Aunt Ruth and the cousins had moved out again, so Grandpa's house would be quieter and cleaner. There would be plenty of hot water. And think of the money you'll save, she said—rents are so expensive. Also, she added softly, she enjoyed my company. She would miss me. Left unsaid was the other reason Grandma wanted me to stay, the saddest reason. She'd come to rely on the buffer I provided between her and Grandpa. I'd never taken Grandpa by the throat, but as I got older I had become proficient at distracting him when he was being mean.

I told Grandma I had to leave. I needed privacy. What I couldn't say was that I also needed sleep. I was groggy from being awakened every other night by her son. I needed a bed that wasn't in Uncle Charlie's nightly flight path. And besides, I wanted to say, but couldn't: Real men don't live with their grandmothers.

Bob the Cop helped me move. Walking into Grandpa's house he cast a cold eye on the bicentennial sofa and the duct-taped furniture and I could see him thinking: I've raided nicer joints than this. He loaded his car with my stuff—six boxes of books, three suitcases—and drove me up Plandome Road. Don handed us the keys to my new apartment. Two tiny rooms, one half bath. The carpet was fecal brown, the "bedroom" sat directly over Louie the Greek's griddle. The smell of pork chops, lamb shanks, gyros, omelets, cheese fries, chocolate cake and Pepsi rose like steam through the floors. It was so smelly, Bob the Cop said, it was noisy.

Bob the Cop plodded back and forth, taking in every detail, as if the apartment were a murder scene. At the back window he peered out the dirty venetian blinds. Parking lot. Dumpsters. Seagulls. A train roared into the station next door, making the walls quiver. He snorted. "Out of the fire," he said, "into the frying pan."

When Bob the Cop told the men at Publicans about my new bachelor pad, and the position of my bed, they razzed me about finding a girl willing to "ride the griddle." They thought I was horny, like them. I informed them that I was lonely. I wanted someone with whom I could go for long walks, listen to Sinatra, read. They stared at me in horror.

I confessed to the men that I had developed an excruciating crush on a copygirl at the *Times*. She reminded me of Sidney. Though she didn't look like Sidney, she had that same ethereal detachment, which I associated with wealth. Copygirl was rich, I believed, or else, because she worked in the business section, her proximity to stories about wealth made her seem so. Either way, whenever she glided through the newsroom in a long tailored skirt and a tight silk blouse, a look of boredom and contempt on her face, all the copyboys stopped separating carbons, and all the male editors (and a few of the females) stopped reading to watch her over the tops of their bifocals. She trailed perfume behind her like a transparent pink streamer, and I purposely walked in her wake to catch a whiff. I couldn't imagine how to approach her, and my helplessness and confusion worried me. My problems with women stemmed from some personality defect, I feared, which I self-diagnosed as hyper-empathy. Raised by my mother, minded by Grandma, influenced by Sheryl, I'd absorbed the female point of view. All the women who had tried to make me a man had done the opposite. This was why I had trouble approaching women. I liked them too much, and I was too much like them, to be predatory.

Rather than reassure me that this was all nonsense, the men concurred. In the war between men and women, they said, I didn't have enough fear of the enemy. I protested that I had plenty of fear, a surfeit of fear, but they said I was confusing fear with awe. Also, they said, I had no plan. Never go to war without a plan. Most men in the bar conceived of romance in warlike terms, because they said it was all a matter of taking something that belonged to someone else, which was the basic dynamic of every military action. Seduction as destruction. All romantic advice from Cager, for instance, tended to be shaped by his experience fighting communism. Broads were like Reds, he said. Inscrutable. Ruthless. Committed to forcible redistribution of your money. Uncle Charlie, meanwhile, thought the Vikings, Huns, and other primitive marauders had it about right. "Just grab the broad by the hair and drag her from the fucking newsroom," he said. He was speaking metaphorically, I guessed. Or hoped. Dalton urged me to adopt a strategy more like the assault on Dresden, and "carpet-bomb" Copygirl with love poems. He'd had great success hiccupping his alcoholic haikus to women. ("Nurses all dressed in white / Sit looking at Publicans tonight / All in a huddle / Like some athletic team / Each with her separate dream of requited desire . . .") But he was handsome enough to compensate for such purple verse.

In the end I decided to simply phone Copygirl from Publicans and ask her for a date. "Your funeral," Uncle Charlie said, stubbing out a cigarette.

Copygirl was surprised to get a call from me, since she didn't know who I was. "Tell me again who you are," she said.

I told her my name again, pronouncing it slowly. I reminded her where I usually sat in the newsroom.

"How did you get my number?"

Since I'd stolen her number from Marie's Rolodex, I pretended I hadn't heard the question. I asked if she was free that Saturday. "I was thinking we might—"

"Actually," she said, "I was going to check out the new clay exhibit, the one everybody's talking about."

"Right, the clay exhibit, sure. But actually I was thinking we might—"

"If you want to meet me there, I guess that would be all right."

We arranged to meet outside "the museum." I had no idea what exhibit she was talking about, nor what museum. I phoned my roommate from Yale, the law student, who now lived in New York, gave him a quick overview (beautiful copygirl, excruciating crush, imminent date), and asked what he knew about some big clay exhibit. "You are such a retard," he said. "Paul Klee. K-l-e-e. A retrospective of his work is opening at the Met this weekend."

The next morning I borrowed a dozen books on Klee from the New York Public Library and read them furtively in the newsroom. After work I lugged them home to Publicans. Colt poured me a scotch and crooked an eyebrow as I opened one of the books. "I was afraid of this," Cager said to Bob the Cop. "Yale found out he doesn't know squat about the Magna Carta and now he has to go back and take summer school."

"It's not for Yale," I said. "It's for—a girl."

Cager and Bob the Cop glanced at each other. Clearly they were going to have to take me out to the parking lot and beat some sense into me. Then Klee's paintings caught their attention. They moved in for a closer look. Cager was intrigued by Klee's shapes and lines, and fascinated when I told him about Klee's experience as a soldier in World War I. Bob the Cop said he liked Klee's use of color. "This one is pretty," he said, pointing to *Twittering Machine*.

I told them what I'd learned so far. About Klee's relationship with Kandinsky. About his fascination with romanticism. About his use of child-like drawing. "This one," Cager said, "looks like a hangover."

I studied Klee with them until last call, then continued studying at my apartment until Louie the Greek fired up the griddle at 4:00 A.M.

I was asleep on my feet as I walked up to the museum, but confident that not even the curators knew more than I about Klee. Copygirl was at the entrance, wearing a trench coat cinched at her waist, twirling an umbrella like a parasol. She was a model whom Klee would have killed to paint, though he might have envisioned her as a pyramid of boobs and eyelashes. I sort of envisioned her that way myself.

We got in line for tickets. I found it hard to make small talk while we waited, my brain both sluggish and overstuffed with facts about Klee. At last we were inside. We stood before the first painting. I pointed to a corner of the canvas, where a stick figure overlooked a fish. I expounded on this symbol of Klee's view of mankind versus nature. We walked along and stood before a pencil drawing. I talked about Klee's debt to primitives, his fondness for crude forms of media like crayon.

"You sure know a lot about Klee," Copygirl said.

"I'm a big fan."

She was scowling at the Klee, her expression not unlike Cager's.

"Don't you like Klee?" I asked.

"Not really. I just wanted to see what all the fuss was about."

"I see."

We left. At a sushi bar we sat over a plate of California rolls and I felt so disappointed about the Klee exam being canceled that I was mute. After half an hour Copygirl said she needed to be somewhere else, and I didn't blame her. If I could have gotten away from me, I'd have jumped at the chance. We parted with a vote-for-me-on-Election-Day handshake.

Back at Publicans Cager asked how it went.

"Not the way I'd hoped," I said.

"Serves you right. Studying for a date."

"What else should I have done?"

He swiveled on his barstool to face me and he pushed his visor back so I could see his face. "Next time some broad tells you to take her to a museum," he said, "take her to fucking Cooperstown."

thirty-four | PETER

"HEY EDWARD R. MURROW-RINGER," A MAN AT PUBLICANS SAID to me. "How come I never see your name in the paper?"

"I use a pen name. William Safire."

He laughed and slapped the bar. "Willie!" he said. "I don't care for your politics."

This man knew why I was never in the paper. Everyone at Publicans knew. How could they not know? They saw me at the bar night after night, putting more effort into the *Times* crossword than I put into anything I wrote for the *Times* news pages. The man asked because he couldn't understand why I'd stopped trying. I'd only begun to figure it out myself.

Like "J.R. Moehringer," the training program was something of a misnomer. There was no training and no program. Shortly after I joined the newspaper the editors decided that the training program didn't make financial sense. Why promote a copykid to full-time reporter, they reasoned, when for the same salary the *Times* could hire any prizewinning reporter in the country? The editors couldn't say this publicly, of course, because the training program was a venerable *Times* tradition, and had been the entrée into the newspaper for many of the editors themselves. How would it look if they pulled the ladder up behind them? Besides, the editors didn't want to kill the program outright, they just wanted to "deemphasize" it. That was the word they used in their secret meetings, the word that leaked out into the newsroom. They enjoyed having a couple of dozen desperate-to-please Ivy Leaguers running around the newsroom. It flattered their vanity to have us fetching their sandwiches and separating their carbons. Thus they simply pretended there was a training program, continued to entice copykids with the false hope of a promotion, then each month or so told another copykid that the secret committee had met and decided he or she wasn't *Times* material. You're welcome to stay, the copykid would be told, so long as you understand we're never going to promote you.

Upon hearing that they were "unpromotable," the other word bandied about, most copykids quit. Ambitious and embittered, they left for other newspapers or embarked on new careers. The editors counted on this steady exodus to stave off mutiny and keep the charade fresh. Whenever another copykid left, scores of new candidates applied for the open slot, and in this way the corps of sandwich fetchers and carbon separators was perpetually replenished. The "training program" rolled on.

No one was supposed to know about any of this, but there are no secrets in a newsroom. Everyone knew, and midlevel editors therefore stopped giving copykids anything to write. Why invest time and energy in a bunch of copykids whom the top editors had come to regard with indifference? Why make a protégé of someone who wouldn't be around much longer? Faced with all this sudden indifference and deemphasis, the copykids might have staged a slowdown, or a walkout, or set the building on fire. Instead we kept trying. We scavenged in wastebaskets for story ideas that reporters had discarded, and groveled for press releases and puff pieces we might turn into something good. When we did find something to write, we polished every sentence like Flaubert, and prayed that the editors might see some ray of promise in our work. None of us could stop hoping that he or she would be the chosen one, the single copykid, sui generis, who would make the editors forget their disdain for all.

For months I tried as hard as anyone. Then, as at Yale, I stopped. This time, however, there was no threat of expulsion. The only consequence of not trying was a faint sense of regret and that old sinking feeling that failure was my fate. Any stronger misgivings about my decision to stop trying were quickly eased by Publicans, which was crowded with people who had stopped trying long ago. The more I moaned about the *Times,* the more popular I became at the bar. Though proud of me when I succeeded, the men celebrated me when I failed. I noted this, then ignored it, as I ignored the fact that my post-Publicans hangover sometimes soured my disposition, hindered my job performance, and reduced my slim chances of being promoted to absolute zero.

Around the same time I stopped trying at the *Times* I did something even more confounding. I stopped phoning my mother. I was in the habit of phoning her every few nights from the newsroom, seeking her advice and encouragement, reading her the top of whatever I was writing. After we hung up I felt a sense of regret, not because she hadn't helped, but because she had. Too much.

I was twenty-three years old. I didn't want to be dependent on my mother anymore. Moreover I didn't want to be reminded that my mother was supposed to be dependent on me. By this time I'd intended to be helping her financially. I'd hoped that by 1988 she'd be moving into the house I'd bought for her, that her biggest worry would be what to wear to her morning golf lesson. Instead she was still selling insurance, still just getting by, and still struggling to regain her energy. I told myself that I wanted to see how well I could do with the men as my mentors instead of my mother, that it was healthy for a young man to distance himself from his mother, but in truth I was distancing myself from unfulfilled promises, from the awful guilt I felt over failing to take care of her.

Embargoing my mother made it easier to rationalize not trying at the *Times* and to turn my full attention to my mother's bête noir, the bar novel, which I was no longer calling *Publican Nights*. The Aladdin motif hadn't panned out. I was now calling the novel *Barflies and Silk Panties,* when I wasn't calling it *Moonshine and Monkeyshine,* when I wasn't calling it *Here Comes Everybody,* a phrase from *Finnegans Wake.* I had loads of material. Over the years I'd filled shoe boxes with cocktail napkins on which I'd recorded random impressions, scraps of dialogue, exchanges overheard in the barroom, like when Colt's brother, filling in for Colt behind the bar, yelled at a customer, "Don't laugh at me! Do not laugh at me, pal. My mother laughed at me and I had her operated on needlessly."

Each night I'd overhear at least one line that would seem an ideal opening or ending for a chapter. "I'm not overwhelmed," a man told his girlfriend. "Right," she said dryly, "you're just the right amount of whelmed."

"So did you fuck her?" Uncle Charlie asked a man. "No way, Goose," the man said. "Honest—she fucked me."

I once heard two women talking about their boyfriends. "He told me I'm a triple threat," the first woman said. "What does that mean?" the second woman asked. "It's some kinda sports term," the first woman said. "He told me I'm really smart, and I have great tits." The second woman counted on her fingertips, then screamed with laughter.

After I stopped trying at the *Times,* I began holding myself to a strict regimen, postponing my nightly trip to Publicans until after I'd spent at least one hour making a stab at my novel about Publicans. Every attempt, however, was doomed, because I didn't understand why I wanted to write about Publicans, why I loved Publicans. I was afraid to understand, and so I was doing little more than rearranging words on the page, an exercise ultimately as meaningless as the Wordy Gurdy.

When the meaninglessness became obvious I would sit and stare at the wall above my desk, where I'd pinned index cards with favorite passages from Cheever and Hemingway and Fitzgerald. I'd grow angry with Fitzgerald. Bad enough that he'd set an unreachable standard of perfection, that he'd already written the Greatest American Novel, but did he have to set it in my hometown? I'd think about my favorite novels—*The Great Gatsby, David Copperfield, The Adventures of Huckleberry Finn, The Catcher in the Rye*—and their brilliance would paralyze me. I never perceived the things they had in common, the thing that drew me to them in the first place: Each male narrator mentions his father in the first few pages. In *Gatsby,* the first sentence. That is where a troubled male narrator usually begins, where I might have begun.

Of course, had I been trying for a debilitating case of writer's block, the conditions above Louie the Greek's couldn't have been better—hot, loud, the walls vibrating with every train pulling into and out of the station, the air vibrating with the aroma of pickles, bacon fat, fried potatoes and cheese. But I wouldn't have fared any better at a secluded writer's colony in the woods, because I was the ideal candidate for writer's block. All the classic defects converged in me—inexperience, impatience, perfectionism, confusion, fear. Above all I suffered from a naïve view that writing should be easy. I thought words were supposed to come unbidden. The idea that errors were stepping-stones to truth never once occurred to me, because I'd absorbed the ethos of the *Times,* that errors were nasty little things to be avoided, and misapplied that ethos to the novel I was attempting. When I wrote something wrong I always took it to mean that something was wrong with me, and when something was wrong with me I lost my nerve, my focus, and my will.

What seems most remarkable in retrospect is how many pages I produced, how many drafts I finished, how hard I tried before I stopped. It wasn't like me to be so persistent and it showed how much the bar mesmerized me, how strong was my compulsion to describe it. Night after night I sat at my desk above Louie the Greek's, trying to write about the voices of the bar, the exhilarating laughter of men and women huddled together in a place they felt safe. I tried to write about the faces within clouds of smoke, how they often looked like ghosts in a foggy hereafter, and the scintillating talk, which could jump from horse racing to politics to fashion to astrology to baseball to historic love affairs, all in the span of one beer. I tried to write about Steve's Cheshire smile, Uncle Charlie's head, Joey D's mouse, Cager's visor, Fast Eddy's way of parachuting onto a stool. I tried to write about the urinals overflowing with money, and the time I fell asleep in the men's room and someone woke me by saying, "Hey! This room's for crappin', not nappin'." I tried to write about the time Smelly brandished a knife at the legendary running back Jim Brown. No matter what I did—naming the character Stinky, changing the weapon from a knife to a lobster fork—the story made Smelly sound homicidal, rather than laughably ill-tempered.

I spent a fair portion of 1988 trying to write about Cager fleecing Fast Eddy. The whole "caper," as Bob the Cop liked to call it, began in the late seventies or early eighties, when "Strangers in the Night" came on the stereo in the bar. "Great song," Fast Eddy said, snapping his fingers. "Guess that's why it won the Oscar." Cager said, "'Strangers in the Night' never won an Oscar." They bet a hundred dollars, dug out the almanac and found that Cager was right. Years passed. The song came on the stereo again one night and Fast Eddy said, "Great song, guess that's why it won the Oscar." Cager laughed. Surely Fast Eddy was joking. Seeing that Fast Eddy was serious, Cager proposed a bet of several hundred dollars. Fast Eddy lost again, and paid. More years passed. Cager buttonholed Uncle Charlie and told him he was behind with the bookies and needed to get even in one fell swoop. Fast Eddy was the swoop. "Fast Eddy has a 'black hole' on 'Strangers,'" Cager said, "so I'm going for the big score. Tonight, when he comes in, you put 'Strangers' on, I'll take it from there, and later I'll give you a slice." But Uncle Charlie wouldn't do it. He didn't want to get mixed up in anything dishonest, he said. Pretty highfalutin talk, Cager countered, for a man who treats Publicans as his own personal betting parlor. Later, when Fast Eddy arrived, Uncle Charlie looked at Cager. Cager looked at Uncle Charlie. Fast Eddy looked at Uncle Charlie. Uncle Charlie served Fast Eddy a beer and started to hum. Scooby dooby doo. "'Strangers in the Night,'" Fast Eddy said, snapping his fingers. "Great song. Guess that's why it won the Oscar." Cager was masterly. He teased Fast Eddy, mocked him, proclaimed to the bar that Fast Eddy didn't know oo-gatz about music, until Fast Eddy had no choice but to insist on a bet sizable enough to salvage his manhood. Neither man ever told anyone how much they bet, but it was a boodle, and when Fast Eddy lost and reached for his checkbook, something clicked. The black hole in his brain flew open and closed like a camera shutter. He didn't remember losing the same bet twice before, but he did remember Uncle Charlie singing, and it wasn't "What Kind of Fool Am I?" Fast Eddy wondered what kind of fool he'd been.

In converting this story to fiction I'd changed the names. Cager was Killer, Fast Eddy was Speedy Eduardo, Uncle Charlie was Uncle Butchie. I'd made Cager a veteran of the Korean War, Fast Eddy an ex-con who may or may not have killed his wife, Agnes, whose name I changed to Delilah. I made the song "Blue Velvet" and the wager a hundred thousand dollars. The story didn't ring true, and for the life of me, I couldn't figure out why.

While I was toiling on yet another draft of "Strangers in the Bar," my phone rang. It was DePietro. "Get down here!" he yelled above the sound of two hundred voices. "The place is crawling with women and I've got primo real estate. Boardwalk and Park Place!" He was referring to the two most coveted barstools, just inside the Plandome Road door, which offered clear views of everyone who came in the front, plus the best chance of getting the bartender's attention.

"Can't," I said. "I'm writing."

"Writing? The fuck about?"

"The bar."

"So? Come down and do some research. Boardwalk and Park Place."

"Can't."

He hung up.

A short time later I heard Louie the Greek shut off the griddle. A low honk, followed by a soft hiss. I went to the window and smoked a cigarette. A light rain was falling. I opened the window and smelled the rain, or tried to above Louie's Dumpsters. Seagulls dove into the Dumpsters. Louie came out the back door and shooed them away. The moment Louie went back inside the seagulls returned. Persistence, I thought. Seagulls have it—I don't. I shut off my computer. A low honk, a soft hiss.

I walked to Publicans, my chapter in a folder tucked under my arm, and consoled myself the whole way with the idea that every writer spends as much time at bars as at his writing desk. Drinking and writing go together like scotch and soda, I assured myself as I walked through the front door. De-Pietro was there, as promised, atop Boardwalk, and beside him, seated atop Park Place, was Uncle Charlie. "My beautiful nephew," he said, kissing me on the cheek. He'd had a couple. Fast Eddy was there, and beside him was his wife, Agnes, who waited tables for Louie the Greek. She was drinking her usual Irish coffee. (She never suspected that the bartenders made her Irish coffees with decaf, "to inhibit her inherent loquaciousness," Uncle Charlie said.) Fast Eddy was telling about the time he'd pitted Agnes against Uncle Charlie in a footrace. Fast Eddy had boasted that Agnes could run circles around Uncle Charlie, and Uncle Charlie had promised to put a bullet in his head if he couldn't beat a "chain-smoking hash slinger," so they tromped to the cinder track at the high school with half the bar in tow. Agnes, draped in towels like a prizefighter, stomped out a cigarette seconds before Fast Eddy fired his starter's pistol. (Why Fast Eddy had a starter's pistol with him, no one thought to ask.) Uncle Charlie beat Agnes but paid a steep price. He lay in the grass, puking, and wasn't right for days thereafter.

I thought that story might be easier to write than "Strangers." I made a note.

Peter the bartender saw me writing on a napkin. Of all the bartenders at Publicans, Peter was the kindest. Ten years older than I, Peter always looked at me with a sort of wince, like a goodhearted older brother who knew I'd done something wrong but hadn't yet figured out what. He had a soft voice, soft brown eyes, soft brown hair, but a hard inner core of something— honesty? sincerity?—that made people lean in close when he talked. No matter how happy he was—and I often saw Peter laughing himself sick—there was always an air of sadness about him. When he looked you full in the eye, even if he was smiling, you could hear him thinking, *It's all fucked, kid. We don't need to go into it right now, we don't need to hash out the details, but I'm not going to lie to you about it either—it's all fucked.* In a bar full of loud and charismatic men, Peter was the quiet one, which made his charisma the most compelling.

"What's that you're writing?" he asked, pouring me a scotch.

"Notes," I said.

"What for?"

"Nothing. Stuff about the bar."

He let it go. We talked instead about his new job on Wall Street, which he'd found through a customer at Publicans. I was happy for him, but sad that one of my favorite bartenders was now working less. He was selling bonds full-time, tending bar only part-time, mostly Saturday nights, to pick up a few extra bucks for his family. His growing family. His wife, he told me, was pregnant. "Yeah," he said shyly, "we found out it works."

"You're going to be a father?" I said. "Congratulations."

I bought him a drink.

"So you're writing about this joint?" he said, pointing to my folder. "May I?"

We traded my chapter for a scotch. *"Barflies and Silk Panties?"* he said. "Catchy title."

"Colt was the inspiration."

"Colt wears silk panties?"

"No! Jesus, I mean, I don't know."

I watched Peter read, analyzing every twitch in his face, every flick of his eyebrows. When he'd finished he handed me the pages and leaned on the bar. He winced, and looked a little sadder than usual. "It's not good," he said. "But there's something there."

I told Peter that ideas and themes swirled around my head the way smells from Louie's griddle swirled around my apartment, impossible to ignore, impossible to identify. I told him I was giving up.

"That would be a mistake," he said.

"Why?"

I gave him an opening to say I had talent. He didn't. He said simply, "Because giving up is always a mistake."

"What have you got there?" Uncle Charlie asked.

"Did you know your nephew is writing about Publicans?" Peter said.

"I thought everything we said in here was off the record," Uncle Charlie growled, joking, kind of.

"Kid's a scribbler," Colt said. "I blame those damned Wordy Gurdys."

"Hand it down," Uncle Charlie said.

"Yeah, let's have a look," Bob the Cop said.

Peter handed Uncle Charlie my pages, and as Uncle Charlie finished reading one he would pass it to Bob the Cop, who would hand it to Cager, and so on.

"I'm missing page six," Cager said.

"Who's got page nine?" Uncle Charlie called out.

"I do," Peter said. "Hold your horses."

Watching the men form a bucket brigade and pass my pages up and down the bar, I made an important decision. The men of Publicans would be my new editors. If the editors at the *Times* were going to deemphasize me, I would emphasize the bar. Every Saturday night I would submit my stuff to Peter and the men. I would set my own deadline, start my own training program.

The decision marked a change in my relationship to the bar, and it brought about a change in the tenor of the bar itself. It had always been true that we brought our stories together at Publicans and shared them, shuffled them, causing a transference of experience, so that in the morning you'd wake feeling momentarily as if you'd fought in 'Nam or fished floaters out of the harbor or owed the mob a hundred grand. But now we shuffled and shared *my* versions of everyone's story, and storytelling—the tricks, the risks and rewards—became the bar's chief topic that summer. The men were exacting readers, and they demanded to be entertained. Words and plots had to be sharp enough, simple enough, to penetrate the penumbra of whatever they were drinking—invaluable training for a young writer. If they weren't as knowledgeable about the rules of writing as the editors at the *Times,* at least they never belittled me for my malapropisms and misspellings.

"The bar is 'like a fart in the badlands?'" Cager said, pointing to one of my pages. "Why is the bar like a fart in the badlands?"

"That's a typo," I said. "Should say 'fort.' Fort in the badlands."

"I think I like it this way. Fart in the badlands. Think about it."

I looked over his shoulder and pondered his suggestion.

"And what's this?" he said. "You wished on a tsar?"

"That should say 'star.'"

"Boy you really can't type. Anyway it's a cliché. *Especially* in Russia."

Mistakes were treated very differently in the Publicans Training Program than in the training program at the *Times.* The difference was brought home to me when I misused the word "panache" in a story for the newspaper. The copyeditor who caught it made me feel a foot tall. Later that night I told

Uncle Charlie and Peter how the copyeditor had dressed me down. "So what does 'panache' mean?" Uncle Charlie asked. "I'm not sure," I said. He set the Book of Words on the bar. "Find out." He walked off to discuss something with Fast Eddy. I flipped to "panache." The definition read "Dashing elegance of manner." Someone had circled the word and written in giant red letters: "SEE CHAS." I showed Peter. He laughed. When Uncle Charlie came back I showed him. "How do you like that?" he said.

"You've never seen this page before?" I asked him.

"You didn't know someone had circled the definition and written your name beside it?" Peter said.

"Nope." Uncle Charlie read the definition out loud. "But it fits, don't it?"

thirty-five | MAJOR LEAGUERS

WALKING INTO GRANDPA'S HOUSE I SAW A STRANGE MAN SITTING at the kitchen table, drinking a glass of milk. "McGraw?" I said.

He jumped up. He was three inches taller than the last time I'd seen him, thirty pounds heavier. He was six-four, at least 220 pounds, and all his baby fat had turned to solid beef. When he hugged me it felt as if he were wearing a shield under his shirt, and his hands, smacking my back, were bigger than Grandma's oven mitts. I was reminded of hugging my father when I was a boy, that sense of being unable to get a grip.

"What are they feeding you in Nebraska?" I asked.

Grandma held up the empty milk container and the bag of Pepperidge Farm cookies he'd just devoured. "Whatever it is," she said, "it's not enough."

I took a beer from the refrigerator and sat across from him. He told me and Grandma about his misadventures on the Great Plains, and had us both laughing. He also told us about learning to be a relief pitcher, the pressure, the intensity, the crowds. I noticed that his stutter had gone from slight to all but unnoticeable.

He asked me about my life. "How's the *New York Times*?" he said. "You a reporter yet?" He asked casually, as if my advancement were as unavoidable as the expansion of his shoulders. I mumbled that it was a long story.

Listening to McGraw, admiring his height and wingspan, and the incredible width of his trunk and legs, I experienced that familiar abandoned feeling, which would come over me whenever McGraw and the cousins moved away. This time it wasn't Aunt Ruth who had kidnapped McGraw, but manhood. McGraw was big and hulking like a man was supposed to be, and I thought of those visits to Rawhide when we were boys, watching the mechanical mannequin cowboys through the chain-link fence. McGraw had joined the mannequins. I was still on the outside, peering in.

Of all the people I loved, I'd said good-bye most often to McGraw. Now it was time to say good-bye again. Good-bye to the chubby-cheeked boy with the buzz cut, hello to this blond superman, who was going to be a problem. By nature, by habit, I looked up to men, but I didn't want to look up to McGraw. He was supposed to look up to me, his older brother, his protector. The only way McGraw could look up to me now was if he lifted me over his head.

Days later I was in my apartment, working on the Publicans novel, when McGraw walked through the door without knocking. "I need to throw," he said. "Keep my arm loose. You up for it?"

He'd brought an extra glove for me. We walked up Plandome Road to Memorial Field, where we spread out, putting about eighty feet between us, then started lobbing the ball back and forth, groaning like arthritics as our shoulders got warm. McGraw rubbed sweat from his brow into the ball. "Slider!" he yelled. The ball sprayed moisture like a sponge as it flew toward me. It veered right, then dipped hard. I barely managed to snare it. He threw another, which seemed to back up and speed forward in midair several times. The thought crossed my mind that McGraw had devised a way to transfer his stutter to the seams of a baseball. As his velocity increased, the ball exploded into my glove with such violence that the bones in my palm felt broken. I stepped into one fastball I threw him, putting everything I could into it, and when McGraw fired the ball back I was embarrassed. His ball had five times the zip. His slider looked like a comet, his curve cut an arc from eleven o'clock to five. Stabbing at his forkball, missing it by a foot, I realized: *McGraw is going to be a professional baseball player.*

In the back of my mind I'd always known this, at least since McGraw was sixteen and his high-school games were scouted by the California Angels.

But that day I saw, and felt in my throbbing palm, that the boy with whom I'd grown up playing catch and worshipping the Mets had raced ahead and stood poised on the verge of achieving our boyhood dream. He'd soon be drafted into the major leagues, probably by the Mets, and his name would be a household word. He'd be the first Met in history to throw a no-hitter. He'd be the next Tom Seaver, while I, Edward R. Murrow-ringer, Mr. Salty, would be the oldest copyboy at the *Times*. McGraw would one day go into the Hall of Fame, and at the induction ceremony the men from the bar would talk in whispers about the two cousins and how different they'd turned out.

I felt a pang of envy, and a rush of pride, but mainly shame. Watching McGraw go through his repertoire of pitches, observing his seriousness and diligence, I understood that my cousin was more than a budding major leaguer. He was a dedicated craftsman, and the rewards he'd gained from hard work went far beyond mastering a slider and a change. He'd mastered himself. He didn't work hard merely because he was talented, but because he knew that hard work was the right path for a man, the only path. He wasn't paralyzed, as I was, by the fear of making a mistake. When he bounced a pitch in front of me, or threw it over my head, he didn't care. He was experimenting, exploring, finding himself, and finding his way by trial and error to a kind of truth. No matter how foolish he looked on a pitch, no matter how badly he missed the target, with the next pitch he was focused, confident, relaxed. He never once that afternoon lost the look on his face that he'd worn when we were boys. He was working hard, but he'd never stopped playing.

Our catch, nothing more than a tune-up for McGraw, was a turning point for me. In one hour he taught me more than all the editors at the *Times* had taught me in the last twenty months. When McGraw returned to Nebraska I returned to the newsroom and became the best copyboy I could be. I drove myself, stretched myself, and by year's end the editors decided I'd earned a tryout. For one month—January 1989—I'd be a full-fledged reporter. Then there would be a formal appraisal of my work. After that, one editor hinted, I might be that one copyboy who emerged from the fake training program. I was overjoyed. Then stricken.

"I'm wigging out," I told Bob the Cop. "My heart is pounding."

"Everyone's heart is pounding," he said.

"Mine's pounding too hard."

"Let me know when it stops pounding altogether."

"There's something wrong with my heart."

"Have a cigarette. Relax."

"Something's wrong, I tell you."

Bob the Cop drove me to the hospital. An emergency-room doctor put an IV in my arm and ran several tests, including an EKG, which came back negative. "Stress," the doctor said as I buttoned my shirt. "Cut down on the stress."

By late 1988, however, my fortress against stress had become a stress factory. The stock market had crashed, suffering its worst single-day slide since the Depression, and Wall Streeters were setting a very different tone at Publicans. Brokers and traders who used to breeze into the bar, putting everyone in a good mood, now sat alone in booths, muttering about their "positions." A meeting place for millionaires had become a refuge for the cash poor. One bright young couple, who used to float into the bar every other night in formal wear, on their way to Carnegie Hall or Lincoln Center, the Gerald and Sara Murphy of Manhasset, now stumbled in, got drunk, bickered. I was there when she threw an ashtray at his head and screamed at him for sleeping with the au pair, and he screamed back at her for spending them into the poorhouse.

For me the crash would always be represented by Mr. Weekend. During the week he wore bespoke suits, starched white shirts and Hermès neckties. From Monday to Friday he never raised his voice or had a hair out of place, and when I saw him on the train he was always reading the *Wall Street Journal,* intently, as if there would be a test later. But every Friday night, without fail, after five days spent vainly trying to recapture his lost fortune, the poor man would walk into Publicans and the bartenders would shout, "Holy shit, everybody—it's Mr. Weekend!" They would seize his car keys while he undid his necktie and for the next forty-eight hours Mr. Weekend would jump on chairs and swing from poles and lounge across tables, singing "Danny Boy," and at some point, for some reason, he would do squat thrusts before passing out in the third booth from the door, as if it were his private berth on an overnight train. I thought many times of introducing myself to him—Mr. Weekend? I'm Mr. Salty—but you couldn't really speak to Mr. Weekend. You could set your watch by him, however, and just as sure as he would arrive Friday night, you could count on seeing him Monday morning, marching smartly up Plandome Road to catch the early train. It was hard to say in that moment if he looked like Mr. Weekend sleepwalking, or like Mr. Weekday just woken from a nightmare.

Few at Publicans were aware, but the one person among us who had been hit hardest by the crash was Steve. His bar in lower Manhattan was in trouble. Steve dreamed up the concept of a high-end Publicans on the Pier when people were using Cristal as Listerine—now everyone was back to clipping coupons. The last thing on people's minds was a juicy overpriced steak and a fancy bottle of overpriced wine. He stood to lose millions. He might lose his house if the banks played hardball. But he'd already lost his most valuable asset. His confidence. The bar in Manhasset had been fine, but Steve had wanted to succeed on the big stage, to be a player, to break into the major leagues. Most likely all the wealth he witnessed in his bar made him think this way. He'd been corrupted by his own customers. He'd watched hundreds and hundreds of people push into Publicans to celebrate their good fortune, and somewhere along the line he'd decided it would be fun to join the party, rather than always be the host. Publicans on the Pier was his chance. Thinking it would be easy, he'd overextended himself, and now for the first time in his charmed life, Steve was failing, and failing big, and Publicans on the Pier was a monument to his failure. There it sat, at the end of the pier, empty as a tomb. A very well-lighted tomb, for which Steve was paying forty-five thousand dollars a month in rent.

"Steve doesn't look good," I told Uncle Charlie a few days before my tryout began.

We both turned to watch Steve, who stood at the end of the bar, angry, wobbly, addled. No Cheshire smile. No trace of the Cheshire smile.

"He looks," Uncle Charlie said, "like Hagler in the late rounds."

Wearing a new pair of suspenders and matching necktie—Christmas gifts from my mother—I was the first one in the newsroom on the first day of 1989. My shoes were polished, my hair was slicked, my pencils were sharp as spikes. The editors gave me a story about a zoning dispute on the East Side, which I attacked as though it were the Watergate break-in. I filed eight hundred words just before deadline, and because I was so nervous the story was a disorganized mess. It read as if it had been written by Fuckembabe. The editors made many changes—sweeping, radical, Professor Lucifer–type changes—and buried the story inside the local section.

On the train back to Manhasset I told myself that I had to find a way to calm down on deadline. I thought of Cager lining up the last shot in a high-stakes game of nine ball. I thought of McGraw throwing a change-up with the bases loaded and the game on the line. I thought of Bob the Cop when confronted with another floater, and Uncle Charlie doing the flamingo tango while mobsters plotted his demise, and Joey D's serene face while beating a drunk senseless. *Relaxkidjustfuckingrelax.* I thought of them all and it helped.

At week's end the editors sent me to Brooklyn, where a teenage girl had been killed, caught in the crossfire of what looked like a gang shooting. I spoke with her friends and teachers and neighbors. She was an aspiring writer, they said. She'd recently started college and dreamed of becoming the next Alice Walker. Her life, like mine, was just beginning, and I felt honored to write about her, and obligated to report her death, which left no time for tensing up. I wrote for an hour and hit the send button on my computer. The editors made a few minor changes and put the story on the front of the local section. Nice work, they said, sounding surprised.

I wanted to stop into Publicans and tell the men about my good day, but I'd vowed to avoid Publicans during my tryout. I tried not to think too much about this vow. I didn't want to admit that the bar could be an obstacle to success, just as I didn't want to examine too closely my difficulty unwinding at the end of a long day. Lying awake at four in the morning, listening to Louie fire up the griddle, I'd ask myself why I was so hot-wired. It wasn't just the absence of alcohol, and it wasn't just stress. Something else was going on. I wondered if it was hope.

As the month progressed I learned to relax on deadline. I even began to enjoy myself, and gained some insight into what had gone wrong at Yale. The first step in learning, I decided, was unlearning, casting off old habits and false assumptions. No one had ever explained this to me, but during my tryout it became obvious. On deadline there was no time for old habits, no time to do what I normally did before writing—making lists of big words and worrying about how I would sound. There was only time for facts, and so the unlearning happened by necessity, almost by force. Before writing a story for the *Times* I'd take a deep breath and tell myself to tell the truth, and I would find the words, or they would find me. I didn't have any illusions. I wasn't writing poetry. I wasn't writing very well at all. But at least what I saw each morning under my byline was different. There was a clarity about it, an authority, which I'd never managed to achieve before, certainly not while working on my Publicans novel.

Halfway through my tryout one of the top editors of the *Times* sent a note to the city editor, who passed it along to me. "Who is this J.R. Moehringer?" the top editor asked. "Please convey my compliments on his fine work."

When I'm promoted, I thought, when I become a full-fledged reporter, Sidney will be sorry. When my byline appears every day in the *Times*, she'll notice, and realize she misjudged me. She'll phone and beg me to take her back.

And maybe I would. After all, I'd changed—maybe she had. In one year I'd gone from barfly to reporter. Who knew what might have become of Sidney?

I went into the men's room at the *Times* and stood before the mirror. I looked different. Wiser? More confident? I couldn't be sure, but it was a distinct improvement. I told my reflection: Soon you'll be earning decent money. Maybe enough to get a real apartment, odor-free, with a kitchen. Maybe enough to send your mother to college. After that—who knows? Maybe enough to court Sidney. And one day buy her a ring.

thirty-six | STEPHEN JR.

DAYS BEFORE THE END OF MY TRYOUT AN EDITOR HANDED ME a small clipping from that morning's *Times*. A man named Stephen Kelley had been gunned down outside his Brooklyn apartment. Police said it looked like a case of road rage. The article was only three hundred words long, but the editor underscored the five or six most important words. Kelley was black, the shooter was white. Worse, the shooter was an off-duty cop. Racial tensions were already high in the city, with memories of Howard Beach and Tawana Brawley still fresh. This shooting had the potential to become another firestorm. The editor asked me to look into it, find out who Stephen Kelley was and write something about him.

I went to Brooklyn with a photographer and we knocked at the door of Kelley's apartment. When it opened we were face-to-face with three McGraw-size men—Kelley's grown sons, including Stephen Jr. I said we were from the *Times* and they invited us in. We sat in their darkened living room, the shades drawn, and the sons told me in gruff, raw voices about their father, who had apparently raised them by himself. He was a tough guy, they said, but also a mother hen, a real worrier, constantly fretting about his "boys." Recently the sons had been planning a get-together for the old man's sixty-second birthday. The sons—there were six in all—lived all over the world, and it was to be a grand reunion, all the Kelley boys returning home for the party. Instead the reunion would take place at their father's graveside.

When it was time to go I promised the sons I'd write a truthful account of everything they had told me about their father. "Listen," Stephen Jr. said, walking me to the door. "Several newspaper stories have misspelled my family's name."

"K-e-l-l-e-y," I said. "Right?"

"Right."

"Believe me, I'll make sure to spell it right. I know how important names are."

I was in the newsroom early the next morning, reading my story over a cup of coffee. I looked up to see the weekend editor on the edge of my desk. "Hell of a job," he said.

"Thanks."

"I mean it. Very nice work. I heard them talking about your story on the radio this morning."

"Really?"

"Keep this up and I see bright things in your future."

He walked away and I tipped back in my chair. Who could have imagined—me, a reporter at the *New York Times*? I wondered if Sidney had seen the story, and if she'd read it. I wanted to phone my mother and read it to her. First I needed to phone the Kelley family.

A man answered on the first ring. I recognized the voice as Stephen Jr.

"Mr. Kelley? J.R. Moehringer from the *Times*. I just wanted to call and thank you for being so generous with your time yesterday. I hope the article was okay."

"Yes. It was fine. But you know, I have to tell you, you spelled our name wrong."

"What?"

"You spelled it wrong. It's spelled K-e-l-l-y."

"I don't understand. At the door, when I said 'K-e-l-l-e-y,' you said, 'Right.'"

"I said, 'Right,' meaning that's how other papers had misspelled it."

"Oh."

My heartbeat was so loud that I was afraid he could hear it. I'd thought my heartbeat was abnormal when Bob the Cop took me to the hospital, but now my heart was knocking against my chest as if it meant to get out.

"I'm so sorry," I said. "I'm so terribly sorry. I didn't understand what you were saying."

"It's all right. But if you could make sure there's a correction."

"Yes. A correction. Of course. I'll talk to the editors. Good-bye, Mr. Kelly."

I went to the men's room and smoked four cigarettes. Then I pulled the towel dispenser off the wall and kicked dents in the metal garbage can and punched the door of a toilet stall until I thought I'd probably broken my knuckles. I locked myself in the stall and tried to decide what to do next. I considered going to the bar across the street and throwing back a half dozen scotches. But there would be plenty of time for drinking later at Publicans. I considered saying nothing, hoping the editors wouldn't notice. But I'd promised the son. Stephen Junior.

Walking back into the newsroom I saw the weekend editor. I went over to his desk. He put a hand on my arm and asked the other editors milling around, "How about this Moehringer, eh?"

He pronounced my name melodically, almost made me like it.

"Well done," the others said.

"Nice job."

"Did you see that the wires tried to match your story?" the weekend editor asked me. "But they couldn't. They didn't get the family. They didn't even spell the family's name right. They spelled it K-e-l-l-y." He laughed mockingly.

"Actually," I said. "I just got off the phone with the family." My voice was shaky. "Apparently, K-e-l-l-y is how they spell their name."

The editor stared. I forged on.

"The son told me yesterday that newspapers had been misspelling the family's name—including this newspaper, by the way. In our first brief about the shooting we spelled the name K-e-l-l-e-y. So I said to the son, 'K-e-l-l-e-y, right?' Meaning, you know, 'That's how you spell your name, right?' And he said, 'Yes,' meaning, 'That's how the other papers have been misspelling it.' It was all a big mix-up."

The editor picked up a pencil, dangled it a foot off his desk, then dropped it. He looked as if he'd like to do the same thing to me. His eyes were screaming, *You're dead, kid.* I held his gaze for as long as I could, then lowered my head. I noticed that he was wearing the most beautiful suspenders. They were beige, with pictures of hula girls. I'd recently seen them in the window of an exclusive men's shop on the East Side.

"We'll have to run a correction," he said quietly.

"Okay."

"I'll write one up and send it to you. Look it over and tell me if it's right."

I returned to my desk and waited for my daily assignment, which never came. The only thing that came my way was the correction. "A picture caption and article on Saturday, about a gathering in remembrance of a Brooklyn man killed in a parking dispute, gave his name incorrectly. He was Stephen Kelly."

Later, sitting at Publicans for the first time in twenty-seven days, I told Uncle Charlie what I'd done. He slammed a bottle on the bar. "How could that happen?" he said. I couldn't tell if he was angry or just disappointed.

I wanted to phone my mother, but there was a line to use the phone, and no one in line had noticed that someone was passed out in the phone booth. Just as well. Only hours earlier I'd been imagining a triumphant phone call, telling my mother to start picking out classes, that I was going to send her to Arizona State University. I needed time to adjust to this new reality.

I was good and drunk when Bob the Cop plodded in. "I've fished floaters out of the harbor that looked better than you," he said.

I told him the story.

"How could that happen?" he said.

"I don't know."

He sighed. "Ah well," he said. "forget it. Honest mistake. That's why they put erasers on pencils."

"You don't understand," I said angrily. "Those poor sons. First, their father is gunned down by some cop, and then I come along with my stupid notebook and make it all worse. And there's no living this down. A million copies are printed. They're out there, everywhere, a million town criers of my stupidity. And when they're all gone, the mistake will live on. Microfilm. Nexus. And I didn't just make a mistake at the *Sacramento Bee*. I made it at The Newspaper of Record. Thanks to my stupidity the record will need to be corrected. And the worst part of all is that I didn't make a mistake about the guy's age or skin color. I made a mistake about his name. Of all things, I should be able to get a man's *name* right."

I'd been aware of Bob the Cop staring at me hard. I'd assumed he was listening intently, but now I realized that my monologue had made him mad. He looked wounded, wronged, and his stare was so intense that it nearly sobered me up. He had something to say, something important. But whatever it was, he swallowed the words. I saw him mentally choose a different tack.

"Why 'of all things' should you get a man's name right?" he asked.

"Because—"

Now it was my turn to swallow words. I might have told him why names were important to me, but I felt exposed enough for one day. When I shook my head and said forget it, we both faced forward and stared at Crazy Jane's stained-glass genitalia, saying nothing. Finally Bob the Cop put a hand on my shoulder. "Go in tomorrow," he said, "and act like nothing happened. No. Don't act like nothing happened. They'll think you're crazy. Act like something happened, but that you're bigger than that something."

"Yeah."

"Trust me. It's no big deal, J.R. You don't know what a mistake is."

thirty-seven | BOB THE COP

WITH THE END OF MY TRYOUT, I ENDED MY DRY-OUT. I RE-turned to Publicans full-time, with a vengeance. I burrowed into the bar, barricaded myself into the bar, became a fixture at the bar, like the jukebox and Fuckembabe. I ate my meals at Publicans, paid my bills at Publicans, made my phone calls from Publicans, celebrated holidays at

Publicans, read and wrote and watched TV at Publicans. On letters I sometimes put Publicans as the return address. I did it as a lark, but it wasn't a lie.

I needed, no less than food and water, that daily hello at the bar, everyone turning and huzzahing as if nothing were wrong, with me or the world. "Well bust my buttons," one bartender would say. "Look what the cat coughed up!" "How are things in Glocca Morra this fine day?" another always said. "Look. Who's. Here," Uncle Charlie would say, my favorite greeting of all. Walking through the door one night I saw Joey D behind the bar. He looked up from his newspaper. "This place is like a lint trap," he said, smirking. "Catches whatever flies through the air." I pointed to Bob the Cop. "Must be why there's so much fuzz." Bob the Cop chuckled, Joey D clapped his hands. "Nice fucking comeback!" he said—*Nicefuckingcomeback!*—and my night was made.

Sometimes the bar felt like the best place in the world, other nights it felt like the world itself. After one especially grueling day at the *Times,* I found the men in a circle at Uncle Charlie's end of the bar. They had arranged cocktail garnishes in the shape of the solar system, a lemon as the sun, and they were moving the olive around the lemon, explaining to each other why New York gets dark before California, why seasons change, how many millennia we have before the whole thing falls apart. I stood behind them, letting their conversation orbit around me. What's a black hole anyway? A thing that sucks up everything in its path. So it's like my ex? Yeah only smaller. I'll tell her you said that. A black hole's like the Grand Canyon with extra gravy. Not gravy, dipshit—gravity. What'd I say? Think of it this way—the universe is held together with gravity, your ex is held together with gravy. Don't use an olive for the earth, I hate olives. Whaddya got against olives? Pits—I don't like food that fights me. Who the fuck ate Mars? Sorry, I see a cherry, I eat a cherry. How big is the fucking earth anyways? It's twenty-five thousand miles around. That sounds almost walkable. You don't even like to walk to the corner for the *Daily News.* You mean to say everyone in this joint is going sixty-seven thousand miles an hour right now? No wonder I feel so fucking dizzy.

The men stopped talking and gazed in wonder at their condiment solar system. The only sounds were a dry cough, a match being struck, Ella Fitzgerald scatting on the stereo, and for a split second I thought I could actually feel Publicans plowing through the cosmos.

I needed the unpredictability of Publicans. One night a famous actor wandered in. His mother lived nearby and he was home for a visit. None of us could stop staring. The Actor had starred in classic films with the best leading men of his generation, and here he was, at Publicans, asking for a glass of buttermilk. He told Uncle Charlie that he always coated his stomach with buttermilk before getting down to some serious drinking. As the night wore on Uncle Charlie teased The Actor about his buttermilk, saying he was the least macho of all the leading men with whom he'd worked. The Actor didn't understand Uncle Charlie's sense of humor. His feelings were hurt. He climbed onto the bar and did military push-ups until Uncle Charlie took it all back and conceded that The Actor was as manly as any man alive.

I needed the quiet times at Publicans. Some of my fondest memories are those dreary, rainy Sunday afternoons, just after my tryout, the barroom empty, a few people having brunch in the back. I'd eat a plate of eggs and read the book review while Mapes, the Sunday bartender, rinsed glasses in soapy water. I'd feel as if I'd walked into my favorite Hopper painting, *Nighthawks*. Mapes even resembled the birdlike soda jerk, stooped over his sink. Eventually Mapes would unfold the stepstool and polish the brass letters that spelled out "Publicans" above the bar, and I'd watch him, envying his concentration. If only I could concentrate on words the way you concentrate on those brass letters, I'd tell Mapes. He'd nod. It wasn't until years later that I realized Mapes never said a single word to me.

On one of those quiet Sunday afternoons I heard someone behind me shout, "Junior!" I turned to see Jimbo, the laid-back waiter with the cherubic face, just home from college. Where did Jimbo get the idea to call me Junior? No one but Steve called me Junior. Then I remembered that Steve was like a father to Jimbo, whose parents divorced when he was young. Jimbo must have overheard Steve call me Junior, and whatever Steve said, Jimbo parroted. I looked at him threateningly—what else could I do? He was too big to deck. He looked like a young Babe Ruth.

He leaned sideways to see the book I was reading. "*A Fan's Notes?*" he said. "What's that about?"

Maybe it was because he'd called me Junior, or maybe it was because I'd had one too many of Mapes's potent Bloody Marys, but I couldn't take it anymore. I let fly at Jimbo. "I hate that question," I said. "I hate when people ask what a book is about. People who read for *plot,* people who suck out the story like the cream filling in an Oreo, should stick to comic strips and soap operas. What's it about? Every book worth a damn is about emotions and love and death and pain. It's about words. It's about a man dealing with life. Okay?"

Mapes looked at Jimbo, looked at me, shook his head.

Jimbo had worked at Publicans since he was fourteen. He'd grown up playing hide-and-seek with Steve's son, Larry, in the tunnels below the bar. "Like Huck and Tom in the caves," he often said proudly. Jimbo had even met McGraw, his best friend all through high school, at a pizza party in Publicans after one of their baseball games. He might have been the only young man in town who loved the bar more than I. He got the same things from it, the same kinds of emotional nourishment from Steve and the men. I'd been trying to write about the bar? Jimbo *was* the bar. He was as good and loyal a soul as you could hope to find there. Remembering all this, realizing that Jimbo was a son of Publicans, and therefore my brother, I felt rotten for berating him. I apologized.

Forget it, he said, and he meant it. That was one of the great things about Jimbo.

Dalton walked in. He was waving a first edition of *The Ginger Man,* which he'd borrowed from Uncle Charlie. "'Today a rare sun of spring,'" he shouted in my ear. "That's the opening line of this novel. That's poetry, Asshole. That's the English goddamn language. I love you, Asshole, but honestly, you'll never write a sentence that good."

"No argument here," I said.

"Dude!" Jimbo said to Dalton reproachfully. "That's harsh."

I looked at Jimbo. Not one minute earlier I'd been berating him, and now he was defending me. That was another one of the great things about Jimbo.

Uncle Charlie arrived. He hopped behind the bar, relieving Mapes, and jumped headlong into our literary salon. He cited his favorite parts of *The Ginger Man,* and soon we were trading lines and passages from our favorite writers, Kerouac and Mailer and Hammett. Someone mentioned the cult classic *Nightwork,* by Irwin Shaw. Someone compared it to a short story by Melville.

"Melville!" Uncle Charlie said. "Oh he's the best. *Billy Budd.* Ever read that one? See, Billy Budd is Christlike." Uncle Charlie rolled his eyes skyward and spread his arms as if being crucified. "Billy goes willingly to the gallows because he knows he made a mistake. Follow? He killed Claggart by mistake and he must pay. 'God bless Captain Vere,' that's what Billy says when they put his neck in the noose, because rules must be obeyed. Without rules you have anarchy. Billy made a mistake and pays with his life—pays willingly, because he believes in the rules, even though he broke them. You follow?"

"I think we read that one in high school," Jimbo said. "Remind me— what's it about?"

He shot an elbow to my ribs. I laughed. Then I spotted Bob the Cop beside the cigarette machine. He had a menacing look on his face, and I knew he must have come into the bar when I wasn't looking, and he must have heard me berating Jimbo. And now he must have thought me a jackass.

The very next night Bob the Cop sought me out at the bar. He pulled me into the corner and practically pushed me up against the cigarette machine. I understood all at once how it would feel to be busted by Bob the Cop. "I was listening to you last night," he said. "Talking about books."

"Yeah. I wasn't in the best mood. I should have cut Jimbo some slack but—"

"I didn't go to college. You know. I went into the police academy right after high school. My father was a cop, my grandfather, so what else was I going to do, right? I don't think about it much, but whenever I hear you guys talking about books I feel—I don't know. Like I'm missing out."

I started to apologize, but he held up his palm. Bob the Traffic Cop.

"I'm a cop," he said. "I am what I am. I'm not kidding myself. But sometimes I think there must be more. *I* must be more. You notice how everyone always calls me Bob the Cop? Never Bob the Father, Bob the Fisherman. And sure as shit never Bob the Bookworm. It irks me. No one ever calls you J.R. the Copyboy."

"Thank God for small mercies," I said.

"Anyway," Bob the Cop said, "I was thinking. I remembered lugging all those books up to your apartment when I helped you move, and I was just wondering if maybe—you know." I shook my head. I didn't know. "I was wondering," he said haltingly, "if you might have any books you're not using."

My first thought was that, technically, I wasn't using any of my books. I saw that Bob the Cop thought of books as tools. He thought of most things as tools. Even his drinks were tools: Screwdrivers and Rusty Nails. I wanted to explain that books didn't have the same explicit purpose as tools, that there wasn't a clear difference between when books were in use and when they weren't. I took pleasure from their presence, enjoyed seeing them lined up on my shelves and floors. They were the only redeeming feature of my squalid apartment. My books kept me company, cheered me up. Furthermore, because every book I'd owned as a boy was mildewed from the basement or missing its front cover, I was fussy about my books. I didn't write in the margins or dog-ear the pages, and I never loaned them, especially not the first editions given to me by the editors of the *Times Book Review* when I did my little author interviews. But I couldn't say any of this to Bob the Cop because it would have sounded ungenerous, so I told him that he was welcome to stop by the next day and help himself to whatever books I wasn't using.

Then I did a bad thing. I selected a painfully dense 842-page analysis of the Middle East, and a hopelessly dull 785-page history of explorers at the North Pole, and the following morning, when Bob the Cop came barging through my door (like McGraw, he never knocked—a big man's prerogative) I told him I'd taken the liberty of choosing two books he was sure to enjoy. I knew that if I gave Bob the Cop those enormous, impenetrable tomes, he'd never ask for more.

Together the books weighed as much as a frozen turkey, and when I placed them on Bob the Cop's outstretched hands he gave me a look of such gratitude and tenderness that I wanted to tell him to wait, I was only kidding, I'd find him some books he'd actually enjoy, books by London and Hemingway and Shaw. Here, take *Nightwork*. Take Nick Adams. Take them all, my friend. But it was too late. With both unreadable books wedged under his massive arm Bob the Cop was already skipping down the stairs.

I didn't see Bob the Cop at Publicans for two weeks and I knew there could be only one explanation. He was cracking his head on those books. The man had reached out to me for help in educating himself, like Helen Keller or

Booker T. Washington, and I'd sabotaged him. Why hadn't I just bludgeoned him to death with the books and been done with it?

A heavy snowstorm shut down New York. Most stores and offices were closed. Publicans, however, was mobbed. Though the roads were impassable, whole families came to the bar on sleds, and stayed most of the night, because they had no lights or heat at home. I was standing at the bar, trying to shed the chill of my apartment, a long scarf wrapped around my neck, when Wheelchair Eddie arrived. "'Rollin', rollin', rollin','" Colt sang. Colt always sang the theme from *Rawhide* when Wheelchair Eddie rolled his wheelchair through the barroom, and Wheelchair Eddie always hated it, which only made Colt sing more lustily. I laughed, then remembered that Wheelchair Eddie lived across the street from Bob the Cop. I asked if he'd seen his neighbor recently. "Yeah," he said. "I just seen him. He's out in his yard making one of them ice huts."

"Say again?"

"One of them huts that them mooks live in at the North Pole."

"What the hell are you talking about?"

"I can't think of the word—you know them people who live at the North Pole?"

"Eskimos?"

"Yeah! And what do you call them huts they live in?"

"Igloos?"

"Right! He's building one of them igloo thingamajigs that them Eskimooks live in."

"In his front yard?"

I was about to trudge downhill and investigate when Bob the Cop himself walked in. He took off his mittens, whapped them on the bar and ordered a drink.

I sidled up to him. "Wheelchair Eddie says you've been building an igloo?" I said.

He sniffed and blew into his fist. "Got the idea from that book you gave me," he said.

"There were igloo blueprints in that book?"

"The book talks about all those British pansies who explored the North Pole in the 1800s and how they kept dropping like flies because they refused to do like the Eskimos did. The British treated the North Pole like it was

Piccadilly Circus, and didn't adapt to the, what do you call, environment. If they had learned to build an gloo, they wouldn't have died. Dumb fucks."

"So you read between the lines and figured out how to build an igloo and decided to give it a try?"

"I tell you, J.R., I cannot thank you enough for loaning me that book. It had me on the edge of my seat."

"It—did?"

"I couldn't put it down. That's why I ain't been around. I've been *reading*."

"And the Middle East history?"

"Read that one first."

He gave me a brief synopsis of the Palestinian crisis.

"I'm glad you weren't inspired to build a refugee camp in your yard," I said. "You finished *both* books? Sixteen hundred pages? In two weeks?"

Bob the Cop shrugged. No big deal. From that moment on I pledged to myself that Bob the Cop was welcome to whatever books I wasn't using.

Bob the Cop was already my best friend at the bar, but the birth that winter of our two-man book club transformed our friendship. We began spending more time together outside the bar. He'd teach me things—how to change a tire, bait a hook, drink a Rusty Nail, a hellish concoction of scotch and Drambuie—and I'd reciprocate by teaching him to rewrite his police reports in clearer prose. It was not an even exchange. Our writing sessions benefited me far more than they did Bob the Cop. I never could convince him that it was better to write "The man said" rather than "The perpetrator stated." And yet it always gave me pause when I heard myself telling Bob the Cop that it wasn't such a good idea to lard his reports with big words.

When we both had the day off, Bob the Cop and I would take his vintage twenty-foot Penn Yan boat to the city. He'd loan me one of his NYPD jackets for warmth, and we'd drift around the Statue of Liberty, fishing for fluke, or float along South Street Seaport. I would stand in the prow of his boat, feeling the spray on my face, watching clouds snag themselves on the tops of the twin towers. Late in the day we'd dock at Pier 17 to get a sandwich or an ice cream. We'd always peek inside Publicans on the Pier, and it was always empty. Bob the Cop would shake his big head at the long row of vacant barstools. "Steve's got trouble," he'd say. "Trouble," I'd say, feeling for Steve, but thinking of Sidney, as I always did when I heard that word.

We were an unlikely duo, the cop and the copyboy, but so much about Bob the Cop was unlikely. The stoic storyteller. The brutish bookworm. The softhearted tough guy. I once heard him tell a story about his kids that was so sweet, Cager was wiping his eyes. Not five minutes later I asked Bob the Cop if his wife ever got suspicious about his being out every night. "Nah," he said. "She knows I'm no Irish fag." I said I wasn't familiar with the term. "Irish fag," he said. "A guy who'd walk past a bar to be with a broad."

Ever since he'd begun borrowing my books, Bob the Cop seemed changed. He was more talkative, more likely to venture an opinion on various esoteric subjects. The books seemed to give him not so much new opinions as new confidence in his opinions. He wasn't happy, exactly, but he wasn't quite so burdened, and even his tread seemed a bit lighter. He no longer plodded into the bar with the world on his shoulders. I was surprised therefore to find Bob the Cop at the bar one night, sorrowful, morose, guzzling Rusty Nails.

"What's up, flatfoot?"

He looked at me as though we'd never met.

"You work today?" I asked.

"Funeral."

His white dress gloves were on the bar.

"Someone you knew?"

He didn't answer.

"You look beat," I said.

"I don't do well at funerals. Especially cop funerals."

He told me about the ceremony. Flag-draped coffin. White-gloved hands crisply saluting. Bagpipes. Nothing in the world, he said, half as haunting as a bagpipe.

"But you didn't know the cop who was killed?" I asked.

"I know them all."

He rubbed his eyes and then drank off the rest of his Rusty Nail, quaffed it like an iced tea. "You never looked me up at the *Times*," he said. "Did you?"

"No."

He waited, as if the words were floating up from deep inside him. As a rookie, he said, about my age, he was on patrol when he heard gunshots. "You know how they talk about everything going in slow motion?" he said. "It's true. You're running and running and your feet feel like they're tied to cinder blocks." He turned down a street, came around a blind corner, and there before him was a man holding a gun on another man. When Bob the Cop yelled, the gunman turned and pointed his gun. Bob the Cop fired, killing him instantly.

"Jesus," I said.

"It gets worse," he said. "The guy I killed was a cop. Nineteen years on the force. Plainclothes. He was trying to collar the other guy."

Friends of the dead cop demanded Bob the Cop's badge, even after an investigation found that the shooting was an accident. An *accident*, Bob the Cop repeated. The friends weren't satisfied. They stalked Bob the Cop, jumped him, ganged up on him, beat him bloody. That's why Bob the Cop transferred to Harbor, he said. He needed a place to lie low, hide.

"Did the cop have—family?" I asked.

Bob the Cop looked deeply into the grain of the bar top. "A son," he said. "He killed himself a year later."

All the conversations I'd had with Bob the Cop came rushing back. I thought how differently I'd have worded every sentence if I'd known about his past. I thought of my tantrum over misspelling Kelly. I remembered calling it a mistake I'd have to live with the rest of my life, and going on and on about making things worse for Kelly's sons—after some cop had gunned down their father.

I told Bob the Cop how sorry I was. He waved off my apology.

"Honest mistake," he said. "Like I told you, that's why they put erasers on pencils. But J.R., believe me. They do not put erasers on guns."

thirty-eight | MICHELLE AND THE FISHER QUEEN

MANY PEOPLE THOUGHT OF PUBLICANS AS THE PLAYBOY MANSION of Manhasset. Like sanctuary, sex was one of the foundational premises of the bar, so it made a kind of sense that people had sex all over the premises. In the parking lot, in the bathrooms, in the basement—people who drank away every inhibition couldn't be expected to resist the strongest urge of all. Even employees were swept away by the hormonal undertow. A waitress and a cook once got caught having sex on the same butcher block where Fuckem-babe packed the hamburger patties. There were many jokes thereafter about how strange the burgers tasted, and Uncle Charlie never tired of asking customers if they *really* wanted their burger "between two buns."

In the spring of 1989, however, the standard sexual energy at Publicans increased tenfold. A virulent epidemic of spring fever broke out, and everyone went staggering around the barroom in a daze, though it took a keen observer to detect how this was different from the rest of the year. Each night we'd stand outside the bar at sunset, in groups of twenty or thirty men and women, watching the April sky turn a dark, ethereal blue—"a Maxfield Parrish blue," one waitress remarked as we all went back inside. After tracking mud and slush into the bar all winter, each of us now trailed into Publicans a patch of that blue sky.

The Actor turned up again. He told us he was home to visit his mother, but it was a lie. He was nursing a broken heart. He'd been jilted by a beautiful starlet, a wildly sexy blond we'd all lusted after. Many nights The Actor would bring his guitar to Publicans and sing mournful Spanish love ballads—he sounded a little like Neil Young—while Dalton would recite Rilke to a gorgeous ash blond from the Upper Hudson Valley, who he talked about marrying. Even Uncle Charlie had a girlfriend that heady spring. He bent himself into the phone booth and sang to her: "My Funny Valentine." He didn't bother to shut the door, so we all had to listen. He also didn't bother to check the time and his girlfriend wasn't happy about being awakened at two in the morning. She let him know it, and he stopped singing to rebuke her for scolding him, then resumed singing, and it all sounded something like this: "'My Funny Valen'—shut the fuck up! 'Sweet comic Val'—shut your goddamn mouth! 'You make me smile with my'—pipe down while I'm fucking serenading you, you bitch!"

Like the chokecherries and black locusts along Manhasset Bay, a fresh batch of women bloomed overnight in the barroom. Uncle Charlie and I watched them appear all around us. "Where do they all come from?" he asked. "Where do they come from, J.R., and where do they all go?" He was asking abstractly, existentially, but the fact was that many of them came from Helsinki and London, to work as au pairs for wealthy families in town. Others were new salesgirls hired at Lord & Taylor. And at least a dozen were new emergency-room nurses from North Shore. There were also scores of college students and grads living with their parents until they could find apartments in the city. Among this last group was Michelle.

She had jet-black hair and warm brown eyes with a spot of cinnamon in the center. Her voice was smokier than the bar, and it made her sound strong, which she was, though she was also shy. She would cower meekly from Uncle Charlie, then turn and mock me fearlessly about my "borrowed" suspenders and ties. I liked Michelle a lot. I liked the way she laughed, silently, her mouth open a second or two before she made a sound. I liked her smile, which in another era would have been called fetching. I liked that I'd known her family all my life—McGraw and I had played Little League with her older brother. After only a few dates I had high hopes for our budding romance, even after Michelle confessed that she'd once made out with McGraw.

"You and McGraw?" I said. "Not possible."

"We were in seventh grade, at a party. Drinking rum and—milk, I think?"

"Yep. That's McGraw."

Michelle was perfect, the best Manhasset had to offer. I should have thrown myself at her, dedicated all my energy to winning her, but I found it hard to be the man she deserved. After Sidney, and several failed attempts at replacing Sidney, I wasn't sure I believed in romantic love anymore. My only objective with women was to avoid being fooled again, which meant remaining aloof, noncommittal, like Sidney herself. Besides, I didn't know what to make of a woman like Michelle—loyal, kind, true. Her virtues clashed with my experience and my lowered expectations.

I held Michelle at bay, therefore, while keeping the occasional rendezvous with a heavily mascaraed woman who was just the right combination of discreet and undiscriminating. At last call she'd catch my eye from across the barroom and give me a thumbs-up with a querulous look. If I gave thumbs-down she'd shrug and wave good-bye. If I gave thumbs-up she'd hop off her stool and hurry out of the bar meeting me five minutes later in front of

Louie the Greek's. When Thumbelina wasn't around I'd spend time flirting and getting nowhere with a snubnosed British au pair who talked like Margaret Thatcher and drew me into long discussions about the Battle of Hastings and Admiral Horatio Nelson. I found her accent distracting, her passion for British history difficult to share, but I was fascinated by her skin, which was like bone china, and her eyes, which were sapphires. I also had a few frustrating dates with a grad student I met in the city, who took a bohemian view of hygiene. Her hair was tangled, her clothes wrinkled, her feet dirty. I overlooked her grubbiness because of her other redeeming qualities—a towering intellect and mesmerizing pear-shaped breasts. When she told me that she was writing her graduate thesis about marine life in New York City, I brought her immediately to Publicans and introduced her to Bob the Cop. She told Bob the Cop what was swimming in the rivers and harbors, and he told her what was floating. The first time she went to the ladies' room Bob the Cop pulled me aside and said excitedly, "I cannot believe you found a broad with cans like those who knows about fish!" Cager, however, did not like my date. He ordered me to break up with the Fisher Queen, immediately.

"Why?"

"She's too—smart."

I scoffed.

"Suit yourself," he said.

Hours later, at my apartment, I lay on the floor with the Fisher Queen, listening to Sinatra. "Why do you love Frank Sinatra so much?" she asked.

No one had ever asked me that question. I tried to explain. Sinatra's voice, I said, is the voice most men hear in their heads. It's the paradigm of maleness. It has the power men strive for, and the confidence. And yet when Sinatra is hurt, busted up, his voice changes. Not that the confidence goes away, but just beneath the confidence is a strain of insecurity, and you hear the two impulses warring for his soul, you hear all that confidence and insecurity in every note, because Sinatra lets you hear, lays himself bare, which men so seldom do.

Pleased with this explanation, I turned up the volume, a recording of Sinatra's earliest stuff with Tommy Dorsey.

"Have you always liked him?" the Fisher Queen asked.

"Always."

"Even as a boy?"

"Especially as a boy."

"Interesting." She dragged a finger through her hair, stopping at a knot. "I've been meaning to ask you. Did your father leave anything behind when your parents split? Any pictures?"

"My mother threw all his pictures out."

"Clothes?"

"He left some turtlenecks. Stuff like that. Junk."

"What else?"

I closed my eyes. "I remember some Italian cookbooks with red sauce stains on the covers."

"And?"

"I remember a big stack of old Sinatra alb—" I turned my head. The Fisher Queen looked sad, but proud, almost gloating, as if she'd guessed the ending of a mystery novel after the first page.

"Yeah," she said. "There had to be a reason."

"I must have started listening to Sinatra when I couldn't find my father's voice on the radio."

I stood and started pacing.

"Have I freaked you out?" she asked.

"You mean Heimliching extremely painful revelations out of me? Nah."

I lay awake most of the night, and in the morning I said good-bye forever to the Fisher Queen. Who knew what disturbing truths she might discover next? The only hard part was telling Bob the Cop, who was hoping to see a lot more of the Fisher Queen. But when I told him the story, he understood. More than most men Bob the Cop believed that things at the bottom of our inner harbors should float up in their own time, of their own accord.

I thanked Cager for warning me, and apologized for doubting him. Unlike the Fisher Queen, he didn't gloat. "Dumb ones," he said. "Stick to the dumb ones, kid."

He was half joking, but that was the moment I decided to stop calling Michelle. I considered it an act of kindness to Michelle, removing myself from her life. I was too confused about women to do anything but waste her time. She deserved the best, and I didn't deserve anyone better than Thumbelina.

Not long after my decision about Michelle, I was drinking with Dalton and his new girlfriend. Peter was behind the bar, reading some of my pages. I told Peter that while his editing was improving, my writing was getting worse. Everything was getting worse, I told him. Peter started to say something encouraging, but like a sleepwalker I went to the phone booth and dialed Sidney.

It was two in the morning. A man answered. Trust-Funder? I said nothing. I listened to him listening to me. "Who is it?" Sidney asked in the background. "I don't know," Trust-Funder said. I was going to ask for Sidney, then burst into "My Funny Valentine." I was drunk enough, bold enough with spring fever, but I wasn't entirely sure that singing was the best way to win Sidney back, and while confidence and insecurity were warring for my soul, the line went dead.

thirty-nine | THE EDITOR

I LIFTED MY SELF-IMPOSED EMBARGO ON MY MOTHER THAT SAME spring. Once again I phoned her regularly from the newsroom. She never asked why I'd stopped phoning, or why I'd started again. She understood, better than I, and picked up where she'd left off, offering encouragement and wisdom. Sometimes I would quote her at the bar—without crediting her, of course—and the men would compliment me on my sagacity.

Keep writing, my mother said. Keep trying. Maybe if I forgot the Kelly Debacle, she said, the *Times* would too. This sounded like too much to hope for, but I followed her advice because I couldn't think what else to do.

Each week the *Times* real estate section ran an obscure feature called "If You're Thinking of Living In . . ." A different town was highlighted every Sunday, and I proposed a piece about Manhasset. The editors gave me the nod, and for weeks I roamed up and down Plandome Road, interviewing people about my hometown. I was glad to be reporting again, and I enjoyed learning things about Manhasset, like the fact that the Marx Brothers used to go there specifically to get drunk. When I sat down in the newsroom with my notes, however, I was more blocked than when I tried to write the bar novel. Haunted by the voice of Stephen Kelly Jr., compulsively checking and rechecking the spelling of every name and word, I couldn't get past the first few paragraphs. Eventually I took the story to Publicans on a quiet Sunday and sat with Mapes, polishing my words while he polished his brass letters. I wrote the whole story in longhand at the bar, which may have been why it started and ended there. The final word of the story was "Publicans."

It ran on a Sunday in April 1989. When I walked into Publicans that night Steve was waiting. He came toward me, his face unusually red. I thought he looked furious. Maybe I'd misspelled the name of the bar. "Junior!" he shouted.

"Yes?"

He gave me his biggest Cheshire smile, the one he saved for his closest friends and his greatest softball victories, and folded me in a hug. "What a nice job," he said.

I saw my story spread across the bar, his Heineken holding it down like a paperweight.

The story was trivial, a dry overview of Manhasset—schools, home prices, that sort of thing—and two mentions of its most important gathering place. But Steve acted as if I'd written *Finnegans Wake*. He said I had "a way with words," and I took a step back, knowing that this was one of Steve's highest compliments. Steve was a word man. It showed in the care he took naming his bar, in naming all of us, and in the crowd his bar attracted. Silver-tongued raconteurs, bullshit artists, florid storytellers. Also, maybe more than all the men, Steve esteemed newspapers, and seeing his gin mill mentioned in the world's finest newspaper was one of the few good things to happen to him of late. I'd briefly taken his mind off the other Publicans, the dying Publicans, which had all but gone bankrupt. He was so appreciative, so kind, that I got carried away, and told Steve that I hoped to write a novel some day about Publicans.

He responded with about as much enthusiasm as my mother had when I made the same announcement to her, at about the same spot in the barroom. "Uh-huh," he said. His reaction puzzled me, and thinking it over later I wondered if Steve believed that Publicans already *was* a book. Walking through the door always did feel like entering a sprawling work of fiction. Maybe Steve intended that feeling when he first named the bar Dickens. He'd created his own Dickensian world, complete with a Dickensian fog—clouds of cigar and cigarette smoke. He'd even named all the characters. Maybe Publicans was Steve's Great American Novel and he didn't see the point of someone writing another novel about it.

Then again, I thought, maybe Steve just had a lot on his mind.

The editors liked my Manhasset story, but not quite enough to forget my past sins. I was told that my case would soon be coming up for final review. The secret committee would meet and decide once and for all if J.R. Moehringer was *Times* material, and to help them in their deliberations I was "asked" to write a one-page letter, addressing the following question: "Why does a Yale graduate have so much trouble spelling?"

Bob the Cop shook his head when I told him about this humiliating assignment. I was considering writing the secret committee a letter in which I used a few well-chosen four-letter words, each spelled correctly, but he told me to stay cool, do whatever the secret committee asked. Steady as she goes, he said. You're in the home stretch.

Working late in the newsroom one night, drafting my I'm-sorry-I'm-such-an-idiot letter to the secret committee, I got a call from Bebe, my barroom-loving friend from college, the only one of my friends who had ever "met" JR Maguire. She invited me out for a drink. We met at a Broadway bar we both liked. She threw her arms around my neck when I walked in. "Let's get smashed," she said.

"Twist my arm."

We ordered martinis. They came in glasses as big as upside-down dunce caps. Bebe caught me up on the gossip from our class. I asked about Jedd Redux. She'd seen him recently at a party and he looked swell. While talking she kept one eye on the bartender. Whenever our glasses were half empty, she'd signal him to bring another round.

"Whoa," I said. "I haven't eaten any dinner. I'll be flat on my back."

She told the bartender to ignore me, keep the martinis coming.

As I finished my third martini she rocked forward and asked, "Are you drunk?"

"God yes."

"Good." She rocked back. "Sidney's getting married."

There are 206 bones in the human body and I was suddenly conscious of each one. I looked at the floor, then Bebe's feet, then the bartender, who was standing with his arms folded, eyes narrowed, watching me closely, as if Bebe had warned him ahead of time what was going to happen.

"Honey, I wasn't sure if I should tell you," Bebe said tearfully.

"No, you did right. Tell me what you know."

She knew everything. She heard it all from a friend of Sidney's best friend. Sidney was marrying Trust-Funder.

"Have they set a date?"

"Memorial Day weekend."

"Okay. That's enough. I don't want to know any more."

I wanted to pay my check and hurry to Publicans.

The Friday before Memorial Day weekend I was separating carbons in the newsroom, thinking about Sidney and how to survive the next seventy-two hours, when I looked up. Beside me stood the secretary for the editor in charge of the training program. "He was just looking for you," she said, pointing her pencil at the editor's glass office.

"I've been right here."

"I looked. You weren't."

"I must have gone for sandwiches."

"That's a shame. He wanted to see you." She widened her eyes to indicate that the editor's desire to see me was important and without precedent. "But he's gone now. Left for the holiday weekend. Are you free Tuesday?"

"Is it good news?"

Her eyes still wider, she pursed her lips and turned an invisible key.

"It is good news?" I said.

She turned the key again and threw it over her shoulder. Then she gave me a warm and congratulatory smile.

"I'm going to be promoted!"

"Tuesday," she said.

How perfect. How fitting. On the same weekend Sidney became Mrs. Trust-Funder, I would become a reporter at the *New York Times*. If only I'd been at my desk when the editor wanted me, I might have spent the weekend reliving the happy scene, which would have helped blot out the recurring image of Sidney walking down the aisle.

No, I told myself, this will be better. The anticipation will be sweeter.

. . .

It was Game Six all over again when I announced at Publicans that I'd been promoted. The men threw napkins in the air and cheered. They tousled my hair and begged Uncle Charlie for the privilege of buying the reporter his first drink as a reporter. Steve insisted my promotion had something to do with my story about Manhasset, which he kept referring to as my "story about Publicans."

I decided to spend my last weekend as a copyboy visiting college friends in New Haven. Still woozy from the big celebration at Publicans I caught a train early Saturday morning. I felt sad when the train stopped in Sidney's hometown, but it was a sadness I could manage. Things were working out for both of us. We'd been traveling different roads, and now we'd reached our separate destinations at the same moment. Everything made sense. Everything had happened for a reason. Had I been wooing Sidney the last three years, fighting to wrest her from Trust-Funder, I wouldn't have had the energy necessary to become a reporter at the *Times*. Still, I thought, she must look lovely walking down that aisle, her blond hair up, her face breathtaking as Trust-Funder lifts the veil. I couldn't imagine how much more agonizing these visions would have been if my own special day weren't hours off.

Before seeing my old friends at Yale, I visited my oldest and steadiest friend, my spreading elm. I sat beneath the tree, drinking a cup of coffee, feeling how far I'd come. I walked around campus, pausing at every bench and stone wall where I'd despaired as an undergrad. I visited the courtyards and street corners where Sidney and I had laughed or kissed or planned our future. I listened to the bells of Harkness, ate lunch at my old bookstore café, and I felt more grateful, more alive, than the day I'd graduated, because I considered this graduation, from copyboy to reporter, a greater miracle.

Tuesday morning I presented myself to the editor's secretary at nine sharp. She made a motion for me to wait, then walked into the editor's office. He was on the phone. I saw her point to me. The editor smiled and waved. *Come in, come in.*

He motioned to a seat across from his desk. "Overseas," he whispered, pointing to the phone. I sat.

The editor in charge of the training program was a former foreign correspondent, and trotting around the world for many years had given him a worldly air. Though bald, his scalp was deeply tanned and the vestigial hair around the perimeter of his head was thick and yellow. He made baldness chic, enviable. His suit was custom-made—London, no doubt—and his shoes, chocolate brown lace-ups, had clearly been hand-sewn in Italy. Someone had once told me that this editor had been buying his shoes from the same old cobbler in Italy for years. I wondered if this was true. I'd also heard rumors about his affair with a notoriously trampy movie star, and his profound disenchantment when he discovered that her breasts were fake.

He hung up and folded his hands on his desk and asked about my holiday weekend. I told him about visiting Yale. "I'd forgotten you were a Yalie," he said. "Yes," I said. He smiled again. A Steve smile, almost. I smiled.

"Well then," he said. "As you've probably suspected the editors have had a chance to carefully review your work—and it's terrific. Truly, some of the pieces you've done for us have been outstanding. That's why I wish I had better news. As you know, when the committee meets to consider a trainee, some editors voice support, others do not. A vote is taken. I'm prevented from telling you who voted how, or why, but I'm afraid the end result is that I cannot offer you a position as a reporter."

"I see."

"The feeling is that you need more experience. More seasoning. A smaller newspaper, perhaps, where you can learn and grow."

He made no mention of pretzel fires and Kelly misspellings. He didn't cite my ebb-and-flow productivity, didn't refer to my I'm-sorry-I'm-such-an-idiot letter. He was a model of compassion and tact. He stressed that I could stay at the *Times* as long as I liked. If I chose to leave, however, if I wanted the kind of gritty writing experience that could be gotten only through daily deadline writing, the *Times* would certainly understand, and the editors would wish me well and send me off with glowing letters of recommendation.

He was right of course. It had been preposterous, and presumptuous, to think I was qualified to be a reporter for the *Times*. I did need seasoning, plenty of it, more than he knew. I thanked him for his time and reached across the desk to shake his hand. I noticed his fingers as they came toward me. They were slender and manicured. His clasp was firm, the skin soft, but not too soft, not effeminate. They were the hands of a concert pianist, or a magician, or a surgeon. They were the hands of a mature man, unlike my hands, with their split cuticles and tobacco-stained fingertips. Mine were the hands of an urchin. His hands had tapped out whistling dispatches from war zones, and fondled the breasts of movie stars. Mine had committed appalling errors, ludicrous misspellings, and had routinely turned to claws with a kind of creative rigor mortis. I wished we could trade hands for one day. And hair. Then I despised myself for this wish. The man had just told me I wasn't good enough, and yet I couldn't stop liking him, and coveting his body parts. As he offered me a few final words of encouragement, I wasn't listening. I was telling myself, *Get mad!* There would be something healthier, I thought, in shouting at the editor, or cold-cocking him. Joey D would lunge at this guy, I thought, right over the desk, feet first. Joey D would take the editor by that yellow hair, that silky, luminous fringe—*how much did the man spend on conditioner?*—and swab the desktop with him. I wished I were Joey D. I wished I were this editor, who was now guiding me out of his office and closing the door in my face.

I walked around Manhattan, trying to think, for hours. Eventually I phoned my mother from a bar in Penn Station. She said she was proud of my efforts. "Why don't you come to Arizona?" she said. "Get a fresh start."

"I'm going to Publicans."

"I meant in the future."

But Publicans was as far into the future as I could see.

forty | SECRETARIAT

I TOOK A WEEK OFF FROM THE *TIMES* AND LOCKED MYSELF IN MY apartment. I left just twice a day, to get breakfast at Louie the Greek's and to pad down to Publicans at dusk. The rest of the time I sat in my boxer shorts, drinking beer and watching old Cary Grant movies on a handheld black-and-white TV. I never was so grateful for my two rooms above the diner. I no longer minded the smells, nor the fact that Dalton took naps in my bed when I was out. For all its shortcomings the apartment was my home, and it came as a heavy blow, therefore, when Don and Dalton told me they were expanding their practice and needed the space. For the price of a few books Bob the Cop helped me move back to Grandpa's.

The house was crowded—Aunt Ruth and several cousins were living there again—but I told myself it wouldn't be bad. I'd save money on rent. I'd be a few steps closer to Publicans. And I'd see more of McGraw, who would soon be home from Nebraska for the summer. We'd share a bedroom again, for the first time since we were boys.

Best of all, McGraw was finally legal. The New York State Legislature had done everything possible to keep McGraw out of Publicans, raising the drinking age every time he was on the verge of another birthday. But in 1989 the lawmakers finally stopped at twenty-one, leaving McGraw, who had just turned twenty-one, free at last to visit the bar. His first night home, a week after I'd moved back in, we coated our stomachs with one of Grandma's gelatinous casseroles, doused ourselves with cologne, and sprinted to the bar. I held the door for McGraw.

"After you."

"No, after you."

"Please."

"I insist."

"Age before beauty."

We walked in side by side. A cheer went up along the bar.

"Look. Who's. Here."

"Oh brother," Cager said. "Adult swim is over. The kiddies are in the pool."

The men pulled bills from their piles and waved them at Uncle Charlie. It looked like a run on the bank. "Nephews!" Uncle Charlie said. "You're backed up on everybody."

The men shouted questions at McGraw. How's the arm, stud? What kind of season you have? Bang any farmers' daughters lately? McGraw answered each question smoothly, deftly, as though giving a locker-room press conference. I stepped aside, into the barroom shadows, which seemed a shade darker that night because of the golden aura surrounding McGraw. He was a star at Nebraska, and everyone knew he had set a school record for most appearances by a pitcher in a single season. Uncle Charlie wanted to know all the details of this record. How many appearances? What was the previous record for appearances? Uncle Charlie said McGraw would be a pro within three years. He'd get a fat signing bonus, buy a sports car, burn up the minor leagues, and before long we'd all be meeting at Publicans to catch the train to Shea, where we'd watch McGraw mow down major-league hitters.

Despite the warm reception they gave him, the men weren't quite sure how to take this new McGraw. Like me, they were proud and intimidated at the same time. They went back and forth between kidding him as if he were still ten, and deferring to him as if he were their king. At times I thought they might weave him a crown of cherry stems and swizzle sticks. Cager had marched through minefields in Cu Chi, Bob the Cop had dodged bullets in Brooklyn, Fast Eddy had plummeted to earth at 150 miles an hour, but they all stepped aside for McGraw that night, because becoming a professional baseball player was the summit. Only if McGraw were poised to become the next heavyweight champ would the men have shown him more respect.

No one gave McGraw a bigger tumble than Steve. He shouted when he saw McGraw at the other end of the bar, and rushed toward him like a linebacker chasing a fullback in the open field. "Look at the size of this kid!" Steve yelled. Steve had always loved McGraw. From the time he was a small boy, McGraw's distinctive giggle had delighted Steve, and that summer of 1989 Steve needed all the giggles he could get. He was becoming incoherent with worry. Many of the men were talking about how much Steve was drinking. You had to drink a lot for people in Publicans to notice, and even more for them to talk about it.

Besides hailing McGraw, however, Steve was also ushering him into the Big Man's Club. A big man himself, Steve liked other big men, related better to big men, and his easy way with McGraw made me think about the conspiracy and primacy of big men. I was average size, but standing that night near Steve and McGraw, flanked by Cager and Bob the Cop, Smelly and Jimbo, I felt like a blade of grass in a redwood forest.

Steve asked McGraw if the star athlete ever went to class. McGraw blanched. He loved class, he said. He talked about his studies, his reading, with a passion and defensiveness that reminded me of Bob the Cop. "I read *The Sound and the Fury* this semester," McGraw said. "The whole book. That book's hard. That book's fucked up. Like this one part where Benjy catches Caddy doing it on a tire swing. The professor calls on me in class, and he says, 'What do you think this scene means?' So I told him, 'Sex in a tire swing—that *does not* sound easy,' and the professor said he'd never heard that take on Faulkner before."

Two simultaneous discussions broke out, one about Faulkner, one about steel-belted radials.

That Faulkner was some kind of drunk huh? I really ought to put some new snow tires on the Chevy. All writers are drunks. How much are they getting for new tires nowadays? Maybe I should be a writer then, if all you got to do is drink. You got to know how to read before you can write, dipshit. What's that title mean anyway, *The Sound and the Fury?* I think I saw Michelins on sale at Sears. McGraw says it's from Shakespeare. If they're having all this sex in tires maybe the book should be called *The Sound and the Firestone.* How can Firestone just rip off Shakespeare like that? You mean Faulkner. What'd I say? You said Firestone, Einstein. That would be a good alias— Firestone Einstein. If you're ever in the Witness Protection Program, that's what you can call yourself. He isn't ripping off Shakespeare—it's a literary *illusion.* I need to stop drinking. I'm going to Sears tomorrow and look at those Michelins. I don't remember any fucking Shakespeare play titled *The Sound and the Fury.*

"It's from *Macbeth!*" I nearly shouted, but I didn't want to be the undersize nerd in the corner, spouting Shakespeare. The men cared about McGraw, not *Macbeth,* so I smoked and sulked and signified nothing.

When his coronation was over, McGraw found me at the other end of the bar, talking to Bob the Cop. "So this guy comes along on his yacht," Bob the Cop was saying, "and he sees the corpses strapped to my police boat, and he shouts, 'Hey—what'd you use for bait?'"

McGraw and I laughed. Bob the Cop went off to donate to the Don Fund and McGraw asked what was new in my life. I gave him the unhappy recap, from the Mr. Salty Incident to the Kelly Debacle, ending with Sidney's wedding and my unpromotion.

"Brutal," McGraw said. "Especially Sidney. She's your Daisy Bohannon."

"Buchanan."

"Whatever."

I was shocked that McGraw had read *Gatsby,* and remembered it, and referenced it. He told me that he had a Daisy too, a girl back in Nebraska who had been toying with his heart. "She's so beautiful—she's ugly," he said. "Know what I mean?"

We asked Bob the Cop when he returned if he had a Daisy in his past. He looked baffled. I made a note to bring my copy of *The Great Gatsby* to the bar for Bob the Cop. I thought, God knows I'm not using it.

I'd been looking forward to spending time with McGraw that summer, but I never expected he'd be my shadow. Instead of lifting weights, getting his rest, staying in shape for his final season, McGraw was leaning against the bar at Publicans night after night, right alongside me. When I asked why he was challenging my record for most appearances at Publicans in a single season, he grinned, then winced. He rubbed his shoulder and looked as if he were about to cry. Something was wrong.

He first noticed it while tossing a baseball earlier in the year. A twinge. The baseball went sideways, and he knew. He ignored the twinge, and all twinges that followed, and pitched through the pain, and set the record, but now the pain was unbearable. He couldn't raise his arm. He couldn't sleep. Aunt Ruth had taken him to several specialists, he told me, and they all had diagnosed a torn rotator cuff. McGraw's only hope of pitching again was surgery, which he didn't want. Too risky, he said. He might lose the use of his arm altogether.

Then McGraw shocked me by confessing the main reason he didn't want the surgery. He'd lost his love for the game. "I'm tired," he said. "Tired of practicing, tired of traveling, tired of the pain. *Tired.* I'm not sure I ever want to pick up a baseball again."

With his last two semesters of college, McGraw said, he wanted to read, think, bring up his grades and maybe go to law school.

Law school? I tried to conceal my shock. When I was able to collect myself, I promised McGraw I'd support him, no matter what he wanted to do.

"Thanks," he said. "But you're not the problem."

"Your mother?"

He took a swig of beer. "Ruth's on the warpath."

McGraw said he'd told his mother earlier that day what he'd just told me, and she had come unhinged. As soon as we went back to Grandpa's I saw that McGraw hadn't exaggerated. Aunt Ruth was sitting up, waiting for us. She cornered us in the kitchen and asked if McGraw had told me about his arm.

"He did."

"And what did you tell him?"

"That I support him no matter what he wants to do."

Wrong answer. She raised her hand and brought it down on the kitchen counter, rattling the Publicans glasses in the cupboards. Her eyes darted left and right, as if she were looking for something to throw. Then she threw words, the sharpest words I'd ever heard from her. All Aunt Ruth's screaming of the last twenty-four years seemed a warm-up for that night. She screamed that McGraw and I were cowards, the most despicable kind of cowards, because we didn't fear failure, but success. We were like all the men in the family, she said, and even in my fear of her, I felt for her, because it was clear how many men had disappointed her, from her father to her brother to her husband and now her only son. Her heart was broken. Though I shrank from her, I sympathized with her, and understood her, because she wanted the best for McGraw, as did I. She didn't want him to stop playing simply because he was in pain. She wanted him to push through that pain, keep trying. Like my mother, Aunt Ruth had pushed through pain all her life. She'd endured years of bad jobs and poverty and disappointments, and the misery of constantly sliding back to Grandpa's house, and the only thing that kept her going sometimes was the hope that life would be different for her children, that her children would be different. Now she felt that McGraw was going to be *the same*, and this caused her a pain at least as excruciating as the pain in his shoulder. When McGraw said he wanted to quit baseball, Aunt Ruth didn't hear his voice. She heard a chorus of male voices saying, "I quit," and it made her cut loose with screams of anguish and rage that ultimately sent me running from the kitchen, McGraw a half step behind.

McGraw's mother blocked his path. He ducked under her outstretched arm but she backed him against a wall. He lowered his head like a fighter, doing a kind of rope-a-dope, but you couldn't rope-a-dope Aunt Ruth. She rained words down upon him. She called him a louse, a fool, a failure, a freak, and worse. I tried to step between them, to beg her to stop, but I'd forgotten, after being out of that house, that Aunt Ruth's fury was like the wind. It blew when it blew, stopped when it stopped. And though there had never been anyplace to hide when we were boys, we felt especially exposed now. My apartment was gone, Publicans was closed for the night, neither of us owned a car. Also, we couldn't look for any help from Grandma or Grandpa. They had never been eager to take on Aunt Ruth when they were younger, but now that they were older they stayed well out of her way.

McGraw and I had no choice but to crawl into our beds in the back bedroom and ride out the storm. For a half hour straight Aunt Ruth screamed at us from the doorway, then abruptly stopped and slammed the door. We lay on our backs, trying to steady our breathing and bring down our heart rates. I closed my eyes. Five minutes passed. I heard McGraw still breathing heavily. Then the door flew open and Aunt Ruth started up again.

In the morning we found her at the kitchen table, waiting, ready to go again.

Every night was the same. Aunt Ruth would wait for us to return from Publicans and she would be screaming as we walked through the door. There was only one option. We never left Publicans. We hid at the bar until dawn, and even Aunt Ruth couldn't stay awake that long. Our strategy was foolproof. Aunt Ruth knew we were hiding from her, and knew where, but she was powerless. Even in her turbulent emotional state she recognized the barroom's inviolate neutrality, like a Swiss embassy. She knew that Uncle Charlie and the men wouldn't stand for a mother ambushing her son at the bar, though some nights Aunt Ruth would send one of McGraw's younger sisters into the bar to speak to him, to embarrass him. At such times McGraw's sense of shame and déjà vu, his fear that he'd now officially become his father, was palpable, and it made us all drink a little more.

By midsummer McGraw and I were hatching plans for a more permanent and radical escape than Publicans. He would quit Nebraska, I would quit the *Times,* and we'd backpack across Ireland, staying in hostels when we had money, sleeping in the lush green fields under the stars when we were broke. We'd work odd jobs, preferably in pubs, which would lead to full-time jobs, and we'd never come back. We sketched out the details of our plan on cocktail napkins, with much solemnity, as if it were something nobler and more complicated than a pub crawl. We told the men and they thought it a fine idea. It reminded them of their travels when they were younger. Joey D told us about going to the Caribbean with Uncle Charlie. A voodoo lady took one look at Uncle Charlie and said, "Him bad magic." The memory made Joey D so weepy with laughter that he had to wipe his eyes with one of the cocktail napkins on which we'd drawn up our Ireland plan.

I phoned my mother and told her about Ireland. She sighed. You don't need a vacation, she said, you need to get back on the horse. Apply to small newspapers, do as the *Times* recommended, then reapply to the *Times* in a couple of years. This sounded like the same old try-try-again nonsense that had gotten me nowhere, and I was saying good-bye to all that. I explained to my mother that I was "tired," consciously borrowing McGraw's line, while forgetting that it was a word charged with meaning for her. She'd been tired for twenty years, she said. Since when was being tired an excuse to stop trying?

Now McGraw and I had something else in common. Besides coming to the end of our careers at the same moment, we'd both run afoul of our mothers. Again and again that summer we turned to the men at Publicans, and like an underground railroad for prodigals, they hid us, not just in the bar, but at Shea, Gilgo, Steve's house, and especially Belmont, where we got a crash course in the sport of kings from the King of Belmont—Cager.

Cager loved the track. Cager lived for the track. Cager spoke about the track in a romance language that McGraw and I longed to learn, and sometimes I would take notes on the back of my racing form, trying to capture Cager's vocabulary, his cadence, his voice. "See the trainer on this five horse? He's good with two-year-olds, so I love the five, I might put twenty on his schnoz, but that seven, boys, he's going off at eight to one, and that's a sweet price for such a speed demon, let me tell you. Now that little railbird inside me says take the seven, take the seven, but *then* I look down here at the morning workouts on the four and he ran a forty-nine while we were still sleeping off the effects of last night at Publicans, and that's flying. On the other hand, or the other hoof, nine is probably going to get away like a bandit, because he loves the slop, he's always loved the slop, and see how it's starting to rain? He could be having a Budweiser at the finish line when all these other little piggies come home. So. I'm thinking I might do a ten-dollar exacta, nine-four, or else box the five and the nine and put ten dollars to win on the seven. What do you say, boys, let's hit the windows, 'cause you know what they say: The track's the only place where the windows clean the people!"

We got a late start to the track one day and McGraw was nervous that we might miss the first race. Walking up to the front gate Cager stopped at the giant statue of Secretariat to pay his respects. McGraw hopped from foot to foot as if he needed to pee. "First race starts any minute," McGraw said. Cager, not looking away from the statue, told McGraw calmly that there were two rules every horse player must always heed, and the first of these rules was: "Never hurry to lose money."

"What's the second rule?" McGraw asked.

"Always make sure you have enough at the end of the day for a hot pretzel."

After three races Cager was ahead a few hundred dollars. McGraw and I were down one hundred. We watched Cager fold his wad into the breast pocket of his shirt. "What are you going to do with all that money?" McGraw asked.

"Invest it."

"Really?"

"Yeah. In Budweiser."

Between races Cager propped his feet on the seat in front of him and asked what we were thinking we might do with our lives, now that we'd been spurned by our mothers and careers. We mentioned Ireland. We told Cager we were hoping to win enough at the track to make a pilgrimage to our ancestral homeland. "Then what?" Cager said. "Can't sit in a pub the rest of your lives. Wait—what the hell am I saying?"

McGraw said he was thinking about law school, or maybe the army. I mentioned the Yukon. I'd heard the *Alaska Daily News* was looking for reporters and I'd sent them my clips. I'd gotten an encouraging letter from the editor. Cager rocked forward and struggled not to spit beer through his nose. Then he said very gently that I wouldn't last ten minutes in the Yukon.

We watched the horses being led to the starting gate and loaded in. The jockeys, all in a row, leaning over the horses' withers, looked like busboys sitting at the bar. I asked Cager if he remembered when Secretariat galloped to his spectacular win at Belmont. "Like it was this morning," he said. "I was here." He described the race, every thrilling furlong, and though I'd read stories and seen film, nothing rivaled Cager's account. He made the hair stand up on my neck. He spoke of Secretariat in the reverent tone he reserved for two people—Steve and Nixon. "Secretariat's *statue* could beat these other horses," Cager said. He pointed to the exact spot where Secretariat had separated himself from the pack. I could see the horse's ghost racing for home, putting a few football fields between himself and the others. I could hear the crowd and feel those thousands of eyes trained on one striving thumping beast. "People had tears in their eyes," Cager said, tears in his eyes. "He was thirty-one lengths ahead at the wire! *Thirty-one*. He was *there*—the rest were down *there*. What a performance. Anytime one athlete separates himself from the pack like that, it sends chills down your arms. What heart."

I noted how Cager stressed that word—heart—and thought about how heart can compensate for other things. All the details at the track, speed and talent and weight and weather, all the factors that decided who wins and who loses, were swept away by heart. I wished I had a Secretariat kind of heart. I felt ridiculous, envying a horse, and yet, man or beast, it would be fine to earn the respect of a man like Cager. To do that, I asked myself, would I have to be a winner? Or was it more a matter of separating myself from the pack?

By the last race McGraw and I had lost all our money. "You hoped to win enough for Ireland," Cager said, "and you don't have enough for an Irish coffee. That's racing, boys."

"But we do have enough for a hot pretzel," McGraw said proudly, holding up three crumpled dollar bills. At the pretzel cart outside the track McGraw turned to me. "That one looks burned," he said, pointing to a smoking pretzel. "You want to phone it in to the *Times*?"

"Ouch," Cager said.

Later that night, after closing time, McGraw and I tried to win back some of our money playing Liars' Poker at Publicans. The other players were Cager, Colt, Don, Fast Eddy, Jimbo, and Peter, who was tending bar. "How's the writing?" Peter asked me.

"Never better."

"Really?"

"No—but this is Liars' Poker. Get it?"

He and McGraw looked at me with pity.

Pulling a bill from the pile Uncle Charlie would put it to his forehead like Carnac the Magnificent. "Without looking," he'd say, "I bid three fours."

Then he would look at the bill, and light a match to see it by, because all the lights in the bar were off.

"Four fives."

"Five eights."

"Challenge."

At dawn the milk truck pulled up to the back door. "Last hand," Cager said. McGraw and I tipped Peter, counted our money and found that we were the big winners. We didn't have enough for Ireland, but we did have enough to go back to Belmont. Walking home I carried our winnings, hundreds of singles, like a clump of dead leaves. I looked at the moon. That moon is beautiful, I told McGraw. Whatever, he said. We need to tip that moon for being so beautiful, I said. I threw all the bills at the moon, chucked them as high as I could into the sky, then stood in the middle of Plandome Road, arms wide open, twirling as they cascaded down.

"What the *fuck*," McGraw said, running circles around me, scooping up the bills. As he went darting after a dollar that was fluttering down the double yellow line, the milk truck almost hit him. "McGraw killed by a milk truck," I said. "Now *that* would be ironic."

Hours later McGraw found me on the back stoop, drinking a cup of coffee, holding my head. "Dude," he said, lighting a cigarette, "that's as drunk as I've ever seen you."

He hadn't seen anything yet.

forty-one | HUGO

THWARTED BY OUR STRATEGY OF HIDING ALL NIGHT IN PUBLIcans, Aunt Ruth opened a second front. She began calling in sick to her job as a receptionist in the city. Now she could scream at McGraw all morning and afternoon. McGraw begged her to leave him alone, but she promised not to stop until he agreed to have that operation on his shoulder and continue playing baseball. McGraw told his mother that he couldn't take any more screaming, he wanted to go back to school. She said he was never going back. She wouldn't buy him a plane ticket until he had that operation.

At the start of August McGraw surrendered. Anything to stop the screaming, he moaned, sitting between me and Jimbo at the bar. She wins, he said, and Jimbo and I both noticed that his stutter had returned.

Aunt Ruth took McGraw to the hospital days later, a stifling-hot morning. He looked numb when he left, and frightened when he returned that afternoon. He was certain that he'd never regain the use of his arm. I was more worried about him regaining his giggle. He wanted to lie down and rest, but Aunt Ruth had one more task for him. She insisted that he go to some fleabag bar in Port Washington and get his father to sign some papers.

We met Jimbo at Publicans that night for dinner. McGraw, groggy from pain pills, nearly weeping from the stress of the day, could barely raise the fork to his mouth. I thought of Jedd telling me why cacti add arms. "Losing" an arm had definitely cost McGraw his balance. Go home, I told him. Go to bed. He wouldn't, and he was candid about why. He *needed* to be in that bar. Now that he'd had the surgery, he said, Aunt Ruth would be after him about the rehab. She'd nag him about getting ready for the baseball season. She'd never stop. He had to leave Manhasset, he kept muttering. Right away. Tonight. Now. He talked again about the army. He talked about hitchhiking to Nebraska.

That won't be necessary, I told him. I hated the idea of saying good-bye again to McGraw, but I promised to buy him a plane ticket back to school first thing in the morning.

McGraw started packing ten minutes after his mother left for work. Jimbo came for us in his Jeep and we sped away, looking nervously out the plastic back window, as if Aunt Ruth might be waiting behind the bushes, poised to leap out and give chase like a cheetah after three gazelles. Three very hungover gazelles.

We had six hours before McGraw's plane left, and we decided to kill the time at Shea. A day game against the Padres. The summer heat had lifted and it was one of those August afternoons that seems like a trailer for the movie of fall. We bought seats behind third base and summoned the beer man. Don't stay away too long, I told him, hearing the echo of Uncle Charlie in my voice. The first cold beers went down like milk shakes. By the sixth inning we were feeling fine and the Mets were rallying. The crowd rose, roaring, and it was good to hear people scream in happiness, rather than rage.

We better go, McGraw said sadly, looking at the clock on the scoreboard. His flight. As we walked up the steps McGraw turned for one last look. Saying good-bye. Not to the Mets. To baseball.

That night, at Grandpa's, I lay in bed, looking at McGraw's empty bed, feeling desolate. The door flew open. Aunt Ruth, the hall light behind her, was screaming. "You won't get away with this! Sneaks! Cowards! Meddlers! You and Jimbo think you're helping him? You're *ruining* his life!"

She went for more than an hour.

It was the same every night. No matter when I came home from the bar, no matter how quietly I crept into the back bedroom, the door would fly open a minute later and the screaming would start. After a week my nerves were shot. I phoned Bebe from Publicans and told her I needed help. Within hours Bebe had located a friend on the Upper East Side with a room to rent. It's small, Bebe said, but it's in your price range.

I couldn't ask Bob the Cop to move me again. Besides, this felt like a job for Jimbo. I found him at the bar, halfway through his Rock à l'Orange, a cocktail he'd invented (Rolling Rock, Grand Marnier chaser). He claimed it had magical and medicinal properties that cured heartbreak. Jimbo had his own Sidney, a girl at college who had wrecked him.

"Jimbo," I said, a hand on his shoulder, "I need a big one."

"Name it."

"I can't take another night of the screaming. I need to evacuate."

Without hesitation, leaving his drink unfinished, he walked with me to Grandpa's.

Along the way I peeked at Jimbo out of the corner of my eye. I'd spent a lot of time with him that summer, and I'd come to know him, to rely on him. I wanted to thank Jimbo for always coming to the rescue in his trusty Jeep, and to tell him there should be a big red cross painted on its side. I wanted to say how much he'd come to mean to me, that he was like a brother to me, that I loved him, but I'd missed my chance. Only at the bar could such things be said between men.

Walking into the back bedroom Jimbo looked around and asked, "How you want to tackle this?"

"Pack like the house is on fire."

Jimbo drove me to the address Bebe gave me and helped me run my stuff upstairs to the apartment. Since he was double-parked, there wasn't time for a long good-bye. We stood in the street and hugged, that contagious-disease hug that young men give each other.

"Come home soon," Jimbo said, peeling away from the curb.

I watched his Jeep disappear in traffic.

"I will," I said. "I will."

Bebe's friend was a Columbia law student named Magdalena, who started almost every sentence with one-word rhetorical questions. "Actually?" she said, opening the door to my room. "It's not really a room, per se, but a converted water closet."

"What's a water closet?"

"Frankly? It's a bathroom. But there's a bed, and a—well, a bed. But it's really cozy, as you can see."

I assured her it was a very cozy bathroom.

She explained that she'd be at her boyfriend's apartment most nights. She turned and motioned to her boyfriend, as if he were Exhibit A. He was so quiet that I'd forgotten he was there.

"You mean I'll have the apartment all to myself?" I asked.

"Yes," she said. "Of course, my mother might drop in now and then."

Her mother lived in Puerto Rico, but sometimes flew to New York, to shop and see friends. She slept on Magdalena's sofa. "Honestly?" Magdalena said. "She's quiet as a mouse."

I thanked Magdalena for renting to me on such short notice, and told her I was going to take a hot shower and go to bed.

"Seriously?" she said. "Make yourself at home. If you need anything we'll be studying in the kitchen."

The working bathroom was on the other side of the apartment. To get there from my bathroom-qua-bedroom I had to walk through the kitchen. Wrapped in a towel I smiled shyly at Magdalena and joked with the boyfriend. "Just passing through," I said. He made no reply.

I ran the hot water full blast and sat on the edge of the tub as steam filled the bathroom. Jimbo would be at Publicans by now, I thought. Uncle Charlie would be breaking out the Sambuca. General Grant would be lighting his first cigar of the night, and Cager would be flipping channels on the TV, looking for a good game. Colt would be in the phone booth, Fast Eddy and Agnes would be ordering dinner, Smelly would be throwing meat cleavers at lazy busboys. I looked at myself in the mirror over the sink. Just before my face disappeared in the steam I asked myself: Is it possible—is it wise—to feel homesick for a bar?

I stepped into the shower. The hot spray instantly opened my pores and soothed my mind. I held my face to the water and sighed with pleasure. A scream cut through the roar of the water. Aunt Ruth. She'd followed Jimbo and now she was there in the bathroom. I screamed too, like Janet Leigh. I jumped back, slipped, and reached for the shower curtain to steady myself. I pulled it off the hooks and fell out of the tub, onto the floor, bending the shower curtain rod and, I felt sure, breaking my elbow. Looking up through the clouds of steam I saw, perched on the showerhead, a parrot the size of a chimpanzee. It spread its wings, a sound like an umbrella opening.

I wrapped a towel around myself and ran into the kitchen.

"I forgot to tell you about Hugo," Magdalena said, biting her thumbnail.

"Hugo?" I said.

"Hugo lives in the bathroom. He likes the steam."

Dripping wet, clutching the towel around my waist, I asked her to remove Hugo from the bathroom. I didn't feel comfortable, I said, being naked in close quarters with any wild animal that had a Ginsu knife for a nose.

"Frankly?" she said. "I can't do that. Hugo lives in the bathroom."

I looked to the boyfriend for help. Nothing.

I went for a walk and when I returned Magdalena and the boyfriend were gone. Hugo, however, was still there. I poked my head into the bathroom and he eyed me ominously. I could tell he was mad as a wet hen that I'd tried to have him evicted. I went to bed, but couldn't sleep, beset by nightmares of screaming parrots and aunts.

As I walked into the newsroom with a box full of sandwiches I heard the weatherman on TV say a major storm was brewing in the Atlantic. Hurricane Hugo, he said. I laughed at myself. I must have misheard. I had Hugo on the brain. Then the weatherman said it again. Hurricane Hugo was gaining strength as it churned across the Atlantic. Exactly what was the universe trying to tell me now?

I slept badly that night, and when I woke a strange woman was making coffee in the kitchen. Magdalena's mother, I gathered. Her English was poor, but I managed to learn that she'd left Puerto Rico in a hurry. Fleeing Hugo, she said. "Aren't we all?" I said.

Over the next several days I read about Hugo, tracked its path, worried about the havoc it might wreak. I didn't know why the storm obsessed me, why I dreaded it as much as people who lived on stilt houses in the Outer Banks. Maybe it was lack of sleep, maybe it was living in a water closet, maybe it was being forced to shower in terror, but I let Hurricane Hugo become a metaphor for my life, and then I let it consume my life. As if its low-pressure system had collided with my high pressure, the storm gathered up all my unhappiness about McGraw and Aunt Ruth and Sidney and the *Times* and focused it into one tight eye. From morning until night I could think of nothing but Hugo.

When Hugo blasted ashore in late September 1989, I was at the *Times*, reading wires, monitoring TVs, like a copyboy for the National Weather Service. I stayed in the newsroom and watched CNN until after midnight, and when the janitors started vacuuming I went to Magdalena's apartment and watched TV with her mother, who appeared to be just as traumatized as I. Even Hugo seemed traumatized by Hugo. Hearing his name repeated again and again on TV the parrot would caw frantically, and with his cawing, and the wind howling, and Magdalena's mother wailing in Spanish, it was a long and harrowing night.

As skies over South Carolina cleared the next morning, as the damage was revealed, I grieved for all who had lost their lives and homes. But while compassion is healthy, what I felt was something else, something disproportionate and irrational. It occurred to me that my thinking was skewed, that I might be on the verge of some kind of breakdown. Then this thought was quickly overtaken by new images from Hugo's swath.

Days after Hugo hit I was watching TV again with Magdalena's mother, both of us drinking whiskey and chain-smoking, and I noticed we were running low on smokes. I went to the market for a pack, stopping into a bar along the way. It was raining hard, the remnants of Hugo now drenching New York City. Returning to the apartment I found the living room in shambles, furniture broken, sofa cushions ripped open, broken glass strewn across the wood floors. I called out for Magdalena's mother and heard whimpering from the bedroom. I ran down the hall. The mother lay on her stomach in the bedroom, which had been ransacked. I knelt beside her and asked if she was all right. "I call everybody," she said. "No one home! No one love me!"

She held the phone in one hand, her address book in the other, and kicked her feet like a child having a tantrum.

"*You*—did this?" I asked. "You trashed the apartment?"

"I call everyone!" she cried, mascara cascading down her cheeks. She threw the address book at the wall. "No one give a shit about me!"

Relieved that she hadn't been assaulted, I went to the kitchen to get each of us a glass of water. I heard the mother breaking more glass and realized that she might harm herself. On the refrigerator was the number of Magdalena's boyfriend. I phoned and told her that her mother wasn't well and suggested she come home. She didn't bother to ask what was wrong, and I surmised that this wasn't the first time her mother had done something like this.

Magdalena arrived, with the boyfriend, who stood passively in a corner while she crept toward her mother. "Mother?" she said. "Mother, what's wrong?" By now her mother was babbling. Magdalena dialed 911 and the apartment soon filled with cops and paramedics. They looked around and maybe noticed, as I did, that the devastated apartment evoked images that had been flickering on TV for days. "Who are you?" a cop asked me.

"I rent the bath—spare bedroom."

Everyone gathered around the prostrate mother, who was tearing her address book into pieces, and tearing the pieces into smaller pieces. A cop asked the mother what was wrong and she repeated what she'd told me. She'd phoned everyone she knew, looking for someone to talk to about Hurricane Hugo, but no one answered.

"You want us to take her to a hospital?" a cop asked Magdalena.

"Hospital?" the mother screamed. "You no taking me to no hospital, you motherfucking nigger assholes!"

And that was that. The cops took one giant step backward and the paramedics fell upon the mother with a straitjacket. She thrashed, scratched, fought them, but within ten seconds they had her trussed tight. Hugo cawed, Magdalena wept, the boyfriend said nothing, and I jumped aside as the paramedics hoisted the mother over their heads and carried her out the door like a Christmas tree on the day after New Year's. She was on her way to Bellevue.

Magdalena and the boyfriend and I sat at the kitchen table. I told her I was sorry for her troubles, and didn't bother saying I was going to leave. She knew. Boyfriend knew. Hugo knew.

"Seriously?" she asked. "Where will you go? Bebe said you had nowhere to go."

forty-two | STEVE

I SLEPT ON BEBE'S COUCH FOR A FEW WEEKS BEFORE GOING BACK to Manhasset, back to Grandpa's. By then Hurricane Aunt Ruth had been downgraded to a squall. My aunt was relatively calm and left me alone, and I was calmer too. The sight of Magdalena's mother in a straitjacket had a sobering effect.

Also, it was soothing to be within 142 steps of Publicans again. The bar had never been better than it was that fall, every night another office party or family reunion or just an unusually entertaining ensemble of characters and personalities. On the first night of November I could barely squeeze inside the door. A solid wall of people. A steady roar of laughter. The only one not laughing was Steve, who stood in the middle of the barroom, just back from bowling. I saw him leaning against the bar as though he or it were about to collapse, and I must have stared too hard, because he looked up as if I'd called his name. He smiled, not his Cheshire smile. Something was wrong with his smile, though I couldn't tell what from across the barroom. He waved me over.

We discussed McGraw, whom we both missed, and McGraw's arm, which hadn't healed after the surgery. The question of McGraw continuing to play baseball had been rendered moot. We lamented the loss of Jimbo, who had just moved to Colorado days earlier. I could tell how much Steve missed Jimbo. He'd made a bid to keep Jimbo in Manhasset, offering to find him a job on Wall Street. One phone call to any of fifty men who hung out in Publicans would have set Jimbo up for life. But Jimbo wanted to be a ski bum. Steve understood.

While talking with Steve I held myself rigid, afraid he might bring up our meeting of a week earlier, the last time I'd seen him. Just after I returned from the Hugo apartment Steve had summoned me down to his basement office.

We sat across from each other at his desk and he handed me a stack of checks I'd cashed at the bar over the summer, each one stamped *Insufficient Funds*. Steve feared I'd deliberately passed bad checks across his bar, and he feared this for my sake, not his. His distress had nothing to do with his money problems. Steve believed in trusting people. Every ticket in his restaurant was handwritten, every drink called by voice. There were no computers, no records, and customers and employees alike abided by a rough-and-tumble honor system. When a busboy got caught taking a bottle of expensive champagne from the bar, Steve's staff handled it "internally." They beat the shit out of the busboy.

I told Steve the truth. I hadn't been thinking clearly, and didn't know from one day to the next how much money was in my checking account. I was disorganized, not dishonest. "Junior," he said, leaning back in his creaky old desk chair, "we all miss the float once in a while. But this is no good. No good at all. *This isn't the kind of man you want to be.*" His words echoed in the basement, and in my head. "No sir," I said. "It isn't." I waited for him to say something more, but nothing more needed to be said. I looked into Steve's watery gray-blue eyes. He held my gaze, the longest we'd ever made eye contact, and when Steve saw what he wanted to see—what I suppose he needed to see—he sent me back upstairs to the barroom. The next day I left an envelope at the bar, filled with cash, to cover my bad checks and any penalties he'd incurred from his bank. I was officially broke, but I was square with Steve, and that was all that counted.

Now, that first night in November, Steve made no mention of that awkward business. Ancient history as far as he was concerned. When we finished talking about "the boys," as he called McGraw and Jimbo, he patted my shoulder, told Colt to "buy Junior a drink," then stumbled away. "Kid," Colt said, "you're backed up on Chief." I felt a surge of love for Steve, and for Colt, and for all the men in Publicans, because I finally figured something out. I'd always assumed the men hadn't heard Steve call me Junior, but of course they had. They simply hadn't adopted the nickname, because they sensed its significance to me. Steve didn't understand, and they didn't explain—the men of Publicans never explained. They just let Steve continue calling me Junior, and they never did. Not once. It was a break with protocol, an act of tenderness, which I'd failed to recognize. Until that night.

I sat at Uncle Charlie's end of the bar, trying to tell him about Steve and my bounced checks. Yuh, he said, as if in a trance. He was staring at the TV. Suddenly he let out an awful wail. His team—the Celtics, I think—had blown an easy three-on-one fast break. He covered his eyes. Earlier in the week, he said, he had *heavy* timber on a football game, and all his team needed to do was take a knee and run out the clock. Inexplicably they threw a pass, which was intercepted and run back for a cover-blowing touchdown. Uncle Charlie poured himself a Sambuca and said, "Everyone is *fucking* me."

Down the bar I heard Steve growing louder. His face looked like the Grand Canyon, striated layers of red, orange and purple, accentuated by the gaping purple hole of his mouth. That was the thing I'd noticed earlier about his smile, but hadn't been able, or willing, to acknowledge. Years of drinking had damaged Steve's teeth, and he was due to have oral surgery. In the meantime he was supposed to wear dentures, but the dentures made his gums bleed, so that night he went without them, setting them on the bar beside his Heineken. He was talking with Dalton, who was drinking a bottle of wine. Dalton poured Steve a glass, the last thing Steve needed. The wine, mixed with ten or twelve Heinekens and twenty-four months of stress, sent Steve over the edge. He grew so unintelligible and belligerent that Uncle Charlie cut him off. Steve couldn't believe it. *Here now—cutting me off at my own bar?* You're done, Uncle Charlie said. Sweet dreams, Chief.

Joey D offered Steve a ride home. Steve refused. Joey D slinked away, muttering dejectedly to his mouse. A busboy offered Steve a ride. Steve accepted. The busboy led Steve through the dining room. As they tottered out the back door Colt spotted Steve's teeth on the bar. "You forgot your chompers!" Colt yelled. But Steve was gone. Someone remarked that Steve had left his smile at the bar. It sat before us, smiling. You couldn't help but think of the Cheshire Cat in *Alice in Wonderland,* appearing and disappearing without warning, its smile always the first thing visible, and the last.

Minutes later the phone rang. Steve's wife, Georgette, said Steve had come home without his teeth. "We've got them right here," Uncle Charlie told her. The phone rang again. Georgette again. Steve fell, she said. He hit his head. They were taking him to North Shore Hospital.

People fall down a lot in Publicans, I thought, saying good night to Uncle Charlie and wobbling back to Grandpa's.

Early the next morning I woke to Uncle Charlie's voice coming from the living room. I wrapped a robe around myself and went to find out why he was up at that hour. He was sitting on the edge of the bicentennial sofa. His face was white as a bone. The veins in his skull were visibly pulsating. He took deep, harsh drags of a Marlboro and stared at me, through me, through the wall behind me, as he repeated what he'd been telling Grandma. Steve was in a coma and wasn't expected to live.

It happened this way: When Steve got home Georgette heated up a plate for him. He ate, drank a glass of milk, and talked with her about the disaster Publicans on the Pier had become. Disconsolate, Steve left the table, headed off to bed. Georgette heard a thud. She ran to find Steve in a heap at the bottom of the stairs.

"How old is he?" Grandma said.

"Forty-seven," Uncle Charlie said. "One year older than I."

The sidewalks on both sides of Plandome Road were three-deep, as if for a parade. Car traffic was backed up for miles. Mourners descended from every direction on Christ Church at the top of Plandome Road, which sat catty-corner from St. Mary's. The church was large, with room for two hundred, but five times that many converged on its doors. Joey D served as usher, though there was no ushering to be done. Hours before the funeral began every pew was filled.

I wedged myself through a side door in time to see Georgette come in, leaning against her children, Brandy and Larry. I spotted Uncle Charlie against a far wall, talking to someone. Suddenly his eyes rolled skyward as though he were doing Billy Budd. He fell backward. "Man down!" someone shouted. Several people helped Uncle Charlie out of the church. I followed and watched them laying Uncle Charlie on the grass, propping him against a headstone with a full head of furry green moss. Nearby was a headstone from the early 1700s, its epitaph faintly legible: HE GIVETH HIS BELOVED SLEEP.

Back inside the church I pushed into the crowd and caught a glimpse of Steve's casket. There was a whoosh like crashing surf as people sniffled and gasped and wept. A procession of large men ascended the altar and read aloud from the Bible, followed by Jimbo, who fought back tears as he spoke.

Watching Jimbo, hurting for him, I realized something, with such force, such staggering clarity, that I wanted to go outside and lie down in the grass beside Uncle Charlie.

I'd always thought of Steve as our Gatsby—rich and mysterious and throwing wild parties for hundreds of strangers on the Gold Coast of Long Island. And this idea was only reinforced by his violent and untimely death. But as with Gatsby, Steve's true character was revealed at his funeral, and it was Jimbo's eulogy that made me see. Steve had been a father to Jimbo, and one way or another he was a father to us all. Even I, who didn't know Steve all that well, was a son in his extended family. A publican by trade, Steve was a patriarch at heart, and maybe that was why he was so intent on naming us. Maybe that was why Uncle Charlie lay propped against a headstone, and why every man from Publicans looked less like a mourner that day than an orphan.

As the service ended we filed outside, mumbling prayers, hugging each other, then drove to the cemetery. The funeral cortege moved slowly past Publicans. Though the bar wasn't on the way, there was a feeling that Steve needed to go past the place one last time. After Steve was lowered into the ground we returned to Publicans, en masse, hundreds upon hundreds of people. Some had urged Georgette to close for the day, in honor of Steve, but she said Steve wouldn't have wanted that. Steve always vowed that Publicans would remain open—through renovations, recessions, blackouts, blizzards, ice storms, market crashes, and wars. Staying open was Steve's mission. Shutting down was his darkest fear, the fear that some blamed for his death. With so many question marks surrounding Steve while he was alive, his death was inevitably shrouded in mystery. Most people thought he died from a fall down the stairs, and some in Manhasset would always think so, no matter what. Georgette thought so too, at first. But doctors assured her that an aneurysm had killed Steve, not a fall.

In Steve's honor Georgette didn't merely keep Publicans open after his funeral. She declared the bar—*open*. No one would pay, no one would dare speak the words "Last call," and the drinking would continue until no one was left standing. A lavish, extravagant gesture, it was also alarming. An open bar in Manhasset? A town that guzzled liquor like seltzer? It struck me and others as a reckless and dangerous idea. Like building a bonfire in a town of pyromaniacs. Georgette, however, wouldn't brook any arguments. She hired bartenders from the other bars on Plandome Road to work that day, so Steve's bartenders wouldn't need to, and she invited—ordered—the town to drink. Manhasset was backed up on Georgette.

Publicans had never been so packed, so loud, so happy and sad at the same time. As the liquor flowed, and the grief grew, and the laughter mounted, a type of hysteria set in, though some of the hysteria may have been caused by lack of oxygen. The air was so thick and hot with sweat and smoke that breathing was an effort. The barroom looked like Dante's Manhasset. Eyes bulged. Tongues lolled. Every five minutes someone dropped a bottle, and large sparkling lagoons of booze and crushed glass began to form. Tables of food were set up along the walls, but no one went near them. Everyone was too intent on drinking. "They're drinking like they're going to the chair in the morning," Colt said. And yet I also heard someone complain that the liquor wasn't working. In such a sea of sadness, it seemed, all the free whiskey in the world was but a drop.

I wended my way through the barroom, feeling as if I were in a wax museum crowded with sallow replicas of the most important people in my life. I saw Uncle Charlie, or some waxen version of Uncle Charlie, his necktie askew, his back hunched, still limp from his fainting spell. He was drunker than he'd been after Pat died, drunker than I'd ever seen him. He'd achieved a new plateau of drunkenness, a transcendent drunkenness, and it was the first time his drunkenness ever scared me. I saw Don and Fast Eddy talking in conspiratorial whispers, and Tommy just behind them, a stupendous frown on his face, his features plunging down the drain of his chin. He looked seventy-five years older than he had the day he escorted me onto the field at Shea Stadium. I saw Jimbo consoling McGraw, who was sobbing. I saw Bob the Cop in the center of the barroom, talking to Cager, and just beyond them was Dalton, leaning against a pole, seemingly lost without a book of poems to read or a woman to flirt with. Joey D was talking to Josie, a détente brought on by Steve's death, and his cousin General Grant stood nearby, in a black suit, needing only the solace of his cigar. Fuckembabe, also wearing a suit, his face scrubbed and his hair combed, may have been the soberest person in the place. I heard him talking with a few stockbrokers and he sounded almost articulate. The eloquence of grief. I saw Colt and Smelly leaning against each other, and DePietro near them in a booth talking with some fellow Wall Streeters. I saw Thumbelina and avoided her gaze—and her thumb. I saw Michelle, lovely as always, eager to leave. I saw Crazy Jane, designer of the stained-glass genitalia behind the bar, emerging from the basement, trailing the smell of pot. I saw people I recognized, whose names escaped me, and people I had never seen before, talking about favors Steve had done them, charities he'd supported, meals he'd provided, loans he'd floated, wisecracks he'd made, pranks he'd orchestrated, students he'd secretly put through college. I thought, We've learned more about Steve in the last few hours than in all our years of talking with him and standing with him at his bar.

I saw Peter and rushed toward his side, relieved. I planted myself next to Peter, my editor, my friend, needing his special brand of kindness and sanity. I plotted how I might contrive to stay by Peter's side all night without annoying him. He asked how I was doing and I started to answer, but Bobo pulled me away. I hadn't seen Bobo in years. He was telling a Steve story, but I couldn't understand. He was drunk and still suffering the aftereffects of his fall down the stairs of the bar, his face still partly paralyzed. I wondered if he equated Steve's fall with his own. When Bobo released me I said something to Peter about how often people fell down in Publicans. Before Peter could respond we both heard Georgette, near the back door. She was crying and saying over and over, "We lost our Chief. What are we going to do without our Chief?"

The stereo was playing dirgelike classical music. Someone shouted that we should be listening to Steve's kind of music. Elvis. Fats Domino. Johnny Preston. One of the bartenders dug out a tape with all Steve's favorites. The songs made everyone feel cheerful, and awful, because they brought Steve to life. Surely Chief was there. We'd have a big belly laugh with him about how weird all this was, if only we could find him in that crush of drunken humanity.

I got another scotch and stood beside Bob the Cop, who was drinking Rusty Nails.

"How long do you think this joint will last?" he asked me.

"You think Publicans will close? God. I hadn't thought of that."

Which wasn't quite true. The thought had been eating at me, I just hadn't wanted to face it. When Bob the Cop said it aloud, however, I understood my grief better, and everyone else's. There was an element of selfishness about it all. We missed Steve, and mourned him, but we also knew that without him Publicans might die too.

My legs buckled. I looked for a place to collapse but there wasn't a seat to be had. I was going to be sick. Everything in the place suddenly repulsed me. Even the long polished wood bar made my stomach lurch, because it reminded me of Steve's casket. I shouldered my way out the front door and stumbled to Grandpa's, where I collapsed in the back bedroom. When I opened my eyes hours later I had no idea where I was. Yale? Arizona? Sidney's? My place above Louie the Greek's? The Hugo Apartment? Gradually the pieces of my mind fell into place, and I remembered that I was at Grandpa's. Again.

After a long hot shower I put on fresh clothes and returned to Publicans. By now it was three or four in the morning, but everyone was right where I'd left them, though they were melting and imploding, as if the heat had been turned up too high in the wax museum. I fought my way to the center of the crowd and found Bob the Cop and Cager in the same spot at the bar. They didn't realize I'd gone home and come back. They didn't know what time it was, or what day, and they didn't really care. I drank with them until sunrise. Still they made no sign of leaving, but I needed air and food.

I walked up to Louie the Greek's. The counter was filled with commuters, all sharp-eyed and eager to start the day after eight hours of sleep. I saw the British au pair I'd dated, the one who talked like Margaret Thatcher. Her hair was wet. Her cheeks were russet apples. She was nibbling a muffin and drinking a hot cup of tea. She gawked at me. "Where are you coming from?" she asked.

"Funeral."

"Bloody hell, love, *whose*? Your own?"

forty-three | SMELLY

WALKING DOWN PLANDOME ROAD WEEKS LATER I SAW A PALE, bloated moon rising from Publicans. The moon was wobbling, as if it had been overserved. Always watchful for signs, hypersensitive to their meaning, I should have had no trouble interpreting this one. *Even the moon is leaving the bar.* But I ignored it. In the weeks after Steve's death I ignored everything, treating all signs and unpleasant facts as Joey D treated loud-mouths. I simply refused to serve them.

And yet Steve's death—the squalor of it, the waste—couldn't be ignored for long. At least once a day I'd think of Steve, of the way he'd died, and I'd wonder what he might say, now that he had all the answers, about the way we were living. I'd always held to the romantic notion that we were hiding from life in Publicans. After Steve's death I couldn't stop hearing his voice asking: Are we hiding from life or courting death? And what's the difference?

Many times that November I would look down the bar, at all the hollow-eyed and ashen faces, and I'd think maybe we already were dead. I'd think of Yeats: "A drunkard is a dead man, / And all dead men are drunk." I'd think of Lorca: "Death / is coming in and leaving / the tavern, / death / leaving and coming in." Was it a coincidence that my two favorite poets depicted death as a barroom regular? Sometimes I would catch my own hollow-eyed and ashen reflection in one of the silver cash registers. My face was like the moon, pale and bloated, but unlike the moon I never left. I couldn't. I'd always seen Steve's bar metaphorically, as a river, an ocean, a raft, a ship, a train carrying me to some far-off city. Now I saw the bar as a submarine trapped on the ocean floor, and we were running out of air. This claustrophobic image was chillingly reinforced when someone gave Uncle Charlie a tape of whale songs, which he played incessantly on the bar stereo, cranking the volume as high as it would go. The screeches and clicks were so earsplitting that the humpbacks seemed to be just outside, floating along Plandome Road, as if the front win-dow of the bar were a porthole. "Isn't this mellifluous!" Uncle Charlie would say. "You don't mind if I say 'mellifluous,' do you? Isn't it beautiful how they communicate with each other?"

We weren't communicating half so well among ourselves. A bar full of virtuoso talkers was now an echo chamber of long and uncomfortable si-lences, because there was only one thing to say and none of us was brave enough to say it: Everything had changed. Steve's death had set off a chain reaction of *change,* the thing we were least equipped to cope with. His death had changed us in ways we didn't understand, and changed the bar in ways we couldn't deny. The laughter was shriller, the crowds thinner. People didn't go to Publicans anymore to forget their problems or ease their sadness, because Publicans reminded them of death, Steve's death, the saddest event in Manhasset history. Bob the Cop had questioned if the bar could survive Steve's death, but what was already gone, forever, was our notion of Publicans as sanctuary. In the time it took a man to fall down, Publicans had devolved from a sanctuary to a prison, as sanctuaries so often do.

The more these thoughts would nag at me, and unnerve me, the more I would drink. The binge drinking of Steve's funeral lasted two days for most of Manhasset, but I was still in binge mode a month later. Riding the train to the *Times,* suffering another paralyzing hangover, I'd talk to myself, question myself, grill myself. Invariably these self-interviews ended with the same hard question. *Am I a drunk?* I didn't think so. If I was dependent on anything it was the bar. I couldn't imagine life without it. I couldn't conceive of ever leaving. Where would I go? And if I went, who would I be? Who I was had gotten mixed up with where I was, and the idea of throwing it all away, the bar and my image of JR-in-the-Bar, terrified me. After thinking along these lines on the morning train, then working all day at a job in which I had failed and had no future, I couldn't wait to get back to Publicans, to drink away my ambivalence about Publicans. Sometimes I'd get a head start, slurping cocktails in Penn Station and then grabbing two or three tallboys of Budweiser for the ride home. Occasionally I'd pass out on the train, sleep through my stop, and a conductor would wake me in the middle of the night after the train had parked in the freight yard. Shaking my shoulder the conductors always said the same thing: *End of the line, pal.*

I no longer made any pretense of drinking to bond with the men, or to blunt the cares of the day, or to participate in male rituals. I drank to get drunk. I drank because I couldn't think what else to do. I drank the way Steve drank at the end, to achieve oblivion. I was a few sips from oblivion on a cold night in December 1989—I don't remember if it was days before or days after my twenty-fifth birthday—when the bar finally decided it had seen enough. The bar had filled every need I'd ever had, and needs I didn't know I had, and now I needed one more thing.

I was standing with Cager and Smelly. General Grant was behind the stick. It was around three in the morning and we were talking about war. I mentioned how often we seemed to talk about war, even when we were ostensibly talking about something else. Cager said it was only natural, since

war is the Big Topic. Life, he said, is war. An endless sequence of battles, con-
flicts, ambushes, skirmishes, with all-too-brief interludes of peace. Or maybe
General Grant said this. Then Cager said something about the Middle East,
and I took issue with his opinion, not because I disagreed but because I worried that if I didn't keep talking my forehead would hit the bar.

"Why don't you shut the fuck up?" Smelly said.

Everyone stopped talking. Cager, standing between Smelly and me, told
Smelly to take it easy.

"No," Smelly said. "I'm sick of this punk thinking he knows everything.
He went to Yale so he's Mr. Fucking Know-It-All? He don't know shit."

"Settle down," General Grant said.

"Fuck that!" Smelly said. Bull-necked, swag-bellied, he walked around
Cager and came toward me.

What wire in Smelly's mental fuse box had I accidentally cut? I tried to
say something in my own defense, but at that moment words couldn't stop
Smelly. Bullets couldn't stop Smelly. He covered the six feet between us in
two steps, surprisingly lithe for a man of his girth. Reaching out with both
hands he grabbed my neck as if it were a rope he intended to climb. He
squeezed hard and I felt my throat close. I thought that Smelly might crumple
my larynx and permanently damage my voice, that thereafter I'd sound raspy
or hoarse, like Mr. Sandman, and this scared me more than the prospect—
the likelier prospect—of strangulation.

Smelly pushed me backward, twisting my neck harder now. His hands
reeked of garlic and meat. *Smelly's hands are smelly.* I hoped this wouldn't be
my last thought ever. I reached up and tried to pull his hands from my neck
but they were also slippery, and his grip was iron. I thought about pasting
him one, but I didn't want to make him angrier. I looked deep into his eyes—
there was no deep in Smelly's eyes. They were black dots, the eyes of a cartoon character. Between them, forming a perfect V, his orange eyebrows were
vibrating, and like his orange mustache and the orange hair on his head, those
eyebrows were glistening with sweat. He was overweight, overwrought, overserved, and as orange as a glass of Minute Maid. He was a cross between
Yosemite Sam and Son of Sam, and this, I was sure, would be my last thought
ever, because Smelly was determined to kill me.

Even as Smelly wrung my neck I didn't hate him. I loved Smelly no less than I loved all the men in that bar, and as I began to lose consciousness I felt hatred only for myself, because I loved him, loved any man who paid attention to me, even when that attention took the form of murder.

Smelly rose. He floated toward the ceiling like an avenging angel, and I thought this vision was surely the first sign of encroaching death. Then, over Smelly's shoulder, I saw Cager. He had Smelly by the waistband of his pants and was lifting him with a classic clean and jerk. Smelly let go of my neck and air rushed into my lungs. My vocal cords twanged. I fell to the ground, followed a second later by Smelly, who landed much harder, because Cager jabbed him into the wood floor like a spear.

Cager stood over Smelly, pushing up his sleeves. "Touch him again," he said to Smelly, "and I'll kill you."

Lying on my back, holding my neck, I looked up at Cager. I'd never loved a man more. He adjusted his visor, strolled back to the bar and took a swig of his Budweiser.

"Now," he said. "Where was I?"

I walked to Grandpa's, head down, counting my steps—170. *That's 28 more than normal, which means I'm zig-zagging.* On Grandpa's dining room table I found a present waiting for me. It was from Sheryl. She'd recently gotten married, and starting her own family had inspired her to think about our family, and to rummage through Grandpa's home movies, converting the most interesting ones to video. She'd left me a tape with a note attached. *Thought you'd get a kick out of this.*

I pushed the tape into the VCR and lay back on the bicentennial sofa, holding a can of beer against my neck, where I could still feel Smelly's fingers. The screen went white, then a picture formed. Grandpa's house. The image was so clean and bright I thought it must have been filmed that morning. But the roof didn't sag, the paint wasn't peeling, the trees were saplings and the driveway didn't have a lightning crack. Now Uncle Charlie walked across the screen with a pompadour and the time frame seemed prehistoric.

The camera wavered crazily, left to right, back again, before settling on a pretty slip of a woman seated on the stoop. She had a baby on her lap. She bounced him, cradled him, whispered something in his ear. A secret. He jerked his head toward her. My mother and me, twenty-four years before. My mother looked at her nine-month-old son, then gazed straight ahead, at me, her drunken twenty-five-year-old son. I felt caught, as if she were peering into the future and seeing what became of me.

Clearly this had been filmed right after my mother had come to live at Grandpa's, shortly after my father had tried to kill her, but that wasn't possible, because there was no trace of fear in my mother's eyes. She looked happy, confident, like a woman with money in the bank and a bright future on the horizon. Hiding her feelings from Grandma and Grandpa, I thought. She didn't want to worry them. Then I understood. It wasn't them she was trying to fool.

My mother's first lie to me, caught on tape.

How did she do it? With no education, no money, no prospects, how did my mother manage to look so *fierce*? She'd just survived my father clamping a pillow over her face until she couldn't breathe, and lunging at her with a razor, and though she must have been relieved to escape him, she must also have been aware of what lay ahead—loneliness, money worries, the Shit House. But you wouldn't know it to look at her. She was an inspired liar, a brilliant liar, and she was also lying to herself, which made me perceive her lies in a whole new light. I saw that we must lie to ourselves now and then, tell ourselves that we're capable and strong, that life is good and hard work will be rewarded, and then we must try to make our lies come true. This is our work, our salvation, and this link between lying and trying was one of my mother's many gifts to me, the truth that always lay just beneath her lies.

My mother fussed with her nine-month-old son, then held him up, admiring him, and twenty-four years later I admired her in brand new ways. I'd always believed that being a man meant standing your ground, but this was something *my mother* had done better than anyone. And yet she'd also known when it was time to go. She'd left my father, left Grandpa's, left New York, and I was always the beneficiary of her restless courage. I'd been so focused on getting in, I'd failed to appreciate my mother's genius for getting out. Sitting forward on the bicentennial sofa and looking into her green-brown eyes I understood that every virtue I associated with manhood—toughness, persistence, determination, reliability, honesty, integrity, guts—my mother exemplified. I'd always been dimly aware, but at that moment, with my first glimpse of the warrior behind my mother's blank face, I grasped the idea fully and put it into words for the first time. *All this searching and longing for the secret of being a good man, and all I needed to do was follow the example of one very good woman.*

I looked away from my mother, at my nine-month-old self. How did that helpless baby turn into this helpless sot? How did I travel so far and wind up only 142 steps away, having my neck wrung by Smelly? And what was I going to do about it? The tape was ending. My mother told her nine-month-old son something else, something important, and his face contorted into a questioning scowl. I knew that scowl. I stood and checked the mirror over the fireplace—there it was. I looked back at the screen, where my mother was holding her son's hand and waving it at the camera. Again she whispered in his ear, again he scowled. Though he heard her voice, her words, he couldn't make out her meaning.

But I did. Twenty-four years later I read my mother loud and clear.

"Say bye-bye."

Each man reacted differently when I told him on New Year's Day, 1990, that I'd quit the *Times* and was leaving New York. Fast Eddy was nonchalant. Don was kind. Colt was cool. General Grant puffed his cigar and told me to give 'em hell. Cager was proud. Peter asked me to send him a chapter now and then. Joey D was worried and looked at me the way he'd looked at McGraw swimming to the sandbar: I was going out too far, too deep. I told him I'd be fine, and thanked him for everything, and he said a bunch of sentimental things about "you boys" to his mouse, things I would have liked to have heard.

If Smelly reacted at all, I didn't notice.

Bob the Cop looked down at his big feet and shook his big head. "Place won't be the same without you," he said. But we both knew, with or without me, the place would never be the same, and that was the whole point.

Fuckembabe hugged me and said, "You'd better leggerish your terpsichore, you hear, my young fiendish? And always go easy on your lackey. And take care that your mindy is always screwed on strape. Your harken will be down some days, and others days it'll be upstarch. Cozening? But whatever cumbles—you lessening?—don't let me hear that you hopped a wabash or slitched your licklechick in a flammery, all for your blooey grubstake! Right? And rememberize, always rememberize: Fuck 'em, babe. *Fuck* 'em."

Dalton's reaction was the most unexpected. "You have no idea what horrors await you out there," he said, pointing to the window. "Did you know that in some parts of this country, last call is at one in the morning? One! Out there, in places like Atlanta, and Dallas, they come up to you and take the martini glass right out of your hand—*with booze still in it.*"

"I'll try to remember," I said.

He wasn't kidding. And he was angry that I wasn't taking him seriously.

"Laugh all you want," he said. "But you know that saying 'People are the same wherever you go?' Well they aren't."

" 'But they are difficult things with which we have been charged,' " I said. "Rilke."

Dalton's face lit up. "You'll be okay," he said, giving me a shove. For emphasis, for old times' sake, he added tenderly, "Asshole."

Uncle Charlie was working. We drank a shot of Sambuca and I told him I was going to visit my mother, stay with her a while, then go see my father, who was living in North Carolina, doing a talk show on the radio. When Uncle Charlie asked why, I told him something was wrong with me, and I wanted to figure out what, which meant going to the source.

Smoke shot from Uncle Charlie's nostrils. He put a hand to his temple. "Your father was in here once," he said. "Did I ever tell you?"

"No."

"He came to Manhasset to talk with your mother right after they split up. I think he was seeking a rapprochement. On his way back to the train he stopped in for a drink. Scotch. Neat. Sat about there."

I looked at the stool where Uncle Charlie pointed. I asked what they talked about, what my father was wearing, what was his attitude. "It's funny," Uncle Charlie said, elbows on the bar. "The only thing I remember about your old man was that amazing voice. That beautiful set of pipes. Isn't that strange?"

"Not really. That's all I remember too."

Uncle Charlie lit another Marlboro. He couldn't have looked or sounded more like Bogart if he'd tried, and it hit me—he *was* trying. The resemblance was no accident. He must have started when he was a boy. He must have discovered *Casablanca,* as I had, and fallen under Bogart's spell, and started talking like him, acting like him, until the imitation became second nature. Which meant that my occasional imitation of Uncle Charlie had been a secondhand imitation of Bogart. I perceived how complicated these chains of imitations could become. We were all doing our private homage to Bogart or Sinatra or Hemingway, The Duke or Yogi Bear or Ulysses Grant. And Steve. Since all the bartenders were partly imitating Steve, and we were all partly imitating the bartenders, maybe Publicans was just a hall of mirrors filled with Steve impersonators.

I didn't stay until last call. I had packing to do before my flight left the next morning. I kissed Uncle Charlie good-bye. He smacked the bar and pointed at my chest. I went down the barroom shaking hands, a lump in my throat. I hugged Bob the Cop, and Cager, but they weren't huggers. It was like hugging two old cacti.

Keep in touch, they said.

I will, I said, walking out the door. I will.

forty-four | MY FATHER

I WAS DYING FOR A DRINK, BUT I COULDN'T ORDER ONE. MY FATHER had been sober for years and I didn't want to seem disrespectful, downing a double scotch in front of him. We sat in a corner of the restaurant, sipping Coke, and I told him about Steve's funeral, and leaving New York, and my recent visit with my mother. Seeing her was great, I said, but awkward, because living with my mother, even for a few weeks, made me feel like Uncle Charlie, which made me feel bad about myself and Uncle Charlie at the same time.

I didn't tell my father about the long talk I'd had with my mother, in which I'd apologized tearfully for being unable to take care of her. I'd wept against her neck and she'd assured me it wasn't my job to take care of her, that it had never been my job, that I needed to stop feeling responsible for her and find some way to take care of myself. I wanted to tell my father all of this, but I didn't, because the subtext of the story was the continuing legacy of his disappearance, and I was still determined to avoid that topic with him.

I talked about McGraw, who had graduated from Nebraska and moved to Colorado to live in the mountains with Jimbo. I envied their closeness, I said, and their freedom. My father grunted. As I rambled on, as I struggled not to think about how delicious a glass of scotch would taste, I tried not to notice or care that he wasn't responsive. He wasn't listening. He was digging at his cuticles, breaking the long breadsticks into little breadsticks, ogling our waitress's ass. Finally he reached toward her. I thought he was going to grab her ass, but he tapped her arm. "Can I get a double vodka martini?" he asked. "Up. Two olives."

I stared.

"Oh," he said. "Right. I forgot to tell you on the phone. I'm letting myself enjoy a cocktail from time to time. See, I realized I'm not really an alcoholic. Yeah. It's good. When the mood strikes me, now and then, I can *enjoy a cocktail.*" He kept repeating this phrase, "enjoy a cocktail," possibly because he thought it sounded reassuringly banal.

I was alarmed at first, but by the time my father had enjoyed half a cocktail, he'd begun to enjoy me. Suddenly he was responsive. He was listening. More, he was offering advice, making me laugh, doing his funny voices. Before my eyes he was turning into a different man, into one of the men at Publicans, and so I urged him to enjoy another cocktail. Hell, I told the waitress, as if the thought had just occurred to me, I think I'd enjoy a cocktail myself.

I spent a week lying around my father's apartment, reading his books, smoking his cigarettes, listening to his show on the radio. It was the realization of a boyhood dream, hearing his voice and knowing that when he signed off he'd come home. We'd go for dinner, enjoy many cocktails, stagger home late at night, arm in arm. We'd listen to Sinatra, have a nightcap, maybe catch a rerun of *The Rockford Files*. My old man loved *The Rockford Files*. There were old publicity photos of himself around the apartment, and I saw that at his best he'd once looked something like James Garner.

He was still a chef, and a gourmand, and after a night of drinking he often liked to whip up some dessert, like Amaretto cheesecake or cannolis. The desserts were delicious, but the real treat was assisting him in the kitchen, learning from him how to cook. We were pals, doing stuff together, like Rockford and his dad. I knew that cocktails were the cause of our newfound closeness, but so what? Cocktails helped us relax and overcome whatever guilt we felt about loving each other. Cocktails made it possible for us both to forget all that he'd done, and all that he hadn't. What objection could there be to cocktails if they could accomplish all that?

At the start of the weekend my father said he wanted me to meet his girl-friend. We had a few cocktails at a roadhouse before going to her place, a low-slung shack in the woods. She opened the door and her jaw dropped at the sight of us, arms flung around each other's neck, grinning. "I see y'all started the party without me," she said.

She was painfully thin, all right angles and bones. Not pretty, but very sexy. Her twelve-year-old daughter, standing behind her, was extremely plump, as if she'd eaten all the meals the mother had skipped.

We went into the kitchen, where the daughter resumed her seat at the table, bent over a book. It was a *Choose Your Own Adventure,* she told me. Each time you came to a turning point, she said, the book made you choose. Want to go into the forbidden cave? Turn to page 37. Want to float down the river? Turn to page 42. "I only read *Choose Your Own Adventure* books," she said. "Because I'd rather make up my own story."

While my father prepared dinner, his girlfriend gave me a tour, which took three minutes, since the house was no bigger than Publicans. Hanging in the hallway was a framed and shellacked jigsaw puzzle, which the girlfriend showed me as though it were an original van Gogh. Returning to the kitchen we both knew something had happened. My father had changed. His eyes were smaller. His cheeks were flushed. Had the daughter said something? Had she nattered on about her *Choose Your Own Adventure* book and annoyed my father?

"What's wrong?" I asked.

"Nothing," he said.

The girlfriend remarked under her breath about my father's "mood swings." Big mistake. He called her a name. The daughter told my father not to speak that way to her mother. He called the daughter a name. I tried to step in, tried to calm him down, and he told me to "shut the fuck up." I'd had about enough of men telling me to shut the fuck up. I told my father to shut the fuck up, and that was the moment everything changed forever.

He rushed toward me. Like Smelly, my father was bull-necked, swag-bellied, and surprisingly lithe. I stepped back and got set. This time would be different, I promised myself. This time I wouldn't let my attacker get the jump on me. When Smelly attacked, I'd been sad and unprepared. This time I was mad, and loaded for bear. All the fighters I'd ever known flashed through my mind. Bob the Cop, Joey D, Cager, even Uncle Charlie swinging at his imaginary Haglers. I tried to recall the pointers Joey D had given me about bar fights, and all that Don had told me about wrestling. I wondered if my father and I were going to punch it out or wrestle. I looked down to see if he was cocking his fists and saw the carving knife in his hand.

In some remote corner of my mind I realized this was the very same specter my mother had once faced—my crazed father wielding a blade. I'd always assumed that I understood how frightened she must have been, but I didn't have the foggiest idea until I saw that knife in my father's hand. Was this my chance to avenge her? Was the universe telling me to settle an old score by disarming my father and chasing him around the woods with that knife? I knew that my mother wouldn't want me to do anything of the kind. *If she were here she'd tell me to run.* But I couldn't. There was no turning back. Whenever my father made his move, something bad was going to happen, and whatever that something was, I only knew one thing for sure. I was going to be the last one standing.

He dropped the knife. The blade hit the kitchen floor with a sickening clatter. He stormed out of the house, got into his sports car and sped away. The girlfriend looked at me. I looked at her. We both looked at the daughter, who was shaking. We all held our breath, expecting him to return any second. When he didn't, I asked the girlfriend, "Can you drive me to the airport?"

"Sure."

"Can you take me to his place first? To get my stuff?"

"He'll be there!"

"No. He's not there."

I knew with certainty that within minutes my father would be at some bar, and that he would be at that bar for a very long time to come.

We sped to my father's apartment. The door was locked but I climbed in a side window. I'd barely unpacked in my week there, so it took minutes to throw everything into my one bag. Then we drove along dark roads. As if in a horror movie we kept checking the rearview, waiting for headlights to materialize behind us. The daughter was lying on the backseat, either asleep or rigid with fear. The night was moonless and uncommonly dark and I couldn't see anything but stars, though I knew we were driving through farm country because I smelled freshly turned soil and manure and every few hundred yards I glimpsed in the distance the yellow lights of a farmhouse. When we reached the airport the girlfriend pulled up to the curb and yanked the parking brake. We sat for a few moments, trying to gather ourselves. "You know," she said at last, "I gotta say—y'all don't seem nothin' like your dad."

"If only that were true." I kissed her good-bye and wished her luck whenever my father returned.

The airport was closed, no flights until morning. All the stores and bars were closed too. A janitor ran a waxing machine over the linoleum floor. I stretched out on a row of plastic chairs in the waiting area and closed my eyes. When I opened them again it was dawn. I smelled biscuits and fresh-brewed coffee. Stores were unlocking their gates. I bought a razor and shaving cream and went into the men's room. In the mirror I saw a different face. There was that familiar scowl—but the eyes were more aware. Of what? I wasn't sure.

I thought of Bill and Bud. They had warned me that disillusionment was the great danger up ahead and they were right. But that morning, rid of lifelong illusions about my father, and about a few other men, and about men in general, I found myself whistling as I patted shaving cream on my jaws, because being disillusioned meant I was on my own. No one to worship, no one to imitate. I didn't regret all my illusions, and I surely didn't shed them all in that airport men's room. Some would take years to pare away, others were permanent. But the work had begun. *Your father is not a good man, but you are not your father.* Saying this to the young man in the mirror with the shaving-cream beard, I felt independent. Free.

I bought a cup of coffee and sat with it in the middle of the airport, under the board that listed all the arrivals and departures. So many cities, so many places to start over. Maybe I'd go back to Arizona and tell my mother about braving my father. Maybe I'd go back to New York, watch the men's faces as I walked in the front door of Publicans.

Then those four oddly emboldening words ran through my head. *Choose your own adventure.*

I phoned McGraw and Jimbo in Colorado. As I told McGraw about my fight with my father, he giggled. McGraw had gotten his giggle back. The sound of him giggling made me giggle, and I knew just where I wanted to be.

. . .

"Junior!" he said, hugging me as I stepped off the plane.

"Jimbo," I said, "you're saving my life."

Only eight months had passed since I'd seen him, but he was barely recognizable. Bigger, older, redder, he no longer looked like a young Babe Ruth, but like a young Steve. He had that familiar swagger, that take-charge quality, and he was developing his own Cheshire smile.

"Where's McGraw?" I asked.

"Working. Your cousin is the newest towel boy at the local hotel."

I laughed, then caught myself. "What am I laughing at? Do they need another towel boy?"

It was a brilliant June afternoon. The sky was a hard sheet of blue, the air tasted like ice water. Jimbo had the top off his Jeep and as we climbed into the foothills outside Denver our hair whipped around crazily. Coming over a steep ridge the Jeep made a jarring, thunderous noise. I looked to the right and saw that it wasn't the Jeep making that noise but a herd of buffalo rumbling alongside the highway. Then, straight ahead, I caught my first sight of the Rockies. Camelback was a pimple by comparison. I howled, and Jimbo smiled as if he'd put the mountains there. I hoped those mountains, like certain men, weren't more impressive when viewed from a distance.

Over the Jeep engine Jimbo shouted a question about the gang at Publicans. I was all set to tell him about Smelly, but I felt as if I'd been in darkness a long time, and now I wanted to bask in this glittering mountain sunlight and say nothing to cast a shadow over the moment. Besides, we were meeting McGraw later at a bar. I'd tell them both then.

I sat back and listened to Jimbo's tape in the stereo. Allman Brothers. "Blue Sky."

You're my blue sky.
You're my sunny day.
Lord you know it makes me high
When you turn your love my way, yeah

Jimbo picked an air guitar, steering with his knees, and we both sang as the Jeep ascended into alpine meadows. Rams, perched like haughty ballerinas on the high rocks, looked down on us. My head started to feel like a balloon on a string. Jimbo said it was the altitude. The Jeep groaned as it crested a steep pass, which I assumed was the Great Divide.

"Got a surprise for you," Jimbo said. He pulled out his Allman Brothers tape and slammed in another. Sinatra's voice burst from the speakers. Jimbo laughed and I slugged him on the shoulder.

A few miles farther the Jeep sputtered. Jimbo looked at the gauges. "Shit," he said, throwing the wheel to the right and bouncing onto the shoulder. He jumped out and popped the hood. Smoke billowed from the engine.

"We may be here awhile," he said, peering at the sun lowering on the horizon.

He sounded worried. For once I wasn't. While Sinatra's voice echoed off the sheer slopes of rock, I was perfectly content to sit on the roof of this unavailing star and savor the sun. I didn't care how much time we had until it disappeared behind the mountains. For one beautiful moment—and who could ask anything more of life?—I needed and wanted for nothing.

EPILOGUE

Keep me away from porter or whiskey
Don't play anything sentimental it'll make me cry
I've got to go back my friend
Is there really any need to ask why

—Van Morrison, "Got to Go Back"

epilogue | ONE OF MANY

O N SEPTEMBER 11, 2001, MY MOTHER PHONED ME FROM ARI-
zona with the news. We stayed on the phone together, watching TV,
and when we were able to speak we wondered with dread how many people
from Manhasset must be in those towers.

It was worse than we feared. Nearly fifty people from Manhasset died in
the attacks on the World Trade Center, among them Peter Owens, the bartender who had been such a kind editor and friend to me. Also, my cousin
Tim Byrne, the strong, charismatic son of my mother's first cousin, Charlene.
A broker at Sandler O'Neill, Tim was in his office on the 104th floor of the
south tower when the first plane hit the north tower. He phoned his mother
and said he was fine, not to worry. Then the second plane hit his tower and
no one heard from him again.

I was in Denver at the time. I drove to New York for the funerals and me-
morials. Along the way I listened to radio call-in shows, stunned by how
many people were calling not to talk but to sob. Outside St. Louis I tried to
tune in McGraw, who was a talk show host for KMOX, one of the largest
stations in the United States. I wanted to hear what he'd have to say about the
attacks, and simply to hear his voice, which I felt would give some comfort.

I'd lost touch with McGraw. When Grandma and Grandpa got sick, several years after I left New York, my mother and McGraw's mother battled over their care, and the bitterness of that fight, which landed in court and didn't end until both grandparents died in 1997, split the family in two. McGraw and his sisters, Sheryl included, no longer spoke to me, because they sided with their mother, and I sided with mine. Driving across Missouri in the middle of the night, I turned the dial back and forth, and thought for a second I had found McGraw in that welter of sobs and voices. But then I lost him.

I shut off the radio and phoned everyone I knew in New York. My college roommate told me that Dave Berray—the supremely confident Yale student I'd dubbed Jedd Redux—had been killed in the attacks. He had a wife and two young children. I phoned Jimbo, who was living outside New York City. "Remember Michelle?" he asked. I hadn't talked to Michelle in years, but I could see her face as plainly as the Coca-Cola billboard up ahead. "Her husband is missing," Jimbo said.

"Does she have any children?" I asked.

"A son."

When I arrived in Huntington, Long Island, at the condo that Tim had bought for his mother, Aunt Charlene was crying, the kind of crying I could tell would last for years. I spent the week with her, trying to help, but the only way I could help Aunt Charlene and the Byrnes was to put their loss into words. I wrote a story for my newspaper, the *Los Angeles Times,* about Tim, about how he'd led his family after his father died. I still remembered his father's funeral, when Tim shouldered more of the weight of his father's casket, and more of the responsibility for his mother's comfort. He'd continued in that role, helping and guiding Aunt Charlene, financially and emotionally, being the kind of son I'd strived to be. Above all he'd been a patriarch to his siblings. He'd filled in for their father, then become their father, and among the many chilling coincidences surrounding Tim's death, the most improbable was that his father's birthday had been September 11.

At the close of that cruel week I met up with Jimbo and we went to the memorial service for Peter. When Jimbo pulled up to my hotel I was speechless. I'd lost touch with him, as I had with everyone from Publicans, and after not seeing him for years I could barely believe his metamorphosis into a red-faced Steve Redux. He seemed, in fact, to be wrestling with where Steve's identity ended and his began. He told me he'd already opened one bar called Dickens, which failed, and he was thinking of trying again.

Driving up to the church we talked about Steve, because the scene was so reminiscent of Steve's funeral. Mourners converged from every direction, many more than the church could hold. I recognized dozens of faces, including one man who looked like an older version of Colt. Of course it *was* an older version of Colt. For some reason he was walking down the middle of the street. Jimbo and I waved, and a gray-haired Colt waved back as if in a dream.

Jimbo parked and we ran to the church. There was no point in running. Every seat was already filled, and people were spilling out of the doors. The top step of the church looked like the bar at Publicans, circa 1989—Cager, Joey D, Don. I hugged them and shook their hands. Inside we heard Peter's father struggling through his eulogy. We stood on our toes to see. When Peter's father became too distraught to continue, we looked away and wiped our eyes.

Afterward Jimbo and I met Steve's widow, Georgette, at the former site of Publicans. Steve had been deeper in debt than we knew, and business had dropped off faster than we feared, but Georgette had held on longer than anyone thought she could. She tried everything, including live rock 'n' roll bands, before finally letting the place go in 1999. Long before selling, however, she'd had to fire Uncle Charlie. He couldn't work for anyone but Steve, she said. His flamboyant rudeness had become something else, not funny, just disagreeable.

He'd become a poor caretaker of Grandpa's house too, worse than Grandpa. While living there alone, he'd set fire to the house by accident, or else one of his creditors had done it on purpose. I heard all kinds of rumors around town. When the fire-damaged house was sold, Uncle Charlie left New York, drifted into a restless retirement, then disappeared altogether. I suppose that in the back of my mind I always feared that Uncle Charlie might disappear, that he'd be another member of my family to make a mysterious and dramatic exit. But when it happened, when he just dropped out of sight one day, it still came as a shock.

The new owners of Publicans had renamed the place Edison's and remodeled the barroom in dozens of subtle ways. I felt as if I were encountering an old friend who had undergone needless plastic surgery. "At least the long bar is still here," Jimbo said, rubbing the wood.

"And the same stools," I said.

We sat at Peter's end, toasting his memory. I toasted with ginger ale.

"You're not drinking?" Jimbo said.

"No."

"Since when?"

"Ten years. Give or take."

I didn't go into a long explanation. I didn't want to list all the reasons that drinking—along with smoking and gambling and most other vices—had lost its appeal after I left Publicans. I didn't want to tell Jimbo that sobering up had felt like growing up, and vice versa. I didn't want to say that *drinking* and *trying* felt like opposite impulses, that when I stopped the one I automatically started the other. I didn't want to say that sometimes, late at night, remembering Steve, I got a cold feeling in the pit of my stomach, because I wondered if he'd died for our sins. Had Steve lived, I'd have gone on living in his bar, and maybe a bar in Manhasset wasn't the best place for me after all. An old-timer at Publicans used to tell me that drinking is the only thing you don't get better at the more you do it, and when I left Publicans the sensibleness of that statement came home to me at last. I didn't say any of this to Jimbo because I didn't know how. I still don't. Deciding to quit drinking was the easiest thing I ever did. Describing how I did it, and why, and whether or not I will drink again, is much harder.

But the main reason I didn't say anything to Jimbo was that I didn't want to profane Publicans. In the wake of September 11, I felt grateful for every minute I'd spent in that bar, even the ones I regretted. I knew this was a contradiction, but it was no less true for being so. The attacks complicated my already contradictory memories of Publicans. With public places suddenly described as soft targets, I felt only fondness for a bar that had been founded on the antiquated notion that there is safety in numbers. In my black suit, sitting amid the ruins of Publicans, I loved the old gin mill more than ever.

I asked Georgette to tell me about the last official night of Publicans. "Oh, everyone cried," she said, especially Joey D, who was so distraught that he had to leave early. He went on to become a public-school teacher in the Bronx. Fourth grade. On his first day in class, Joey D would tell me later, he wrote his name on the blackboard, then wheeled around. "All these faces were looking at me," he said. "And I thought, Okay, I can do this." *Icandothis.* He'd spent his life staring out at a sea of thirsty faces, and now he was confronted with a wall of faces hungry for knowledge He would make a fine teacher, I thought. The children would be fascinated by his pet mouse. And woe to any little hooligan who started a brawl on Joey D s playground.

Fast Eddy insisted that he be the one to buy the last round at Publicans, Georgette told us. When the last glass was washed, the last cigarette extinguished, General Grant shut off the lights and locked the doors. I could picture his cigar floating through the pitch-dark barroom like the brake light of a motorcycle on a country road. I looked at the booths and stools—they were all empty, but I could *hear* the laughter. I could hear the voices from that last night, from every night, going back decades. I thought, We used to haunt this place, and now it will always haunt us.

Georgette ordered another glass of wine. Jimbo and I ordered cheeseburgers. They didn't taste the same, because Fuckembabe and Smelly weren't back there packing the patties. Fuckembabe was dead and Smelly was working at a place in Garden City. I asked about Bobo. Neither Jimbo nor Georgette knew where he'd gone or what had become of him.

Georgette asked about my mother. I told her that my mother was doing well, still living in Arizona, and though she still battled fatigue and a few other health problems, she hoped to be able to retire soon. Georgette then asked about me. What had I been doing with myself the last eleven years? I told her that in 1990, after a few months living with Jimbo in the Rocky Mountains, McGraw and I had moved to Denver. I'd gotten a job as a reporter at the *Rocky Mountain News,* where I spent four years learning the basics I'd lacked at the *New York Times*. McGraw went back to Nebraska and found work at a tiny radio station, where he conquered his stutter and discovered his calling. He always was a talker, Georgette said, smiling. A charmer, I said. A ham, Jimbo said. But now he was a star. His giggle could be heard in forty states.

In 1994 I became a reporter for the *Los Angeles Times,* and in 1997 I was promoted to national correspondent, based in Atlanta. From there I went to Harvard on a journalism fellowship in 2000. While at Harvard I took one more pass at the book about Publicans, which I'd decided to write as nonfiction. As always, the book eluded me. When my fellowship ended, the editors at the *Times* asked me to be their western correspondent, to cover the Rocky

Mountain region from Denver. I'd just arrived in Denver for a visit, to see if I could picture myself living there again, when the towers were attacked.

"You can't ever predict the future," Georgette said in a half whisper.

I thought I could, I told her. The night I left Publicans forever, I'd boasted to Cager and Dalton and Uncle Charlie that I knew two things for sure about my future: I would never live in California or the South. When I became the southern correspondent for the *Los Angeles Times,* I knew that the universe had been eavesdropping on us in Publicans, and the universe had a bizarre sense of humor. Georgette smiled wistfully. True, she said.

It was getting dark. Georgette had to be getting home. Jimbo and I walked her out to the parking lot. She kissed us both and said Steve would have been proud of how we'd turned out. Stay in touch, she said.

We will, we said. We will.

I couldn't move to Denver. Not yet. I couldn't leave the East Coast without first writing something about my hometown and how it had been changed by the attacks. I kept my apartment at Harvard, but essentially lived in Manhasset, in a hotel outside town, and spent my days walking up and down Plandome Road, interviewing strangers, renewing old acquaintances. Most of the old gang from Publicans, I heard, gathered in a new joint on Plandome Road. I stationed myself there at happy hour and one by one they came through the door, a bit grayer, a lot sadder. I'd been reading *David Copperfield* again, for distraction, for comfort, and I was reminded of a line toward the end of the novel when David laments "the wandering remnants" of his surrogate childhood home.

DePietro walked in, wearing a black suit, returning from his twentieth funeral. Don, also in a black suit, said he knew a man who had attended fifty. We talked for hours, and someone at the bar described for me the way ash from the towers had floated all the way across the water. I thought of the marshy stretch of land just outside Manhasset, which Fitzgerald had dubbed the Valley of Ashes. That description now seemed a terrible prophecy.

I asked about Dalton. He and Don had dissolved their partnership, and Don was happily going it alone above Louie the Greek's. The last Don had heard, Dalton was somewhere in Mississippi, trying to bring out a volume of his own poetry.

Cager walked in, looking exactly the same, his hair still red and still tumbling out of what appeared to be the same visor. He shook my hand and asked how I was—and if I was still going to the track. "No," I said. "I've stopped doing things I suck at."

"And yet," he said, "you're still a writer." He swatted me on the back and offered to buy me a drink, and he didn't tease me when I ordered a Coke.

We talked about the state of the world, and all the men along the bar joined in, while TV sets above the bar flashed footage of the towers burning, and of people holding photos of loved ones who were missing. I noticed how quickly every conversation hurtled back through time to the 1980s, and not simply because that was our common link. We were all masters at idealizing places, and after September 11 there was only one place left to idealize, one place that could never disillusion us. The past. Only Colt didn't care to discuss the past, because he couldn't remember it. "Don't talk to me about the eighties," he said. "I wasn't there."

Later that night, standing between Cager and Colt, I felt a heavy arm land on my shoulder. I turned. Bob the Cop. His hair had gone completely white and he looked exhausted. "Where are you coming from?" I asked.

"Ground zero."

Of course.

He sat beside me and stared deep into my eyes.

"How are you?" I said.

"Twenty-five years on the force, I thought I'd seen it all." He continued staring at me, then closed his eyes and shook his head slowly from side to side.

In time I worked up the courage to phone Michelle. I told her I'd heard about her husband and asked if there was anything I could do. She said she could use a drink. I drove to her parents' house, where she and her eleven-month-old son, Matthew, had been living since the attacks. She opened the front door and looked exactly the same. Matthew, hiding behind her leg, had her big brown eyes with the spot of cinnamon in the center. He stared at me as if we knew each other, and in a way we did. He looked as if someone important had just left the room and he was wondering when that someone was coming back.

I took Michelle to dinner in Port Washington and she told me about her husband, Mike Lunden, an energy broker who loved bow ties and cigars and hockey and weddings and Chicago and fine wines—and her. She described their courtship and happy marriage. Though they lived in a studio apartment with a newborn baby, she said, they never once got sick of each other. As Michelle talked I noticed that she was yet another graduate of the Publicans Storytelling Academy. She had me laughing one minute, swallowing a lump in my throat the next.

She asked about me. Had I gotten married? I told her I'd come close once or twice, but I'd had some growing up to do first. Also, it had taken me a long time to get over my first love.

"Right," she said. "What ever happened to—?"

"Sidney." I cleared my throat. "She phoned me out of the blue when she heard I was at Harvard. We met for dinner."

"And?"

"She was exactly the same."

"And?"

"I'd changed."

Sidney had explained, carefully and honestly, her decision not to choose me years before, saying she'd been apprehensive about a young man so enthralled by a bar. I told Michelle I thought Sidney had been right to be apprehensive.

After dinner I took Michelle for a nightcap to the site of the old Publicans. We sat in the booth nearest the door and I could see Michelle's spirits lift, ever so slightly, as good memories drifted back. But her thoughts quickly returned to her husband. He was such a good man, she told me, repeating those words, "a good man," several times. And he was thrilled about Matthew, she said. Now Matthew would know Mike only through letters and photos and stories. She worried about her son growing up with no father, how that void would define him. "At least he'll have his uncles," she said with a sigh. "And his cousins. He's crazy about his cousins. And in school he'll know many other children who lost fathers, so he won't feel—different."

I slumped against the back of the booth. It hadn't hit me until then. Manhasset, where I'd once felt like the only boy without a father, was now a town full of fatherless children.

I'd been working on my story about Manhasset for months, shuttling back and forth between my Harvard apartment and my hotel room outside Manhasset, and my time, my editors said, was up. They needed me in Denver. I sat down and wrote at last. I wrote about the endless funerals, still taking place months later. I wrote about the mood along Plandome Road, where the bars and churches were unusually full. I wrote about the widow who couldn't bring herself to retrieve her husband's car from the train station. Week after week the car sat there, covered in candles and ribbons and notes of support and love. Now and then she would appear and try in vain to drive the car away, and people along Plandome Road would watch her sit behind the wheel, staring straight ahead, unable to turn the key. I wrote in a fever, a trance, about my hometown, the first time I'd experienced writing as catharsis. The words poured forth, no effort finding them. The hard part was shutting them off.

When the first draft was finished I went for a drive. I started at Memorial Field, where I sat in the sun, dizzy with nostalgia and fatigue. Staring at the baseball diamond, I remembered seeing the Dickens softball players for the first time when I was seven. I remembered all the Little League games with McGraw, and our pivotal game of catch when we were in our twenties. I snapped out of my reminiscing when four people arrived to play basketball—three men my age and a boy about eleven. The boy's eyes were large and bright, his smile crooked, and his way with the men told me he wasn't related to any of them. They began to play two-on-two. The boy, who wore thick glasses, didn't have many moves. But he was quick, and determined, and holding his own. The men were just out for exercise, but the boy was having an experience he'd remember forever. He might have been thinking the same thing, and so he wasn't paying attention when one of the men threw him a no-look pass. The ball whacked the boy in the side of the face, knocking off his glasses and stopping him cold. The men ran to him. "You okay?" they said. "Fine," the boy said, smiling shyly, rubbing the spot where the ball had left a red mark. "Aw," one of the men said, "he's a tough guy," and the other men applauded, and patted him on the back, and the boy looked at them all, one by one, with such ferocious love and gratitude that I had tears in my eyes.

I got back in the car and drove to Shore Drive and looked at the water. The man who owned the most opulent waterfront house in Manhasset had been killed in the attacks. He'd phoned his wife minutes before he died, and she was said to be in seclusion inside that big Gatsbyesque palace, haunted by the sound of his voice. I followed the route my mother and I used to take in our T-Bird, from Shore Drive up Plandome Road, to Shelter Rock, and all along the way I saw American flags draped in every window, yellow ribbons tied to so many trees. I kept going, farther east, to Aunt Charlene's, and spent the afternoon with her, drinking coffee and watching a video of Tim graduating from Syracuse.

Driving back to my hotel through the beautiful winter twilight, I listened to the radio. The local classical station was playing Debussy's "Clair de Lune." I'd always gotten emotional while listening to that piece, which Bud had introduced me to. But that night it seemed unbearably sad. I knew from Bud that "Clair de Lune" was Debussy's musical portrait of the moon, but suddenly it seemed a song about memory, about the unearthly sound that the past makes when it drifts back to us. Hitting the scan button I came upon a man explaining how to make "the perfect cannoli." He was funny, giving recipes in a preposterous Italian accent. I had to laugh. It was my father. We hadn't spoken in years. I'd heard he was in New York, but I hadn't known he was doing a cooking show on Sunday nights. I was tempted to call in, but the temptation passed. Three weeks later he died.

I couldn't bring myself to attend his funeral, for many reasons, but especially because I couldn't face that open casket. I went instead a few days later to Calverton National Cemetery, on the eastern end of Long Island, a wilderness of white crosses. It was a cold February day, a biting wind blowing in off the ocean. The office was closed, but a machine told me my father was in Section 23, Grave Site 591. He had never been so easy to find.

Section 23 was the newest in the cemetery. My stomach rolled when I saw the many open graves, waiting. I walked along, reading names, until I came to a freshly covered grave. JOHN JOSEPH MOEHRINGER, PVT., AIR FORCE. My father had told me that he'd changed his name legally to Johnny Michaels and that he'd been a marine. Two lies, dispelled by one headstone. I jammed my hands into my pockets, turned my collar against the wind. I looked down at my father's name, at the fresh footprints of the workmen who had buried him, and tried to think of something to say, but I couldn't. I stood quietly for half an hour, waiting for the words—and the tears—but they would not come. "Well," I said, turning to go, "I hope you're okay, Dad. I hope you've found some—*peace.*"

Why it should have been this word that set the tears flowing, I don't know, but they came in a torrent, so suddenly, so violently, that I had to drop into a catcher's crouch. Rocking back and forth, my hands over my face, I felt that there was no end to those tears, that I could sob all day and into the night if I didn't will myself to stop. I was embarrassed, and troubled, by the power of my reaction. "I'm sorry," I said to my father, "for making such a scene at your—for making a scene."

The wind was whooshing through the dead leaves in the branches of the trees. A sound like static. Somewhere in that white noise is your old man. I tried to believe this. I tried to hear my father's voice telling me—what? That he was sorry? That he understood? That he was proud of me? That it was normal to feel sadness about your father? That we all do, and that such sadness is part of the hard work of manhood? It was wishful thinking, hearing these things, hearing his voice, but as I left the cemetery I granted myself that last wish.

I said good-bye to the gang from Publicans. In many ways it was harder saying good-bye this time than it had been years earlier.

When are you coming back? they said.

Not for a while, I said sadly.

Don't disappear this time, they said.

I won't, I said. I won't.

I promised the Manhasset story to my editors by the end of the week. Before I let it go, there was just one more thing I needed to do. One last interview. A Manhasset man named Roko Camaj had been a window washer at the World Trade Center, and he was on the job when the planes hit. His twenty-three-year-old son, Vincent, still lived in Manhasset. Just behind St. Mary's.

I phoned him and said I was writing about my hometown and how it had changed forever.

He wouldn't talk. Reporters had already written about his father, he said, and most had gotten it wrong. They had even spelled the family name wrong. I promised I'd get at least that much right. I pleaded with him to meet me. He sighed.

"Okay," he said. "Where?"

I mentioned a few restaurants in Port Washington. I suggested Louie the Greek's. I named places near his house, places not so near. He was silent. I was silent. Finally he said, "There's a place my friends and I like to go."

"Name it."

"Do you remember where the old Publicans used to be?"

ACKNOWLEDGMENTS

Like its author, this book has been rescued many times by a number of extraordinary people.

First, Roger and Sloan Barnett. Their love and generosity at the outset made all the difference. When the book was just an unformed idea, they introduced me to Mort Janklow, the archangel of literary agents, who immediately understood the story I wanted to tell. He embraced me, inspired me—and commanded me to write a book proposal. More, he told me how. I'm forever in his debt.

It was Mort Janklow who sent me to Jeff and Tracy Smith, the Nick and Nora of Watermill. They clipped lines from Somerset Maugham for me to pin above my computer, and let me set up my computer in their empty Pond House, where I wrote a rough draft while watching their frozen pond thaw.

During my stay at the pond I did much of my reporting, visiting Manhasset countless times, interviewing most of the people who appear in these pages. My thanks to Bob the Cop, Cager, Colt, Dalton, DePietro, Don, Georgette, Joey D, and Michelle. They, and many others from Publicans, spent hours confirming or correcting my memory, and helping me piece together long-ago conversations. They also granted me permission to use their real stories and real names. (Only three names in this book have been changed—Lana, Magdalena, and Sidney.)

As drafts progressed I showed them to a group of careful and thoughtful readers. Jackie Griggs, Bill Husted, Jim Locke, McGraw Milhaven, Emily Nunn, Jim Newton and Amy Wallace each helped in unique and essential ways. I owe a special thanks to Harvard professor John Stauffer, who gave me a list of rare old memoirs to read, then sat with me in his campus office through long winter afternoons and explained to me the American memoir. Those were among the most pleasant hours of my life.

From the start my editors at the *Los Angeles Times*—John Carroll, Dean Baquet, and Scott Kraft—have been unwavering in their patience, support and interest, even granting me a book leave at a time that was very inopportune for them. I can never thank them enough.

At one particularly anxious moment I was fortunate to meet with Hyperion's editor-in-chief, Will Schwalbe, who set me right with a brief tutorial in the "architecture" of story. Another pivotal meeting, with *Los Angeles Magazine* editor Kit Rachlis, The Master himself, helped me finish at last.

In the fact-checking stage, Yale spokeswoman Dorie Baker and Saybrook dean Lisa Collins were kind, gracious and tireless. They are what Yale is all about.

Through it all I was pushed, coached, charmed, needled, educated, dazzled and edited as never before by the miraculous Peternelle van Arsdale, my editor at Hyperion. As rare and symphonic as her name, she did two things no one else had ever been able to do: She made me believe in the story, and through the sheer force of her faith, she made me keep writing.

Finally, my mother. Though a private woman, she answered hundreds of my questions with honesty and astonishing recall. She let me write about some of her toughest days, and shared with me her decades' worth of family diaries, photos, cassettes and letters, without which this book might not have been possible. Above all, when the way was lost, she was my beacon, calling me back to the words, the simple words. It has been my great fortune in writing this book, as in entering this world, to have had her as my primary source.